Stuff Theory

Stuff Theory
Everyday Objects, Radical Materialism

Maurizia Boscagli

B L O O M S B U R Y
ocn 857981592
NEW YORK • LONDON • NEW DELHI • SYDNEY

Bloomsbury Academic

An imprint of Bloomsbury Publishing Inc

1385 Broadway	50 Bedford Square
New York	London
NY 10018	WC1B 3DP
USA	UK

www.bloomsbury.com

Bloomsbury is a registered trade mark of Bloomsbury Publishing Plc

First published 2014

© Maurizia Boscagli 2014

Library of Congress Cataloging-in-Publication Data
A catalog record for this book is available from the Library of Congress

ISBN: HB: 978-1-6235-6268-7
PB: 978-1-6235-6225-0
ePub: 978-1-6235-6630-2
ePDF: 978-1-6235-6057-7

Typeset by RefineCatch Limited, Bungay, Suffolk, UK
Printed and bound in the United States of America

To Enda, Francesco, and Biba

Contents

Introduction

Of Jena Glassware and Potatoes:
Matter in the Moment

"Stuff" ("*La Roba*") is the title of a novella by the Sicilian novelist Giovanni Verga. Published in 1883, it is the story of a poor and dispossessed day laborer, Mazzarò, who, through his cunning and hard work, manages to acquire all the possessions ("*la roba*") of his employer, the Baron. Although he has become immensely rich, Mazzarò keeps on living like a pauper, eating bread and onions, and anxiously watching over his lands, harvests, and animals for fear of being robbed by his employees. When he grows old and is advised to forget about his stuff and rather "think about his soul," he gets angry, and running in the yard like a madman, "he began to hit all the ducks and turkeys with his cane to kill them," shouting "Stuff, my stuff, come along with me."[1]

This parable of late nineteenth-century materialism centered on the figure of the peasant entrepreneur in post-feudal Sicily is a story of class *ressentiment* and subaltern determination that stems directly from Mazzarò's own suffering, his recognition that the value of his stuff equals the slave-like labor it took to acquire it. Mazzarò's identification with his possessions ("It seemed as if Mazzarò's body was stretched down all along his land, and that one, walking through the countryside, was in fact walking on his body") is more than the delusion of a miser or fetishist. He is almost touching in his attachment to the stuff that, in the narrative of humanism, doesn't "make" man, his refusal of the idea that your possessions are what you leave behind, and that *ce qui reste* is really the spirit. Mazzarò's connection to stuff is economic *and* affective, abstract *and* somatic. When he invokes a paradoxical immediacy in his cry "Stuff, my stuff, come along with me," we know that Mazzarò and his stuff share a deep proximity and commonality: having lived together, they should die together. In this image of untranscended matter, and of a man both dominating and dominated by it, the story opens a vista to a traffic between subject and object at odds with the classical dialectical opposition of these terms.

Verga's story anticipates a relationship between human and non-human, animate and non-animate, subject and object that is only now becoming visible. This new relation of the subject and his stuff, brought about by new types of technology, new forms of capital, and a new sense of the planet's finitude, is the topic of this book. This understanding of materiality put in place by the revised relation between people and things has far-reaching cultural, social, and political possibilities. I call this new materiality stuff: matter whose plasticity, its transformative potential, comes into being, inextricably, with the human. The notion of the human as participating in matter, the idea of the human–object connection as a technogenesis, rather than as a tale of origins and domination, has been one of the chief claims of contemporary critiques of science. The time has come to study this new, plastic materiality in the sphere of the everyday and as part of the contemporary culture of capital, where artefactual matter never ceases to be a commodity.

By now, stuff seems to be everywhere, ready to overwhelm us, and at the same time it appears to be an illusion, melting into air. On the one hand, the proliferation of commodities, to buy, use, eat, or wear, is unprecedented, and the disposal of the mountains of cast-off stuff has become a global problem. On the other, the rise of the knowledge and service industries as central to western economic development has meant that the material world is harder to grasp than ever. We are unsure whether the objects we desire are about to overwhelm us, or whether the object has become obsolete and interest in things only confirms its disappearance; either way, stuff endures. At this juncture in modernity, stuff is palpably dangerous. *Stuff Theory* shows how culture has seized on the dangerous instability of stuff to radically recast accounts of the encounter between human subjects and objects, and between objects themselves.

In recasting this encounter between subjects and the material world, the book considers how culture has focused not on matter in general, but on stuff more specifically defined as those things which we own, but which have shed their glamour as shiny commodities, yet which we are unwilling to dispose of and relegate to the trash heap. This book records the flash appearance of an assortment of such objects: a piece of his own rib bone, removed in an operation, which Roland Barthes tosses from his balcony; the cool abstracted bottle and pipe "object types" of Le Corbusier's paintings; the designer hat included in the 1940 Cupaloy Westinghouse time capsule, destined to be opened in five thousand years; antique furniture; the bobbing plastic bag in Sam Mendes' film *American Beauty*; the clothes in a wardrobe in a locked house, still bearing the shapes of their wearers' bodies, in a Virginia Woolf novel; Italo Calvino's philosophic garbage can; and the door handle turning in empty space in Jacques Tati's film *Playtime*. All this stuff is protean, volatile, always on the verge of becoming valueless while never ceasing to be commodified, awash with meaning but always ready to become junk or to mutate into something else. Its instability in the everyday makes the conventional split between subject and object impossible. It implies scenarios in which material stuff and human subject make contact in ways that are intensely intimate, somatic, and unpredictable. Stuff in this sense is a materiality out of bounds, which refuses to be contained by the western philosophic, scientific, and semiotic order of things. It is a hybrid objectivity that declines its role as the eternal sidekick of the subject, the role to which that order has confined it historically. This unruly stuff, intruding in works of culture, radically recasts fundamental questions of human and material agency in modernity.

In recent years, a set of critical languages has emerged to discuss this materiality; these are now attaining critical mass under the rubric of the "new materialisms." In literary studies the "thing theory" of Bill Brown and others offers a complex reading of the emergence of things into the cultural field of vision since the end of the nineteenth century. In anthropology, theorists from Michael Taussig to Daniel Miller have theorized the persistence of magical thing-thinking in settings from the Colombian rain forest to central London. The Heideggerian phenomenological focus on the *quidditas* of things as embodied materiality is being rethought as "object oriented ontology" by a group of younger philosophers in rebellion against Derrida's focus on language. A range of thinkers inspired by Gilles Deleuze, from Elizabeth Grosz to Brian Massumi, are revisiting the thinking of Bergson, and Spinoza and others before him, to construct a counter-narrative of a quasi-vitalist materiality in lively interaction with subject actants. A related vitalist strain has emerged as political theorists consider how we engage with the physical world as they construct viable models of ecological politics; Jane Bennett's *Vibrant Matter* is the best known example. The work of scientists and historians of science on matter and its interaction with human subjects has been crucial in recasting received notions of materialism. In particular, the work of Bruno Latour in France and Donna Haraway in the US is key. Latour's notion of the quasi-subject quasi-object—that is, of a radically other (dis)order of things in which friable subjects and mutable objects intervene in each others' being—may be the pivotal idea of the new materialism. Each of these theories presents versions of the material as unruly: they refuse to play by the rules that define materiality as passive matter. Their sense of a world in which matter is in flux, offering promising new versions of subject–object entanglements, is one this book proposes to develop further.

This development has two axes. First, these theories have, with some signal exceptions, recently found their home in the critical discourses of the sciences; this book asks what insights are gained when we return to the space of culture and aesthetics. Second, these science-oriented discourses, considering matter as such, engage less and less with the fact that this volatile materiality takes shape and gets assembled and disassembled in the only possible cultural-economic context: that of modern capital. The techno-scientific ontology of the hybrid object, its ecology, is always already a part of a political economy. Culture asks us to look again at the messiness of matter. This matter is not simply technonature, but technoaesthetics. By technoaesthetics is meant, first, that aesthetics is an important technology of matter, a *dispositif* through which materiality comes into being; second, that the new forms of matter are also aesthetic, that is, that they have been shaped by artistic production; third, that materialities have been accessed primarily through the senses, apprehended synaesthetically, affectively, and somatically through a perceptive apparatus that dismisses any hierarchical separation between soma and matter. The commodified and aesthetic version of materiality takes us into the middle of the everyday, and allows the critic to gauge with more clarity the effects of matter as a force operating through different network flows of power—economic, technological, scientific, libidinal, affective, collective, and individual. I call this everyday matter with style, accessible to the subject's senses and produced also by aesthetic practice, stuff. This book insists that the aesthetic, both as practice and mode of perception, because of its own plasticity, is a very apt sphere in which to recognize, articulate, and study hybrid materiality in its positivity and contradictions.

To affirm that stuff as we encounter it is by definition already culturally constructed is to remind ourselves also that behind the new materialisms there stands the (often unacknowledged) other account of the relation of materiality and human subjects in modernity, what is known as "historical materialism" itself. For the historical materialist, the subject's experience of materiality in modernity is governed by reification—the subject's alienation from the sensual real, brought about because matter, once commodified, had its true nature, the labor involved in producing it, hidden. The new materialism throws open this monologic narrative, but it should not lose sight of the fact that stuff is already worked-upon, hence aestheticized, matter, that exists inside the cycle of commodity circulation under capital. The older materialism insists that under the system of capital every object is always already commodified; the new materialism insists on the fungability of matter and on the plasticity possible at the moment of subject–object interaction. Stuff, as the mish-mash of objects at the borders of commodified matter, both eloquently testifies to the effects of commodification and at the same time tests its limits. To acknowledge that stuff is always already commodified is to consider materiality as part of the historical, cultural, and economic regimen of capitalism, but not necessarily, as historical materialism did, to understand this produced matter for sale as invariably a source of false consciousness. Rather, the new understanding of materiality I have been outlining creates a whole new environment for the commodity, or, we could say, it creates the commodity as environment,[2] potentially capable of producing, rather than blocking, experience. The point is not to soberly recoil from the siren song of the object for sale, but to use the energies it liberates at the affective, somatic level, in order to enlist them, hopefully, for emancipatory ends. To call this new commodified, ebullient materiality stuff, therefore, is to foreground its plurality and instability, the volatility of its value, and the event-like quality of its meaning, to privilege its plastic and transformative power.

By focusing on stuff we take the theorization of materiality into the everyday and into the open air of history. The word "stuff" appropriately expresses the everydayness of hybrid materiality: it has a mundane ring that also speaks, nevertheless, of the potential threat that all our possessions pose to us. "You have all that stuff?"; "What are you going to do with your stuff when you are away?"; "Too much stuff!" we cry, so that the image of the proud self-made owner-accumulator fades into the banality of the consumed consumer of objects we feel obliged to buy, and soon discard, in order to become the subjects we think we are. This is the fate of objects in cultures of abundance, so that, as the comedian George Carlin points out in his skit "What to Do with Your Stuff,"[3] the houses we live in have become merely containers for objects: "If you didn't have all that damned stuff you wouldn't need a house ... houses are piles of stuff with a roof on them." Stuff is the satellitary system of objects that continually accompanies and never leaves us; these are the prosthetic things that fill our pockets and purses, closets and trunks with which we furnish the self and the spaces we inhabit. Stuff is the expendable and necessary appendix that tells us that we exist and function, and yet weighs us down. It designates the useless and "used up" on its way to being thrown out, as we sense on contemplating the contents of a drawer of bric-à-brac. Stuff is unstable, recyclable, made of elements put in place by different networks of power and meaning, that encounter one another by chance and cohere only temporarily by affinity: Lucretius' atoms meet the glass shards of the smashed door in Tati's *Playtime*.

This is a materiality that refuses to behave according to the rules of the "order of things" of modernity. Uncontainable by the *tabula* through which, as Michel Foucault describes it in *The Order of Things*, matter is made into epistemological fields and taxonomies of knowledge, stuff designates those forms of hybrid materiality that defeat, with their plasticity and unceasing traffic with the human, the long western history of systematization of the object. Under the terms of the new materialism, such potential for uncontainability should be discernible in any material object. In the lived conditions of the real world, however, some objects are more amenable to plasticity than others. It is such liminal objects, piled at the borders and the transit routes between subjects and "proper" objects, between organic and inert matter, between glam object and garbage, that we term "stuff" here. Stuff refers to those objects that have enjoyed their moment of consumer allure, but have now shed their commodity glamour—without yet being quite cast aside. They exist brazenly as neither one thing nor the other: not quite saleable, and certainly not garbage, not monumental or important objects, but still bearing traces of a past, of desire, of life, and of the interactions between subject and object that formed them and wore them out. Not particularly useful but not useless enough to cast off, these are objects that we are not quite ready to let go of—or that are not ready to let go of us. They complicate the old totalizing account of the blanket duplicity of commodity culture offered by historical materialism, but they are also certainly much too shopworn to qualify as the pristine materiality dreamed of in some environmentalist accounts of nature. They are the characteristic used goods of modernity, where nature's materials have all already been commodified. They are, in short, stuff, and it is in attending to their folds and enmeshments, to their eagerness to mix it up with other objects and with subjects, and to their eccentric attractiveness, their willingness not to be contemplated but to be touched, that we may find, in their complex concreteness, a template of a materiality to come.

Let us consider two examples to illustrate the difference between the tendency to take the object as commodified and hence "perfect" within the existing order, and on the other to discern its energized materiality, a materiality so enmeshed in time, place, and the subjects who have dealt with it that it is eloquent. The first is a set of glass beakers in a photograph by the German photographer Albert Renger-Patzsch, the second the image of the sprouting potatoes in Agnés Varda's film *The Gleaners and I*, which I discuss at the book's close. Renger-Patzsch's most famous and influential work is his 1928 book of photographs *Life Is Beautiful*, a prime example of *Neue Sachlichkeit* ("New Matter of Factness") or Weimar documentary realism, in which the photographer meant to record reality phenomenologically. His intent was to capture "the essence of the object"[4]—in exact and clinical images of industrial objects and locales. Despite the claim of realism, it is evident that his camera eye, in such a famous photograph as "Laboratory Glasses, Schott Glassworks, Jena, 1934," (Figure 0.1) makes matter ascend to the sphere of Art.

Here reality is remade cosmetically; the photo finds beauty, unexpectedly, in the ordinary and overlooked. The viewer consumes this surprising image and is caught in an ecstatic contemplation of reality as it is—which, in a logic

Figure 0.1 Laboratory Glasses
Albert Renger-Patzsch, "Laboratory Glasses, Schott Glassworks, Jena, 1934."

shared by the relatively new genre of advertising photography, turns out to be extremely photogenic. Here realism, frozen into the spectacularity of the common object made auratic and heroic, turns the object into a fetish, pointing in the direction of the commodity and its advertisement. In their algid isolation, detached from any story or history, the laboratory glass vessels announce themselves as Things, unproductive materiality consumable primarily as spectacle, capable of a sidereal life of their own. Photographic technique disappears into the perfection of the products, objects without past or future, immobilized in the fetishistic present. No tactility is possible here: these are absolute objects that can be accessed only visually, only at a distance. They do not wish to be used, displaced, destroyed: only admired. Any memory of their use is coolly superseded by the radiance of their image. Their everydayness washed out, their use value erased, the lab glasses have become hyperobjects of beauty allowing no traffic, no movement.

This art-as-advertising reading of these photographed objects is supported by the fact that Renger-Patzsch did indeed make much of his income from advertising photography; the Schott logo is discreetly legible on four of the beakers, and this photo appeared in a company catalog in 1937. It is also the reading suggested by none other than Walter Benjamin, in his comments on Renger-Patzsch in "The Artist as Producer," where he criticizes this glorification of the object as commodity fetishization in an art that should know better. Finally, it is appropriate that these flasks are made of glass, for glass, promising transparency, light, health, smoothness, and cleanliness, as we will see in the third chapter, is *the* key and most characteristic material of modernity. This photograph of glass beakers on a glass table presents objects of exquisite purity, aloof, elegant, rarified, and calling silently for the tribute of distanced contemplation, straining for the status of the well-lit beautiful commodity.

And yet . . . the photo might also be seen to cry out for a counter-reading of these glass spheres and cylinders, one that discerns disorder at the edges of their clean lines. The beaker's very glassiness, in this second look, multiplies their presence, once they are crowded together, as a kind of haunting; every one is reflected in its dream-reversal, in the glass surface of the table; for every one of them, its separateness is compromised by the back-shadows cast by its companions. As a composition, this photo is a mélange of tangled lines, shadows, lacunae, and frayed curves in which each object decomposes, raises cloudy radiances behind and around it, fades in and out as we gaze, lost in this object-diffusion. Then too, the objects are left there—by whom? The collection bespeaks work, science, experiment, chemical reaction, tasks begun, glasses washed, handled. This is therefore a photograph of matter which has been worked on, of matter with a history and a use, of matter which fades into other matter, with object curving round object in the white-to-grey shadowland of the photograph. Not cool, still, and distinct at all, then, but emergent matter—emergent to the extent that these laboratory glasses, bunched here, are stuff, unruly objects with their own stories and their own latent, but discernible, affective charge.

With other objects, the plasticity of hybrid materiality can be celebrated from the start. For an example, consider the heart-shaped potatoes which Agnés Varda serendipitously finds discarded after the harvest, in a French field during the making of her 2000 documentary *The Gleaners and I*.

These are examples of what Bruno Latour, celebrating the hybrid qualities of both parties bred of the mutually osmotic relations of subject and object, calls "quasi-subjects quasi-objects." They lie at the crossroads of a series of networks that include aesthetics, social solidarity, and politics, as well as the environmental and economic conditions of their planting and harvesting. The potatoes are discarded for "aesthetic" reasons, because they are considered misshapen, non-standard, and so unmarketable. Nonetheless, like any hybrid, they have power: to bring together others who encounter them, here the poor

Figure 0.2 Heart-Shaped Potatoes
Agnés Varda, *The Gleaners and I* (2000) (screenshot) heart-shaped potatoes.

who assemble in the field to glean; to inspire one of them to work at the *Restaurants du Coeur*, the "Restaurants of the Heart," for which he is collecting potatoes the day he meets Varda. Examples of heavily networked materiality, the potatoes are excluded from the economic and aesthetic grid of dominant culture. They are examples of improper beauty, a beauty that doesn't manage to conceal the fact that materiality is a process, not the Thing itself, which is still very capable of affecting others and of signifying, but not on cue. Varda herself, delighted with these chance finds, tries to contain their materiality into the image of a curiosity that she will preserve with her film. For her the potatoes become miraculous curios that she installs as private museum pieces in her home, exhibited for her own pleasure as a still life without a painter. But no photographer's light can freeze the potatoes into immortality: Varda's camera simply registers their decay. The home museum display turns into a *memento mori* that reminds the director of her own finitude: when she returns from a trip abroad, the potatoes have sprouted and withered. From the withered potatoes her camera moves to her own withered and aged hands, shifting the image of the impermanence of the aesthetic artefact to that of the impermanence of the body.

Figure 0.3 Director's Hand
Agnés Varda, *The Gleaners and I* (2001) (screenshot) close-up of the skin of the director's own hand.

As the camera moves, the object as hybrid materiality vacillates; following the sprouted potatoes with the director's hands has the effect of making her too a quasi-subject quasi-object, facing the vulnerability of her own materiality. Both the potatoes and Varda are hybrids, and both refuse to occupy their assigned space in the grid of meaning and value: the potato is nature that trespasses into art and then, decaying, contradicts the durability of art. The director puts herself into the object's position when she films herself with her handheld camera to make art from decaying nature: the potatoes' and her own. It is her own decaying hands, filming, that make the art.

The ennobled industrial object of the "New Matter-of-Factness," whose photographically created perfection makes it seem an atemporal ideal, appears to beautify the ordinary into forgetfulness of its own production and history. Yet even here the object, frozen into a cultural artefact, waits patiently, available to be read against the grain. Varda, over sixty years later, delights in the hybridity and in the complex, multiple status of materiality as she moves her camera, her film, and her audience into heterogeneous realms, knotted together at different moments of the continuum of forms of power. Technoaesthetics: her camera, itself the techno-object which we don't see but sense at work, is also an integral object mixing it up with the other glimpsed objects Varda uses to question the systems of power and signification she portrays.

I. Critical Stuff

What defines stuff is its amorphousness as accumulation, assemblage, jumble of objects; a blur between borders and defined categories, what's left in the aftermath of (now waning) cultures of abundance. As part of stuff the object loses its contours, the armor that had defined it in relation to the subject, or as a commodity for sale. Once objects cease to be objects, as Bill Brown suggests, they become things. The disactivated objects that participate in stuff, however, never attain this kind of "thinginess," the *quidditas* that sets them apart from the human, from their function in relation to people. Rather, stuff is better defined by its liminality between the human and the non-human. *Stuff Theory* locates this liminality in the midst of history, society, and aesthetics. Stuff's materiality is not only a question of production and consumption, or of our ethical connection to nature; rather it takes shape through a set of relations that are social, affective, aesthetic, technological, and sensate, and both individual and collective. The newer scientific and ontological approaches to materiality tell only one part of the story. We need to also study vital matter from the perspective of what is common, to imagine its potential for praxis. What does stuff produce? What are its effects? What kind of practices does it put in place? Beyond the gaze of the new materialism fascinated by matter, we need a politics of materiality.

If amorphousness is stuff's signature figuration, its prototype in the twentieth century is the materiality with which Walter Benjamin engages, when he writes of his collection of toys, his library, and the out-of-fashion commodities of the arcades. Benjamin's thoughts on things are the starting point for a modern genealogy of stuff. Through the out-of-fashion objects he observes, materiality proliferates into unexpected intimacies and encounters. His ex-commodities no longer speak the language and the desires of consumption: the dysfunctional ex-commodities promise to detonate the unrealized future contained in the past, to expose in the objects themselves the realization of the utopias of generations past. Surrealist stuff, appropriated by Benjamin, becomes a social holograph politically charged, waiting to flash out its utopian potential. Here the plasticity of stuff, its assembling and disassembling in new formations, opens a new scenario for praxis, where the subject and the object both recognize their undeniable co-participation in materiality, and, in Baudrillard's phrase, the *objet* is the precedent of the *projet*. Benjamin's early twentieth-century dialectical image as *Wunschbild* is a template for a twentieth-first century political ecology of stuff. His vision of the power of the arcades' *bibelots* anticipates the quasi-subject quasi-object. For him the haptic quality of the dream image and the tactility of the profane illumination do not only concern the individual's body, but open it to collective experience and praxis. If we take his version of matter as the prototype of hybrid materiality, what do these stuff-objects promise today? What can the quasi-object quasi-subject, and the materialism of the event, which now wants to replace the teleology of the dialectics, promise?

To think the everydayness of the quasi-subject quasi-object, we need to change the perspective from which hybrid materiality becomes visible to the scattered, fragmentary, and singular perspective of the street. There, hybrid materiality takes shape and is experienced, knotted through different encounters, deterritorialized, and reterritorialized. From the perspective of the street these material assemblages of human and non-human, animate and inanimate, reveal themselves to be matter with style: not "naked" materiality, nature purified, but always technological and imbricated in the body aesthetically, through lines of affect that redefine subjectivity away from the detached autonomous rationality of the spectator. At street level, hybrid materiality produces affect and can be affectively invested. This materiality is both technological and "natural;" it speaks the languages of science *and* aesthetics. Its mode of existence, the way it comes into being by skipping between the human and the non-human, is a technoaesthetics. This aesthetics is a technology of matter, through which both human and non-human materiality, far from being an inert object of representation, develops into a flexible formation that claims attention. What counts as materiality is triangulated by the technological *and* the aesthetic. Neither human nor non-human materiality can exist, be perceptible and capable of perceiving, without being embodied in a sensate, aesthetic form.

Twentieth-century art, beginning with the experiments of the avant-garde, enacts in its texts this very traffic between the subject and her "outside," between the human and the non-human. If modernist aesthetics is a material and embodied practice that brings everyday reality to bear on the artwork, then its aesthetic operates as the testing ground for the new materiality. This aesthetic highlights the plasticity of matter, and illuminates what the narrative of the quasi-object quasi-subject tells in the sphere of science and technology. The modern texts studied here are, in different ways, haptic: they generate and record affective and somatic responses both in their characters and in the audience, from Elfriede Jelinek's use of fashion as arousal machine to Peter Greenaway's display of bloodied books. They show how the "deep" materiality of the object, its stuff quality, comes into being and functions in synergy with the body, to become live matter that changes the traditional understanding of the subject as alive and the object as inert. Aesthetic practices also show that stuff has an agenda, that the vitality of hybrid matter, from Benjamin's disactivated commodities to the sprouted potatoes of Varda, might break down the protocols of capitalist materiality.

What kind of politics does the technoaesthetics of matter allow? It seems clear that negative dialectics cannot only be envisioned in the terms laid down by historical materialism, which invested the capacity for critique solely in the worker who fashioned the object. In the era of the quasi-object quasi-subject and of late capital, a new idea of negativity might recognize a critical power in what may be called the political ecology of materiality. Hybrid materiality does possess an oppositional power, a volatile form of "electricity by contact" that emerges, ad hoc, in the contact zones of the encounter. Our task is to record these moments, moments that still produce the spark of negativity that flickers at times of danger, always under threat of disappearing. Stuff challenges us to rethink negativity in terms of its plasticity. Such negativity is not a state achieved, a category fixed in an always recognizable identity, but a mobile one, capable of signaling dissent, but not from the hypostatized position of the object. The quasi-subject quasi-object gets its negative potential from its ungovernable nature, its unruliness, its becoming in the juncture of which it is part. Especially today, when capital seems to move at the same speed of rhizomatic expansion as vital matter, by giving up the need for the negative, critical theory risks echoing and reproducing the logic of capital. The critique of the present through stuff, then, demands the same plasticity that organizes the object of this critique. The materialities of stuff are not automatically and joyously productive, but may also be produced, corralled into a specific state, reterritorialized into submission. The production of materiality can be either emancipatory or oppressive. To let stuff speak dissent is not only a matter of pushing the quasi-subject quasi-object out of the closet of metaphysics, but of allowing materiality the role of liminal go-between connecting what that metaphysics has read as a fixed masterful subject on the one hand, and an inert universe of matter on the other. This dynamic role is more disturbing than any static image of negativity, more powerful than a dissent turned positivity, because it cannot be easily reterritorialized and put to work.

Let us try, then, another definition of this category, stuff. Stuff is an assemblage of quasi-objects quasi-subjects, forms, flows, and events that supersede the object as it has been defined, whether in Newtonian physics or the Hegelian dialectic. Thus it points to a matter that is continually becoming, through an increasing production of contact zones, an increasing criss-crossing of flows of power that continually and necessarily compromise its individual identity. At the same time, stuff blurs the contours of the object into a dangerously valueless materiality-as-mass: what you bought as unique and new will soon become unfashionable, and chances are it will leave your house in lump form, saleable only by weight. Stuff, whether as post-Newtonian matter or as outmoded paraphernalia, foregrounds the instability of materiality; in each case an image of permanence melts into a liquid circulation of matter. But the question remains: are these two instabilities one and the same? This book proposes an already existing form of liminal objecthood, stuff, as a test case for the new materialist designation of all matter as liminal, active, rhizomatic, and emergent. Stuff, as unruly-object horde, might in this sense seem the ideal candidate for rebellion, leading more proper objects into a more intimate, subtle, and dangerous relation to the subject—and all material into new kinds of subject–object encounters. The reality, however, is more complex: stuff is not a designation for one type of matter, forever fixed, but a category into which various objects can enter, and exit, in different historical circumstances. Stuff, then, is made up of objects that have been through the mill, have interacted with the world and its subjects, and have a story to tell. This story, which all matter, as it were, knows is its destiny in modernity, is both that of the dynamism that infuses all relations of modern subjects with every kind of materiality, and that of the dehiscence of this complex, hybrid materiality into the valueless.

Stuff as mass becomes a continuum from which value can no longer be extracted and recognized; it turns into a conglomerate that cannot be invested affectively in a proper manner: it simply becomes the unspecified form into which materiality as stuff presents itself daily—the mess in the house, the impacted closet, the crowded attic. Its ancestors could be found in Dickens' *Old Curiosity Shop*, as well as in the amassed goods ready to be destroyed in the potlatch ceremonies Marcel Mauss describes and Georges Bataille cites in "The Notion of Expenditure." Stuff, therefore, can represent a threat—and a productive one. It is a particular kind of lively matter resulting from the conditions of a specific historical moment: the overflow of commodities from the successive stages of overproduction and overconsumption in consumer culture.

If, therefore, materiality in the new vision offered by the new materialism is to be understood as immanently productive of the always new, stuff reminds us that this unarrestable proliferation is also counterbalanced and at times stalled by points of blockage, resistance, contradiction. As examples, consider the somewhat different effects of the recurrence of the same type of materiality, in the two following examples of massified matter, in both of which the individual object loses its "self." The first comes from the sculptor Michelangelo Pistoletto's "Venus of the Rags" (1967) *arte povera* installation, which critiques a whole tradition of artistic beauty.

Venus, her iconic beauty contained in the cool perfection of white marble (merely cited by the artist in cheaper plaster), faces away from the spectator to gaze over a pile of old clothes amassed at her back. Displaced into the space designated for aesthetic exhibition, the rags stage an iconoclastic protest against art as institution, a call to bring the street into the museum, and to complicate established notions of beauty and artistic value. The classical ideal of beauty is defied by the abjection of the rags, soft beside the hardness of the plaster Venus' body, soft as the bodies that once occupied and have now vacated them. Art's auratic value is questioned by the junk's valuelessness, in one stroke reminding us of the ephemerality both of bodies and of traditional notions of taste.

Now consider how this heap of clothes as *arte povera* returns with a vengeance in another, quotidian image of stuff that we have all seen. The stuff in this case is also old clothes, which are always evocative of lived material lives. In the case I have in mind they are crammed into a small truck that I often spot at the local gas station. These chance encounters, the reappearance of the truck, might be a portent, a particular moment of illumination for this student of unruly and scandalous stuff. The first time, I noticed only a long board on the roof (another surfer?); then the occupant of the car, a middle-aged blond woman, a little disheveled (but who am I to talk?), a figure *à la* Duane Hanson, emerged. I glance into the back of the truck, jammed with stuff flattened against the windows, in unexpected formations and combinations. The intertwining of these clothes makes them look like rags.

Figure 0.4 Venus of the Rags

Michelangelo Pistoletto, "Venus of the Rags," 1967.

Courtesy of the Tate Modern.

Among the rags are small appliances, books, shoes. This image, more aleatory than that of the Venus, also stands as a critique, but a sharper one than that of any art installation. Both images of stuff, however, pose questions concerning materiality that the new materialisms must take into account if this theory of subject–object interaction is to matter in the real world. These questions are not about the dissolved solidity of the object, or its possible sentience; they concern the indissoluble "weight" of materiality, in the sense in which Pierre Bourdieu uses the phrase "the weight of the world"[5] to mean the burden of poverty, of denied access to material goods in the midst of plenitude, shared by the poor. On the one hand there is the challenge to the *status quo* posed by the introduction of rags into the museum. On the other note the materiality of displacement, of homeless nomadism, of coping, amidst a superabundance of objects, with not having the capacity to encounter objects in the way capital says we should, by owning them.

How can we differentiate between these two versions of stuff? How can we talk about their different meanings? How can we account for the very different contexts that put them in place? How do different forms of stuff, even if configured in the same way, assume a different value, and affect users differently? Finally, how can we, as critics, distinguish between different forms of materiality, go beyond the functionalist and ontological perspective and its inclination to describe, to recognize the production of matter as simply "machinic"[6]: to be able to assess and recognize its history and the effects of its productivity? It is only by naming the contexts and the circumstances that contribute to the piling up of the rags that we can read reality in a way that is not simply a description of its productivity. We need to reconstruct the conjuncture that put in place the volatile stuff we see, and work to intervene in that event, to change it.

II. Object, Thing, Hybrid: The Case of the New Materialisms

The image of a traffic between the human and the non-human that characterizes the new materiality has, in the western philosophical tradition, been the site of some of the fiercest debates about what it means to be modern. Marx lays out the stakes in the *Economic and Philosophic Manuscripts of 1844*,[7] where he talks of "the practical creation of an object world, the working over of inorganic nature, [which] is the confirmation of man as species-being, that is, as a being that relates to the species as to himself, and to himself as to the species." Even in his power of objectification "over" inorganic nature, man, as Marx points out, is never outside of, or above nature itself, but rather partakes of it through his corporeality. Thus alienation is not only a matter of value, but of "stolen materiality ... It alienates from man his own body," in his phrase. Yet Marx's nineteenth-century historical materialism, with its totalizing sweep, was a theory of its era; now, when global resources are known to be finite, when their flow has created an immense level of global traffic, and when the commodification of every resource, from food to human feelings, into commodity objects is pursued at an unrelenting pace, the theory of reification, and its account of the unvarying commodity at the heart of it, is both more compelling than ever and in need of expansion. An alternative, new materialist tradition of thinking about materiality, from Spinoza to Bergson to Deleuze, more adaptable to a world of matter in flux and to accounting for new versions of subject–object entanglement, is now being recanvassed. An aim of this book is to consider how the now classical tradition and the new can learn from one another, and to see how the new materialist insights might align with the cultural critiques which, stemming from historical materialism, have set the stage for them.

The older materialisms, whether dialectical, historical, mechanicistic or culturalist, were developed in the era before the current truly massive proliferation of commodities; from a time, therefore, when a separation of forces could still credibly be apprehended in thinking the subject–object encounter. New object formations—from frozen embryos to digital machines, from floating islands of plastic waste in the world's oceans to grim scenes on the same seas of refugees without papers crammed into leaky vessels, accompanied by a growing sense of imminent environmental catastrophe in a world overwhelmed by things—call for theories capable of understanding the new assemblages of contemporary materiality. Now subject and object on our small planet with its finite material resources stand in an inextricable proximity to each other. Their shared materiality is made by their coalescing into temporary aggregations that produce not stable objects, but events. Most strands of the new materialist critique insist, from different disciplinary perspectives, on an ontology of the material that centers on the positivity and productivity of the event. Some define the new hybrid materialities in terms of subjects' interaction with technology. In contrast to the older materialisms, many, however, are wary of critique.

While the emergence of a new notion of matter, and the search for new critical languages capable of making it visible, has intensified recently, it has been on the agenda of theorists, scientists, and artists at least since the early twentieth century. Between 1880 and 1918, new energy-using technologies—the cinema, the car, the airplane—gave a new sense of fluidity to everyday experience and gave rise to a kinetic apprehension of space. This mobility was theorized in physics and practiced in aesthetics; both Einstein's theory of relativity and Futurism's sculpture and architecture, from Boccioni to Sant'Elia, considered space as a field of forces and energy without any substratum against which these forces could emerge. In this space the concept of Newtonian matter as solid was superseded by fast movement, which, by accelerating and decelerating, produces object-effects. Matter here has no defined, a priori form, but rather could be thought of as temporarily aggregating into an event. "The event is there where space suddenly differentiates itself," as Sanford Kwinter sums up this line of thinking. In this new vision of fluid materiality, fixed form was superseded by a new order of becoming, in which matter is acknowledged to be in flux, "a momentary and metastable constellation of forces (or force-lines), that originate outside and continue beyond it."[8] These forces, in their perpetual multiplicity, mobility, and differentiation, generate the object and the subject effect. Mobility is acknowledged by Bergson, and, decades later in the work of Deleuze and Guattari, as the chief quality of the new materiality, and has marked all its critical languages: that of flows, networks, intensities, deterritorialization and reterritorialization, and change. This account of dynamic matter has lately begun to propel new analyses of the colonization of life under the terms biopower, biocapital, and biopolitics, redrawing the boundaries between what Marx calls "the world of men" and "the world of things." This new interest in flux needs to be taken into account if the implications of the new materialism are to be understood.

If Bergson and, later, Deleuze are the most influential theorists of this fluid materiality, their vision is anticipated by a whole alternative philosophical tradition of materialism, which begins with the atomism of Epicurus and Lucretius, and reaches into the work of Spinoza, Rousseau, Marx, Nietzsche, Heidegger, and Althusser. This genealogy of alter-materialism is what Althusser in his later writings calls "the materialism of the encounter,"[9] or "the materialism of the rain," an allusion to the way Lucretius' "rain of atoms" encounter one another "*nunc hinc, nunc illinc*" ("now here, now there") through the random intervention of the *clinamen*, the swerve or differentiation. It opposes any teleological and dialectical view of matter, refusing the proposition that reality is organized by any *causa prima*, or causality in general, regarding reality as aleatory and always becoming.

The materialism of the encounter acknowledges something that had always existed beneath the radar of western metaphysics, without ever being recognized. This is the condition of what Bruno Latour, following Michel Serres,[10] calls the quasi-subject quasi-object. Quasi-subjects quasi-objects, for Latour, are hybrid actants which, while necessary to the dominant order, have always been relegated to the invisibility and subalternity of the nameless and the unrepresentable. There has been no place for these volatile entities in the taxonomic system of modernity.[11] We could think of contemporary discourses of materialism as attempts to make place for these hybrids. In the pioneering language of Donna Haraway, influential for Latour, they are the cyborgs, breaching the established *tabula* of knowledge and representation. For Haraway the cyborg is a critical figure that helps us inquire into the wordliness of technoscience. Figuration, rather than representation, is how materiality takes shape in a series of spaces that include "literature as well as biology, and philosophy ... places where the ambiguity between the literal and the figurative is always working."[12] In *We Have Never Been Modern* (1993) Latour points out that the subject–object split has been naturalized by centuries of western science and philosophy, becoming the ground on which hierarchies of difference, built upon the rigid differentiation of an active authorizing subject controlling and manipulating inert matter, have multiplied. Explaining that the hybrid has never been admitted into this grid, Latour highlights the marginalizing aspects of power as well as the merely "productive" ones. The assumed "order of things" upon which the western logic of valued knowledge is founded has been a means of (not) naming matter in order to dominate it. He shows that there is nothing natural about this: this order of things owns its stability to the exclusion of the hybrid and marginal quasi-object quasi-subject, while depending upon it.

An interest in this newly discerned hybrid and in its plasticity is what has given contemporary critiques of materiality their radical potential.[13] The pioneering work in the anthropology of material culture by Arjun Appadurai and Daniel Miller, and in "thing theory," by Bill Brown, are important blueprints for the new materialism. Appadurai and Kopytoff's[14] discussion of the social life of things, Miller's absorbing work on stuff, and Brown's beautifully nuanced critique of things[15] all champion the material in its assumed struggle with existing social forces and norms. Appadurai looks at commodities and their after-human life in terms of materiality's rebellion against the effects of consumer culture, whereby the object is subtracted from the jurisdiction of the subject, and thus liberated in part from its passive fate under capitalism. The anthropologist Daniel Miller understands stuff, a term he intentionally refuses to define, in structuralist terms. He traces the history of material culture back to Marx and Simmel, insisting that materiality exists "not through our consciousness or body, but as an external environment that habituates and prompts us."[16] Objects always exist as part of a system, and their "humility", their tendency just to be there and fade out of focus, teaches us to behave appropriately in our culture, so that "culture comes with stuff" (52). Brown aims at recuperating "the thing" on the terrain of art and literature in order to grant materiality a particular status of independence: "The thing is what is excessive in objects." Thus when materiality is separated from its use for humans, it can emerge in all its sensuousness and metaphysical presence. With the claim that the thinginess of things makes them unavailable to a cultural reading ("Things lie beyond the grid of intelligibility the way mere things lie outside the grid of the museal exhibition, outside the order of objects"[17]), Brown's approach counters the anthropological view. His is less a case of the social life of things than the secret life of things, which go on strike on the subject and enjoy an existence of their own.

Each of these critical positions anticipates current discussions of materiality in that they paradoxically salvage the relationship between subject and object while giving more preeminence to the object. The problem now is not to turn the relationship between subject and object on its head, or to recuperate the object and give it new primacy, but rather to reconfigure this relationship in terms of relationality and entanglements. Following this lead, the discourse of new materialism has been growing exponentially, reaching into the fields of philosophy, geography, bioethics, sociology, environmental studies, and politics. Recent interventions, including the work of Jane Bennett,

Diana Coole and Samantha Frost, and Sarah Whatmore and Bruce Braun,[18] have channeled the current discussion of materiality in the direction of political theory and biopolitics, repositioning technoscience in the social and public domain.

This move in contemporary materialism is symptomatic of an ontological turn of contemporary theory. All the new materialisms are interested in a view of materiality as force, a form of post-Spinozian vitalism and deterritorialized nomadism based on an ontology of materiality. Bennett, for instance, poses "thing power" as "the agentic capacity of a matter that is alive and whose ontology needs to be taken into account" (4). The vivid image of materiality with which her book opens, a serendipitous assemblage of a glove, a dead rat, a plastic lid, and a spool of thread, is programmatic: her encounter with materiality in the gutter allows her a glimpse of "a culture of things irreducible to the culture of objects. I achieved for a moment what Thoreau had made his life's goal: to be able to be surprised by what we see" (40). Second, the new materialists show a renewed attention to the now demoted subject, attempting to redefine what counts as the human now, when the human and the non-human are no longer clearly separable. As Braun and Whatmore note, "There is no moment in which humanity comes to be contaminated by technical objects and practices . . . because there can be no human without them. The history of the human animal—and indeed the history of culture—is thus necessarily the history of the stuff that is, from the beginning, part and parcel of human life" (xix). The genesis of the individual is necessarily also a technogenesis. Third, the new materialisms imply a desire to get beyond recent iterations of the historical materialist analysis of materiality, especially the now superseded "cultural turn." These latter are considered as forms of abstraction that reduce matter to language, culture, discourse, unable to reach the solid bedrock of reality.

The contestation of a more orthodox materialism in this work follows the trend of forty years of poststructuralism and feminist criticism and so is unsurprising; the associated rejection of "constructionism" and the cultural, however, begs some questions. Inflected by the language and inquiry-protocols of the sciences and social sciences, the new approach may offer a new rapprochement between the dominant "hard" sciences and the humanities. At stake in what sometimes amounts to an object-oriented ontology is a materiality that does not compromise itself by dealing with the imprecise and spurious quality, or the impressionism, of everyday experience. This perspective has tremendous political implications, for example in rethinking sustainable development, yet the productivity of actual matter and its plasticity don't always and automatically square up with lived day-to-day experiences of subjects and materialities. Working out the implications of the new materialisms for the variegated sphere of the everyday is still a work in progress, in which this dynamic view of matter might take into account the heterogeneity of the street and of politics from below. To fully speak its potential, the new vitalist materiality will benefit then from being brought into liaison with the kinds of subaltern politics which the "culturalist" turn made visible. The celebration of the "immanently self organizing properties of matter" (13) will have more immediate purchase for such areas as a biopolitics of health and wellbeing, or for the labor issues of affect work, once the new materialism takes into account the different conditions in which specific relationships between matter and subject groups are produced. For this, new materialism could take on board the cultural turn's well developed strategies for discerning the marginalized subject and object beyond the conventional disciplinary fields of vision, subjects, and objects which, though marginal, are no less material. It is this reintegration of insights of the cultural with the breakthrough of the new materialism that this book hopes to effect.

Without some such version of the cultural and the everyday, the project of "giving matter its due" always risks doubling up into a rejection of critique. As Coole and Frost point out, " a further trait of new materialisms is its antipathy towards oppositional ways of thinking . . . [in favor of] the creative affirmation of a new ontology" (9). Now that, according to the editors, "the radicalism that came into being with the cultural turn is . . . more or less exhausted" (6), the new materialist has full license to embark on the ontological turn; while the radical cultural critic analyzed the world in hopes of changing it, however, the ontologist analyzes it in order to trace the directions of its unpredictable mechanisms. Yet can such an ontology aspire to any more than an ethics as self-interest, in which one is cautious in intervening in the material world because such intervention might come back to harm oneself? Ontology recognizes, and tries to account for, the multiplicity of new intersections, new relationalities, new events; its danger is a descriptive presentism which in the end might only confirm and ensure the permanence of the status quo. A strength of the new materialisms is the suggestion that novel kinds of political organization and new horizons of the political, such as the biopolitical regime of the care and wellbeing of the self and of the environment, need new analytical frameworks to do them justice. This project is more indebted to the cultural turn than its advocates admit, especially since that turn was a movement as complex, contradictory, and multivocal as are the new materialisms today. The work of Gramsci or Althusser, or a tradition of feminist materialists, from Judith Butler to Eve Sedgwick and Elizabeth Grosz, for example, goes well beyond analyses of representations to theorize critical interventions at the material level. When the cultural is short-circuited as the terrain of otiose fantasies that have no track with the physical, economic, and social spheres that give force to materiality, and the materiality of cultural production is dismissed, history itself gets sidelined. To matter in the real world new materialisms must be open to the history of how any given matter has already been worked on and produced; that is, made into culture.

Culture matters, as it provides a purchase on history, including material history, the history of matter itself, of subjects' encounters with it and vice versa. An historicization of the productive, inventive capabilities of materiality would show that these capabilities both coincide and collide with the inventiveness of capital. The innovative forging of new relations that characterizes contemporary supple matter also characterizes today's forms of labor, and is co-generated by contemporary forms of neoliberal capitalism. What do we make of this coexistence, of the changing juxtapositions of matter and subjects, and the struggles, cooperations, and chance explosions that take place between them? How do we recognize the creativity of material life in its different circumstances and effects?

In making distinctions between different kinds of subject–object contacts the question that Catherine Malabou asks in her book of the same title, "What should we do with our brain?"[19] comes to mind. Malabou takes to task neuroscience's analysis of the plasticity that characterizes another form of materiality, that of the brain. The brain's plasticity, she points out, could be an incredible resource, which, if used by an aware subject, could help change reality. However, this plasticity is always co-opted by capital, whose modalities are similarly plastic, innovative, always producing new synapses. Malabou decries this kind of suppleness which demands the subjection of the individual to the flexible laws of capital, and which must be resisted. She defines plasticity, on the contrary, as the productive-destructive, and therefore oppositional, potential of the brain. Drawing on accounts of how modern management techniques rework tropes of 1960s counter-culture,[20] she sees the flexibility demanded of the worker as a perverse capture of neuronal plasticity, in which creativity and freedom are recast as a means of enslavement to the dominant system.[21]

"What should we do with our brain?" she asks. (Her choice of the verb "to do," *faire*, implies praxis, and thus is eminently political[22]). Let us ask, likewise, what should we do with new materialities, once we have acknowledged the multiplicity of subject–object connections, and the unexpected interconnections of objects leading to unanticipated events? Now what? What is this materiality for? Both questions, Malabou's and ours, take the material out of the serene, clean, and disinterested sphere of science and into the space of politics and the everyday. As she notes, her question is not for scientists, "it is a question 'for anyone' [in that] ... it seeks to give birth in everyone to the feeling of a new responsibility" (14), to ask: "*What should we do so that consciousness of the brain does not purely and simply coincide with the spirit of capitalism?*" (Italics hers, 12). Similarly new materialities are for everybody, or they should be, and they should take the fluidity of the event to the everyday level, where power itself becomes material. It is only there, where capitalism is a force making matter flexible, that versions of matter's fluidity can be judged and, if necessary, contested and opposed.

Once we admit that the unlimited freedom, innovation, and plasticity of materiality often works in unison with that of capital, what do we do? We cannot stop at the ecstatic response: the chief affect of new materialisms cannot be just fascination in front of the vibrancy and the marvel of a materiality that works by itself, because we declare that its mobility always produces something new. We cannot afford to contemplate the fluidity of matter as spectators, without recognizing its uneven effects. How do we differentiate between the two energies of materiality, the one emancipatory, the other merely enslaving, which Malabou outlines? How can we do so without a notion of contradiction and negativity? Could these categories be reimagined as immanent, rather than external to reality? We still need a politics of matter's plasticity, whether it be that of the brain or of any other materiality. Certainly negativity is no longer carried by a designated historical subject, which Georg Lukács had imagined to be the proletariat. For the historical materialist, the fate of matter under capital was invariably one of commodification and reification. The new, more adaptable account of a fluid materiality reads matter's active role as a magnetic pole for any number of social, historical, and physical forces as well as affects, pleasures, and desires. Yet the fact remains that under capital most matter has already suffered the transformations commodification implies. What new traits, we then need to ask, does the language of the new materialisms afford to commodified materiality? How can we rethink commodities as matter that is alive, and not as simply bearing in its form the ever-same fetish-logic of consumer capital? How can the discourse of mobile materiality help us reconceptualize the commodity at a time when its actual materiality and, we could say, its embodiment, is more and more volatile and immaterial? For example, in the contemporary knowledge and service economies, do information streams constitute matter, even as they are bought and sold? Similarly, in a commodity culture centered on advertising, itself more often than not virtual, the object for sale is presented preeminently as image, so that the actual material component of what we consume is evermore deferred. The interchange of commodity as material object and its simulated image, the fading out of the object for sale behind the glossy photoshopped image of its dream existence, may be part of the continuum of its vibrant plasticity. We cannot avoid intervening in its flows.

The materiality of the commodity in fadeout, and the way it circulates affect through its somatics, takes us to the issue of aesthetics. Malabou gives us an indication of how to rethink materiality as inextricably implicated in the aesthetic. Through the new materialist and cognitivist language of connection of neuronal synapses and of network flows, she outlines a model of the brain's materiality that includes memory, conflict, contradiction, domination, and resistance. This is a materiality with a history, itself capable of making history precisely through its "style," a term which in her work signifies agency and praxis, the power to change and to make reality, through the chief function of the aesthetic, that of giving form. In her words: "The resource of giving form, the power to create, to invent or even to erase an impression, the *power of style*" (13). Style: the way matter exists, comes into being as what Haraway calls a "figure," sensate and communicating. Style is simultaneous with matter, encoded in it. It's not superimposed from outside, but part of matter's self-generativity, through which materiality takes shape and offers itself to its actants. The materialization process does not happen only in the sphere of the sciences, or in response only to the empiricism of data, but also in the aesthetic dimension of materiality itself, in its "style," which finally gives plasticity a name and a semiotic dimension. Materiality also takes shape, or melts into formlessness, in writing, in art, in cinema images, either in its affirmative immanence or in its similarly immanent resistance. This matter with style is what we, as critics who question what is to be done with the materiality at hand, should read to differentiate between alternative formations of power and of materiality. Discerning style, we can distinguish between what another theorist of hybridity, Antonio Negri, calls the trajectories of force and power.[23]

The new materialisms' relative silence about aesthetics is therefore an opportunity; likewise, strategies developed during the "cultural turn" to discern subaltern voices need to now be reharnassed to the task of reading the styles of matter's roles in the subject–object encounter. If the biopolitical body in its materiality were to be studied only from the impersonal statistical perspective, from the point of view of its governance and administration, rather than from the perspective of those who are struck by the policies of biopower, this approach would be in danger of merely replicating the procedures of the powers that first set the new regimes in place. To fully understand how the social body is constituted by, for example, State policies that want to maximize a population's health, we need to make visible those bodies that are made "flexible" by various forms of power. A discussion of "bodies without organs" must cite reports on organ traffic, medical reports, statistics on the most stricken social and racial groups, but it would also not be complete without a reading of how Kazuo Ishiguro treats organ harvesting in his sci-fi pastiche *Never Let Me Go* or how Stephen Frears engages the organ trade and immigrant lives in his film *Dirty Pretty Things*. We need to evaluate materiality at all levels, including the aesthetic; we need to demand that its styles be historicized, in order to grasp the effects of the events it generates. Materiality needs to be understood as always in the process of transformation; the critical languages that render matter's new suppleness need to be maximally supple and inclusive themselves. Critiques branded as aesthetic, and therefore impressionistic, are necessary in discerning all of matter's lines of flight.

What exactly can an aesthetic perspective contribute to the new materialism? Since *Stuff Theory* attends to ordinary objects, a sprouting potato and a broken door handle that morphs into a begging bowl, let an ordinary image illuminate the value of the aesthetic. Aesthetics might be thought of as the clothing of the quasi-subject quasi-object, signifying the traces of its social, cultural, physical, political, affective, and economic environment which every object, through its dynamic interconnectedness with other objects, enfolds. It can manipulate these traces to turn them, explosively, against themselves. The object's aesthetic character can run smoothly along the grooves of power, gliding over them with the sleekness of a lubricant; or, like the rough side of a Velcro strip, it can attach to other materialities whose affinities become the means either of tight connections or of abrasive stresses. Whether as attachment or slippage, the aesthetic marks the thick, potentially explosive point of contact: recall Malabou's image of plasticity as a means of destructive deflagration.

By excluding culture from their horizon, justified by the hope of more direct access to the real, new materialisms risk falling into the myth of transparency,[24] that dream of raw, unmediated access between subject and world. The unpredictability which for the new materialists is key to the ontology of matter—even to the celebration of how atoms aggregate into unpredictable configurations—can simply double back to an outcome which turns out to be already known and foreseen. Aesthetics and the idea of a stylized matter do not simplify things, but make the unpredictability of lively vitalist matter messier still. Historically, aesthetics has worked both for and against the forces in power: either as a narcotic, cosmetically occluding the unevenness of reality, in order to maintain a fetishistic unity of surface,[25] or, in the opposite direction, to illuminate this same unevenness, often through experiments with style. This second option is the aesthetics of stuff. On the one hand, stuff reproaches the environmental, untouched purity of matter with its commodity swagger, however defunct that has become; on the other, it reproaches the sleek and confident commodities of capital, as a leftover with no resale value that refuses to leave the stage. This stuff, bursting out all over in a world of overproduction, challenges any fatalist tendency to the apolitical, or the anaesthetic, in the new materialism. The ontology of matter can thus keep the pulse of power; with a more ambitious and political move, culture can read the heterogeneity of matter in order to intervene in the social scenario to which it belongs. Stuff, as high-tension matter that slides beyond the smooth styling of commodification or the shock styling of the bricoleur, names the object-state where we can catch culture off guard in modernity.

III. *Tchotchke* Overflow: Materiality in the Twentieth Century

There is a late modern history of stuff from Mazzaròs "la roba" to the useful and useless *tchotchke* that still clutter our pockets and rooms like a talisman hoard left over after the end of the sacred. It is neither a teleology nor a narrative of progress. Rather, hybrid objects have existed all along, even if largely unrepresented as such. Their emergence into visibility relies on particular historical and cultural conditions. Stuff as dangerous materiality *ex-tabula* has managed to emerge intermittently, to punctuate the orthodox narrative of political, scientific, and aesthetic "proper objects." This book marks stuff's intermittent appearance, in a constellation that includes clutter, memory objects, fashion, glass architecture, home décor, and junk in its recyclable and unrecyclable forms.

Stuff Theory focuses on the crisis points of the century when stuff came into cultural view: first, the modernist era of the 1920s and 1930s, when consumerism was being consolidated around the time of the economic crash; second, the mid-century moment of postwar reconstruction and the economic boom; and third, the end of the century, era of global flows, digital networks, and the fast traveling of objects, bodies, information, and power across more and more blurred national boundaries. We might think of these as centered on moments of economic crisis: the crash of 1929 and the crash of 1973 that preceded the postmodern era of globalization, with the economic boom of the 1950s and 1960s in the middle. All are moments of economic and cultural disruption, when the hybrid flashes up, illuminated by the historical conjuncture to which it belongs, to expose the fragility of the conceptual system that traditionally has defined, and often minimized the importance of, materiality in western modernity.

The first historical knot of materiality examined here comes at a moment of intense industrialization, when modernization stands above all for technological progress and urbanization. Yet this accelerated tempo of modernization still coexisted unevenly with the slower temporality of rural life and the premodern reality of the colony.[26] The sense of jarring unevenness that resulted is discernible in the structure of modernist materiality, from Surrealist objects forgotten in the Arcade des Panoramas, to the feminine accouterments of the late-colonial female consumer in 1904 Dublin. The 1950s period of postwar reconstruction witnessed a wave of Americanization, "efficiency," and the standardization of life in home and workplace before the conspicuous consumption of the 1960s; in this phase, the contrast between trajectories of power and the desire they incited was intensified. By now, the ethos of efficiency of a new class of white-collar workers—the *cadres* of mid-century France, for example—was augmented by the commodity's call to pleasure and waste, and countered by memories of a life of multiple, slower rhythms. The third temporal knot takes in the contemporary scenario of global capital, with its overproduction and overconsumption, when the world's problem of materiality is now that of waste and its management. Despite the economic homogeneity that globalization claims to produce, this is a new moment of glaring economic and social unevenness, not only between the North and the South, but also within the affluent west itself, where precariousness produces new kinds of marginality and, in Zygmunt Bauman's words, "wasted lives."[27] At these moments, stuff proliferates, its plasticity a palimpsest of the forces in tension across the uneven terrain of power of its time.

The chapters of this book trace the repeated emergence, in different styles, of hybrid materialities as stuff in the twentieth century and since. Benjamin inaugurates the stuff conundrum. He portrays the encounter of western subject and object as shot through by the subject's weakness before the allure of the commodity, but also by the frailty of that allure once the commodity lapses into the quasi-commodification of the marked-down, second-hand, unfashionable—that is, once it becomes stuff. He takes the magic of the commodity fully on board with what I call a "homeopathic" logic, by which the allure of the commodity is used against itself by the critic as a form of inoculation. In this move he grants himself access to the force of modern materiality without being blinded by its capitalist gloss or mystical energies. While Benjamin's mystical strain has often been noted, his absorption of the work of such contemporary vitalist thinkers as Henri Bergson, who wrote of the *élan vital*, of the relation of energy and experientiality and of how memory adheres to matter, needs to be noted also. In Bergsonian mode, Benjamin appears as an avatar of the energetics of Deleuze, the chief forerunner of the new materialism. Deleuze follows Benjamin when he shoots Bergson's vitalism through more static accounts of materialism. Benjamin, however, provided his Bergsonism off-kilter: he is fascinated with "innervated materiality," the somatic matter that makes the human subject hybrid when the energies of commodity and subject are sutured to each other. The energy of matter is concentrated in the commodity; once that commodity has been cast off, this energy turns sluggish—but has not disappeared. Benjamin discovers different modalities of energy in his delighted explorations of the subject–object encounter, but he is never under any illusion that that object in consumer culture is not always already a commodity. For him the possibility of experience relies upon a contact between innervated materiality and the subject's synaesthetic capacity. The innervated energy of the object meets, in his work, the innervated exhaustion of the modern subject.

The work of Benjamin, reread, is however only a point of departure. For example, when, at the very moment that mass consumerism became the order of the day in the west, he tore open the nineteenth-century materialist one-size-fits-all reading of the subject's encounter with the material as commodity, one of the first complications he allowed to enter was that of gender. While he elaborates a complex theory of the fetish-object as capable of action, finessing Marx's view of fetishism, he discerns less frequently how the commodity fetish encodes desire and sexuality. In reappraising the Benjamin-effect on materiality studies, this book interrogates this silence, examining instances of the encounter when materiality is figured as female, from the prostitute, to Baudelaire's *passante*, to Benjamin's own lover, Asja Lacis. In each case the critic retrenches; threatened before female sexuality, he shows the force of the affective-libidinal structures that proliferate under the aegis of the commodity, to which he himself is not immune.

In the deft interplay of wholly gendered subject and possibly gendered matter, which fetishism spans in different registers, how do desire and innervated energy coincide? The second chapter of *Stuff Theory* uses the gender issue to stress-test the limits of Benjamin's new flexibility on the subject–object encounter. At issue is the libidinal charge of commodified materiality and its effects on the gendered body. By focusing on a single episode of Joyce's *Ulysses*, "Nausicaa" (1922), in which a girl plays out the implications of her designation as object of male desire, and on Elfriede Jelinek's ferocious, tough-minded novel of modern Viennese sexuality, *The Piano Teacher* (1983), we trace how the commodity spectacle as clothed, fashionable female body can deviate from the protocols of mimetic western visuality and tactility. Each text establishes its own hybrid exchange with materiality, via the glam-porn show of the defective female body in "Nausicaa," and of the female masochist in *The Piano Teacher*. In both, fashion is no longer simply a chief phantasmagoria of modernity, marking, as Benjamin claims, the hellish time of the "always the same," but the stuff of a radical critique of femininity, of sexuality, and of objectification itself. The forms of fashion allow for the female subject's rematerialization of experience. Benjamin's flexible theory is pushed to its limits as a specific coalition of subaltern subjects and unruly stuff rechannels desire and potentially recasts existing gendered power relations in the material world.

These texts illustrate the possibilities of subjective intervention in the material realm at moments when a residual sense that there might still be objects not wholly subsumed by capital was still available even to the subaltern subject. By the 1950s, however, planned national economies on the one hand, and the advent of a high-gear culture of consumption on the other, narrowed the possibilities for recalcitrant objects and subaltern subjects to deploy. In this changed scene, stuff came to be demarcated as "past" objects, would-be souvenirs from a time of more quaint relations between subject and the material world. The heyday of the antique, whether attic relic or museum piece, as sublime stuff, had arrived. By now, the spread of consumer culture meant that commodification inhered not only in objects for sale, as it had already done, and not yet in services and affects, as it would do later in the century, but in spaces. Space—with urban zoning, with the rise of bland "non-spaces" and mass tourism, the new speculation in housing—became commodified. Materiality at the level of space itself, rather than simply at that of objects, became the site of possible contestation. In Chapter 3 we move to another locale to read the effects of this new moment of the history of materiality. The place is Paris, the time is the 1960s, a moment of intensified consumption and of regulated forms of work, and a massive reorganization of urban spaces to maximize the smooth flows of goods, services and money. This era's official style was glass architecture, tubular steel, and minimalism. What could now count as unruly stuff, fomenting a counter-narrative?

The postwar call to function and efficiency was simultaneous with a rebellious youth culture which denounced every type of authority, including the illusory democracy of consumption. Cultural critics, especially Barthes, Baudrillard, and Debord set the critical agenda; the Situationists, with Henri Lefevbre, forcefully opposed the abstraction of space with the image of the old and residual "unmodern." Anomalously unmodern objects in the films of Tati, from the child's whistle in *Mon Oncle* to the souvenir-of-Paris scarf in *Playtime*, and the antique furnishings described in Georges Perec's novel *Things*, illustrate how, in a world saturated with objects which are allowed to float free of tangible places, some objects still exist in which notions of desire, happiness, and youth can circulate in new forms. In Bertolucci's film *The Dreamers* (2000), a retrospective meditation on the time "before the revolution" of 1968, the glorious mess of clutter, another name for stuff in the era of clean lines, foregrounds the relation between stuff and space. Pointing to the mess of the body and of sexuality, this stuff itself incites to action, urging the protagonists onto the barricades. Stuff as clutter overspills the apartment of the young protagonists, contradicting the sleek functionalist spaces of the era with a flat utopian charge. This stuff could hardly effect change, but it could invade the sleek new spaces and in them sound the jarring note to incite it.

The "vintage" quality of stuff, as antique, "time capsule," or out-of-date fashion, lingering in the amnesiac new paradise of mass consumption, reminds us that it harbors the weak radioactivity, at once ominous and desired, of memory. Materiality incites remembrance with a complex circuitry of reminders and amnesia; the object in which memory lingers is lost and found, and lost again, by the modern subject. The failure of the souvenir as memory object at the end of the nineteenth century, evidenced for example by the modernist disdain for the souvenirs in Victorian parlors, allowed various modernisms to renegotiate the connection between time and materiality. In the well-known memory-texts of Marcel Proust and the somewhat less familiar ones of Virginia Woolf to which I turn in Chapter 4, the disruptive presence of "bodies without objects" and "objects without bodies," a sundering of the material and the subjective in the text, presents opportunities for a new rapprochement in which the object works as memory bank. At the same time the mundane civic object which is the time capsule, an evocative stuff-filled memory object which reached the height of its popularity in the early- to mid-twentieth century, returns matter-as-remembrance to the fetishistic self-importance accorded to it in consumer culture. Reworking his own time capsule at the century's end, in the prop-opera *One Hundred Objects to Represent the World*, Peter Greenaway ironically questions the time capsule's claimed universalism, to critique how representation upholds mnemonic materiality. His anti-representation, nevertheless, does not deny that multiple narratives have already always adhered to every object; the point is not to imagine that one can dissolve representation and thus discern pure materiality, but to ask how representation twists our perception of the material.

At the mid-century, stuff as memory object and as history-teller over time could still be taken earnestly even by the officials planning the contents of a civic time capsule. Thus stuff, as unruly clutter or silent reminder in the midst of streamlined modernity, might still have some resistant charge. By the close of the century, however, the postmodern dreamscape of consumerism had no such lingering respect for stuff, so that it could unabashedly be rejected as nothing more than junk. The final chapter here analyzes the most contemporary image of materiality in all its threatening proliferation: as rubbish. The trashed object, without any lingering sentimentality whatsoever, is cast out of the smooth circle of commodity culture. Yet this rough handling is what makes it valuable and, in cultural terms, voluble as the last halting-stage of stuff. Trash highlights the status of materiality as fluid and unstable, an instability replicated in the "viscous" condition of postmodern life. The incorporation of everyday waste in art famously defined the adversarial stance of the modernist avant-garde, from the littered "throwaway" in Joyce's *Ulysses* to the broken ceramics used by the sculptor Nikki de Saint-Phalle to build heroines and monsters. In the twentieth-century fin-de-siècle the aesthetization of waste, marginality, and poverty has tended, instead, to be a means to tame the political force of waste, to purify it into an object of contemplation. Consider the floating plastic bag bobbing through Sam Mendes' film *American Beauty* (1999), which I juxtapose with the misshapen potatoes and hands in Agnés Varda's extraordinary *The Gleaners and I* (2000). Mendes' film manages the unruly power of garbage through the aestheticizing camera eye of one of the characters; Varda's does the opposite, and uses waste to imply a thorough social critique, but not at the expense of aesthetics. The way the narrative of her film articulates at once the world's burden and the subject's enjoyment, need and desire, pleasure and praxis, aesthetics and politics, brings full circle the dance of contact between subaltern subject and unruly stuff that Benjamin had only tentatively and provisionally intuited a century earlier. Varda's work testifies that despite all of the totalizing efforts to control materiality and make it move smoothly, stuff still exists as the other of consumerism, and that engagement with it in ways which match its unruliness with unruly action will continue to pressure the existing system of power.

Notes

1 Giovanni Verga, *Tutte le Novelle*, 1883, http://www.liberliber.it/biblioteca/v/
   verga/tutte_le_novelle/html/roba.htm, p. 2 (my translation). Subsequent
   page numbers in the text.
2 See Scott Lash and Celia Lury, *Global Culture Industry: The Mediation of
   Things*, Cambridge, Polity Press, 2007.
3 George Carlin, "What to Do with Your Stuff", http://www.youtube.com/
   watch?v=JLoge6QzcGY.
4 *Albert Renger-Patzsch: Photographer of Objectivity*, Ann and Jurgen Wilde
   and Thomas Weski eds., with an introduction by Thomas Janzen,
   Cambridge, MIT Press, 1998, p. 12.
5 Pierre Bourdieu et al., *The Weight of the World: Social Suffering in
   Contemporary Society*, Stanford, Stanford University Press, 1999, *La Misère
   du Monde*, Paris, Editions du Seuil, 1993.
6 See Nigel Thrift, *Spatial Formations*, London, Sage, 1998, Ch. 7 and 8.
7 Karl Marx, *Economic and Philosophic Manuscripts of 1844*, in David McLellan
   ed., *Karl Marx: Selected Writings*, Oxford, Oxford University Press, 1977, p. 62.

8 Sanford Kwinter, *Architectures of Time: Toward a Theory of the Event in Modernist Culture*, Cambridge, MIT Press, 2002, p. 65.

9 Louis Althusser, *Philosophy of the Encounter: Later Writings, 1978–1987*, trans. G.M. Goshgarian, London, Verso, 2006. Paris, Gallimard, 1993.

10 Michel Serres, *Statues*, Paris, Francois Bourin, quoted in Bruno Latour, *We Have Never Been Modern*, trans. Catherine Porter, Cambridge, Harvard University Press, 1993, p. 51.

11 Bruno Latour, *We Have Never Been Modern*, trans. Catherine Porter, Cambridge, Harvard University Press, 1993:

> Linking the two pools of nature and society by as many arrows and feedback loops as one wishes does not relocate the quasi-object or the quasi subject . . . On the contrary, dialectics makes the ignorance of that locus still deeper than in the dualist paradigm since it feigns to overcome it by loops and spirals and other complex acrobatic figures. Dialectics literally beats around the bush. Quasi objects are in between and below the two poles, at the very place around which dualism and dialectics had turned endlessly without being able to come to terms with them. Quasi objects are much more social, much more fabricated, much more collective than the "hard" part of nature, but they are in no way the arbitrary receptacles of a full-fledged society. On the other hand they are much more real, nonhuman and objective than the shapeless screens on which society, for unknown reasons, needed to be "projected." (p. 55).

12 "Interview with Donna Haraway", in Don Ihde and Evan Selinger eds., *Chasing Technoscience*, Indianapolis, Indiana University Press, 2003, p. 48.

13 By now materiality studies have expanded exponentially. Here is a selection of recent work: Isabelle Stengers, *Power and Invention: Situating Science*, Minneapolis, University of Minnesota Press, 1997, and *Cosmopolitics I*, Minneapolis, University of Minnesota Press, 2003; Nigel Thrift, *Non Representational Theory: Space/Politics/Affect,* London, Routledge, 2008; Sanford Kwinter, *Architectures of Time: Toward a Theory of the Event in Modernist Culture*, Cambridge, MIT Press, 2002; Karen Barad, *Meeting the Universe Halfway: Quantum Physics and the Entanglement of Matter and Meaning*, Durham, Duke University Press, 2007; Michel Serres, *The Birth of Physics*, Manchester, Clinamen, 2000; and *The Parasite*, Baltimore, Johns Hopkins University Press, 1982; Bruno Latour, "From *Realpolitik* to *Dingpolitik*", Introduction to *Making Things Public: Atmospheres of Democracy*, Latour and Weibel eds., Cambridge, MIT Press, 2005; *Aramis, or The Love of Technology*, Cambridge, Harvard University Press, 2004; *Politics of Nature: How to Bring the Sciences into Democracy*, Cambridge, Harvard University Press, 2004; Mario Perniola, *Sex Appeal of the Inorganic: Philosophies of Desire in the Modern World*, New York, Continuum, 2004; Bruce Braun and Sarah J. Whatmore eds., *Political Matter*, Minneapolis, University of Minnesota Press, 2010; Timothy Bewes, *Reification or The Anxiety of Late Capitalism*, London, Verso, 2002; Roberto Esposito, *Bios:*

Biopolitics and Philosophy, Minneapolis, University of Minnesota Press, 2008; Zygmunt Bauman, *Consuming Life*, London, Polity Press, 2007; Nikolas Rose, *The Politics of Life Itself: Biotechnology, Politics and Culture and Subjectivity in the Twenty-First Century*, Princeton, Princeton University Press, 2006; Brian Massumi, *Parables for the Virtual: Movement, Affect, Sensation*, Durham, Duke University Press, 2002; Nancy Wacquant and Lois Scheper-Hughes, *Commodifying Bodies*, Thousand Oaks, Sage Publications, 2004; Melinda Cooper, *Life as Surplus: Biotechnology and Capitalism in the Neoliberal Era*, Seattle, University of Washington Press, 2008; Bruce Sterling, *Shaping Things*, Cambridge, MIT Press, 2005; David Harvey, *The Limits to Capital*, New York, Verso, 2006; Victor Buchli, *The Material Culture Reader*, London, Verso, 2002; Gay Hawkins, *The Ethics of Waste: How We Relate to Rubbish*, Sydney, University of New South Wales Press, 2006; Jane Bennett, *Vibrant Matter: A Political Ecology of Things*, Durham, Duke University Press, 2010; Daniel Miller ed., *Material Cultures: Why Some Things Matter*, Chicago, The University of Chicago Press, 1998; Daniel Miller ed., *Materiality*, Durham, Duke University Press, 2005; Christoph Asendorf, *Batteries of Life: On the History of Things and Their Perception in Modernity*, Berkeley, University of California Press, 1993; Brian Wallis ed., *Damaged Goods: Desire and the Economy of the Object*, New York, The Museum of Contemporary Art, 1986; *Les Objets du Siècle*, special edition of *Libération*, Paris, Dec. 17, 1999. See also the extensive work in object-oriented ontology by Graham Harman and others.

14 See *The Social Life of Things: Commodities in Cultural Perspective*, Arjun Appadurai ed., Cambridge, Cambridge University Press, 1996.

15 Bill Brown ed., *Thing Theory, Critical Inquiry*, 28, Autumn 2001.

16 Daniel Miller, *Stuff*, Cambridge, Polity Press, 2010, p. 51.

17 *Thing Theory*, Bill Brown ed., *Critical Inquiry*, 28, Autumn 2001, p. 5.

18 Jane Bennett, *Vibrant Matter*, Durham, Duke University Press, 2010; Diana Coole and Samantha Frost eds., *New Materialisms: Ontology, Agency, Politics*, Durham, Duke University Press, 2010; Bruce Braun and Sarah J. Whatmore eds., *Political Matter: Technoscience, Democracy, and Public Life*, Minneapolis, University of Minnesota Press, 2010.

19 Catherine Malabou, *What Should We Do with Our Brain?*, trans. Sebastian Rand, New York, Fordham University Press, 2008.

20 Luc Boltanski and Eve Chiappello, *The New Spirit of Capitalism*, London, Verso, 2005, trans. Gregory Elliott; Paris, Editions Gallimard, 1999.

21 Here is the core of Malabou's argument:

> Plasticity is situated between two extremes: on the one side the taking on of form (sculpture, molding, fashioning of plastic material); on the other the annihilation of form (plastique, detonation) . . . essentially today we must think this double movement, contradictory and nonetheless indissociable, of the emergence and disappearance of form. At the core of the constant circulation between the neuronal, the economic, the social,

the individual ought to occupy the midpoint between the taking on of form and the annihilation of form—between the possibility of occupying a territory and accepting the rules of deterritorialization, between the configuration of a network and its ephemeral, effaceable character. We live in an epoch in which identity is defined no longer as a permanent essence but as a process of autoconstitution, or "fashioning", . . . a process at whose heart a multiplicity of possible figurations unfolds . . . Self-fashioning implies at once the elaboration of a form, another face, a figure, and the effacement of another form, another face, another figure, which precede them or are contemporaneous with them . . . The plasticity of the self, which supposes that it simultaneously receives and gives itself its own form, implies a necessary split and the search for an equilibrium between the preservation of constancy (or, basically, the autobiographical self), and the exposure of this constancy to accidents, to the outside, to otherness in general (identity, in order to endure, ought paradoxically to alter itself or accidentalize itself). What results is a tension born of the resistance that that constancy and creation mutually oppose to each other. It is thus that every form carries within itself its own contradiction. And precisely this resistance makes transformation possible. Malabou, *What Should We Do with Our Brain?*, trans. Sebastian Rand, New York, Fordham University Press, 2008, pp. 70–71.

22 "By the verb 'to do' or 'to make' we don't mean just 'doing' math or piano but making its history, becoming the subject of its history, grasping . . . a new meaning of history." Malabou, *What Should We Do?*, p. 13.

23 Antonio Negri, *Insurgencies* distinguishes between force (*potere costituente*) and its deterritorializing capability, which as a form of Spinozian vitalism pushes the multitude to create the political as the new, and power, which tries to give fixed form to force. Force is the plasticity of matter translated into political terms. See *Insurgencies*, trans. Maurizia Boscagli, Minneapolis, University of Minnesota Press, 1998.

24 "Beneath the shifting profusion of appearances there lies, accessible through proper operations, the finite, essential pattern of the real", Kwinter, *Architectures of Time*, p. 97.

25 The phrase is Buck-Morss, in Kwinter, *Architectures of Time*, 2002.

26 See Fredric Jameson, "The End of Temporality", *Critical Inquiry* 29, Summer 2003.

27 Zygmunt Bauman, *Wasted Lives: Modernity and Its Outcasts,* London, Polity, 2004.

1

Homeopathic Benjamin: A Flexible Poetics of Matter

Small glass balls containing a landscape upon which snow fell when shook were among his favorite objects. The French word for still life – nature morte – could be written upon the portals of his philosophical dungeons. Philosophy appropriates this fetishization in the commodity for itself: everything must metamorphosize into a thing in order to break the catastrophe of things. Benjamin's thought is so saturated with culture as its natural object that it swears loyalty to reification instead of flatly rejecting it.
   The glance of his philosophy is Medusan.

Theodor Adorno, "A Portrait of Walter Benjamin," *Prisms*[1]

Marionettes at a fair in Lucca, dust, plush, iron works in Paris, figs in Capri, *shlock* in Moscow "radiating" from market pavements, red neon reflected in street puddles in Berlin. More: collected books and toys, the chocolate-dispensing machine of his childhood, "the infamous carved wooden battlements" over the door of his classroom, panoramas, transparencies, wax figures, and at the end of his essay on Surrealism, the clock with human features. Nothing (no-thing) eludes Benjamin's Medusan glance. One of the great *detailistes* of the twentieth century, as Naomi Schor defines him,[2] he looks at material culture from a double stance of delight and criticism, and even disgust, as in the case of the heavy bourgeois interior. As he admitted to Adorno, "I am not interested in people, only in things."[3] The world of commodities, and even more its debris and residue, all that the *nouveauté* cult of modern consumerism has cast as outmoded and marginal, is the fulcrum of his intellectual production. Benjamin's critical romance with material culture led him to relate to the object beyond the protocols established by the bourgeois order, the existing order of things. This order sentences matter to a position of submission and instrumentality.[4] Through his critique of the object, Benjamin addresses instead how the system of capital still allows its users to articulate desire and pleasure, both at the individual and collective level. Further, by looking at historical reality, either through the lens of a

Surrealist or Brechtian avant-garde politics of representation, or as an avatar of the Deleuzian-inflected notions of a rhizomatic matter, Benjamin reclaims materiality from consumption's logic, outlines a new concept of subjectivity, and describes an alternative encounter of subject and object. His modernist object lessons thus anticipate debates on materialism and aesthetics of the late twentieth century and since. They laid the groundwork for the cultural materialisms of the 1980s and 1990s, and they have an enormous resonance for the even more radical versions of materialism being mooted in the new century.

Benjamin is the point of departure for any analysis of matter in modernity, and the time has come for a reappraisal of the significance of his work, if only to underline his importance for the new stage of materialist critique. Benjamin's work is critical for the new materialisms because he is one of the first theorists to base his analysis of the subject–object contact on the assumption that commodification—the value given to the object under the consumer regime of buying and selling—was not a totalizing phenomenon, which condemned the object to an invariable fakery and the subject to an endless alienation. Rather, for Benjamin, the subject–object interaction was wily, unpredictable and open-ended, with the plasticity valued by recent theories which seek to recast this relation. No one is better than he at offering full-dress experiments in the open-ended and complex choreographies of contact, by turns agonistic and desire-infused, between the modern subject and the commercial object of urban culture. His is a philosophy of the everyday and of the improvisational gesture, as opposed to the impressively totalizing and aphoristic sweep of the work of his friend Adorno. His eagerness to interrogate multiple aspects of the tremulous touch of subject and object is needed now when the definition of the object itself is up for grabs. Benjamin, uniquely among materialist thinkers, is willing to bring himself and the display of the frailties of his own subjecthood into view. Thus while we can on the one hand place him next to Bloch, Adorno and Lukács, we can align him on the other with the great modernist artists and writers, from Mann, Kafka, and Joyce, to Barnes and Woolf. These modernists each gave us at least one minutely described *flâneur*: Aschenbach, Gregor Samsa, Clarissa Dalloway, Robin Vote, Leopold Bloom. Benjamin presents us with the most evocatively delineated of all, but he did not have to fictionalize, as this *flâneur* is himself. Displaying himself in his work as he enacts his *flânerie*, Benjamin dramatizes the inevitable plasticity of the everyday urban subject who never tamps down his desires, fears, and hopes before the next tantalizing object in the commodity carnival.

Benjamin's work can be read therefore as a seismograph-text which measures the energies released when desires flow and dreams materialize as the variegated object world, by turns gaudy, shoddy, uncannily alive, and recalcitrant, either draws or repels the subject. Benjamin's reports from this riven contact zone nevertheless maintain two constant themes: a commitment, of varying intensity throughout his career, to a broader collective, hence political, reading of his milieu, and a fidelity to the specific force of the object attended to at any given moment. The interpenetration of these Benjamin-effects has been read by his new historicist followers as the outcome of a struggle between his weak-charged historical materialism and Scholem-inspired messianism. This is useful in understanding the underpinnings of the concept of 'profane illumination" Benjamin provides, but if it is clear that he is a somewhat reluctant Adornian and only a lukewarm mystic, then the field opens.[5] In particular, his indebtedness to Bergson, a thinker whose fate as a Jewish Parisian has tragic parallels to his own, but who took mysticism more seriously than Benjamin did, is worth considering. Benjamin pays Bergson a backhanded compliment at the opening of "On Some Motifs in Baudelaire." While he notes that Bergson's *Matter and Memory* towers above the turn-of-the century philosophic attempts "to lay hold of the 'true' experience as opposed to the kind that manifests itself in the standardized, denatured life of the civilized masses,"[6] he nevertheless critiques him for refusing any historical or collective determination for memory. Yet Bergson's interest in *Matter and Memory* in versions of materiality as a grounding for experience, his philosophizing on a generalized version of vitalism with scientific bases and mystical overtones, his interest in the sensory, the tactile, and intuition, all with overtones of the poetic, as a grounding for experience (which won the admiration of William James), all find their reflection in the liveliness of Benjamin's philosophic approach. In a sense, the *flâneur*-figure "Walter Benjamin" dramatized in Benjamin's writings is a test case for a range of Bergsonian concerns. When we recall that Bergson died from a chill contracted after standing for hours in a queue for papers as a Jew in Nazi-occupied Paris, we can grasp the urgency before a mounting state of emergency which infuses the later writings of each. From the point of view of new work on materiality, to acknowledge Benjamin's Bergsonism is also to see his work as a precursor to that of Deleuze, who always described Bergson as a forebear. Deleuze's focus on change, to be achieved through a peculiarly malleable vitalist materialism, may have its roots in Bergson; nevertheless, especially in its dedication to an innovative kind of historical materialism, it may be said to be equally indebted to Benjamin. If the new post-Deleuzian materialisms are to carry forward and reimagine the historical materialist tradition, then it is crucial to explore the example of Benjamin as precursor in the work of experimental materialism.

To begin this work, let's start with the notion of the "homeopathic" Benjamin. Vitalism, as a belief in the "life-spark" inherent in organic matter, is a tradition which science, as it grew more established, treated with increasing suspicion as a residue of religious or mystical thinking at odds with narratives of scientific causality. Its mystical-religious genealogy likewise hardly endeared it to historical materialists eager to assert their claims' scientific basis. Attributing to the commodity not just the shrouding "mystery" which Marx saw as the basis of its deceptiveness, but a fascination which made it seem almost animate, Benjamin toys with the unlikely and even paradoxical possibility of a vitalist materialism. This toying is homeopathic— that is, based on the notion that an agent which ingested in large doses would prove fatal to the subject can, if taken in minute, carefully calibrated amounts, actually help the subject to combat the threat. (This formulation of fluctuating power relations between subject and matter is the "minor" version of the concept of immunity—a version of the subject–matter relation advanced in the work of Roberto Esposito[7]). Benjamin's implicit vitalist materialism is homeopathic in that it allows him to tarry with the commodity and suffer its wiles in small intense doses as an immunization mechanism to fend off the totalizing phenomenon which any given commodity represents.

Benjamin provides an understanding of materiality and the commodity form that is interested in *what to do* with things and the pleasures they provide, and in what things can do, rather than in how the subject simply consumes and is consumed by the fantasies they circulate. He aims to reappropriate the power of phantasmagoria and its relation to the unconscious away from commodity fetishism, to use it instead to realize collective and individual desires, and for social change.[8] What he's asking of the object is to reactivate a sleeping historical memory, a dream of social justice still alive in nineteenth-century industrial culture and its technological modernity.[9] In this project, his interest in stuff—the marginal version of the commodity, its detritus—is key. He seizes upon junk, the outmoded bric-à-brac of the Parisian arcades, to awaken the dreaming collective to the desires and utopias that the previous generation, their libidinal energy derailed and appropriated by the logic of consumption, never saw come true.

If the nineteenth century, the century of the second industrial revolution, is the time of progressive dreaming through materiality, the twentieth becomes the time when the same materiality produces nightmares. Now through commodity fetishism the inanimate becomes not only the medium for social and human relations, but also the model for a new and expendable mass individuality. The subject, always a suspicious category for Benjamin because suggestive of bourgeois *ratio*, is refunctioned by capital as a consumer who is seduced and interpellated by the commodity. This demands of the critic a double gaze: first, the Medusan gaze of the allegorist, who exposes the "progressive" quality of modern objectivity as decay, and second, the adversarial gaze of the modernist intellectual, who scours the thing-world of modernity to salvage its talismanic qualities. He shows how a mimetic relation to commodity-culture's debris can be used to reactivate messianic powers, a relation of libidinal energy, "magic", fantasy, chance. In Benjamin's privileging of the thought of the French utopian socialists Saint-Simon and Fourier, and in his unorthodox Marxism,[10] is an implicit ambivalence toward the outcome of the nineteenth-century European revolutions, and even more of the October revolution, whose aftermath he observed firsthand during his 1927 trip to Moscow. What should for him have been the revolution's outcome—happiness, fantasy and unpredictable new forms of existence—he then sought to discern in the encounter of subject and stuff.

Benjamin's is modernist salvage-work on materiality. It emerged at the moment when avant-garde aesthetics revealed bourgeois reality to be porous, so that in its fissures hints of resistance could be envisaged. In the writings of the Parisian cycle,[11] Benjamin addresses this historical conjuncture along two axes: the question of the individual subject caught between the demise of its bourgeois version and its return in the image of the consumer, and the idea of the dreaming collective as a historical entity now waning into the reproducible multiplicity of the masses. Both the dreaming collective and the desirous individual, as figures of modernity, are organized around the element that bourgeois *ratio* had censored and made inaccessible to its subject, the unconscious. On the terrain of the unconscious the twin axes of Benjamin's theory of materiality, the individual and the collective, converge. Thus his thought is a reflection on the political value of the unconscious, as the space where *Erfahrung*, the fullness of experience, can be recuperated. This space is a future-anterior utopia, the paradox of a past that has yet to happen. It must be redeemed as dream-memory, and brought to the threshold of consciousness. It is never once and for all realized, but always in the process of becoming. In his fullest conception of the subject–object encounter he renders it almost as a form of permanent revolution.

Benjamin's work on objects, then, denounces a loss. At the same time it aims at redeeming both the individual subject and collectivity away from the shape that they have assumed under early twentieth-century capitalism. The allegorist's power of vision, and the famous, Surrealistically inflected profane illumination, are about recognizing something that the history of the victors has occluded. By taking the phantasmagoria of the commodity fetish seriously, Benjamin imagines a new relationship between subject and object *against*, and not outside, the logic of reification. To dereify the object, and the subject, in his fetishistic individuality, means for him to reinstate into the field of vision, both conscious and oniric, what has been erased; it means to redeem the memory of what has been made forgettable by capital, relegated to the space outside our field of vision, from which it can only be inferred. Benjamin's allegorical gaze expresses the urgency of stopping and reversing a process that is still ongoing, not yet concluded.

The material world and the object as talisman carry the fingerprints of the collective, at the level of both production and consumption. The material and technical culture of the nineteenth century was supposed to bring social and economic emancipation and the "classless society" of which Benjamin speaks in the 1935 *Exposé*. Instead the dream of collective happiness was managed by capital, and fragmented into the image of the atomized mass of solitary consumers. The notion of the dreaming collective remains problematic for Benjamin,[12] and he acknowledges this difficulty and historical inadequacy. For instance, as Miriam Hansen notes, in the last version of "The Work of Art in the Age of Mechanical Reproduction," he replaces the phrase "Das Kollektiv" with "Die Masse," signaling his compromised faith in the political power of the multitudes.[13] But if he lets go of the collective, he certainly doesn't let go of the unconscious. Throughout all his work, he challenges the modern articulation of the unconscious as private. His attention is equally split between the public dimension of material culture, with its spaces and monuments, the arcades, the panoramas, the exhibitions, as architectures of the collective, and the individual one. Through his analysis of the commodity form, in the figure of the prostitute or of the Baudelairean *flâneur* as its alter egos, he addresses a micrological form of desire, while simultaneously exposing and questioning the colonization of the unconscious. The dereification of materiality, which is his aim, is not a matter of stripping the object of its phantasmagorical quality, just as his recuperation of historical memory through dream is never a matter of moving from "false" to "true" consciousness. Rather, both imply reclaiming the potential of the phantasmagoria, and its capability as a form of traffic between matter and spirit, animate and inanimate.[14] Benjamin's aim is to reconnect the phantasmagorical quality of the object, its "immateriality," which might also be its residual vibrancy or energy, to the libidinal flow of *collective and individual* desire that he sees traversing outmoded and marginal commodities. In stuff, made ex-centric by the culture of consumption, he intuits a collective unconscious which he accesses through a tentative, often consumerist, contact.

To unravel the density of commodity fetishism Benjamin proposes a counter-discourse of the object as talisman, which in the next section I call homeopathic fetishism. The point of Benjamin's counter-memory is not to wake the subject up to consciousness of reality. The twentieth-century intellectual knows that the modern real has been constructed as a seamless positivity, while it's always already troubled and complicated by what it censors.[15] It's from within the space of the unconscious that this mechanism of censorship and displacement upon which bourgeois reality, and realism as its chief mode of representation, is founded, can be recognized, and its yet-unrealized past remembered. This is why Benjamin plans to write of the commodity as a "poetic object," and why he is interested in its phantasmagoria as one of the crucial spaces of the unconscious in modernity. He takes the commodity fetish seriously because he knows that the battle for political and cultural hegemony in the twentieth century is being fought on the ground of the unconscious. Critiquing the individualization of desire at the hands of commodity fetishism, and the reformulation of bourgeois individuality in the image of the consumer, he wants to reclaim the unconscious, on the contrary, as a source of collective agency. Dream, phantasmagoria, and fantasy have for him a collective potential that simply cannot be relinquished to capital. He reclaims the phantasmagoria of consumption as a political virtual reality, a way of giving the visual and tactile presence of one's body to an unrealized past.

Benjamin uses different tactics to make visible, at the threshold between dream and wakefulness, the shards of the past that he sees frozen in some outmoded and marginal objects, in stuff. These, in turn, should unblock and circulate the subject's memory as well as desire, or better, unblock libidinal energies as a form of memory. The equation between memory, the body, and the stuff in question, is never fully established, but lingers in Benjamin's thought. What is actually redeemed of the past is the body, and the way its very tactility contributes to the recuperation, and the fullness, of experience. Thus historical memory is a form of libidinal energy for Benjamin: what the unhinging of the commodity from the logic of capital should accomplish is the circulation of unfixed, unchanneled desire. Whether it be the dusty objects of the arcades or the Surrealist *trouvaille*, the unpredictability of the object stands as a form of chance capable of unsettling the system of use and exchange value with which the fetish is saddled in modernity.

To beat capital at its own game, and to recover for object and subject a materiality that the abstraction of reification has dissipated both at the level of production and circulation, Benjamin "hallucinates" the commodity into a multifaceted object. First, to newly make the commodity into a fetish, he studies it as a dialectical picture puzzle where different, opposed notions of value stand in an unresolved opposition, in a clashing montage that Dada-like and stereoscopically produces a new meaning. Then he turns his Medusan gaze to alternative symbolic economies of the object, at work, for instance, in the mimetic quality of children's play, in the Surrealist *trouvaille*, even in drug-induced hallucinations. He situates the object at the intersection of three force fields: commodity fetishism, outmoded stuff, and folk or artisanal objects. These, in turn, are structured through a number of recurring motifs, principally the theatre, the threshold, and magic. Through these motifs he reimagines the commodity as a talisman in the anthropological sense, in a move that exposes the "magic," the irrational quality of capitalist modernity itself, a cultural element that had been censored by the Enlightenment and its rationalism. In this Brechtian counter-magic of "showing the showing," reinstating into the field of vision what had been elided, he also sets the agenda for the production of a new subject, predicated upon a different articulation of the encounter.[16] This new relationship between subject and object is the point of both departure and arrival in his critique of materiality. The new subject is shaped by the encounter with materialities of which he is always already part. This encounter, as we will see, does not simply promise happiness, as does the commodity in its perverse game of postication, but shows it as within reach. Happiness in the subject–object encounter can be experienced through an erotics of nearness and distance. In a flash, this affect suggests a space that can be inhabited, at least provisionally, by the subject.

Commodity fetishism and reification both render abstract what should be tactile and affective. Both the producer's praxis and the consumer's cathexis have these living, lively qualities. But these are neutralized with the reinvestment of that social relation represented by value into a fetish, an object through which the consumer vicariously and indirectly imagines a stunted version of her own materiality. The commodity's fetishistic aura contains all of the above: the operation of abstraction and occlusion is its past, its history. In its present, instead, the commodity claims immediacy while producing further alienation, and addresses and captures the polymorphous quality of the subject's libido while channeling its flow in the direction of matter. By attending to the outmoded object as a talisman, Benjamin attempts to unblock the libidinal traffic between materiality and abstraction, past and present, nearness and distance. He foregrounds the structural instability of the commodity, an instability that can potentially provoke the subversion of the economic, affective, and aesthetic order affirmed by capital. Dependent on the chance quality of the unconscious, the commodity's coherence is always threatened by the breakdown of the order of value, representation, and subjectivity that sustains it. This is what is at stake in Benjamin's reclaiming of the commodity as aesthetic object, capable of a semiotic instability that can potentially disrupt the mimetic quality of realist textuality.[17]

In order to contest the realism of the commodity and the referentiality of bourgeois mimesis, Benjamin turns to avant-garde aesthetics. No longer a spectacle to contemplate, but rather a dialectical image, the commodity becomes a space where the past can be encountered through the open door of the unconscious, but also a place where one can experience plenitude, and a here-and-now happiness. Further, no matter how intractable a category it might be, Benjamin does not entirely relinquish the subject. In the image of the child at play mimetically relating to objects, of the *flâneur*, of the allegorist, of the collector, or of the hallucinating Surrealist, the subject remains as the repository of historical memory, and the carrier of the allegorist's gaze that sets the aura of the commodity aflame. At the same time Benjamin's subject, in his encounter with this thoroughly acted-upon matter, embodies a new type of synaesthetic identity, centered on the unconscious. While inhabiting the threshold between sleep and wakefulness, he is capable of critique because of the special power of vision he acquires by seeing reality from within the dream. Through the filter of the kaleidoscopic montage of the dialectical image, he recognizes and reclaims what dominant culture has made utopian and invisible, and degraded because dreamlike. Working at the limit of symbolic and political economy, social critique and aesthetics, Benjamin takes the risk of outlining praxis through the dream, politics through the unconscious, "in earnest," as he says in his essay on folk art, trying to build upon the ruins of the bourgeois order.

Benjamin is a new kind of creative materialist, an immensely rich thinker on the issue of the subject as actant encountering the vibrancy of matter. He is by no means merely a "culturalist," which is to say that while he fully acknowledges the spectacle of the commodity, he invariably focuses on the object itself in its provocative and particular enhancement of materiality. He is completely aware that matter in consumer culture is never merely natural, but has always, before it reaches the metropolitan citizen of modernity, been acted upon in advance—and changed. Its vital intractability, even its utility, has been modified once it is introduced to the circuit of buying, selling, and making profit, so that its magic has perversely been twisted, but not extinguished altogether. It arouses in the subject who encounters it new, intriguing energies, at all levels, unconscious, libidinal, somatic, social, and aesthetic. These, reconfigured in new and plastic formations can lead not only to new affects and desires, but to new actions: a flexible fetishism.

I. Homeopathic Fetishism

Instead of trying to cleave what is taken to be sober from intoxicated thought, why not seize upon the intoxication itself? . . . As Walter Benjamin, following the Surrealists, might have elaborated on his insight into modern society, as animated by the new mythic powers located in the tactility of the commodity-image, the task is neither to resist nor to admonish the fetish quality of modern culture, but rather to acknowledge, even to submit to its fetish powers, and attempt to channel them in revolutionary directions. Get with it! Get in touch with the fetish!

Michael Taussig, *The Nervous System*[18]

Even more directly than *The Parisian Arcades* and the 1930s *Exposés, One-Way Street* stands as the best point of entry into Benjamin's engagement with modern material culture, because there he shows most directly his ambivalence about the object's allure, while implying a subject-consumer almost Deleuzian in his deterritorialized openness before the object. Written between *The Origin of German Tragic Drama* (1925), and the essay on Surrealism (1929), this book foregrounds the gaze of the allegorist, fixed on the scene of modernity. Margaret Cohen, reading *One-Way Street*,[19] focuses on the way Benjamin both endorses and resists the Surrealists' discovery of the marvelous in the everyday; we will focus on a number of nodal points in the work where Benjamin rethinks Surrealist ideas on materiality.[20] In the text, he assumes a double, almost schizophrenic position toward the world he is analyzing. When he affirms that "objects are closing upon us, they are coming too close," (446) he shows a near-Lukácsian sensitivity to reification as the defining condition of twentieth-century modernity and a characteristically modernist fear of the encroachment of the material upon the tremulous, threatened subject. Yet, except for his account of the funereal clutter of the nineteenth-century upper-class apartment,[21] Benjamin is not really afraid of the proximity of objects. The artefacts of modernity may in fact allow new conditions of existence and perception for the subject, conditions potentially capable of debunking reification's logic. Benjamin is definitely open to learning from modern objectivity. The new subject he lets us glimpse among the fragments and aphorisms of *One-Way Street* is alienated from bourgeois interiority, subjected *to* nervous impulses, an individual-as-body almost convulsed by the shocks of modernity. This nervous, somatic subject almost suggests a figure of deterritorialized anti-Oedipal—that is, Deleuzian—corporeality. No longer in touch with his self and his feelings, this subject doesn't look for some source of authenticity. Rather—anticipating Žižek—he learns to emote from the technological artefactuality of American films: "just as people whom nothing moves or touches any longer are taught to cry again by films" (476). This is the subject who, fascinated, watches the decay and return of experience in the reflection of a red neon sign in a puddle of water on the asphalt. What Benjamin makes clear is that there is no outside to the enchantment of reification. Rather than retrenching into a paranoia, he thinks instead of how to work from within, to envision a new sensorium for new forms of subjectivity.

At the same time the critic never forgets that the artefacts capable of producing a new subject and a new sensorium are often also commodities, and that it is the logic of capital that circulates through them: the mesmerizing reflection of the red neon advertises an object for sale. When he looks at modern enchantment and its potential to produce a new level of experience, he knows that in modernity the marvelous and magical is foremost that of the commodity itself. It is not, therefore, a question of "sobering up" the commodity, and tearing through the veil of its phantasmagoria, because the phantasmagoria is where the unconscious as shield and magnifying glass, as homeopathic shock-reabsorbing device and optical unconscious, operates. If the commodity is to undergo a process of disenchantment that will expose the bankruptcy of its way of producing affect and value, it also needs to be re-enchanted in terms different from those established by capital, in order for the materialist critic to reclaim its libidinal energy. Benjamin's work on materiality is a critique, but not a rejection, of the object and its *promesse de bonheur*: what he wants is to unmake the fetishism of the commodity form with another form of fetishism, homeopathically. How Benjamin conceptualized this other fetishism is the topic of the next section. Through a play of disenchantment *and* re-enchantment the commodity is transformed from an object carrying the inscription of capital, that is, an object whose materiality has been irreversibly disembodied and abstracted, to a fetish which carries traces of the past collective dream.

Benjamin's object-critique has three different but connected dimensions. In the semiotic-epistemological dimension, his understanding of objectivity produces a new way of signifying and knowing reality, experience and history in open antagonism to bourgeois realism and positivism. Here he participates in the avant-garde's dismantling of the arbitrary coherence of signifier and signified in favor of the uncaptioned presentation of the materiality of the dialectical image. This recast semiotics of the object affirms that representation can be other than realist mimesis, an imitation of the real, but a means of changing it. Next, in the somatic-libidinal dimension, contravening the sex appeal of the commodity, Benjamin reclaims pleasure by looking at the object as a visual-tactile phenomenon, to be approached synaesthetically through all the senses rather than through the mind or the eye. Domination of the object over the subject and vice versa is replaced by mimetic interaction,[22] and by seduction as a game of distance and nearness. This dialectic of tactile and visual immediacy and distance in turn invokes two different libidinal economies: the Oedipal one of the body properly sexualized by the protocols of heteronormativity, and another, centered on a pre-, or anti-Oedipal perverse and polymorphous sexuality, where the distance between subject and object is phantasmatically bridged by the infant's capability to inhabit and fuse with the object. Here Benjamin reclaims the body through a dialectic of desire and happiness, in opposition to the way capital inscribes sexuality onto the commodity. Third, consider how the semiotic and libidinal qualities converge in the political dimension of the object. The object's tactility produces a new sensorium with which to encounter reality, and a new form of subjectivity. By regarding materiality as something that can be approached and known primarily through the senses, that is, somatically and aesthetically, he proposes a tactile epistemology of the material, where the body enters meaning, and where meaning is produced *in* the object rather than through it, or at its expense. Through this sensate knowledge experience the past may be reached and redeemed.

This double perspective of critique (of commodification) and re-enchantment (via tactile sensuousness) with which Benjamin approaches materiality, affirms the need to unhinge the object from the ideological hooks that give it meaning in western culture. On the one hand this had involved imagining matter as dead, a passive object of observation upon which the subject's mastery, knowledge, agency, could be erected. On the other, its logic was presided over by the all-powerful commodity fetish, whose magic, reification, reduces the subject into an object and reduces him to passivity and powerlessness, making him inanimate. By envisioning the commodity as a "poetic object" he prospects a new living relationship to living matter, organized as mimetic exchange rather than domination, as tactility and distraction, rather than the contemplative and rapacious visuality of bourgeois art and science. By these same means, he also envisions a politics of resistance.

To talk of the "poetics of the commodity"[23] is to attribute to it an aesthetic quality that makes it, to all effects, a fetish whose semiotic and affective structure is extremely unstable, and whose "magic" quality defeats the sutured logic of facts. For the historical materialist the fetish quality of the commodity implies its doubleness, its illusory and delusional fakery. Michael Taussig, instead, inspired by Benjamin's elastic thinking on the subject, brilliantly flips this doubleness into a dynamic configuration. He recasts reification, the way things and people exchange features and human labor gets transformed into the abstraction of value, as an unstable traffic between subjects and matter. Taussig here anticipates new materialism's interest in dynamic encounters of subjects and matter: "The matter of factness of production becomes anything but matter of fact, and facticity itself is rendered marvelous, mist-enveloped regions of frozen movement, . . . in which things that come from the hands of men change place with persons ... commodities erase the social nexus imploded within and become self-activated spirit, even God-like 'things in themselves'" (5). For Taussig, Georg Lukács' emphasis on reification as a death is only half of the story: what he is interested in is "the restless metamorphosizing from matter to spirit and back ... the epistemological flip-flop back-tracking over the capitalist moonscape of subject and object" (5). This wrestling of the subject with the fetish, and the object's corresponding reversibility from matter to spirit, continues the project inherent in Benjamin's notion of commodity fetish as dialectical image. Taussig champions a different understanding of materiality which puts it in step with the "nervous system," a term that for him signals the asystematicity of any structure of power and matter under capitalism. He stresses the flip-flopping character of the fetish, and he orders the subject to go with its flow. Reveling in "the power of arbitrariness of social conventions battling it out with the physical wallop of their effects" (6), he learns from Benjamin how to read the shamanistic healing pictures of the Putumayo nights he encountered on his fieldwork in Colombia. After Benjamin, with Taussig and his Putumayo nights we can reconceptualize the power of magical thinking in modernity.

Benjamin's commodity as a poetic object in these terms is a new kind of fetish, whose "magic" is neither debunked nor brought back to reason. As its history shows, the fetish is an object whose *hybridity* questions, and disturbs, any supposedly reasonable economy as a fixed system of order. William Pietz's genealogy of the fetish makes clear that since its emergence in the seventeenth-century Dutch African trade,[24] it has stood as a form of hybrid materiality which defies and unsettles western economic and religious value-systems, disrupts the circulation and commensurability of prevailing protocols, and thus signals the possibility of understanding that things are capable of overpowering human beings and of undercutting their control. Peter Pels tells how merchant ethnographers such as William Bosman transformed the *fetisso*—a functional object in African trading relationships— into the fetish, the central feature of what they decided was African religion. "European ethnographers," he writes,

> tried to bring this object's hybrid inexplicability under control by making the fetish into something essentially "African;" the same discourse gave the fetish a life and a career that eventually allowed it to migrate from Africa and (un)settle down in two of the most important intellectual landscapes of western modernity, Marxism and psychoanalysis. Even in this diaspora it retained some of its original identity ... [as] an object of *abnormal traffic*.[25]

The fetish's abnormal traffic confers upon this materiality the status of quasi-object. It is related to another quality of the fetish, which Pietz notes in "The Problem of the Fetish, I": its artefactuality and artificiality as an object whose genealogy is grounded in the act of making. Noting the relation of *facere*, "making," and fetishism, Pietz brings to the fore the issue of praxis and of the making of the subject and object, which in turn brings us to the issue of agency. We have here two readings of the fetish, one where the agent is the subject or collective, inscribing its sentiment onto the artefact, and the other where the agent is the object, capable of disrupting meaning and overpowering the subject. The fetish as poetic object in Benjamin's terms blocks traffic, and juxtaposes different economies, of value, sexuality, and signification, blurring the line between the authentic and the fake, the factual and the factitious, the real and the marvelous. It's the talismanic—as in the "mana", the factitiousness—quality of the object that Benjamin wants to restore to modern materiality, so that it will exercise upon the subject a power different from that of the commodity. Instead of being seduced by the sex appeal of the inanimate, so that he becomes himself frozen into thinginess, the subject is fascinated and made alive by the wonders that the object, now re-envisioned as an object closer to the anthropological fetish or medieval relic, can perform. The subject is no longer stuck in the death-in-life space of reification, but suspended, doubled, in the endless, restless flip-flop reversibility of material and immaterial, agency and passivity. Whereas Marx, in the famous passage of *Capital* Vol. I where he describes the commodity and all its "metaphysical subtleties and theological niceties," tries to fit the fetish's alterity into the gridlock of western value-making, and uses this alterity to prosthetically support the western distinction between artificiality and authenthicity, Benjamin, like Taussig later, is instead interested in the exchange between these two codes of representation, the real and the fake, and in the way they might challenge the exclusionary logic of meaning-making. This is why Benjamin invites his reader to look at the fetish in a premodern light, either as baroque emblem, whose allegorical powers defy the totalistic semiosis of the symbol,[26] or as a disordered and inordinate artefact, whose ontological and epistemological status is situated in the midst—and the mists—of fact and fiction, authenticity and fakery. He wishes to encounter it as it was encountered before these categories had been made antagonistic by the eighteenth-century scientific desire to classify objects and knowledges.[27]

Benjamin's understanding of the object as fetish and emblem traces a genealogy that takes us back to the seventeenth-century curiosities: objects that elicited wonder, standing between fetishes and the museum pieces, difficult to classify.[28] These curiosities had performative power: instead of representing nation, history or nature as museum pieces, they were, like relics, supposed to make things happen.[29] With what Pels calls the eighteenth-century urge to taxonomy, the curiosities' aesthetic of wonder and performance was displaced onto the trifle and onto bric-à-brac; with the rise of the modern museum, these came to be regarded as worthy only of degraded forms of collecting practiced by children, women, and amateurs. The fetish thus represents a pre-eighteenth-century economy of perception and reception that sees the object as animated, performing, capable of acting upon the subject, and affirming the possibility of "thinking of an untranscended materiality of things."[30] In the modern era, the Benjaminian fetish as elaborated by Taussig likewise gives a specific kind of nervous agency even to commodified objects. Naming capital a "nervous system," it posits that this agency exists on a somatic and synaesthetic continuum with the tremulous modern subject.

These are some of the qualities that Benjamin restores to materiality in his critique. In this sense, his object bears the trace of the premodern. However, both modern and premodern registers of the object-fetish, the fetish as magical and animated because it still has the premodern life of vibrant matter at its disposal, and the commodity fetish whose magic comes from its fake glamour which hides its history, are each recorded by Benjamin as the very conditions of his structural critique of the object. From his earliest writings, he portrays matter, nature, and objectivity as not only existing in their own right, but as capable of making the human being the subject of her own agency. Toward the end of his career the animistic perspective comes to the fore, especially with the melancholic view of the Proustian aura in "On Some Motifs in Baudelaire." This not only makes his thought an avatar of the problematic materiality of the fetish in recent debates in anthropology and cultural studies, but offers the new materialism a model of nuanced thinking on the possible agency of matter, and the ways in which matter is transformed by subject-actants, in a world where raw materiality is always already worked on by capital's force of abstraction.

The fetish does not simply "represent" itself to the subject, because the structural contradiction of the fetish, as both the product of human transcendence and as a form of dangerous, untranscended materiality, is inscribed in the notion of the commodity as "poetic object." The word "poetic" here obviously points to an aesthetic dimension of the object. It outlines an experiential protocol that is sensuous, in the sense of the Greek verb *aisthanomai*, to feel, rather than ideational or rational. At the same time, the Greek verb *poiein*, to which the term "poetic" refers, can be read in both an active and a passive sense, both implied in Benjamin's notion of the object as fetish. First, the poetic object is one that actively makes things happen, and "makes," structures, the subject. Second, insofar as it is itself "made", the fetish is a factitious, talismanic object, whose power is social. The fetish acquires religious and magic power because of its sociality: it becomes sacred through an act of social inscription. This structural contradiction of Benjamin's version of the fetish therefore implies a disruption of conventional signification and agency both for the subject and for the object. This fetish performs a double role. It appears as a self-activated object, whose claimed autonomy and sutured seamlessness stands as a blueprint for both restrained bourgeois subjectivity and for less contained desires. The subject, mirroring back this fetishism, also works fetishistically, deploying systems of both semiotic and libidinal organization. The Medusan gaze of the allegorist, however, performs another magic, this time an act of *dénouement* capable of unmaking the *maleficium* of capital: now the commodity appears as dialectical image, bearing the inscription of the utopian wishes of the past generations. The signifying commodity fetish is used by Benjamin to bypass the whole conventional story of representation, to reach instead an unmediated (but not immediate) relationship between materiality and commodity.[31] This unmediated relation establishes the object as untranscended materiality, enacting meaning and performing reality rather than "representing" it. By bypassing representation, Benjamin sunders materiality from the semiotic gridlock of merely culturalist interpretation.[32] Now the fetish's meaning is by far more unstable: deeply compromised as it is by the object's aesthetic and libidinal charge, it is up for grabs, in particular the grab of the "shamanistic" modernist as visionary subject. This subject in Benjamin is capable of recognizing the profane illumination that electrifies the object, and of interpreting the shock that the dialectical image can produce. Further, this subject is part of Benjamin's "dreaming collective," which recognizes the meaning of a specific object only unconsciously, in an ideological penumbra where materiality, as in the structural duplicity of the fetish, is denied and affirmed at the same time. This double move takes us back to the key characteristics of the fetish, its reversibility, its flip-flopping between spirit and matter, again to the issue of agency.

As labor abstracted into an object, and imperceptibly rematerialized into a thing as consumable image, calling the consumer to desire and identify with it, the commodity is founded upon an excess of meaning, desire, and value that makes the boundaries of its facticity, its empirical existence, unstable. This excess constitutes its "poetic" quality, that uncontained, unorganized element that relates to the subject's own unfixed desire. For Taussig, Benjamin's critique of materiality under capitalism is therefore a poetics. In practice, it is a mnemonics of the commodity, against the mimetics of capital. In this poetics of matter, capital's effort to suture the gap between reality and its representation is contradicted by the excessive quality of the commodity's phantasmagoria.[33] This is the semiotic and libidinal instability that marks the object as the space of the unconscious, and that, by haunting the aesthetic factitiousness of the object, exposes its man-made, apparently naturalized, order. Insofar as it is a fetish, the commodity conceals and at the same time flaunts its pocket of excess. In thinking materiality as simultaneously carrying the logo of capital and the inscription of antagonistic forces such as desire and the collective utopia of the past, Benjamin looks at the commodity as an object torn between competing forces, animated by a traffic between meaning and a libidinal volatility, charged by alternating currents of reason and magic, matter and spirit. This volatility and reversibility, as opposed to the congealed state of reification, is what Benjamin is after in his work on objects. This is why, no less than Taussig, he decides to "get with the fetish," and look for a magic that can homeopathically overcome abstraction without sobering up the fetish and waking the dreaming subject. Matter matters for Benjamin exactly for its capability to transfigure itself into the space of the unconscious: the phantasmagorical power of the fetish cannot be relinquished to capital.

Flip-flopping between inanimate and untranscended matter, Benjamin's fetish functions differently from the commodity, as it is built on different notions of subject and object. Commodity fetishism relies ideologically upon a stark division between human and inanimate. This is clearly visible in Lukács' anxiety about the dangers of reification: humans become things and things acquire human traits, but human and nature are opposed, so that human beings and materiality are seen as sharing no qualities or traits. This safe separation implies, paradoxically, the same frozen fixity that in the culture of consumption the object is supposed to impart to the human subject. Benjamin's version of fetishism, instead, relies on a notion of movement and fluidity, on an unarrested traffic between matter and spirit that violates any fixed boundary between human and thing, subject and object. Here, as Pels points out when he suggests that the interaction between people and things is "best studied in terms of aesthetics: the material process of mediation of knowledge through the senses" (101), the point is that the subject too is matter, and partakes of the same materiality as the object. "Not only," affirms Pels, "are humans as material as the material they mold, but humans are themselves molded, through their sensuousness, by the "dead" matter with which they are surrounded. It is in this way that I understand fetishism, which confers a measure of plastic power to things" (101). Fetishism, in these terms, becomes nothing less than the precondition, in modernity, of plasticity: the object as fetish has the complex energetic charge to act on the matter that is subjectivity itself.

This fetishism thus produces an erosion of the boundaries that, through centuries of rationalism and humanism, have separated human beings from objects. Through the problematic of the fetish and its contradictions, Benjamin establishes a middle ground between animism and untranscended matter, which allows him to theorize a similarly ambiguous and open middle subjectivity, while attributing power of agency to the object. To what ends? Now neither fully a self-possessed, transparent, autonomous subject, nor fully a "patient'—although capable of suffering in relation to the object—the individual allows himself to be acted upon and shaped by the object. For Benjamin, the materialist critic of bourgeois modernity and capitalist culture, political economy passes through the object via aesthetics and its magic. Benjamin's bewitched and highly vibrant matter makes things happen, and the subject, without becoming reified, is acted upon, and becomes part of the action, too. This fluid and osmotic relation between subject and object, the existence of a middle ground between subjectivity and objectivity, is not however merely a matter of epistemological or ontological indeterminacy, or a form of modernist sublime. Rather it means multiplying possibilities of change, partly by opening up the terrain of memory and, for Benjamin, history, for those upon whose defeat the hegemony of the victors has been built.

II. Fetishism, Contradiction, and the Desiring Subject: The Problem of Gender

If the Benjaminian fetish manages to find life, and life of a complex and potentially powerful kind, in the commodity object that earlier materialists had seen as reified dead matter, where does this leave the subject, and, particularly, her or his desire? If Benjamin manages to find a balance for the object between the contradictory qualities of the fetish—"animated" by human agency, capable of its own agency—by establishing a middle ground where their opposition is unmade, how does he deal with the mirror contradiction that informs the materialized subject? This subject must negotiate between the cognitive and the libidinal, *ratio* and desire, vision and tactility, and, last but not least, the individual and the collective. Benjamin solves these contradictions through the apparatus of the dialectic at a standstill. In this standstill swirls a problematic notion of the role of desire. We need to grasp the persistence of desire in Benjamin, to understand the limits as well as the possibilities of the subject–object fluidity he inaugurates.

If Benjamin's stuff theory articulates the somatic and synaesthetic in the subject, it does so within a discourse of sexual desire. Against the remorseless power of the commodity to structure desire and identities under capitalism, Benjamin's discourse of materiality attempts to recuperate the agency of things away from reification under the existing relations of production and culture. The outmoded commodity is for him capable of a mnemonic power: the power to unmake the forgetting produced by commodity fetishism, and a libidinal power capable of restoring desire to its free-floating, unfixed form. In turn this unfixed desire, when sparked by specific objects, should create an "combustion" that renews the individual's lost connection both to the past and to the collective. Thus the commodity's pernicious interpellation of the subject into a passivity that freezes and fixes the political and libidinal potential of his desire is overcome. However, it is the collective dimension of the object, its capability to act at the social level, that matters most to Benjamin. With the focus on the social and collective power of the fetish rather than on its libidinal aspect, this latter always appears, instead, connected to the degraded "individuality" and sexuality of the commodity. This might be seen as a disciplining of the object into a productive function: the commodity, now an object with nothing to hide, transforms desire into meaning, libido into history, the individual fantasy into collective utopia. Such at any rate is how the ideal Benjaminian subject–object relation might be sketched. Nonetheless such a liquidation of the commodity as commodity and the desire that it references turns out to be impossible: a residue of its power simply as a commodity, and of how it organizes the body, always remains. Benjamin's own analysis, as I will show, does not escape this power of the commodity, where it remains as a residue—the dirt that cannot be put under the carpet, a touch of shame.

If we analyze the slippage between the anthropological and psycho-analytical registers of the fetish in Benjamin's discourse of the object, we can see that the sexual charge of the fetish, which is the way the commodity speaks desire, is not erased but only displaced. This displacement constitutes a telling problematic in his view of matter. In brief, his theorization of the object's potential to produce happiness, in contrast to the always unfulfilled *promesse de bonheur* of the commodity, voices his diffidence regarding the role of Oedipal sexuality as a step in the production of a gendered subjectivity. His discourse of the object as fetish, suspended between animated and untranscended matter, subjectivity and "pure" objectivity, harks back to a pre-Oedipal version of libidinal desire. This version is dominated by the image of porosity, an important trope in his work. Pre-Oedipal porosity characterizes the traffic between subject and object, and even the dialectic at a standstill. Now a commitment to such porosity in the subject–object relation, and to a polymorphous pre-Oedipal libidinality as a model of the subject's sexual desire, might seem utterly appropriate to a theoretical project that would unsettle both subject and object. Yet the subject's structure of desire, just like the object's fetishistic vibrancy, also always already exists within a set of preexisting power relations—in the case of sexuality, those of gender. While he brilliantly develops a viable account of the plasticity of the commodity object, he seems more impressionistic when developing an account of the other side, that of the subject and his desire. Just as the commodity object always, literally, has a price, so too the subject's libidinal desire is not (despite what humanism may long have claimed) priceless either. As we shall see, the price Benjamin's theory of subject–object relations has to pay for his gingerly handling of the subject's desire is the problematic nature of his concept of the collective unconscious.

What is at stake in this discrepancy between what Benjamin describes as the commodity fetish on the one hand and the subject desiring that fetish on the other, is brought to the fore by Christina Kiaer's claim, in her essay "Rodchenko in Paris,"[34] that Benjamin's object is not a fetish and that his consumer is not a fetishist at all. In her brilliant discussion of the Soviet Constructivist object, Kiaer pits Rodchenko against Benjamin, and juxtaposes their views of materiality. Rodchenko the Bolshevik goes to Paris in 1925 to the International Exhibition, and returns to Russia full of both admiration and disgust for the western object world. The desire staged by the commodity in the west, and the way the commodity is sexualized and gendered by its collapse into the figure of the female body, then makes for the conflicted quality and complexity of the Constructivist object.[35] Kiaer contrasts Rodchenko's ambivalence with Benjamin's delight. Benjamin, the westerner, travels to Moscow in 1927, and is seduced by the Russian object world "of the rickety market kiosks" (19). Kiaer's acceptance of Benjamin's all-too-politically correct reading of the "comrade objects" he finds in the Soviet State is what allows her to claim that he is no fetishist: "In the analysis of industrial modernity, Benjamin discovers a political force in the way that the fragile and fleeting formations of individual fantasy congeal into, or are centered upon, objects that individuals share, objects that are all alike, and whose very sameness and reproducibility inspires the dream of a collective dream-image." The individual, in Kiaer's view of Benjamin, is now quickly and automatically sutured onto the collective, and while Rodchenko's Constructivist object lets itself be questioned and complicated by the interaction with the western commodity (31), Benjamin's object seems to have already unproblematically overcome this interaction. Kaier contrasts the desire at play in the western commodity, about which Rodchenko was so conflicted, with Benjamin's reading of the Soviet object as transparent, tactile, and as "useful coworker", which doesn't try to seduce you as does the "dark slave" the commodity. In this contrast, Kiaer claims for the Constructivist object and its maker a hybridity from which Benjamin's fetish, and Benjamin as the subject, is excluded. If this is true in the case of his reading of the Soviet object, might it not be equally true of his reading of western commodity objects? Kiaer's valorization of Benjamin is therefore double-edged: her reading of Rodchenko leaves her too polite regarding Benjamin's views. When Kiaer, and Benjamin himself, thinks of the desiring subject, we witness a contradictory slippage between the intention to unfix desire from the logic of the commodity, and the image of an individual in control of his wishes. Individual desire, in other words, is not in Benjamin a pattern of collective desire, and the slippage between the two remains unexamined. The image of the collective paradoxically dreaming the added-up dream of many individuals, and dreaming outside and against the fantasies circulating through the commodity, is in fact an inverted image of systemic, and supposedly, in Benjamin, automatically coherent individual subjective desire.

Not to acknowledge this—as Rodchenko did in his letters to his wife about his reaction to western commodity displays—is what allows Benjamin to leave unexamined the ease with which he changes his tune about Soviet, as opposed to western, commodities. And the price is a relatively unexamined assumption of collective dream power, as a result of unexamined inferences about the working of individual, libidinal desire. As might be expected, for both Rodchenko and Benjamin, the implications of each of their analyses of desire in relation to the object reveal themselves when the subject is the writer himself and the object in question is the body of a woman.

Both in Benjamin and Rodchenko the commodity is associated with the degraded femininity of the prostitute and of the Parisian consumer, and represented as a form of false consciousness, lacking transparency, and as an index of decayed modern experience. However, the commodity and the subject's desire for it returns, and is present, albeit displaced, in certain thick moments of Benjamin's thought, when the encounter with the alterity of matter, and with nature, is figured as the encounter with the woman as object. This is especially so when, as often in his writing, he himself is the self-dramatized subject. In these instances, the agency of the female figure perverts and refigures what Kiaer sees as Benjamin's egalitarian, ascetic relationship to the object, so that the fetish becomes active with a vengeance: not only it is an agent, but it can harm the subject. This vengeance is carried on by a female figure which resists the subject's interpellation, no matter how benevolent and well-meaning. The more intriguing vision of an affect-charged, synaesthetic relationship between subject and object here seems to be taken over by an old script, that of the fetishized *femme fatale*.

The prostitute, however, has about her for Benjamin the aura of Bauman's "wasted lives." And it is in this attraction to the marginal, to the wasted and excessive, to stuff, that Benjamin manages to salvage his new vision of the magical vibrancy of the fetishized commodity object. Here, his focus on stuff, on the unruly, *outré* and cast-off, rather than the one still preening under its gloss and glamour, is crucial. It is as if he has entered so profoundly into the spirit of the fetishized commodity in consumer culture that he has intuited that all commodities are excessive, wasteful, or at least aspire to the condition of waste. (This might be his legacy from the *fin-de-siècle* decadents). Benjamin's outmoded commodity reflects the conflictedness of an uneven economy, which in the west, for example, can be reflected in the way it switches from the political to the libidinal in a moment. If in Moscow he had sung the praises of the handmade peasant toys, when he returns to the west,

Benjamin focuses on hybrid materialities, on objects that are commodities but whose outmoded and marginal commodification either don't measure up to or exceed the fully regulated system of commodity fetishism, and thereby can leave space for individual fantasy. The consumers' relations to these commodities can also be marked by unruliness, and in this unruliness fetishism can be exaggerated and flipped over, between individual "private" fantasy and collective goals. As both positions of subject and object become more unstable in the exchange between material and immaterial, the frozen "death in life" of reification is jeopardized. It is the encounter with the woman as object that, as I will show, fully exposes the possibilities of Benjamin's baroque model of the contact between subject and object.

Finally, where does this leave the issue of the subject as part of a collective? By focusing on stuff, Benjamin contests the object's claimed neutrality by seizing not upon the commodity, but on a commodity now outmoded, a fragment. Against the excessive, marginal quality of stuff, he then memorably and persistently offers us the vision of his excessive, marginal self. With a bold inversion that testifies to his investment in fluidity, in the flip-flop (strategic, this time) between the categories—reason vs. sleep-dream; agency vs. inactivity; subject vs. object—which dominant culture claims are opposites, the self-presence of the individual as reader of reality is displaced onto the shamanistic figure of the allegorist. Meaning in Benjamin comes from two *loci*: a social collective which is asleep, and an individual awake with dreams and visions, a self isolated from and at odds with the system. This individual inhabits a porous social position that makes him both a thief *and* a saint, as Genet is for Taussig, an upper bourgeois *and* proletarian, as is Benjamin himself, and a dispossessed eccentric *and* the consciousness of his time, as Baudelaire was for Benjamin. His multiple positions—allegorist, criminal, innocent child "seeing the new anew," *flâneur*, continual border crosser, whore, *démodé* poet, collector—gives him power to be illuminated both by the unconscious and by his own problematic and contradictory stance in the social whole. In all these hybrid figures Benjamin projects the notion of an unstable, outlaw, porous "middle subjectivity" that is a match for the vibrant fetishism of the frail, cast-off commodity as stuff object. Stuff and subject meet on the middle ground, the porous space that Benjamin himself inhabited in his own life, and with which he experiments, as in his attempts to find a new perceptive dimension with drugs. All along he theorizes a subject position where contradiction and Surreal illumination mix, so that science and vision, Enlightenment and magic, subject and object become part of each other, or at least come halfway toward each other.

Benjamin's talk of the object is always necessarily fetishistic, that is, double, unstable, moving between two different categories, reason and the unconscious, science and magic, collective and individual. The object, the *res*, remains the lightning rod of fantasy and desire, but no longer according to the logic of the commodity, or as the subjected dead matter that the scientific gaze of the Enlightenment demands. His object is a flexible fetish, presiding over, and reshaping, different economies of value, affect, and sexuality. Through a mnemonics and a mimesis of the object, Benjamin then tries to redefine subjective desire against the "sex appeal" of the commodity fetish. Nonetheless, no matter how hijacked by consumer capitalism, this very sex appeal is the irreducible residue of Benjamin's theory of materiality, the libidinal charge he himself experiences, and which needs to be held to account in his discourse of the object.

III. The Erotics of the Encounter: Hysterical Contact and the Ascetic Swerve

We will now examine specific moments at the margins of Benjamin's own philosophic project when the theorist's own libidinal desire does not necessarily match that of the projected desire of a hypothetical collective. So far, we have spoken of the inevitability of the subject–object encounter. This encounter has, in the work of a line of radical thinkers, been liberated from being a scenario involving fixed subject–object positions, with the living, powerful subject acting on dead, abject matter. This study speaks of stuff as that recalcitrant matter that itself falls outside the hierarchical, rationalist account of the way in which subjects and objects relate, so that it incites us by its very existence to rethink subject–object contacts in new ways. One danger of this way of thinking, however, might be that stuff is merely what the powerful subject, acting within the old model of how subjects relate to matter, casts off and designates, disdainfully, as such, precisely to preserve his power over the rest of "proper" matter. One value of the new materialism, then, is that its theorists invoke the alternative philosophical tradition, from Lucretius to Spinoza to Bergson, Deleuze and Latour, to insist, rightly, that matter, however designated by the official order of things, is not only malleable but itself active, that it cannot be prevented from merging with other matter or with subjects, and that it can—as stuff—fight back. Yet we should not underestimate the resourcefulness of the hegemonic subject who has profited from the dominant order of subject–object relations. One simple strategy for this subject to fight the object's liveliness is to avoid contact with the object altogether. This asceticism has a long tradition in western thought and practice. The ascetic impulse, valorizing such categories as "purity," denial, fasting, and self-abnegation, is an important if implicit undercurrent not only in various "magical" practices and pre-rational traditions, but persists also in the classical materialist suspicion of the commodity as a duplicitous object which masks its own history. It continues today in various dreams of living outside consumer culture altogether. Asceticism has also always been associated with the expression of libidinal desire. To explore the power of the ascetic impulse we need to consider how the libidinal can mark the limit of free subject–object encounters.

When Benjamin, often poignantly, describes his own encounters with women whom he objectifies, an ascetic impulse comes into play. Literally, the Chaplinesque *flâneur* philosopher enacts a gesture, a movement, of passing them by. This trope of "passing by" I take to be the mark of the ascetic in Benjamin. To be a *flâneur* is to make the act of passing by an expected gesture. Yet to the extent that it is a practice of everyday asceticism, is it a viable version of the human subject's relation to matter over time? My working hypothesis here is that it is not, that the refusal of contact with matter is the subject's illusion, and even more, that the notion that one can avoid contact with matter as commodified objects is, in western consumer culture, an illusion too. The ascetic gesture of passing by the alluring object does not grant to the subject a freedom from the effects of commodification or reification, but rather signals, in Benjamin's case in the first instance, a version of traumatized ambivalence which leads to even more baroque enfoldings of subject and object, psyche and matter. Does asceticism, then, have a future in the brave new world of subject and matter? It would seem that the ascetic gesture can narrow the zone of contact between subject and object, but it cannot foreclose it—and that this narrowing only makes the actual contact more unruly, more fraught and friable, more intense.

If the encounter between human subject and matter is a charged one, then we can be sure that desire will enter into the equation. On the one hand, to see matter as hybrid is in part to anthropomorphize it, to humanize it, so that the matter of sexual desire gets greater scope to be in play. On the other, the living allure of the object makes one, as subject, want to imitate it, to *be* the object, to objectify oneself, and to present oneself as an object in a world where objects are almost always the most alluring things there appear to be, in order to incite others' desire. Finally one may objectify another subject, whether to exert dominance or simply to conform to the order of things in which commodity objects *are* invested with glamour. The more open the subject–object relation is, the more any and all of these possibilities are likely to be activated. This makes a new order of subject–object relations liberating, but also dangerous. One of Benjamin's most courageous moves is to unabashedly cast himself in each of these roles. In the process, he makes of his philosophic persona a character even more fascinating than Mann's Aschenbach or Joyce's

Leopold Bloom—because he did not, if we believe him, invent the dramas of his desiring life, but actually lived them. Anticipating new relations between subject and matter, he plays out the scenarios with himself as actor and actant. We see him not only hoarding his book collection or his collection of toys, but also being the lover (jilted and not), ogler, desirer, and possessor of women whom he often objectified, and whose allure he certainly read in the context of the charge of desire passing between subjects and objects in the commodity world. Almost invariably, in his accounts of these relations, the dominant trope throughout is the swerve, the act of "passing by." The desire relation switches on an ascetic impulse.

Often in Benjamin, the libidinal seems to be converted and channeled into the productivity of the political: the mimetic relationship of non-identity between subject and object gives the encounter a performative, rather than erotic, character, which seems to exclude desire and its pathologies. Yet the passage from the individual to the collective in his work seems all too smooth; the question of desire and sexuality provides a different perspective on such categories as the subject–object encounter, the coexistence of a sense of loss and a sense of totality, the relation of individual and the collective, and the cohabitation of eros and power. What, then, is desire in Benjamin? If the perverse libidinality of incorporation and identification with which the commodity endows the inanimate is outskirted by Benjamin in his critique of the object, it reappears elsewhere, uncannily, when the object of the same encounter is female. What happens when the encounter gets eroticized, as it often turns out to be, through the figure of the mother, lover, prostitute? How does this feminization and sexualization of the object interrupt the act of seeing things as they are in their *quidditas* vs., comprehending them as containing the seeds of diverted dreams and future possibilities? What happens to the male subject, and to Benjamin's theory of materiality, when the object is a woman? In this instance the unstable play of non-identity that has so far marked the relationship between subject and object is further complicated by the desire to be the object, *and* to have the object, to incorporate it, as well as by the subsequent revulsion that this desire inspires.

Here the dialectical theatre of nearness and distance, which Benjamin tries to adjust throughout his work, is distorted in a frantic telescoping between approaching the object and refusing this approach. This time the perpetual present of the erotic encounter doesn't serve the purpose of "detonating" the past into the future, as we see when Benjamin dramatizes his encounter with actual objects, but rather freezes the subject in a melancholic state. The examination of the libidinal dimension of Benjamin's stuff theory, through the specific body politics that sustain it, makes visible a more complex, less constructive side of his thought. In the erotics of the encounter with the female object, the stress is on loss, and, as we will see, on a defensive politics of passing, as both a form of transience and of performance. The erotic female object implies the impossibility of utopia and of happiness itself.

The images of the erotic encounter we will now analyze here—fragments of *One-Way Street*, Baudelaire on prostitution as described in Konvolut J and in *Central Park*, Benjamin's reading of Baudelaire's sonnet "*À Une Passante*," and last but not least Benjamin's autobiographical account of his relation to Asja Lacis—are structured as moments, and acts, of passing by.[36] The impermanence of modernity is presented as the passage of the beloved, a passage that is often imagined as the encounter, actual or hallucinated, of man and woman. Benjamin's interest in waning phenomena, and in historically transient figures, that is, figures that are passing out of history, helps explain the temporal quality of the category of "passing." Note that all of the passing characters are male: the *flâneur*, the collector, the storyteller, the lyrical poet in the era of high capitalism. At the same time, in his work this category becomes spatialized in the attempt to become, to "pass as" the object, in coming to inhabit its space, in trying to incorporate the corpse—of the prostitute-as-commodity—which, Benjamin notes, happens in Baudelaire. Here the temporality of loss, in which the critic, poet, and male subject are entwined in his desire to merge with the object, to identify with it, becomes for him a way to reinstate his own permanence.

At the heart of his version of the erotic encounter are the tactics through which Benjamin faces the transience, the impermanence, and the loss of the object. These are forms of displacement and sublimation, comprising scenarios of desire and sexual violence, as in the case of the allegorical representation of the prostitute's body. They are also tactile and visual, as in the dream of fixing the desired object in memory in the sonnet by Baudelaire to which Benjamin devotes some of his most eloquent criticism, "*À Une Passante*." All are centered on the female body. Finally, the loss of the passing object in the erotic encounter is sublimated and exorcised in the displacement of desire onto political agency.[37] Kiaer's claim of an Apollonian notion of desire in Benjamin, always gesturing to the collective, social, and socialist utopia, and founded on the claimed transparency of the object is however, in the Benjaminian everyday, complicated and clouded by a more Dionysian eroticism. His sexual politics and his representation of women says that the ascetic or sadistic desire of the male allegorist, talking politics when he is talking of objects and collectivity, cannot be separated from the desirous individual, and that talking of objects does not and cannot exclude talking of sexuality. The desirous individual divided between *Angst* and *Lust* toward the object, and fetishistically sublimating its loss, should not be taken as an odd element of disturbance in his critique, but rather should be seen as what further interrupts (again, dialectically) an already fraught and not at all transparent balance between subject and object. For Benjamin as subject, the optimism of utopia as the path to fulfillment is balanced by the pessimistic realism of loss.

The erotic aspect of the encounter is a *memento mori* of what appears, at times, a too automatic notion of collectivity in Benjamin. It reminds us that the sum of individual fantasies and desires doesn't immediately amount to the collective utopia,[38] and that the collective doesn't erase individual desire. In contrast to the image of the subject mimetically recuperating the object in a joyful, perfect balance of nearness and distance, there is always, also, his attempt to deny loss by trying to masquerade as the object, to become it, to pass as it. This desire to disguise oneself as the object, and in that way to close the gap between subject and object, as well as between the verbal and the figural in his writing, is perhaps the only truly ascetic, even puritanical moment in Benjamin's thought. This theorist, eager to contaminate the solitary modern subject with the materiality of things, and to reintroduce aesthetic sensuousness, somatic affect and the tactility of matter into philosophy, so that thought can be articulated only through objects, in its concreteness,[39] reaches a telling limit point when dealing with libidinal desire. Through the displacement of the sexual onto the political, Benjamin seems to perform a cleansing of the libido away from the erotic into a "productive," constructive force. In fact, this ascetic choice backfires.

IV. Modernist Gender, Modernist Objects

What are objects for? If "commodities ... store the fantasy energy for social transformation in reified form," as Susan Buck-Morss puts it,[40] the sexual politics of the encounter indicates that objects also have an important function in the subject's personal history, and are even at the core of this history. Helga Geger-Ryan writes of Benjamin that his work "is ... a search for the moulds of objects which have shaped people in the same way that a baking tin forms cookies ... The inner space, this dimension between soma and phantasma, is firstly created by objects." She goes on to note that in *Berlin Childhood* Benjamin shows us how the subject is formed in the construction of an imaginary cosmos by dealing with objects and spaces, during childhood. First pre-Oedipal abjection, then the mirror stage: at this point the child has a sense of himself as a unified body—"under the reassuring gaze of the mother" (122).

Instead of focusing on *Berlin Childhood* to trace the formation of Benjamin's imaginary and the sexual politics of his theory, let us turn to two passages of *One-Way Street*, where the encounter is clearly eroticized in the way Benjamin describes his relationship with his lover, and to the maternal figure. In these fragments the relationship to the object is in each case structured by loss, presented both as shockingly unredeemable and as a source of pleasure, that which gives the object a special radiance. The farewell scene he describes confers an aura upon the leave-taker: "How much more easily is the leave-taker loved! For the flame burns more purely for those vanishing in the distance, fueled by the fleeting scrap material waving from the ship or railway window. Separation penetrates the disappearing person like a pigment, and steeps him in gentle radiance" (*OWS* 450). With the waving handkerchief as synecdoche, its stuff and the lover fade into one another as aura-bearing objects. This melancholic pleasure in the disappearing other is replaced, soon, by a different pleasure, that of the loss of the self. Looking at the beloved, Benjamin experiences a sense of an "erotic optical unconscious," which decenters the loving subject. He finds himself no longer in the commanding position of feeling; rather, feeling is experienced and resides in the object, which now enables perception and structures the subject's identity:

> Wrinkles on a face, moles, shabby clothes and a lopsided walk bind him
> [to the loved one] more lastingly and relentlessly than any beauty . . . And
> why? If the theory is correct that feeling is not located in the head, that
> we sentiently experience a window, a cloud, a tree, not in our brain but
> rather in the place where we see it, then we are, in looking at our beloved,
> too, outside ourselves. But in a torment of tension and ravishment. Our
> feeling, dazzled, flutters like a flock of birds in a woman's radiance. And
> as birds seek refuge in the leafy recesses of a tree, feelings escape into the
> shaded wrinkles, the awkward movements and inconspicuous blemishes
> of the body we love, where they can lie low in safety. And no passer-by
> would guess, that it is just there, in what is defective and censurable that
> the fleeting darts of adoration nestle (*OWS* 449).

This fragment evokes a contradictory moment of intense reassurance and anxiety, but it is one already shot through by the sadism of the prior allegorical representation of woman as whore. Rather than being idealized, the body of the lover is stripped of its beauty and shown in its defective reality: only the lover's self-abandonment to its space can confer a new radiance on it.

Benjamin's reflection on the prostitute as a figure of modernity starts early in his career. In a 1913 letter to Herbert Belmore[41] he looks at prostitution as a cipher of all human life under capitalism. His silence on the gender-specificity of the prostitute he mentions implies his participation in early twentieth-century discourses of male anxiety in the face of modern femininity and the emancipation of women;[42] occasional images in his work of a sterile modern femininity, transgressive of more "natural" roles, show that he was not immune to the ideological and visual regimes of mysoginistic modernity. Nevertheless, he also clearly transgresses the boundaries of a patriarchal modernism by reinscribing abjection into his text, and by becoming himself an abject in his own life.[43]

This masculine abjection, this capability of inhabiting the space of the corpse (that is, of looking at history from inside its rubble), returns in his writing on the figure and poetry of Baudelaire. Both images, of abjection and corpse-habitation, speak of the same "impure" traffic with the abject, to which both Benjamin and Baudelaire as Benjamin's alter ego are committed. For both authors prostitution testifies to the death of the organic and the fall of love: all that is left of the human and of nature in the sexual encounter between the client and the prostitute is his shame, while the woman is seen as entirely reified.[44] Modern women's autonomy is presented as a form of reification that turns them into massified industrial products, while taking up the place of men in the public sphere.

As the victim of the historical disorder signaled by the phallic femininity of the whore-commodity, the now impotent male subject as disowned poet, in Benjamin's formulation, is forced to go on the market. He becomes himself like the prostitute. He becomes a victim whose passion sanctions his impotence and his solitude.[45] He retrenches, like the prostitute-as-commodity, into the position of masochistic victimhood. By claiming the abject feminine space of the object-corpse, the male subject can also assuage his womb envy, which in Baudelaire, via Benjamin, is quite literal: "It belongs to the Via Dolorosa of male sexuality that Baudelaire perceived pregnancy, in some degree, as unfair competition. On the other hand, solidarity between impotence and sterility" (*Arcades Project*, J57, 1, 331). Retrenching, he also elaborates violent strategies of containment of femininity, of the transgressive maternal force that, by refusing to stay in its place—at home or in the abject space of the pre-Oedipal—has caused the fall of the natural, and has perverted love into demonic sexuality.

Ultimately this perversion of maternal femininity has the effect of introducing death into life, Thanatos into Eros, and the pre-Oedipal denial of distance turns into the deadly embrace of the Oedipal mother-prostitute, or into the impossibility of approaching her. What then is the male subject to do, other than masquerading as the object, in the impossible fantasy of once again inhabiting the maternal body, a body now become a skeleton, the grotesquely decorated and made-up skull of the baroque stage? The subject's masquerade is about himself, a way of dealing with his fear and sense of loss, but how does he deal with the woman figure? In two opposite, but equally counterphobic and therefore fetishistic ways: by punishing and allegorically disfiguring her into the image of the whore, or by sublimating her erotic danger into a spiritualized femininity. These two images are correlative: they are two different projections of the perverted maternal figure, whose Oedipal eroticism has been split into the fallen sexuality of the prostitute, and in the asexual figure of the woman as spiritual guide, from Dante's Beatrice to Breton's Nadja.

The two extremes of femininity Benjamin projects are both present in Baudelaire, suspended between the image of the whore and that of the veiled woman in the sonnet "*À Une Passante*," which Benjamin describes in Konvolut J of *The Arcades Project* as "one of Baudelaire's most perfect love poems" (J21a, 4, p. 267), and the only poem which he reprints in its entirety. It is only by considering a passage from his essay on Surrealism that the implications of this version of perfection are made clear. In Benjamin's reading of Nadja, the destitute prostitute and *voyante* who introduces Breton to the Paris of his unconscious in the latter's novel of the same name, ("I saw a young, poorly dressed woman walking toward me, she had noticed me too, or perhaps had been watching me for several moments"[46]) this figure exists only to show things to the writer, to make him "see." Breton first notices her eyes ("She was curiously made up, as though beginning with her eyes, she had not had time to finish, … What was so extraordinary about what was happening in those eyes?" (Breton, 65)) and goes on, in describing her seizures and visionary power, to idealize and disembody her, so that she comes to represent to him a projection of his own mind that shocks him "out of himself." So too Benjamin explains Breton's use of love and of the figure of the beloved, as means to profane illumination. Through the "mystical beloved" the poet doesn't try to satisfy sexual desire, but to approach "an illumination." "The dialectics of illumination," he continues,

> are indeed curious. Is not perhaps all ecstasy in any world humiliating sobriety in the world complementary to it? What is it that courtly *Minne* seeks (and it, not love, binds Breton to the telepathic girl), if not to make chastity too, a transport? … The lady, in esoteric love, matters least. So, too, for Breton. He is closer to the things that Nadja is close to, than to her (210).

That the "telepathic" beloved, on the stage of Surrealist materialism, brings one close to things, means that she remains a medium. Her power is superseded, and her Medusan female gaze, blinded by the vision, can no longer petrify the male subject. This same decreed blindness of the female other returns, but with a twist, in Baudelaire's "*À Une Passante*" to negotiate the erotics of distance and nearness of the encounter; in his reading of it, Benjamin explores this erotics more painstakingly than anywhere else in his work.

Benjamin's commentary on the sonnet comes in two different versions of his work on Baudelaire: the essay "The *Flâneur*," in "The Paris of the Second Empire" of 1938, and its 1939 revision "Some Motifs in Baudelaire," in "Paris Capital of the Nineteenth Century."[47] It has become a *locus classicus* of modernism, affirming the transience, if not impossibility of love and connection under the conditions of existence in the modern city. In the poem the poet catches sight in the crowd of a fascinating female figure in mourning. Their encounter lasts only for the moment their eyes meet: after that flash she is lost again, carried away by the crowd, and the poet is left with the image, the memory of her, and a promise—his own—of eternal love. The loss is what makes the encounter erotic: "The delight of the city dweller," comments Benjamin, "is not so much love at first sight, as love at last sight" ("The *Flâneur*," 1938, 45). This motif is anticipated ten years earlier in *One-Way Street*, when Benjamin writes: "The only way of knowing a person is to love that person without hope" ("Arc Lamp," 467). Here the sentimentality of the aphorism hints at Benjamin's thought on reading Baudelaire's sonnet: the best encounter is the one where the subject and the object don't actually meet, an encounter that takes place *in absentia* for one or the other. This is what makes the sonnet, for Benjamin, "the most perfect love poem." For the anxious male critic, the encounter doesn't happen; he alone does all the looking and the talking. The poem is then a fetishistic male fantasy about the power of the gaze in structuring the relationship to the other. Benjamin's work charts different moments in this relation, from the protective reciprocity of the (defective) body of the lover and of the maternal imaginary in *One-Way Street*, to the sadistic allegorizing of the sexuality of the prostitute in Konvolut J of *The Arcades Project* and in *Central Park*. In reading the sonnet he further negotiates the split between love and sexuality, reciprocity and domination, allegory and symbol, to keep at bay maternal abjection. In his reading he sees new strategies of containment of the *passante*, strategies destined to fail. Perhaps this desired, if not planned failure, represents his truly dialectical negotiation between different images of femininity and modalities of the encounter.

In a fragment of Konvolut J, Benjamin explains how the agency of the crowd is countered by that of the male viewer: "Baudelaire introduces into the lyric the figure of sexual perversion that seeks its object in the street. What is most characteristic, however, he does this with the phrase 'trembling like a fool', in one of his most perfect love poems, "*À Une Passante*" (*Arcades Project* J21a, 4, p. 267). The "figure of sexual perversion" seeks its object in the street and finds "love." But love, understood as something that affects, makes the subject suffer, is assuaged in two ways: the object is re-enveloped by the crowd and taken away, and then the crowd becomes the medium for something else, a higher vision that generates the productive sublime of poetry. Notably, the object is not fully accessible to the poet. The gaze that incinerates and makes him "tremble like a fool" perhaps never takes place. In Benjamin's 1938 reading, the poet is only nominally "touched" by the sight of the beautiful woman, but he is not at all changed by her: "The 'never' marks the high point of the encounter," writes Benjamin, "where the poet's passion seems to be frustrated but in reality bursts out of him like a flame. He burns in this flame but no Phoenix arises from it" ("The *Flâneur,*" 1938, 45). The woman passes, then, in order to allow an experience, an after-effect, in the poet, which is productive of a kind of work, but also enables him to merge with the crowd. Here, then, the passer-by maintains her sublimated and sublimating power as medium, spiritual guide to Platonic love, which connects the lonely individual to the totality as represented by the crowd. In this sense, I agree with Melissa Marder's interpretation that the sonnet is for Benjamin resolutely about the crowd, rather than about love or the woman.[48] Crowd merging allows a swerve, a lack of contact with the woman.

However Baudelaire's, and Benjamin's, resistance to reading the female figure, his bypassing her description, must be interpreted symptomatically. Consider the strategies through which a Baudelaire-identified-Benjamin tries to stave off suffering and subjection at the hands, or rather, the eyes, of a woman. He recuperates his displacement of her image onto the crowd, and her passing by, as positive: love is about loss and the impossibility of "having" a dangerous object. He focuses on how the danger is transfigured, turned into the safe haven of art, which presupposes the poet as its active agent. "What makes his body twitch spasmodically is not the excitement of a man in whom an image has taken possession of every fiber in his being, it partakes more of the shock with which an imperious desire suddenly overcomes a lonely man" he decides ("The *Flâneur,*" 1938, 45). This resistance to "being taken possession of" by an image is however disrupted in his 1939 commentary on the sonnet, where Benjamin closes ranks against the powerful female figure. In "Some Motifs in Baudelaire" (1939), the unscathed, untouched male figure who gets burned in flames, but is no Phoenix, is no longer there. Now contact is subsumed by alienation: "What makes his body contract in a tremor ('*crispé comme un extravagant*') Baudelaire says, is not the rapture of a man whose every fiber is suffused with eros; it is, rather, like the kind of sexual shock that can beset a lonely man" ("On Some Motifs," 1939, 125). Now the terms of Benjamin's earlier discussion are inverted: the rapacious possession of the man by an erotic image had been rendered as the rapture of love, pervading, and not taking over, his body, and is now acknowledged as impossible. What we are left with is the shock of sexuality which, guaranteeing no connection, leaves the lonely man even more lonely. The axes of submission and domination now become those of reciprocity and disjuncture. The reciprocity of love cannot be had, the pre-Oedipal pleasure of the maternal will not happen. Again, what is the male subject to do? He can fake and hallucinate this reciprocity, or he can fixate on its painful passing, in order to turn it into some kind of permanence. Replaying both moves, Benjamin recuperates the female as object, perhaps even to "inhabit" it, in a move toward an abject identification. Yet he must try to avert her burning and petrifying gaze. (As we will see, he manages to do so in his writing, but not in his life).

I may have fallen into the trap of Benjamin's argument: the discussion has been, so far, mostly focused on the crowd and on the male subject. I want to go back to *la passante*, because it is for, and against, her that all the critical apparatus in both versions of Benjamin's interpretation of the sonnet has been shored up. My hypothesis is that she is not truly fully accessible, and that the male subject might in fact be hallucinating the reciprocal exchange of gazes: "In a widow's veil, mysteriously and mutely borne along by the crowd, an unknown woman comes into the poet's field of vision." ("Some Motifs," 1939, 125). What remains unexplained is what exactly each of them sees. The "widow's veil," that goes unmentioned in Benjamin's 1938 commentary, would actually bar the view of the woman's face, which the poet can only imagine. Acting as a mirror, as Marder proposes, the woman's veil directs the gaze back to the crowd, in a frustrating circularity that excludes the woman, and makes her unknowable, and inaccessible.[49]

It's the unavailability of the object that elicits two only apparently contradictory responses in Benjamin's 1939 commentary: on the one hand, his refusal to focus his analysis on the *passante,* and on the other, obliquely, his bringing her back as a degraded figure, not worth desiring. What is the meaning of this mixture of denial and affirmation? The doubling implies that either the encounter did not take place, yet that is for the best, or that the encounter did, in fact, occur; Benjamin wants to have his Baudelairean abject cake and eat it too. This final, footnoted reinstatement of the reciprocity of the impossible encounter is a way of desiring contact while avoiding it, or a way of avoiding the female gaze while claiming to be exchanging it. The "perversion" of the modern lover, as he says in Konvolut J, is not that he is looking for love in all the improper places, such as the street, only to lose it the moment he finds it. Instead, the problem is that the male subject is himself creating the conditions for the impossibility of love, because he desires love from the street, from the female figure as prostitute (and failed spiritual guide), who can only provide sex instead.

What is the effect of this man-made impossibility? It certainly does not solve the split between eros—love, nature, sex—and the petrifying, castrating power of the bad mother, whore, or commodity. In fact, if anything, eros seems to be taken over by sex. What else, then, does this impossibility produce for Benjamin? It produces the irremediable sadness of loss, to be assuaged *and* maintained through the work of melancholia. The most conspicuous act of the *passante* is not her returning the gaze of the poet in the crowd, an exchange that seems to be always already short-circuited, but her *passing*. This passing, says Baudelaire, is fixed in the photograph-like image of arrested movement it becomes for the viewer, ("A flash! Then nothing"), and for us, so that the very poem is a verbal photograph. As verbal snapshot pre-dating the era of snapshot photography, it becomes a form of relative and tainted permanence, what is left of the moment. This is the passing of the female other sanitized of her actual presence; nonetheless, the male subject as poet cannot yet fully let go of this presence, and sublimate it, as Breton does, under the sign of esoteric love. Rather he lives in relation to her trace, melancholically renewing, as the only form of possible permanence, the experience of loss. In this repetition neither death, as the ultimate passing, nor the other, as woman, can be transcended. We return, then, to the image of untranscended matter, the quality with which Benjamin endows the object and affirms its difference. The passing woman stands as the image of a desired object that cannot be had, of a loss that cannot be sublimated. Yet, this image of disruption is also consolatory. On the one hand we have the suspicion, and denial, of fulfillment: the object passes and the poet cannot "pass" through it, become it, or take shelter in it. On the other, the passing (of) woman becomes a frozen image of the poet's desire, a perhaps narcissistic image of his own subjectivity outside himself: its suspension, rather than his frustration, is a response to the fact that the object cannot be had.

V. The Striking of the Match: Benjamin on Fire

The scenario of the erotic encounter occurs once more in Benjamin's life and writing.[50] Describing his feelings for Asja Lacis, the "engineer," as he calls her, to whom *One-Way Street* is dedicated ("The Street is named Asja Lacis Street after her who, as an engineer, cut it through the author"), he deploys the same images and terms as he did in his analysis of the Baudelairean encounter. Prominent in his account is the romantic cliché—and, this being Benjamin, the salvific kitsch—of the "burning" of passion, the exchange of gazes between the two lovers.

Benjamin met Lacis in Capri in 1924. At the time he was married to Dora Pollack, and they had a child, Stefan. In Capri, where he went to complete his

Habilitationschrift on German tragic drama, he fell in love with Lacis, a Latvian Bolshevik, an actress and theatre director in post-revolutionary Russia, an active figure in the avant-garde intelligentsia who had worked with Brecht's Expressionist theatre in Munich. The street that Lacis cut into Benjamin was that of Marxism via Lukács, whose 1924 book *History and Class Consciousness* they read together. They also co-wrote the essay "Naples," published in 1925. The affair lasted until 1927, when Benjamin went to Russia to visit her, and to write an article about Soviet post-revolutionary life. Their story ended badly, with Lacis' nervous breakdown and her *ménage à trois* with Benjamin and Bernhard Reich, an Austrian dramatist who had immigrated to Russia.

It is important to speculate on this last, biographical version of the encounter, because Benjamin's representation of his love for Lacis helps illuminate his final understanding of the aura in "Some Motifs in Baudelaire," of 1939, and his final word on the relation of subject and object. The double affect of *Angst-Lust* which had for him characterized the erotic encounter returns in *One-Way Street* in his account of a key moment in his relationship with Lacis, his visit in Russia:

> I had arrived in Riga to visit a woman friend. Her house, the town, the language were unfamiliar to me. Nobody was expecting me; no one knew me. For two hours I watched the streets in solitude. Never again have I seen them so. From every gate a flame darted; each cornerstone sprayed sparks, and every streetcar came toward me like a fire engine. For she might have stepped out of the gateway, around the corner, been sitting in the streetcar. But of the two of us, I had to be, at any price, the first to see her. For, had she touched me with the match of her eyes, I would have gone up like a powder keg. (*One-Way Street*, "Ordnance," 461)

The scenario of "*À Une Passante*" is brilliantly repeated and transfigured in this passage: the solitude of the *flâneur* in an unknown city is animated by the fear and desire to meet the lover. In this amplified cityscape, where we expect, with Benjamin, the coming of a portent, *the* portent, the radiance of the female passer-by is exchanged for the burning flames that Lacis' eyes will spark. By claiming the need to be first to impose his gaze upon the other for fear of being burned, the male subject preempts the female gaze, where there is no veil to shield him. The violence of his modernist imagery ("every streetcar came towards me like a fire engine"), where passion is represented by the image of technology, measures the amplitude of love. Yet it also denotes its danger. Therefore he tries to see before being caught unaware. To occupy the scopic position of feminine passivity also guarantees recognition, and as such it is feared and desired.

When Lacis, at the end of their relationship, does not return Benjamin's gaze, he experiences a moment of true, irreparable loss: "His last days in Moscow," writes Buck-Morss, "were preoccupied with buying Russian toys for his collection. His last meeting with Lacis was as indecisive as all the earlier ones. His last words in his diary are these: 'At first she seemed to turn around as she walked away, then I lost sight of her. Holding my large suitcase on my knees, I rode through the twilit streets to the station in tears.'" Buck-Morss sees this moment as one of "wise impotence" for Benjamin, but the fact is that it is a different impotence from that of the Baudelairean poet. Here there is no veil, except that of his own tears, to allow him to hallucinate the reciprocity of the lover's gaze. He cannot fake it. The mechanics of address is reversed: the man veiled only with his own tears is ignored by the love object, and her irrevocable passing cannot be photographed and sublimated. The missing flash prevents any melancholic freezing of this passing, or of the object—an object which in any case plays the part of the subject itself.

This definitive passing of the female figure in Benjamin's life resonates, ten years later, with another irrevocable passing, that of a moment in history when social change and utopia are still possible. In the face of advancing totalitarianism in Europe, and of Benjamin's disillusionment with Soviet politics after the Hitler–Stalin pact, the history of the victor seems to definitely occlude the field of historical visibility that could have brought the utopia of the past to combustion in the present. This failure of the historical *promesse de bonheur*, refracted in the object's refusal to return the gaze, produces an urgency which drives all Benjamin's work of 1939–40, especially the militancy of the *Theses on the Philosophy of History* and the melancholic view of the aura in "Some Motifs in Baudelaire." This is the endpoint of years-long theorizing for Benjamin. The cosmic dimension of the aura, as the balance of nearness and distance, yields to its social quality; it is finally reduced, via Proust, to the function of reconquering not a collective historical dimension, but a personal one, the dimension of individual experience. Consider this passage from *Central Park* on the social value of the aura: "Derivation of the aura as a projection of social experience of people onto nature: the gaze is returned" (41). The experience of the aura, "the expectation that our look will be returned by the object of our gaze," ("Some Motifs," 147), becomes private in 1939:

> Experience of the aura thus rests on the transposition of a response common in human relationships to the relationship of the inanimate or natural object and man. The person we look at, or who feels being looked at, looks at us in return. To perceive the aura of an object we look at means to invest it with the ability to look at us in return (148).

This experience corresponds to the data of the *memoire involontaire*. While the first part of the passage still speaks the language of historical materialism and of collectivity, so that the object is dereified by expressing, rather than erasing, the social relations that had produced it, the aura is then subjectivized. It becomes a one-man show, rather than one which makes visible a social relation. The political meaning of the auratic encounter is renounced through a series of displacements. Not only is the act of investing the object with the power to look at us in return a "wellspring of poetry,"[51] but, says Benjamin, nebulously and inconclusively turning to Proust, it is merely a figment of one's mind and fantasy. "Some people who are fond of secrets flatter themselves that objects retain something of the gaze that has rested on them, (the ability, it seems, to return the gaze)," he says. "This chimera, Proust concludes, would change into truth if they related it to the only reality that is valid for the individual, namely, the world of his emotions." After this he goes on to discuss the disintegration of the aura in Baudelaire's poetry. To endow the object with the power to look at us in return is a type of foolproof system of reciprocation, a form of ventriloquism through which the subject tries to overcome and compensate for the actual silence, and possible danger, of the untranscended other. The safety and gratification of the subject comes at the cost of fixing and subjecting the object.

In this perspective, the most accurate and safe image of the love object, of the woman for whom the poet can fall (almost) without danger, is the wax statue in the *Musée Grevin* which fascinates both Breton and Benjamin.[52] At the end of *Nadja* Breton wants to return to the places to which the narrative "happens to lead" (Breton, 151), to photograph them. He wants "to provide a photographic image of them, taken at the spatial angle from which I myself had looked at them"—or, we could say, he wants to freeze them, to represent them from his point of view. Yet he notices that most places resist his desire. One of the places is the *Musée Grevin*, the Paris wax museum, where Breton is piqued by

the impossibility of obtaining permission to photograph an adorable wax figure ... on the left, between the hall of modern political celebrities, and the hall at the rear of which, behind a curtain, is shown "an evening at the theatre": it is a woman fastening her garter in the shadows, and is the only statue I know with eyes, the eyes of provocation etc. (Breton, 151).

This fairytale image of femininity is the embodiment in wax, seventy years after "*À Une Passante*," of both the female passer-by and of the male "photographer" in Baudelaire's sonnet. The denial of the "widow" retrenching behind the veil is compensated for by the wax statue's availability, here making a spectacle of herself for the male viewer, half allegory of femininity and half image of resistant woman. Her eyes of provocation invite, but she cannot be "photographed." Her irrevocable, definitive passing, like Lacis in Benjamin's last encounter with her, is forever suspended not in the possessive and reassuring melancholia of the male photographer, but in the dusty duration of history.

This time the suspension, and interruption, of history, is not the salvific punctuation of the *Jetztzeit*. As Buck-Morss notes: "The wax woman to whom both Breton and Benjamin lost their hearts still adjusts her garter, as she has for half a century. Her ephemeral act is frozen in time. She is unchanged, defying organic decay. But her dress is musty; her figure and her hair are no longer fashionable: she has clearly aged" (369). If the continuum of historical progress failed, so did the possibility of historical redemption. In her uncanny aging without changing, in this ruin and perversion of the secret of eternal youth, the wax figure is a powerful dialectical image of the body of unrealized history still beckoning, calling the viewer to experience, and exorcise, the loss through a fantasy of futurity. Another striking quality of the wax woman Benjamin and Breton fall for, is her *mis-en-abyme* of femininity, her refusal to be photographed. This marks her refusal to point to anything else but herself and her materiality.

This, ultimately, is the function of femininity in Benjamin's work. Rather than just posing woman as a disembodied sign of modernity, symbolically pointing to a higher realm, Benjamin also gives her a body, and, through his materialism, acknowledges, and dangerously affirms, female corporeality in his work, by letting his thought be contaminated by its abjection. Such a move could be interpreted as a further act of sublimation, but only paradoxically so, since the "sublimation" of femininity into work, whether in the subject-Benjamin or in his writing, serves to continually dismantle, rather than contain, an unscathed totality. In the sexual politics of the encounter Benjamin's double stance of *Angst-Lust*, with its counterphobic turns, speaks first of the male subject's imperative to defend and preserve himself. Yet Benjamin on fire is also committed to the risk of getting burned, that is, to a form of expenditure that welcomes the dangers of passion, of suffering, of abjection, and of otherness implied by the nearness of things and of femininity, accepting its risks and the possibility of loss.

The strategies of containment at work in the erotic encounter contradict, but do not nullify, the attempt, throughout Benjamin's work, to create a new, transparent relationship between subject and object, a relationship capable of producing praxis, a collective ideal of utopia. Courageously, *pace* the critics who see his project as a form of asceticism, in his theory of materiality Benjamin acknowledges and tries to encompass, rather than repress, the dangerous and unproductive desires that in capitalist modernity are organized by and through the commodity. If on the one hand he decides to inhabit *en masquerade* the space of the object, in order to maintain a safe distance which is also a form of respect for its difference, on the other he accepts the possibility of being inhabited by the object, and threatened by the dangers of its nearness. His attempt to negotiate the eroticism of abjection through, and not away from, the commodity fetish at the cost of burning his fingers doesn't make him into the picture of the male saint in the terms of the masochistic sainthood of modern masculinity we have seen in Baudelaire. He is no Saint Benjamin. Rather, it establishes his work as a striking attempt to live desire as political.

Notes

1 Theodor Adorno, *Prisms*, Cambridge, MIT, 1986, p. 233.
2 Naomi Schor, *Reading in Detail: Aesthetics and the Feminine*, New York, Methuen, 1987, p. 5.
3 Quoted in Theodor Adorno, "Benjamin the Letter Writer", Gary Smith ed., *On Walter Benjamin: Critical Essays and Recollections*, Cambridge, MIT Press, 1988, p. 333.
4 This is Adorno's and Horkheimer's thesis in *Dialectic of Enlightenment*, which Benjamin subscribes to in his work.
5 See for example, John Mullarkey, "Deleuze and Materialism: One or Several Matters?", special issue "A Deleuzian Century?", Ian Buchanan ed., *South Atlantic Quarterly*, 96, 3, Summer 1997, pp. 439–464.
6 Walter Benajmin, "On Some Motifs in Baudelaire," *Illuminations*, Hannah Arendt ed., trans. Harry Zohn, New York: Schocken Books, 1968, pp. 155–200, p.156.
7 See Roberto Esposito, *Bios: Biopolitics and Philosophy*, trans. Timothy Campbell, Minneapolis: University of Minnesota Press, 2008.
8 The key critic is Susan Buck-Morss, in her seminal *The Dialectics of Seeing*, Cambridge, MIT Press, 1986. See also Terry Eagleton, *Walter Benjamin, or Towards a Revolutionary Criticism*, London, Verso, 1981; Lutz Koepnick, *Walter Benjamin and the Aesthetics of Power*, Lincoln, University of Nebraska Press, 1999.
9 Benjamin writes in the 1935 *Exposé*: "In the dream in which each epoch entertains images of its successor, the latter appears wedded to elements of primal history (*Urgeschichte*)—that is, to elements of a classless society. And the experiences of such a society—as stored in the unconscious of the collective—engender . . . the utopia that has left its trace in a thousand configurations of life", *The Arcades Project*, trans. Howard Eiland and Kevin McLaughlin, Cambridge, Harvard University Press, 1999, p. 4.

10	Adorno attacks Benjamin's Marxism as undialectical and "idealist" in the
	Hornberg letter of August 4, 1935, *Adorno and Benjamin: The Complete
	Correspondence*, Henry Lomitz ed., Cambridge, Harvard University Press,
	1999.

11	The Parisian cycle includes Benjamin's writings between 1925 and 1940,
	from immediately after the publication of his *Habilitationschrift: The Origins
	of German Tragic Drama* to *The Arcades Project*. It marks the most
	materialist and political moment of Benjamin's reflection on modern
	culture.

12	Benjamin's theorization of the collective unconscious (or lack thereof) is
	another crucial point of Adorno's critique of Benjamin's *Arcades Project* in
	the already quoted Hornberg letter, where Benjamin is accused of
	Jungianism. Susan Buck-Morss, *Dialectics of Seeing*, Cambridge, p. 278.

13	Miriam Hansen, "Benjamin and Cinema: Not A One-Way Street", *Critical
	Inquiry*, Winter 1999, p. 320.

14	The way I use the term "naming" in this passage does not fully coincide with
	Benjamin's theory of language in the essay "On Language as Such and on the
	Language of Man", *Reflections*, trans. Edmund Jephcott, New York, Schocken
	Books, 1978.

15	See Francis Barker's discussion of modernity and subjection in his reading
	of early modern textuality (Pepys, Shakespeare, Descartes, Marvell) in *The
	Tremulous Private Body: Essays on Subjection*, London, Methuen, 1984.

16	This term signifies the subject–object relation, and the Surrealist *la
	rencontre*, where the relation is dominated and structured by chance,
	involving the unconscious. The eruption of the repressed is nonetheless
	anchored to historical conditions and reconnects the subject to
	consciousness. See Margaret Cohen, *Profane Illumination: Walter Benjamin
	and the Paris of Surrealist Revolution*, Berkeley, University of California
	Press, 1999, p. 169.

17	See Terry Lovell's critique of realism as an aesthetic and ontological logic in
	Pictures of Reality: Aesthetics, Politics, and Pleasure, London, the British Film
	Institute, 1980.

18	Michael Taussig, *The Nervous System*, New York, Routledge, 1996, p. 122.
	Subsequent page numbers in the text.

19	*One-Way Street*, in *Walter Benjamin: Selected Writings*, vol. I, M. Bullocks
	and M.W. Jennings eds., Cambridge, Harvard University Press, 1996, p. 446.
	Subsequent page numbers in the text.

20	Cohen, in *Profane Illumination,* and Buck-Morss, in *Dialectics of Seeing*, offer
	important interpretations of *One-Way Street*.

21	"The bourgeois interior of the 1860s to the 1890s—with its gigantic
	sideboards distended with carvings, the sunless corners where potted plants
	sit, . . . —fittingly houses only the corpse. 'On this sofa the aunt cannot but be
	murdered.'" Benjamin, *One-Way Street*, in *Walter Benjamin: Selected
	Writings*, vol, I. M. Bullocks and M.W. Jennings eds., Cambridge, Harvard
	University Press, 1996, p. 447.

22 Benjamin's notion of mimesis both encompasses and goes beyond the idea of imitation: it implies the fact that the object is not passive, and that subject and object interact, with reciprocal agency. In the essay "On the Mimetic Faculty", where he reflects on the fading of the human capability of "becoming" the other, he writes: "Nature creates similarities. One need only think of mimicry . . . Children's play is everywhere permeated by mimetic modes . . ." *Reflections*, p. 333.

23 The plan to write a "poetics of the commodity" is announced by Benjamin in *Central Park* and never fulfilled. "Central Park", trans. Lloyd Spencer (with Mark Harrington), *New German Critique* 34, Winter 1985, 32–58.

24 William Pietz, "The Problem of the Fetish, I", *Res* 9: 5–17, 1985; "The Problem of the Fetish, II: The Origin of the Fetish", *Res* 13: 23–45, 1987; "The Problem of the Fetish, IIIa: Bosman's Guinea and the Enlightenment Theory of Fetishism", *Res* 16: 105–23, 1985; "Fetishism and Materialism: The Limits of Theory in Marx", in Emily Apter and William Pietz eds., *Fetishism as Cultural Discourse*, Ithaca, Cornell University Press, 1993.

25 Peter Pels, "The Spirit of the Matter: On Fetish, Rarity, Fact, and Fancy", in *Border Fetishisms. Material Objects in Unstable Spaces*, Patricia Speyer ed., New York, Routlegde, 1998, p. 94.

26 See Taussig, *Nervous System*, p. 153.

27 This desire is a central concern of Michel Foucault in *The Order of Things: An Archeology of the Human Sciences*, New York, Vintage Books, 1973. See also Mary Slaughter, *Universal Languages and Scientific Taxonomy in the Seventeenth Century*, Cambridge, Cambridge University Press, 1982; James Clifford, "Objects and Others", in G.W. Stocking ed., *Objects and Others: Essays on Museums and Material Culture*, History of Anthropology Vol. 3, Madison, University of Wisconsin Press, 1985, and Susan Stewart, *On Longing: Narratives of the Miniature, the Gigantic, the Souvenir, the Collection*, Durham, Duke University Press, 1993.

28 For the "performing" power of the rarity, see Peter Pels, "The Spirit of the Matter: On Fetish, Rarity, Fact, and Fancy", in *Border Fetishisms*; Stephen Greenblatt, *Marvelous Possessions: The Wonder of the New World*, Chicago, The University of Chicago Press, 1991; Hal Foster, "The Art of Fetishism: Notes on Dutch Still Life", in Apter and Pietz eds., *Fetishism as Cultural Discourse*, Ithaca, Cornell University Press, 1993; and Oliver Impey and Arthur MacGregor eds., *The Origin of Museums: The Cabinet of Curiosities in Sixteenth and Seventeenth-Century Europe*, Oxford, Clarendon Press, 1985.

29 "The relic did not represent but *was* the saint", Pels, "The Spirit of the Matter: On Fetish, Rarity, Fact, and Fancy", in *Border Fetishisms*, p. 104.

30 "the possibility of thinking of an untranscended materiality is historically contingent on the emergence of a global trade in objects, in which 'fetish' was the derogatory term." Pels, "The Spirit of the Matter: On Fetish, Rarity, Fact, and Fancy", in *Border Fetishisms*, p. 92.

31 Taussig, *The Nervous System*, New York, Routledge, 1996, p. 154.

32 "Here we are inching toward a critical dismantling of the sign in which the image lifts off from what it is meant to represent." Taussig, *Nervous System*, 1996, p. 128.

33 For a historical and theoretical discussion of phantasmagoria in Benjamin see Margaret Cohen, "*Le Diable à Paris*: Benjamin's phantasmagoria", in *Profane Illumination: Walter Benjamin and the Paris of Surrealist Revolution*, Berkeley, University of California Press, 1999.

34 Christina Kiaer, "Rodchenko in Paris", *October* 75, Winter 1996. The essay is now a chapter in Kiaer's book *Imagine No Possessions: The Socialist Objects of Russian Constructivism*, Cambridge, MIT Press, 2005.

35 Kiaer, *Imagine No Possessions*. Subsequent page numbers are given in the text.

36 Here I play with the meaning of "passing" as used in queer theory, and in drag. On passing in Benjamin see Pierre Missac, *Benjamin's Passages*, Cambridge, MIT Press, 1993.

37 On the sexual politics of Benjamin's work, see Siegrid Weigel, "Eros and Language: Benjamin's Kraus Essay", in Gerhard Richter, *Benjamin's Ghosts*, Gerhard Richter ed., Stanford University Press, 2002; Christine Buci-Glucksmann, *Baroque Reason: The Aesthetics of Modernity*, London, Sage, 1994; and Helga Geger-Ryan, "Abjection in the Texts of Walter Benjamin", *Fables of Desire*, London, Polity Press, 1999.

38 Perhaps the only, volatile, form of totality in Benjamin is the collective. For a discussion of totality, desire, and totalitarianism, see Alice Yaeger Kaplan, *Reproductions of Banality*, Minneapolis, University of Minnesota Press, 1988.

39 See Geger-Ryan ("Abjection in the Texts of Walter Benjamin", *Fables of Desire*, p. 115), and Adorno: "The thought presses close to its object, seeks to touch it, smell it, taste it, and so thereby transform itself . . . The radical reduction of the distance of the object also establishes the relation to potential praxis which later guided Benjamin's thinking." Adorno, *Prisms*, Cambridge, MIT Press, 1986, p. 240.

40 Susan Buck-Morss, *Dialectics of Seeing*, p. 29.

41 Letter to Herbert Belmore, 23 June 1913, *Walter Benjamin: Briefe*, Gerschom Scholem and Theodor W. Adorno eds., Suhrkamp, Frankfurt, 1978, p. 87.

42 See Katharina von Ankum ed., *Women in the Metropolis: Gender and Modernity in Weimar Germany*, Berkeley, University of California Press, 1997.

43 "We could say that the trajectory of Benjamin's life and death was a road paved with continuous expulsions from various collectives . . . He was himself treated as refuse." Geger-Ryan, "Abjection in the Texts of Walter Benjamin", *Fables of Desire*, London, Polity Press, 1999, p. 119.

44 "On the dialectical function of money in prostitution. It buys pleasure . . . But not her client's shame. The latter seeks some hiding place during this quarter hour, and finds the most genial: in money." Walter Benjamin, "Prostitution, Gambling", O1a, 4, *Arcades Project*, 1999, p. 492.

45 "Male impotence—the key figure of solitude—under this sign the forces of production are brought completely to a standstill—an abyss separates the individual from his fellows." Walter Benjamin, "Central Park", *Arcades Project*, p. 47.

46 André Breton, *Nadja* (1928), New York, Grove Press, 1960.

47 Both essays appear in *Charles Baudelaire: A Lyric Poet in the Era of High Capitalism*, London, Verso, 1983, respectively in the sections "The Paris of the Second Empire in Baudelaire", and in "Paris: Capital of the Nineteenth Century".

48 Melissa Marder, "Flash Death: Snapshots of History", *Diacritics*, 27:3, 128–44, p. 129.

49 Marder: "Flash Death: Snapshots of History", *Diacritics*, 27:3, 128–44, p. 135.

50 Both Bernd Witte and Susan Buck-Morss recognize this intertextuality. See *Dialectics of Seeing*, p. 31.

51 Walter Benjamin, "On Some Motifs in Baudelaire", *Illuminations*, Footnote 90, p. 148.

52 "No form of eternalizing is so startling as that ... which the wax figure cabinet preserves for us. And whoever has once seen them, must, like André Breton, lose his heart to the female form in the *Musée Grevin*, who adjusts her stocking garter in a corner of the loge." Benjamin, Konvolut B, "Fashion", B3, 4, *Arcades Project*, p. 69.

2

For the Unnatural Use of Clothes: Fashion as Cultural Assault

Prosecutor: These three women, however, as improbable as it sounds, happen to meet in a boutique one fine day to buy dresses, blouses, and similar items. But instead of indulging in this harmless pastime . . ."
Janine: I don't understand why you define buying clothes as "a harmless pastime." Is that how you buy clothes?"
Prosecutor: "Madam, let me continue without these trivialities."

Marleen Gorris, A Question of Silence

I have to stop this woman from her unnatural clothing habit.

Elfriede Jelinek, The Piano Teacher

In Marleen Gorris' 1982 film *A Question of Silence*, three women, who do not know one another, meet by chance in a boutique and kill the male owner when he, superciliously, finds one of them shoplifting. In court Janine van der Bos, the court psychiatrist, refuses to declare the three women insane: to declare them responsible is to condemn then to life in prison, but also the only way to make visible the unnamable motivation for their crime—the experience of everyday humiliation that as women they all share. In a world where their subaltern status is the norm, there's no language to express their frustration and resentment, and the film turns to silence, laughter, *and* clothes to make visible what it means to be a woman. Dr. van der Bos' insistence on the importance of clothes-shopping jokingly signals clothes' dangerous power to signify female anger. Choosing clothes, far from being an innocent pastime, turns into the ideological task that sparks the women's rebellion: the locale of the murder becomes the crux of this apparently absurd, because too plausible, feminist manifesto.

Shopping for clothes is one of the designated activities for women in western cultures of abundance, fashion the cultural terrain where they are interpellated into femininity and consumption. At the same time, fashion as cultural practice also points to the less predictable and rational realm of fantasy. Thus in Gorris' film shoplifting clothes becomes a way of reclaiming fantasy and value from the power that manages both, and a way of denouncing one's exclusion from the party of patri-capital. As Janine points out, there's no innocence, universality or disinterestedness in fashion as cultural practice: clothes stand as the key element of modern material culture both for turning women into a spectacle for the male gaze, and for signifying the female desire for something other.

This chapter centers on this double value of fashion as the site of female spectacle and of fantasy as mode of dissent against how subjects and objects are supposed to relate. I study how femininity and the commodity relate via the spectacle by examining fashion and the "unnatural use of clothes" in two texts, one from early in the twentieth century and the other late, the "Nausicaa" episode in James Joyce's *Ulysses* (1922), and Elfriede Jelinek's novel *The Piano Teacher* (1983). Both works dwell on the meaning and danger of clothes. Each counters the negative theorization of fashion of Benjamin and others. The fashionable and fashioned spectacles of femininity in these fictions become sites where women working with the object, through style, performance, and the management of one's appearance, produce adversarial constructions of gender. Here are actants who, from below, manipulate their dealings with commodities for their own personal and political ends.

Fashion and its temporality, the new as always-the-same, are for Benjamin a trap that reifies human beings. Fashion freezes them into a fantasy of progress and change that is in reality only capital's time of the eternal present. From a feminist critic's viewpoint, Benjamin's critique of fashion is indebted to orthodox historical materialism. When, as we have seen, he theorizes the commodity fetish in terms of its "poetics," that is, in terms of an aesthetic, but not a libidinal economy, he merely pushes the limits of historical materialism without overcoming them. His revealing blind spot here is the way in which he leaves unanswered the question of how gendered and sexual desire complicates the relations between subjects and objects, and subjects as objects. This is in part an effect of the historical conjuncture in which Benjamin lived and wrote: in the interwar years, there is a sense in which for critics such as he, the door of history is still ajar, and the utopian impulse could persist—but with its own limits.

Further into the century, the economic, political, and social conditions that made possible Benjamin's theory of materiality change: the gaps in the culture of consumption, through which the critic can glimpse the flashes of profane illumination, and, after Fordism, produce the Spectacle Guy Debord incisively denounces in 1967. From now on the idea of revolutionary change becomes more distant and utopian, and is converted instead into the search for a syntax of resistance and denunciation to be signaled by the very signifiers of the culture to which one belongs. *Pace* Benjamin, once the commodity closes ranks on the subject, as happens in the late twentieth century, the practices and desires put in place by consumer culture cannot be avoided, or easily re-functioned. The pleasure and politics of junk from the flea-market and the arcades pursued by the Surrealists become, for avant-garde intellectuals and connoisseurs, a more powerful and thought-provoking affect.

Once junk is recycled as "vintage" or antique, and starts again to produce value as a signifier of taste and class, Benjamin's stuff theory loses its bite. Resistance cannot come only from the side of avant-garde connoisseurship and from the allegorist's vision. The libidinal economy put in place by the commodity cannot be dismissed; it must be dealt with and worked through. Once the commodity saturates experience, fashion must be taken seriously because, as a key semiotic and libidinal system of modernity, it depends on the regime of looking and spectacle. With it, capital as materiality addresses the subject's unconscious. Yet it is a site where the hyper-interpellated individual who has been hailed by the system as commodified materiality coded by fashion's strategies can resist.

The gender acts I study through Joyce and Jelinek show that fashion, when appropriated by the *bricoleuse* in "Nausicaa" and by the female masochist in *The Piano Teacher*, produce at least one of the effects that Benjamin himself had anticipated in his theory of materiality: the moment when the female object denounces her position and refuses her assigned place in modernity. The perverse, unnatural use of clothes can articulate new gender definitions and destabilize apparently fixed notions of reality and materiality, from the nation to individual subjectivity. Commodities, in other words, can be deployed against the cultural, libidinal, economic, and identitarian logic that they also appear to support. As an example of praxis through desire, fantasy, and subversion, deploying fashion for her own ends represents an effective strategy for the marginal subject. In both the texts I analyze, the female protagonist manages to throw off balance a system of signification, of visuality, of gender propriety and social power through an "unnatural" use of clothes. The aim of this disorder of femininity and of its fashioned spectacle is not to show that under the dress there's nothing, which would only be another way of indulging in the Freudian male fantasy of the fetish or in the vertigo of simulation; rather it is to produce a certain critical garrulity, an exposure that might be the beginning of new models of subjectivity and objecthood.

The correlation of the spectacle of the commodity with the spectacle of woman, the presence of femininity as necessarily spectacular in modern commodity culture, has by now been widely studied, and constitutes a whole branch of feminist analysis of visuality and the gaze.[1] Already in the nineteenth century this foolproof system of gender production, in which women decorate themselves into spectacles for the male gaze in order to become marketable for, and exchangeable among, men like commodities, begins to occasionally be countered: see, for example, the beguiling strangeness of the Countess of Castiglione's one thousand photographic portraits, that, between 1856 and 1865, she had taken of herself, in different poses and costumes, by the Mayer and Pierson studio in Paris, and whose excess of spectacularity remains difficult to interpret.[2] But it is in the twentieth century that such aberrations become more frequent and less extraordinary—and imbricated in their historical and cultural contexts so that it is impossible to read them exclusively as inscriptions of an internalized and policing male gaze.

This chapter addresses the meaning of fashion and style in two different contexts: that of late colonial Ireland, and of late twentieth-century post-World War II Austria, that is, in the colony on the verge of becoming an independent state, and in the post-imperial country that reclaims its lost *grandeur* in the face of its recent Nazi past and consumer modernity. Joyce's Gerty McDowell and Jelinek's Erika Kohut are two women who fully pervert the spectacle of femininity and the orthodox uses to which it is put: to support the ideology of the nation, that is, of an imperial British nationalism and an Irish patriotism modeled upon it, on the one hand, and the ideology of class hierarchy and bourgeois cultural elitism on the other. Rather, each turns it into a performance centered on mobility. Gerty complicates the notion of *flânerie* and, in a minor key, derails the circulation and flow of capital at the same time. Erika short-circuits established gender definitions and the logic of visual consumption by partially occupying the mobile abject space of the laboring body, the same space that, as Jelinek points out, is assigned to the Turkish immigrant in Austria, and to the immigrant at large in the globalized world economy.

By perverting the logic of the male gaze through a female appropriation of the visuality of porn, *and* by assuming the position of the female spectator, both Joyce's and Jelinek's characters come to occupy a masculine position, only to dismantle it. In doing so each demonstrates, in fact, the impossibility of the self and of a stable definition of gender, and its necessary incorporation of alterity. As an inverted image of each other at two different historical moments of the twentieth-century culture of capital, Joyce's and Jelinek's narratives directly point to the features at the core of the modern problematic of the object: the question of ornament and fantasy, of ornament as an emissary of fantasy; the organization of libidinal economy through the commodity; the idea of the spectacle as the means to alternative materialities and femininities; and, last but not least, the persistence of visuality as the organizing principle of experience in the twentieth century.[3]

The chapter is organized in three sections. First I discuss the articulation of spectacle, aura, and style in twentieth-century visual culture to show how the technologies and practices that further abstract materiality, such as photography, cinema and fashion, can also produce a "return of the real", to use the art theorist's Hal Foster's expression, capable of compromising the hierarchy of subject and object. Then I focus on "Nausicaa" and its protagonist as a subaltern colonial consumer, capable of fashioning, through the language of advertising and romance, an identity at odds with the feminine stereotype of national-religious purity, of which the image of the mother-virgin was a signifier in the Irish culture of the time. My analysis centers on Gerty's condition as herself a defective, damaged commodity, and her scandalous mobility as late colonial *flâneuse*. If Gerty McDowell's figure marks the shift from nineteenth-century portraiture, whether painterly or photographic, to its "degradation" in the spectacular anonymity of the fashion plate, and to the mobility of the cinematic image anticipated by the Mutoscope girls, Erika Kohut's story further documents the vicissitudes of this mobile spectacle. In *The Piano Teacher* the author, mimicking a version of late twentieth-century gender panic, uses fashion and female masochism to represent the predicament of a woman who is literally barred from femininity by her mother, in the name of the masculine quality of the artistic genius; as a consequence, Erika is incapable of situating herself in traditional gender terms. In the course of the novel, the visuality of the object becomes violently pornographic, and the gendering of the gaze, as well as the reliability of the gaze itself, grows more and more unstable. The crux of the text lies in this instability, and in Erika's attempt to be on both sides of the camera: she wants to be an object seen from all directions, and a subject seeing in all directions. Her unnatural use of clothes finally allows her to take up the most disturbing place, that of the abject. With brutal directness, echoing and elaborating upon the subject–object logic implied in "Nausicaa," Erika's action in a part of the novel is centered on her desire to turn masculinity, and the phallic position, into that of the abject, too. Her attempt to be subject, object, and abject simultaneously is her most transgressive gesture, not easily reabsorbed by the text.

What Erika knows at the end of the story, she already knew at the beginning: her body, the spectacle of her materiality which she so carefully assembles and manages, as well as the spectacle of masculinity she watches, are of her own making. Jelinek's story becomes symptomatic of what women can learn from their condition as objects at the end of the twentieth century; once again, a sobering lesson. In *The Piano Teacher* Erika unlearns how to be a woman through the lesson of the commodity. Femininity, she affirms, is the materiality she desires, and at the same time the ruin of an objectification which never existed except as a male fantasy.

I. Spectacle, Aura, Fashion

Fashion as a particular modality of the spectacle has often been read in terms of its negative power as illusion, as covering over the truth of history and the economies of gender and objectification.[4] Benjamin's view of fashion as a form of extreme reification, sanctioning the hellish time of the always-the-same,[5] uncannily resonates with the Austrian architect and theorist Adolf Loos' vision of the ornament as a form of feminine degradation.[6] Later in the twentieth century, Barthes and Baudrillard also analyzed the temporality of fashion, and its role as a no less coercive structuring—and structuralist—system of social semiosis.[7] J.C. Flugel's 1930 essay,[8] on the other hand, discussed fashion as a system of class and gender difference, and as such has informed recent feminist analysis.

From the nineteenth-century display of commodities in Universal Exhibitions, department stores, and advertisements, to the technological "imaging" of reality in photography, cinema, and now digital culture, materiality gets more and more abstracted into images. This all-pervasive abstraction of materiality and reality into images that, for Guy Debord, defines the spectacle,[9] produces an amnesiac existence where the "thick materiality of sentient experience" dramatically recedes.[10] We can think of the spectacle as the most extreme form of capitalist phantasmagoria. Yet, once we complicate the apparent seamlessness that the article "the" attributes to the spectacle, we see, as I hope to show through my discussion of fashion, that modern spectacularity is not a system without its glitches and its dysfunctions. On occasion it can work against itself to disable one of its most insidious and powerful aspects, the alienation of the corporeal sensorium.

For the materialist critic, modernity is a process of further and further abstraction of, and distancing from, materiality, from matter, the body, nature, and reality. At the center of this process of abstraction stands the subject who claims to be his own point of origin, autonomous from the world around him, and, in particular, not subjected to his senses. The claimed autonomy of *homo autotelus*, as Susan Buck-Morss points out, is predicated upon a "narcissistic illusion of self-control"[11] and of his autogenesis, which she characterizes as "surely one of the most persistent myths of the whole history of modernity." This autonomous subject relies on his sensory alienation, his being without a body and therefore "sense dead."

The synesthetic interdependence of mind and body,[12] self and the senses, and the importance of sensory perception as what *produces* reality and the sensuousness of reality, is occluded when aesthetics turns into a disembodied science of beauty, and especially into spectacle. Spectacle is the deployment of aesthetics by capital, as in advertising. With this new, bourgeois grasp of aesthetics, the modern subject is turned away from his own materiality and the sensuousness of matter, renouncing his own sensorium as what limits reason: instead of a somatic relationship to the world, he is constituted through a sharp separation from alterity and materiality. The history of modern western visuality produces the correlative of autotelic subjectivity through the principle of vision of the *camera obscura*, which operates according to the model of a distanced observer who is apart from the object observed, who establishes himself as a disembodied eye scrutinizing the world at a distance.[13] The gap between subject and object in this scenario, and the privileging of vision over tactility, then necessitates the conventional figuration of the aura, as an image of the unreachable sacred demanding distanced contemplation. This aura invites passive contemplation, rather than corporeal, sensorial subjection and passion that sanctions the co-dependence of subject and object.

This triumph of the autotelic subject over the object in western metaphysics is always at the expense of their synaesthetic relation. Through its progressive aestheticization in the spectacle, the culture of modernity becomes more and more anaesthetic and narcotic, alternating overstimulation as shock, and numbness as shock's reabsorption. The phantasmagoria of the commodity becomes a collectively experienced aesthetics enhanced by technology which, from the bourgeois interior to the fashion plate, to the arcades and the cinema, takes over modern culture and experience. Fully integrated in the spectacle, defused into an endless multiplicity of objects, the aura leaves behind its earlier bourgeois value, without ever being able to guarantee the kind of experience for which Benjamin wished. If in the age of the modernist spectacle the aura is staged by the total choreographies of fascism, and later defused into the immaterial and non-referential post-Fordist commodity, we can also recognize the persistence of auratic traces—and traces of the synaesthetic aura—in both mainstream and "outlaw" instances of modern and contemporary visuality, such as fashion and pornography. In fashion and pornography, the stakes of the aura are not exactly the same as Benjamin's. The persistence of the aura's traces doesn't allow the perfect reciprocity, and balletic proximity, between individual and community, or cosmos and nature, that Benjamin had envisioned; rather, it points to re-establishing a synaesthetic relationship between these two terms that may privilege the senses, the body, and make visible the subject's dependence upon them.

When the spectacle begins to saturate more and more aspects of human experience, the point is not to choose between a non-fetishist tactility and a fetishistic visuality, but to look at fetishism as a possible means to a synaesthetics, and more radically, to consider the synaesthetic, somatic quality of fetishism. This is particularly important from the point of view of the feminist critic interested in a gender and sexual politics that cannot any longer rely on the discourse of authenticity. In other words, the phantasmagorical "sexiness" of the commodity and of the female body, similarly fashioned into a spectacle, are no longer (if they ever were) a bad copy of the original, but historically produced cultural objects, potentially capable of signifying differently from their capitalist inscription. As a form of abstraction, that is, of pleasure alienated from the body and set in place by capital, the spectacle of the commodity and of the female body cannot be simply reclaimed as an impossible "innocence" by the means of abstentious and abstemious tactics. Rather, in the name of the risky principle of "going with the fetish" proposed by Michael Taussig as Benjamin's discovery, both spectacles demand that we embrace the spurious quality of modern materiality. The choice to "go with the fetish" is what the textualities I examine do. For the female subject whose subjectivity is always already implicated in the theoretical morass of fetishism and sexuality, there is no other choice.

In this context, the aura stands as an experience of shock, the shock of a reconquered tactile and synaesthetic relationship to materiality, a rupture of the spectacle's logic, capable, if momentarily, of countering the anaesthetic amnesia of modernity. In this sense fashion, clothes, style, and, possibly, the pornographic, can become a means of recognizing and reaffirming the subject's somatic relationship to materiality, by their ob-scene (off-scene, excessive, disorderly) way of representing the surface-unity of the body, the smooth, seamless surface in which fetishism takes shelter. Thus fashion paradoxically allows us to pursue exactly what Benjamin was after in his work, even if he himself did not have the critical gutsiness to engage with the sexuality which the fetishism of the commodity invokes.

Clothes, as a particular aspect of materiality, partake of the duplicity of the talisman: as aesthetic objects they are charged with intimacy and thus occupy a potentially synaesthetic position in regard to the subject. Fetishistically invested, they *also* speak directly to, and of, desire and fantasy. Benjamin's tendency to an ascetic approach to materiality in the case of the figure of the female implies that the object is accessible only through a politics of abstention that risks once again positing male reason as the *factotum*. Here I insist on the impossibility of this abstention, this passing by, by showing how the spectacle of the adorned female body makes the categories of subject, gender, and materiality shifting and unstable. The unnatural use of clothes illustrated by Joyce and Jelinek puts women in the position of the observer and *voyeur* rather than in that of the object, to forever ruin the party of western philosophy and vision.

"Nausicaa" and *The Piano Teacher* both stage the spectacle of femininity in the debased field of porn. As a particular kind of visuality that exasperates, until it reverses, the narcotic quality of the aestheticized real, porn represents a form of synaesthetic perception that might interrupt the unfurling of the spectacle, and its exclusionary separation of subject and object. The porn image, as an image capable of "moving" the spectator's body, of working with a direct immediacy upon its affects, is the prototype of a visuality at odds with the principle of the *camera obscura*, which is predicated on the distancing of observer from the object observed. A case can certainly be made that the new embodied eye which porn traumatically brings to the fore was also brought about by the new optical technologies generally understood as supporting the self-centered machinery of modern vision and subjectivity.[14] Yet the new vision machines and philosophical toys of the mid-nineteenth century—the thaumatrope, the phenakistoscope, stereoscope, and even the kaleidoscope[15]—also put in place a sense that a new kind of embodied immediacy of sensations was possible, in that they appeared to establish a tactile relation between the subject and the image. These were philosophical toys in that they revealed an "hallucinatory" quality of perception. For example, the image which the human eye sees in one of the simplest machines, the stereoscope, does not exist per se, but is produced by the juxtaposition of two images which the human retina matches in order to create a third one, an "hallucination" with a particularly vivid sense of depth. The stereoscope reveals how vulnerable the subject is to sensations; like other new technologies of vision, it inaugurates a visuality in fact at odds with the principle of the *camera obscura* and its detached observer. This new visuality also created new bodily pleasures which were not only vicarious, as some critics maintain.[16] The visual tactility of the stereoscope, as Linda Williams points out, lay in the fact that it could actually be touched and held by the viewer, as well as in the fact that the image was capable of moving the observer to a pleasure that is erotic, if not sexual, and not exclusively phallic, but diffused, differently localized, and available to women as well as men. The autotelic subject using this technology wanes to make space for an embodied self, somatically and synaesthetically open to an outside world mediated by her own sensations.[17]

It is also exactly because of the way it "moves" the body of the observer, and thus helps dismantle the subject's claim to autogenesis, that pornography is cast as a debased form of representation. Ultimately porn gets disqualified because it affirms, or reaffirms, the intractability of materiality and of the body, both in the object of vision and in the viewer himself, *vis-à-vis* the subject's claims to self-control and detachment from the object. Porn also exposes what Jelinek calls "the banality of fleshliness," the desublimated corporeality that *The Piano Teacher* foregrounds by aligning the spectacular, sexually performing body with objects of various kinds, but particularly with junk, refuse, garbage, and labor. Both refuse and labor are necessarily made marginal and invisible by bourgeois propriety and by the visual protocols of the spectacle, that sanctions the equality and homogeneity—the in-difference—of all things, as long as they can be turned into an image. Jelinek's junk and junky bodies point to time, in contrast to the more frequent amnesia of modernity and late modernity, by reminding us of what comes before and after consumption, so that the flow of the eternal present of dominant culture is interrupted by the desublimated counter-aura of junk objects and of labor.

"Nausicaa" and *The Piano Teacher* do not only represent the dysfunctional body, whether physically in the case of Gerty, or psychologically in that of Erika, as answer to, or breakdown of, the integrated circuit of modern spectacle; they also use the dysfunctional body as the terrain where the object and materiality return with a vengeance, hurting the subject, and dispossessing him of any illusion of autonomy, through a sophisticated and often violent form of virtuality. In both texts the violence of materiality is the most effective way of problematizing the scenario of anaesthetic abstraction of the real in advanced capital, of which the spectacle of femininity is part. Fashion and pornography are, respectively, a straight and an outlaw form of spectacle. On the one hand each is a complete phantasmagoria, a version of the total environment of *la vitrine*, the spectacle-behind-glass of the shop window, exhibition, museum, framed photography, or viewing window at Leopold Bloom's remembered peepshow.[18] On the other, each is a form of dangerous tactility, making visible the traffic between the subject caught in a phantasmagoria, and the way the observer, whether male or female, is moved by the image perceived. Further, in both texts porn represents the body in a shattered, avowedly un-aesthetic form, alienating the subject from her mirror *imago* "back" into untotalizable fragments, where the *corps morcelé* of the fashionista, for whom there's a product for every single part of the body, forever suspends and prohibits any imaginary unity of the subject. For good or ill, this is another instance in which fashion and consumption plot against, rather than toward, the phantasmagoric effect of the surface-unity of the body,[19] and the dress and other feminine accouterments work less as a protective, fetishistic shield, than as means to explode surface and seamless appearance. This lack of unity particularly pertains to the figure and self-representation of Gerty in "Nausicaa." Fashion, under the aegis of excess, perverts the spectacle into a non-unifying, non-homogenizing, heterogeneous force, so much so that *glam*, the unnatural use of clothes, always complicates and compromises the representation of the aura in its fetishistic register. The traces of the auratic I am after cannot compile materiality into a totality, but rather suspend it into an image of rubble.

In this perspective, "Nausicaa" and *The Piano Teacher*, along with other twentieth-century counter-hegemonic discourses, show that the sensing subject is always already permeated by that which is outside him or her. More immediately, the pornographic quality that both texts attribute to the spectacle of femininity unexpectedly establishes two more threatening and destabilizing axioms. First, the object is alive and has lots of fun; she might even perform her spectacle for herself, working or playing toward an identity that throws off balance the theory of narcissism as a form of self-preservation and self-making in a minor key.[20] This is the case of "Nausicaa." Second, the fake, the copy, the image as something other than "the real thing" and therefore incapable of delivering the goods, gives as much pleasure and moves the observer as much as the "authentic" one, to the point that the distinction between real and fake is erased.

This collapse of the distinction between the fake and the authentic produces the demise of the autotelic subject, and as such gestures toward a whole new way of understanding reality and matter. However the potentially denunciatory moments of glam and porn that I have been singling out within the logic of the spectacle, might be merely windows of opportunity, a historically overdetermined fragile flickering, constantly under the threat of being stabilized and reabsorbed by dominant culture, especially when we take into account the relentless intensification of the spectacle during the twentieth century. While this intensification is registered in the texts I study, my analysis concentrates on the blanks, on the incongruous elements of this shift from spectacle to spectacle, blanks that in turn leave open a space where materiality, agency, subjectivity, and gender categories can be revised. In the midst of the overall intensification of the spectacle, from interwar totalitarian media experiments to postwar cultures of consumption, to the niche-marketed and networked webs of simulation of today, I look for rifts in the modern protocols of visuality, moments of break with the bourgeois systematization of subjectivity and materiality indexed by the spectacle itself.

The contradictions of the history of modern materiality and perception become sharper when the center of the spectacle is occupied by a woman. The spectacle of femininity makes visible the modalities of fashion and pornography as critical examples of tactile vision. What's at stake in this critique is a redefinition of the object and materiality, but also of the subject and of what counts as the real. The visual-tactile renegotiation of the real produces a new, potentially subversive form of femininity and female agency modeled in part on the object, rather than on the male subject. "Nausicaa" photographs a time when the image, freed from the shackles of bourgeois mimesis via the phantasmagoria of the commodity and of new visual technologies, has not yet been developed into a total phenomenon, a time when the spectacle of woman-as-commodity can still be questioned and potentially dismantled by the tactility of the new means of mechanical reproduction (in this case, the mutoscope), whose effect will culminate in the postwar era in the obscenity of the spectacle. If the multiplicity and man-made quality of the image in "Nausicaa" questions the stability and ontology of the referent, in *The Piano Teacher*, where referentiality has been compromised and supplanted by television, pornography, and the virtuality of sadomasochistic theatrics, the stakes are even higher. In the post-Fordist panorama of Jelinek's novel, a more claustrophobic and saturating experience of the spectacle demands more extreme and violent means of resistance, inscribed in Erika's own masochized body, but also in the way she subjects others by turning them into a form of spectacle.

The aura persists, both in capital's recycling and appropriation of it, and in the iconoclastic effect of its scattered traces. My discussion pushes the question of the aura beyond the critique of phantasmagoria as false consciousness, in which Benjamin's stuff theory is still partly caught: in the cases I examine, the aura of the female spectacle is not at the expense of the real, but rather illuminates it, makes it visible, by operating according to a logic that is not simply that of capital. The show put on here is not a form of visual and ideological deception, which is how Benjamin thinks about the image of the hellish time of fashion, of the new as always-the-same, and it's also more than female masquerade. Rather, the spectacle of femininity becomes an ephemeral monument, a folly, to the elusiveness and intractability of materiality, once it is no longer fixed to the position of the object. In both texts the representational paradigm of the *camera obscura* fails: the object moves, performs, and moves the spectator too. No safe contemplative position is possible on his part, even at a distance. Note that in neither text are the consumers of porn exclusively men: women are also *voyeuses*, but dealers in a different type of voyeurism, capable of managing the object of desire and themselves as spectacle, through fantasy and hallucination. This *voyeurism* does not simply duplicate that of men. The way women deal with the spectacle and its visuality is not simply a matter of filling somebody else's shoes, of simply taking up somebody else's place, but of challenging and changing the space occupied by the viewer, by the act itself, and by its ends: it's a matter of adding a new style of ornamentation that will make them unrecognizable. Monstrous. And like fashion, all the rage.

II. What Gerty Knew (or, Philosophy in the Outhouse)

The "Nausicaa" episode of Joyce's *Ulysses* has been widely interpreted as a scene of seduction: while Bloom falls for a teenager, a young female consumer, Gerty in turn is interpellated by, and falls for, the commodity and the "namby pamby" sugary Edwardian commercial culture specially fabricated for women.[21] Much fine work has been done on Gerty's resistance to this interpellation, and her limited agency as a consumer,[22] but much less attention has been given to the status of the spectacle and of the object in the episode. For most critics of *Ulysses* it is the "Circe" episode and its carnival of commodities, generally interpreted as the dramatization of what Marx had in mind when he wrote of commodity fetishism, that better than any other episode talks of consumption, femininity, and materiality.[23] And if Gerty is not interpreted as an object, as the embodiment and counter-figure of the commodity, even less is she considered a subject. Rather than arguing over Gerty's agency or passivity, it is better to approach "Nausicaa" from the perspective of the status of the commodity and of consumption in late colonial culture, in order to show how its spectacle shapes an adversarial femininity. This femininity threatens not only the self-contained male subject, but also both the discourses of Irish nationalism and British imperialism. Gerty's fantasies and performance as a spectacle clear the ground for the production of a necessarily open, unstable, and tentative feminine cultural identity at the time when Ireland was about to become an independent state. Gerty's status as an object points to the difficulties and contradictions of Irish late- and postcolonial modernity. But this is not all: Gerty's unnatural use of clothes in this episode, and Bloom's response to it, also calls into question a number of ontological and epistemological claims regarding the status of the object and of reality in the age of mechanical reproduction.

In a culture of abundance, such as consumer culture, the "use" of clothes is always unnatural, for it is *contra* use value, and is, instead, semiotic and libidinal. The syntax of this unnaturalness is fixed in fashion. When we talk of clothes, and of the unnatural use of clothes, we immediately invoke an opposition between function and ornament, fact and fiction, reality and fantasy, materiality and abstraction—a split that in the west has been deeply gendered, so that the useless has been naturalized into the artificial, while the unproductive pleasure of a "decorative" female spectacle has been represented and perceived as illusion. Confronted with this illusion, Bloom in this episode seems to replicate the male subject's dismay at the waning of the visual regime inaugurated by the *camera obscura*, and at the consequent disorientation of male subjectivity. On her side, Gerty actively contributes to the perception and representation of reality as hallucinatory. This hallucination is also the phantasmagoria of the commodity. But while the auratic spectacle of the commodity wants to pass as the real, Gerty's, by painstakingly revealing her process of self-assemblage and packaging into a beautiful image, exposes this aura as artefactual, and complicates the functioning of imperial consumer culture.

When staged in the colony, consumer culture is a double-edged weapon: on the one hand it works as a means of modernization,[24] and on the other it remains, both in economic and ideological terms, a form of further subjection by imperial power.[25] In the age of monopoly capital, the time of *Ulysses*, the colony, as Rosa Luxemburg claims in her theory of imperialism, does not represent primarily a source for raw materials and cheap labor, but a market wherein to circulate home-produced goods.[26] These same goods, through their representation in advertisements, also support the Empire ideologically. Joyce, in reproducing the colonial culture of advertisement, shows that, like recorded history, the culture of consumption and its representation is always the victor's. Thus consumer culture in the colony is a door into a modernity elsewhere—that of the metropole. From the perspective of the Empire, consumer culture is a means of penetrating the colonial imaginary through an attempt to crush and homogenize a native culture in the making. Characterized as progress, this process can hardly be avoided; 1904 Dublin was already folded into the modern urban culture of the European metropolis. At the same time, as a colonial city, it was caught in the contradictions of a consumption predicated upon and practiced in a culture of relative scarcity, characterized by fewer available commodities, and, given Ireland's poverty, less buying power.

As a colony, Ireland provides a context for consumer culture in which the positions of the teenage consumer, Gerty, and the one who incites consumption, the advertising salesman Bloom, are both unstable. Gerty may be the consumer and Bloom the producer of consumer desire, but the way consumption and commodity fetishism work in the colony contradicts their claims to be guarantors of freedom of choice, and of fashioning oneself into "whatever one wants to be." In *Ulysses* it is not the economic agency of the *entrepreneur*, or the agency of the colonial consumer making her choice—of commodities and selves, that the commodity signals. Rather, it highlights the power of both as *bricoleurs*, with an ability to mix and match desires and fantasies to reshape them to the colonial situation. This reshaping, and its failure, shows the shortcomings of imperial and capitalist universalism and of its discourse of modern progress. The same failure has the effect of short-circuiting the very subject position Bloom thinks he inhabits—to which, as a Jew and a colonial subject, he is often reminded he is not entitled in any case.

For Gerty McDowell, fashion, as an aspect of consumer modernity, works as a means of emancipation from the traditional ideal of "national" virginity that late colonial Irish culture made available to women; in the episode, even the image of the Virgin Mary is converted into that of the knowing and fashionable nymph via Gerty's reading of advertisements and women's magazines. But even in her minor consumption, or perhaps because of it,

Gerty turns the protocols of consumer culture on their heads, so that its interpellation of her doesn't work as expected. On the one hand, the erotic spectacle of the commodity that Gerty dramatizes in her performance does not simply produce desire, the desire set in place by an infinite series of equally unsatisfying commodity-objects. On the other hand, the more or less comic fireworks of Bloom's sexual excitement, responding to Gerty, demonstrate that the commodity, in its spectacularity and artificiality, does deliver the goods, even if they are merely *like* the real thing, instead of *being* the real thing. Furthermore, rather than producing the intoxication that is supposed to fog and occlude one's consciousness, Gerty's status as commodity *and* female consumer brings to the fore the contradictions that mark the gender identity of the colonial subaltern. Through the engagement with the world of fashion and romance, among other forms of modern popular culture, Gerty McDowell signifies and negotiates her historically overdetermined identity as a colonial subject. Her turning to Madame Vera Verity and Maria Cummins' nineteenth-century sentimental novel *The Lamplighter*, one of the intertexts of "Nausicaa," is not simply escapism, or a means of forgetting about her status, but of putting her condition into focus and making it manageable and recognizable to herself. Thus the episode throws light on the complexities and contradictions of colonial modernization in Ireland, exploring the costs for different groups of the colony's entry into the circuit of imperial capital exchange, as it anatomizes the specifics of gender production under the same conditions.

We will read the episode symptomatically, as a key moment in the twentieth-century history of unruly materiality being traced in this book. The clash of cultural, political, and representational economies provoked by Joyce's sardonic, if somehow unguarded, figuration of colonial consumption, produces a splintered refraction of the spectacle that forever, and irreparably, compromises its supposedly seamless image. Like other female figures in *Ulysses*, Gerty is poor, uneducated, marginal, and deprived of the tools that would help her understand and make sense of her condition. However, she has access to the elements that make her character contribute to a form of self-construction and possible agency: while Bloom, at the end, discovers that he is not what he thought he was, and is incapable of saying who he is, the initial question "But who was Gerty?"[27] opens a number of possibilities that do not disorient her at all.

At the heart of this episode of *Ulysses*, which itself is close to the heart of the book, the crucial act which Gerty performs is to get up and walk. To pursue the analysis just outlined, we will first focus on Gerty's unstable identity, on her knowledge, and the aura of her spectacle. After discussing the mobility of her image, we will focus on her crucial *moving*, the shift from her condition as a photographic pose to her highly cinematic walk that, in Bloom's eyes, transforms her from titillating erotic image to dangerous live porn. This crucial movement on Gerty's part is the exact reverse of the "passing by," the swerve of the ascetic (male) subject which we discussed in the first chapter. Gerty's capability to move Bloom to satisfaction and shame prefigures the shaking up of an entire epistemological and ontological horizon, visible in the way Bloom thinks of materiality and reality. The shift from the visuality of photography to that of cinema, signaled by Gerty's walk, and her new identity as movable image and hence filmic female body, marks a break in the history of mimetic representation, as well as in the culture of Irish late colonialism. This female body walking out of the frame, out of the male viewer's field of vision, tells a new and unsettling story about the presumed passivity of the object. After examining what is at stake in the mobility of the object, I will conclude by discussing the two protagonists' different ways of coming to terms with the fictional quality of the real, and with the technologies of vision that lead to this new notion of movable materiality.

This episode at the heart of *Ulysses* is Baudelaire's *passante* in reverse: now the subject as object acts, and thereby claims a new subjecthood.

To approach the question of a contested female colonial identity, at odds both with Irish nationalism and British imperial patriarchy, consider the specific elements through which Gerty's figure is articulated. What makes her dangerous, and situates her well beyond the problematic of the hoodwinked female consumer, or of the hoodwinking commodity replacing some apparently "authentic" thing, is the discursive contradiction that marks her position. As a character, Gerty stands at the intersection of different discourses, which make her unstable as a figure, creating that epistemological indeterminacy that so disturbs Bloom in the second part of the episode, provoking his hysterical conjectures and anxious questions as the sun sets.

Enveloped by the mysterious embrace of the evening, Gerty sits on a rock on Sandymount strand, an image of pristine Irish beauty, whose purity cites that of the Virgin Mary. Dressed like Gerty—the issue of originality and imitation is the crux of the episode—the Virgin Mary is prayed to in the nearby church by a crowd of male teetotalers, and the litanies heard through the open door of the church comically intersperse Gerty's thoughts throughout the narrative. When we read through Gerty's enthusiastic reciting of her own litanies of cosmetics, hymns to the *corps morcelé* of fashion items and beauty creams, we realize that neither her beauty nor her Irishness are natural, but made by British products. Similarly, we understand that her purity is actually a disclaimer of her sexual knowledge, and that her lack of self-consciousness, the quality of being caught unaware so dear to the *voyeur*, that so thrills and reassures Bloom, is actually a careful pose long studied in front of the mirror.

Apparently oblivious to anybody but herself and "the gentleman in black," Gerty is constructed as an always already contradictory image of spectacular femininity, partaking at once of different identities: virginal teenager *ingénue*, female Sadean libertine, pursuing her sexual knowledge in front of the mirror and in the outhouse; consumer of B-series commodities and inferior literature; shopper on a budget, starlet, the equivalent of the Mutoscope girls, Virgin Mary, mother *and* daughter. Poured into the container of stereotypical Irish female beauty (after all, she is the Citizen's granddaughter), these different personae do not collapse into one, and neither do they amount to any fixed and clearly discernible identity. Her carefully composed beautiful semblance seems to explode the mold of the self, and compromise any straight notion of identity. She's not properly Irish. Is she a proper consumer? Or a proper, safe to-be-consumed commodity or spectacle? Rendered as camp by two nominally opposed fantasy genres, romance and porn, and fueled by Gerty's unnatural use of clothes, the unruliness of femininity and of the commodity makes in "Nausicaa" for a charged strategy capable of destabilizing any institution from patriarchy and colonialism to the Irish state-to-come, from consumer capital all the way to the western protocols of vision.

Among the elements that contribute to Gerty's instability is her assumption of innocence. This relates to religious imagery, and it invokes abjection; the undecidability of her role as mother or daughter is one of the text's important contradictions because it both blurs the concept of the incest taboo and attacks the concept of order that relies on this very distinction. Enda Duffy points out that female abjection in *Ulysses* is presented as a form of degradation more thorough than any suffered by men, partly because it refers to sexuality, where it is typically signaled by the abjection of the prostitute. When referred to Gerty, however, the virgin-whore dyad is replaced by, and displaced into, that of the virgin-libertine, centered on the Sadean figure of Juliette, of whom Gerty can be considered the counter-figure. The Sadean female libertine gives up her virginity not for money but for knowledge, and the power this knowledge will guarantee her. The scenario of "Nausicaa" and the question of what Gerty knew, reproposes, in reverse, the Sadean scenario of seduction: the pedagogical relationship between the older male libertine and the young female disciple is turned upside down. It is Bloom, after having "blushed like a virgin" at his own base instincts, while only half-suspecting that Gerty's are as base as his, who learns not about power, but about his own powerlessness; Gerty, instead, teaches him something which she knew already. Echoes of the Sadean text also appear, comically, in the scene of auto-erotism which Gerty performs in the bathroom (a sort of "philosophy in the outhouse"), in front of the Halcyon Days calendar, looking at the kitsch image of dames and gentlemen "looking lovely" in eighteenth-century costume—a citation of the aristocratic ethos that Sade himself represented and supported, and about which Gerty fantasizes repeatedly. The culminating sign of Gerty's abjection, her limping when she makes the crucial move, appears later in the episode, fully inscribed upon and enacted by her material body.

To take the full measure of the anomalousness of Gerty's body, consider again the issue of her double role of mother and daughter, Madonna and erotic *ingénue*.[28] Gerty dangerously occupies both places at the same time, and this double stance complicates her status as both image of the commodity fetish *and* female subject. As daughter-virgin she puts herself "on the market" wearing her sexual value on her sleeve (or on her nainsook underwear, as it might be). At the same time, winking to the logic of Irish nationalism, Joyce, in siting her before the church and its hymns, juxtaposes her to the image of Mary Virgin *and* mother. While the ideology of Catholicism tries to anchor this split in the paradoxical dogma of the mother's virginity, the episode lets these two positions clash in the figure of Gerty, without trying to reconcile them. The miraculous status of the mother, both in psychoanalytical and religious terms, as sacred, untouchable and unexchangeable, is demystified by Gerty's daughterly urge to be touched and touch, and to expose herself.

When referred to Gerty, the double role of mother and daughter also signals the dismantling of the opposition between use and uselessness, in a way that dislocates the notion of pleasure away from its utilitarian shackles. This utilitarianism prescribes self-preservation and a reasonable notion of common good against the principle of *jouissance*[29] then designated as self-destructive. In the sense that her double embodiment of mother and daughter overcome this opposition, it is the forbidden sexuality of the mother, and the unavailable pleasure she represents, that finally is invoked by Gerty's defect. In psychoanalytical terms, pleasure is not attained through the *possession* of the object, which is, in fact, impossible to obtain, but is necessarily founded on the continual postponement of the achievement of it, the unattainable thing. It's this non-utilitarian, non-commodified notion of pleasure as postponement that structures Gerty's image as the spectacle both of femininity and of the commodity. In this perspective, the commodity's capability of delivering on its promise is made redundant, and ruled out. If the colonial commodity exists only as simulation, in the sense that the advertisement is the only proof of its existence, while in the colonial market itself it is largely absent, its absence is turned by "Nausicaa" into a figuration of an anti-utilitarian subjectivity, where the self is in Copjec's terms "no longer equal to its traces."[30] The "metaphysical niceties" of the commodity, its phantasmagoria, are now used for a new semiosis of gender, and for remaking subjectivity and cultural identity exactly through the misstep of the subject and its traces, of which the most poignant image is Gerty's limp.

III. Fashion, Tactility, and the "Carnal Density of the Image"

"Nausicaa" replays in reverse, in slow motion, the scene described by Baudelaire in his sonnet "*À Une Passante*." Centering on a scene of "love at last sight," whose ephemeral quality is slightly longer lasting than the encounter in Baudelaire's crowd, the episode is dominated by an act of looking that both invokes and challenges *voyeurism*. We see Gerty looking at herself, in the commonplace image of woman caught in the mirror of consumer culture, passively trying to reproduce an image while being made into one. Gerty's spectacle gains pathos from the naïve confidence with which she grasps the networks of snobbery and populism that marked the newly emerged pop culture of her time. The sentimentality—Gerty's, but also Joyce's own—that laces her more aggressively sexual self-presentation also functions to make visible her social position, so that the *luxe* of the fashion plate is always complicated and disrupted by the protagonist's class status: she is poor, and the painstaking assemblage of her image is an act of *bricolage* having to do with such shop-soiled garments and self-made confections as the "nigger straw hat."

Fashion discourse and the sentimentality of romance converge for Gerty as pleasure and self-awareness in a form of cognitive mapping. Through them she maps the social networks of the city, working *through*, and not at the expense of, fantasy and desire. The rhetoric of *The Lamplighter*, whose protagonist is also named Gerty, becomes here a way of acknowledging her own subalternity, and dealing with her ambiguous role as both daughter and mother to her alcoholic father. Her fantasy of an aristocratic status exists alongside her awareness of her actual class position: if father had not been an alcoholic, she reflects, she might have had the education to which she is entitled by her "natural" *hauteur*. She has, by nature, she feels, the body of an aristocrat—and it is notable that it is only through her body itself that she can think of her social predicament: "There was an innate refinement, a languid queenly *hauteur* in Gerty that was unmistakably evidenced in her delicate hands and higharched instep. Had kind fate willed her to be born a gentlewoman ... Gerty MacDowell would have easily held her own beside any lady in the land" (348). She situates on her body, as both the bearer of her subjectivity and the only object that she, a subaltern, really controls, her dreams of social power. These dreams coalesce around her sense of how she moves, the *hauteur* of her steps; her limp, when she does move, makes the claim of *hauteur* intensely poignant.

The body is her best purchase into social mobility, and it is also her ticket out. Too dressed up and too bodied, Gerty cannot play fully the game of the proper and properly marketable virgin: she wears her desire openly, and wants instant gratification—which she gets, too. All dressed up, she produces a tear in the smooth surface of the commodity image and a slightly shamefaced blockage in the system of capitalist circulation and exchange. Her self-staging actively resists her designated role as circulating object of value and exchangeable daughter-body. Bloom, in turn, has to give up his own implied claim to autonomy when he falls prey to the commodity whose image, because of his job as advertisement canvasser and designer, he can claim he has in part created. By falling for something he knows is not "real," and by denying the very mobility of the artefactual on which both the materiality of the commodity and of the female spectacle is founded, he can only retrench into the alienation of autotelic subjecthood.

We never stop seeing Gerty producing her self-image, in an act of artifice which unmakes the inducement-to-forgetfulness of reification. Similarly, in her self-*mis en scene*, she never lets us forget the labor that gets into her image. The female consumer's self-fashioning is established as an endless process, forever incomplete, whose openness testifies to the unfinished, and hence dangerous, process of self-making. Gerty shows the impossibility of truly being the fashion plate: the ideal recedes to the horizon the more the subject reclaims it. She is always a step—or a misstep—behind, or ahead of it, demonstrating that the subject is never equal to the sum of its traces. The self is a stereoscopically produced reality, relying on the hallucinatory activity of the viewer; no presumed surface-unity is possible. We see in "Nausicaa" the incommensurability between Gerty's spectacle, and the ideal image she's called to inhabit.

Gerty never achieves the naturalized status of auratic commodity or subject; rather, her performance makes visible labor, production, and the ersatz quality of her low-brow effort to approximate the perfection of the ideal and the aura and *luxe* of the aristocracy—both inevitably unattainable. The gap between the body of the individual and its mirror image remains open. In "Nausicaa" this gap becomes a yawning space; negotiating with Joyce's coyness, we are never sure as readers quite how to react to her efforts. The incommensurability between Gerty's spectacle and the dream world offered by *The Princess Novelette* is what Joyce uses to make us laugh at, and to pity her; she is a subaltern, a consumer with no spending power, forever condemned to the shop-soiled, ersatz pleasure of the image rather than the hands-on capitalist success story of ownership. But there is one element that gives back to Gerty her dangerous power as a theoretical projectile, another Dora walking out of Freud's office: her mobility, signified both by her unstable multiplicity as a character and by her actual, physical moving, walking away from the scene of seduction.

Through her multiple hybridities Gerty is already posing in female drag. Her resolute camping of a series of feminine stereotypes defeats any cultural lexicon that might make her fully legible. She knows, and lets us see, the process through which she is assembled as a commodity, so that her spectacle never produces a homogeneous and total self. As a fraught spectacle of femininity Gerty is an image that refuses to serve the purposes and the desires of the male viewer, an object, that is, that refuses to be abstracted and photographed into passivity. In fact, the episode portrays a male subject acted upon by the object, by a spectacle of the other produced through the very codes he thinks he knows and masters. As advertiser, he is the one producing the images that seduce women into buying. As with any fiction, Gerty is supposed to titillate the spectator erotically; instead, to use Roland Barthes' distinction in *Camera Lucida*,[31] the erotic produces a pornographic effect. Here the erotic register of the commodity fetish produces tactility, and its unrealizable *promesse de bonheur* is for once maintained. This is why Bloom *must* masturbate in "Nausicaa." The way in which Gerty's image affects Bloom cannot be recuperated and channeled into proper capitalist consumption as the prelude to profit, and rather turns into a form of expenditure, loss, and destruction of value. As a spectacle of materiality, Gerty affirms the intractability of the object, and the impossibility of reining it in through the available cultural codes of femininity and consumption. Gerty stops being exchangeable at the moment when she seduces Bloom and makes him spend, thus threatening to shatter the self-control of the male subject. This particular quality of Gerty's body as spectacle—its intractability—is made truly material when it is represented as a physical defect, her limping.

At the end of the fireworks show, after a tacit exchange of glances with her putative seducer, Gerty gets up from the rock and starts walking after her friends, revealing that she is lame. The fact that both as a porn image and a commodity she walks away from her assigned space is transgressive, but the limping makes it more so. Sitting on a rock as a *tableau vivant* becoming photographic image, Gerty is trying to reproduce those she has seen in *The Lady's Pictorial*. But then she slowly changes her status into that of an animated image: her "photographic" condition passes through the visuality of the philosophical toys studied by Crary and Williams, and, with her walking, becomes cinematic. At once, the cinematic moment of Gerty's spectacle is taken by Bloom as a way of both negotiating and reiterating the shock of her live porn performance.

The story of Bloom masturbating to a defective body faking an auratic perfection is the story of the autotelic subject in the age of modern consumption, who has lost the upper hand on the product he has contributed to launching. In this sense, the optical unconscious of Gerty-as-spectacle are the Mutoscope girls, dancers Bloom saw when he looked into a machine in Capel St., and whom he mentions later during the panicked and non-sequential observations that follow his sight of Gerty's walk. As such, her image defeats the visual logic of the *camera obscura*, which implies that reality is truly what we perceive by looking at what is in front of us, and nothing else. Her image counters the guarantees that this kind of vision grants Bloom as a male subject. He soon tries to re-establish these privileges through his nervous response to Gerty's spectacle.

Bloom's reading of Gerty's misstep speaks the Freudian language of fetishism and castration anxiety, whereby the male viewer, threatened by what he sees, converts his fear into a suspension of belief. This is the question "Can I believe my eyes?" asked by all the modern and postmodern "great male hysterics," from Yeats to Baudrillard.[32] Revealingly, he switches linguistic register twice, from bodily to economic, to sexual again, when talking about Gerty: she is a commodity "left on the shelf" because defective ("Poor girl! That's why she's left on the shelf and the others did a sprint," and an exceptional, unmarketable object "like a negress or a girl with glasses" (368)). Attributing to women a blindness that is all his own, Bloom tries to exorcise his fear through the effort of finding a code capable of making Gerty readable again— something to minimize the damage that the moving projectile that is Gerty has already inflicted upon his masculine subjecthood.

Bloom tries to reassert himself as male subject and *voyeur* by turning Gerty back into an erotic rather than pornographic image, that is, by trying to defuse her reality effect, and once again affirming "real" and "fake" as separate categories. He does so through his reflections on the Mutoscope girls, the images seen in a peepshow. First, he tries to bolster his masculine prerogative by paradoxically dislocating masculinity into the place of the feminine object. Then, by collapsing Gerty into the more manageable female figures about which he fantasizes, Bloom tries to caption her image, to steady the disordered multiplication of signifiers that compose her character into a single code. Fixed into an image of generically sexualized femininity, as in his thought that all women have their period at the same time, or his vision of "Shoals of them every evening poured out of offices" (368), or made exceptional as a curiosity, Gerty becomes once again manageable, albeit in an aleatory way. At the same time, Bloom revalorizes his masculinity by paradoxically putting himself in the place of the object of desire ("Because they want it themselves. Their natural craving" (368)) and representing masculinity as women's irresistible *desideratum*. By turning himself into the object of feminine desire, the role in which he had at any rate been cast into by Gerty, Bloom abdicates his agency for a different form of power, the presumed active passivity of the female object itself.

The narrative also tries in vain to contain the threat of Gerty's specular instability by having Bloom disavow her defect through a fetishization of the new pop-culture version of female beauty of "those lovely seaside girls." Born as characters in a music-hall song, the "seaside girls" as image of leisure girlhood became a commercial icon in Edwardian advertising.[33] But their reassuring visuality gets complicated by the image of pornographic femininity, that of "the Mutoscope pictures in Capel Street" (368). Out of the blue, in the course of his anxious self-communing after the sight of Gerty's defect, Bloom blurts out the question: "A dream of wellfilled hose. Where was that? Ah, yes. Mutoscope pictures in Capel Street: for men only. Peeping Tom. Willy's hat and what the girls did with that. Do they snapshot those girls or is it all a fake?" (368). The question of the Mutoscope girls is both an ontological and epistemological one: it inquires about the status of the real and of materiality vis-à-vis the fiction made possible by the new means of mechanical reproduction. Bloom tries to assuage and deny "the carnal density" of his vision, to use Linda Williams' phrase, his falling for Gerty's striptease, by assimilating her, with a somersault between fact and fiction, to the image of the Mutoscope girls. Speedily placing Gerty's defect in the realm of implausibility, the threatening reality that scares Bloom in Gerty's spectacle is called fake and dismissed. With this, he disables the photographic reality before his eyes, the live porn which Gerty performs. Paradoxically, he turns to the mutoscope and its mechanically reproduced vision—that is, to the fake— to reaffirm the real he wants to believe in. It is for him a foolproof system: if the girls in Capel Street have been photographed using trick photography, they can take Gerty's place, and reaffirm her image, once shorn of its instability, as real. The terms of this reality, however, are those set by the principles of visual distance and power. In the logic of this traditional gaze, reality can be imaged, that is, abstracted, manipulated and faked, but only if it exists as a steady object in front of the camera eye in the first place.

"Nausicaa" is Joyce's threnody to the changed status of the object, materiality, and the real in the age of mechanical reproduction and monopoly capital, not to mention nascent Irish postcoloniality. It elaborates a new female subject with the ability to strategically negotiate this reordered object world. The entire meaning of the episode is suspended between two questions that sanction the transformation of what counts as the material real, as gender identity, and as subjectivity. First comes Bloom's key pseudo-scientific inquiry into technology and reality: "Do they snapshot those girls or is it all a fake?" This is countered by a line of a poem Gerty finds in a newspaper, and transcribes in her keepsake:

for she felt that she could write poetry if she could only express herself like that poem that appealed to her so deeply that she had copied out of the newspaper she found one evening round the potherbs. "Are Thou Real, My Ideal?" it was called by Louis J. Walsh, Magherafelt, and after that there was something about "Twilight, wilt thou ever?" (364).

In my reading, Gerty's answer to the (male) poet would be: "I hope not," or at least, "Who cares?" Invested as she is in the power of fantasy, and in femininity as necessarily "defective', she exposes, rather than covers over, the unsutured condition of the subject. Gerty is the female subject objectified by her society, whose very existence is only possible in the space of the moving traffic between subjecthood and objecthood, and who works always either to be the self-faked object or the self-made subject, with the unsettling deftness to move off-frame.

In "Nausicaa" Bloom and Gerty each ask a question crucial to *Ulysses*, perhaps the greatest fictional exploration of how complex subjects and hybrid materiality meet in modernity. Each question indicates a different way to negotiate how materiality may be fantasized, and the status of the artefact in strategic display. Bloom signals his discomfort with the "reality of the Ideal" by his reflection on the technological object, as he tries to recover the upper hand as a *voyeur*. He seems afraid that the commodity, as an Eliotic siren, will not sing to him; he also appears unsure about what to do when it does. Disturbed by his physical, bodily reaction to a chance-encountered "defective" body, he first disavows it as artificial, and then tries to bring it under the power of his gaze by substituting for it the controllable image of the Mutoscope girls. Panicked, he would freeze Gerty's sexual power and agency with the Medusan gaze of the peepshow viewer. In this move he tries paradoxically to convert fantasy into fact by focusing away from a real person and her live-show, which he now reads as unreal, to turn, instead, to photographs as reassuring evidence of an empirically and ontologically stable reality. Let us, instead, pause on the value of the defective, as it carries the mark of labor, difference, and an unsutured identity. Bloom's *aporia* is answered by Gerty's ease with fantasy and fiction as the fashion of the subject's materiality. This ease gives her latitude and power: she acknowledges that the theoretical and visual system that supports a certain notion of the real is gone, and so is its aura. Gerty's manipulation of the spectacle breaks the spell of auratic contemplation, and *moves* the viewer to act. Bloom is persuaded to respond to the image physically and synaesthetically, in a way that reaffirms the materiality of both the object and the subject through the tactility of her spectacle. Her performance makes a tear in the fabric of the real, and Bloom is left hesitatingly to patch up this tear, afraid of its consequences, so that we find him tentatively experimenting with the notion of putting himself in the place of the object. To face materiality no longer controllable through mimesis, Bloom needs the aura of the erotic, its sheen and blur. He wants to abstract the object's materiality. Gerty's porn self-*mis en scène*, her camping different material femininities through fashion, has instead a disturbing desublimating effect. She appears auratic to Bloom only during her sitting performance, only insofar as he manages a detached contemplation of her spectacle. When the aura of the object turns into the aura of the abject, he needs to reseparate real from fake, to disavow her "defect" into the inauthentic.

Gerty's misstep implies that the material body as commodity, no less than the self, and any other system of signification and libidinality, is always defective. Bloom may imply in his stream of consciousness that her ersatz nature actually delivers, and can satisfy the viewer as much as the "real thing,'; this doesn't mean that one is duped, or that one settles for less. It means that the distinction between ersatz and real, as an effect of both commodity culture and of the new means of mechanical reproduction that also support this culture, doesn't quite hold anymore. The copy has real, tangible effects, and is as pleasurable as the belief in the real thing. In "Nausicaa" the opposition is no longer between fake and real, but between different degrees of artefactuality within the real. The fake is in this sense always already the real of modernity. This heightened visibility of the artefactual in the twentieth century calls for a new cultural syntax, since the system of perspective, of sufficient distance and confident difference for the individual subject that guaranteed value and plausibility to the bourgeois notion of the real and its systematization of materiality, is now under attack. As part of the aesthetic project of the various modernisms, *Ulysses*, and "Nausicaa," is witness to this change.

What does Joyce's text say about the status of the object and of materiality? How does the representation of the object through a desirous sexualized female body complicate the issue of modern materiality and subjectivity? Here the spectacle of femininity, although articulated according to the modalities of commodity fetishism, emerges as contradictory. Unmaking the opposition of fake and real, itself an effect of the culture of capital and of its means of mechanical reproduction, is Gerty's challenge. Such "aberrant" behavior is her personal management of the spectacle. In contrast to the spectacle which Guy Debord theorizes in the mid-century, Gerty takes visuality beyond abstraction and fetishism. The erotic and auratic quality of the image is revisited with a vengeance: distance—the distance between Gerty and Bloom on Sandymount strand—doesn't imply the fixity of the object and the detached, rational observation on the part of the viewer. Bloom and Gerty co-participate in their exchange, re-establishing the trace of tactility, via a charge of sexual desire that the logic of the *camera obscura* had occluded. The collapse of the opposition between fake and real through tactility brings to the fore a materiality that the bourgeois order had managed to subject and erase—in this case, that of the *jouissant* body. Porn alone seems to provide the syntax through which this unrepresentable materiality can here appear: the pornographic nuance of Gerty's spectacle coincides with her intractability as the object. Her ob-scenity, her being off the scene of the male gaze, makes the object intractable from the viewpoint of the male fetishist, and illegible in the registers of femininity available in her culture. When she steps out of her motionless place as the fetish, which is how Bloom represents her during their exchange, with her limping gait she dismantles the difference between real and artificial. Her shocking movement-image makes her impervious to patriarchal language and to existing notions of gender.

Gerty's defect talks not of the illusion, or of the delusion, of materiality and femininity, but of its elusiveness, of its "not being there" in the terms set by capital and bourgeois patriarchy, which are in Gerty's case imperial and local. It's this elusiveness that unnerves Bloom so much, and shakes his self-confidence, exposing as a side effect the ineffectual subalternity of his professional self. At the end we realize that Gerty's defect is indexical and symptomatic of Bloom's own shortcomings and contradictions as a social and economic figure, as well as, at large, of the system of capitalist circulation and consumption in the colony. As an advertisement designer and canvasser, Bloom is the one who, on behalf of capital, creates the images and the fantasies that make Gerty who she is, only to be himself seduced by the same images he has created. In the case of his lost battle to re-establish the real and the authentic at the expense of the fake, he realizes that he is only a cog in a mechanism that he does not master: capitalist circulation at large, and the process of colonial consumption in particular. His marginality and lack of agency is affirmed twice: at the personal and sexual level, and at the structural one—as a colonial subaltern in the imperial economy. Faced with this double *impasse*, it's understandable that Bloom retreats into the logic of fetishism, as his nervous considerations in the second part of the episode show.

The nexus of consumption, fantasy, *voyeurism*, new visualities, and expenditure, sets the stage for nothing less than the demise of a particular understanding of reality and materiality in the early twentieth century. In the colony, this opened a space of indeterminacy that matched the status of colonial subjectivity in general, whether male or female. While Gerty acknowledges, and profits from, this indeterminacy, and uses fantasy to make sense of her material conditions of existence, as well as to seduce "the gentleman in black," Bloom dismisses it in his fetishistic search for the real—a move that makes him the actual escapist. Gerty's seductive show produces fear together with pleasure: the male libertine pedagogue is taught to admit his insubstantiality and powerlessness by a knowing *ingénue*. By camping gender and the image of a fixed and stable reality, the episode also explores the claim that one is in control of one's identity, of representation, or of the material conditions of one's existence. In this scenario, Gerty occupies an entirely central and yet ex-centric position, at once inside and outside the institutions of national patriarchy and imperial capital. Her defect makes her odd, unmarketable, and so she limps off the circuit of commodity exchange. As a commodity she generates no profit, and only makes her "buyer" spend without any financial return, or any possibility of making him acquire more, thus defying the law of profit and accumulation. Neither mother nor daughter, daughter who "knows," commodity and camp mother (to Father), Madonna of male sobriety *and* intoxication, perhaps Gerty is, after all, the most striking and successful example of colonial resistance in the whole of *Ulysses*. Through her fashion, her unnatural use of clothes, she sees and contemplates her dispossessed state but, even more, makes evident to Bloom his own. Having done her counter-hegemonic work as a commodity through her spectacle as a woman, Gerty simply walks off, and leaves Bloom to patch up the fragments.

Bloom tries, but cannot recognize himself at the end of the episode: his own cracked mirror produces a crisis of self-definition as a man, as a colonial subject, and as an agent of capital. Significantly, Gerty doesn't tread the territory of identity: the final verb referred to her is "to know." The question about her identity that appears at the beginning—"But who was Gerty?"— remains unanswered, and the narrative shows the impossibility and irrelevance of such questions at the historical moment when new postcolonial and gendered relations to the material real were taking shape in Ireland. What Gerty knows, instead, and "Nausicaa" shows us how this knowledge can be articulated through a "bricolaged" manipulation of the colonizer's culture of consumption, becomes the foundation of her power to open the Pandora's box of western materiality through a new understanding and performance of the spectacle of femininity.

IV. Love in Vienna

"Nausicaa," which appeared in *Ulysses* in 1921, and Jelinek's novel *The Piano Teacher* (published as *Die Klavierspielerin, The Piano Player*, 1983) bear witness to two different moments of rupture in the continuum of the modern spectacle of the commodity and its structuring of materiality in relation to gender. As a form of abstraction through which the logic of capital circulates and reproduces itself, the Spectacle[34] increasingly intensifies during the

twentieth century. Confronting this intensification, the two texts I examine
center on the reorganization of the gaze and of touch, and so reassign a new
meaning to materiality. In both, clothes and fashion as a social syntax become
weapons of cultural assault.

Both texts represent women made transgressive by their use of clothes.
Each is a post-imperial text: while *Ulysses* is written from the perspective of
the colony on the verge of independence, *The Piano Teacher* hails from the
other side of the colonial spectrum, the imperial metropolis well after the end
of the Habsburg Empire. Jelinek's novel darkly mocks the national melancholia
which forbids Austria from relinquishing its vaunted past; she depicts it as a
country caught in a stuffy snowglobe image of urban gentility, and of ersatz
natural beauty. Each text exposes the economic undergirding of imperialism,
in a *denouement* through which the language of imperial and colonial
greatness lowers its ideological guard to show its actual interest: its investment
in the circulation and accumulation of capital. Further, both "Nausicaa" and
The Piano Teacher center on female spectacle and pornography as the means
for foregrounding and making tangible the materiality of the body. In both
cases, materiality is signified exactly by the wounded and defective female
body. Gerty's limp and Erika Kohut's self-inflicted cuts each stand as a
memento realitatis that concerns modern subjectivity at large. This material
real in each case refers to the unbound materiality of the body, sentient,
perceiving, and perceived, *jouissant*, in pain, as signified by the spectacle of
the subaltern, the marginal, and the abject. Gerty's colonial performance of
femininity, as well as Erika's transgressive stance as the female artist and
genius, stand as missteps in the continuum of heteronormative representation.
In this optic woman-as-commodity is not the allegory of modernity, as
Benjamin affirms, but its best allegorist and diagnostician, playing this role
better than any male intellectual.

The "unnaturally" decked out female body makes visible that misstep, that
out-of-sync relationship to the material, which characterizes representation
in the age of the spectacle. It gives the lie to naturalistic constructions of
gender, subjectivity, and commodificaton itself. In "Nausicaa" the consumer
of images is also a producer, while the producer-subject turns out to be
consumed by Gerty and by his own body, by his passions and his desire. The
way the episode deploys visuality opens for discussion the status of
the material, and of the viability of the distinction between real and fake
at this point of capitalist development. With fashion and a new pervasiveness
of vision and spectacle, the image appears to become more important than
the thing. Traffic between images and reality, however, does not imply a
slippage of materiality into simulation, as a common caricature of the
complexities of post-Fordist visual culture often claims.[35] The despatialized

and detemporalized contemporary visual horizon progressively undermines what the art critic Victor Burgin calls "the integrity of the semantic object,"[36] but does not do away with the object altogether. On the contrary, disenfranchised from the diktats of bourgeois mimetic and anaesthetic representation, materiality is given a chance to *move*, and become more dangerously unstable and volatile.

The Piano Teacher is set in the late twentieth century, at a very different stage of the culture of capital and of the history of materiality than *Ulysses*. Now visuality has become ubiquitous, and the spectacle is no longer simply fueled by photography or by the philosophical toys, from stereoscope to mutoscope, that give vision its peculiar quality in *Ulysses*, but rather by such technologies as cinema, photographic advertisements, and television and computer screens. As a form of non-coercive control through which capital establishes alienation and abstraction, the spectacle has now colonized perception, production, and memory, so that simulation appears to have taken over, and the screenscape of the video arcade triumphs. In the new *fin-de-siècle*, the shock of the mechanically reproduced image has become everyday exceptionality; similarly, the auratic has become the quality of *any* represented object, and subjectivity itself appears as a function of the virtual. The vast spread of advertising imagery, most recently through the viral flows of digital media, has produced an epochal change in the modes of perception and representation well beyond what Benjamin had envisioned in his work.

After simulation, whither the material? Once the society of the spectacle is taken as a cultural given, contact with the material carries on, if in further alienated terms which must constantly be negotiated. Jelinek is a sharp diagnostician of this condition. Her novel analyzes the spectacle in detail, delineating the constellation of forces, institutions, and permutations of matter which define and support it. Jelinek makes it possible to talk of a material politics of the spectacle. *The Piano Teacher*, instead of steering away from the real as the logic of simulation demands, turns the spectacle back to materiality and sexuality, away from the apparently seamless and genderless neutrality of the virtual. To challenge the vinyl universality of the postmodern, she fixes her gaze on the particularities of the object and of power, especially when the object reclaims for herself the position of the subject, and attributes to herself a power denied her by culture.

V. Ornamentality (is an Austrian Thing)

Erika Kohut, heroine of *The Piano Teacher*, now in her late thirties, lives a decorous life in the name of art: her days are dedicated to teaching piano at the Vienna conservatory, her evenings to the coziness of watching TV with her mother, with whom she lives. She has never managed to become a pianist, a career performer, and her genius, long frustrated, has been achieved at the expense of her femininity and sexuality. Now, from her gender-uncertain position as a *voyeuse*, Erika pursues her sexuality in the seedy scenarios of peepshows and porn theaters which she enters during her nighttime escapades. Her relationship with Walter Klemmer, her student who is ten years younger than herself, turns into a brutal tug of war staged as a sadomasochistic struggle, where her search for power manifests itself in her desire for subjection.

Written in a breathless, voracious style, punctuated by a vitriolic humor aimed at the protagonist as much as at her culture, *The Piano Teacher* has been interpreted as a scandalous case study of what Jelinek herself calls "the tragedy of an older woman in love with a younger man," or the story of a complicated relationship between mother and daughter that exposes the hypocrisies, xenophobic anxieties and sexism of contemporary Austria.[37] The cultural critique evident in all her work aligns Jelinek with such Austrian writers as Karl Kraus, Thomas Bernhardt and Peter Handke. Her writing shows how conservative Austrian culture reifies its Nazi past into forgetfulness aided by its affluent and sexist present. She foregrounds a kitsch, postcard picture of Austria as the land of Alpine lakes and Vienna as "city of music," with which the Austrians, she makes clear, are happy to identify. Her work comically perverts both of these kitsch spectacles of the nation, to foreground what is left out of the picture: the economic and sexual labor of women and migrants upon which capitalist patriarchy rests. Punctuating this novel, for example, are the encounters of Erika and the Turkish *Gastarbeiter*, especially when Erika, having internalized the xenophobia of her culture, snubs him as an abject.

Women in this universe are caught between family and State in an impossible place, whose political economy is the topic of the novel: it's a matter of surviving in a context where other codes have been superseded by economic value, of which the spectacle is the index.

In *The Piano Teacher*, materiality, as experienced by the late-modern female subject, may be said, literally, to hurt. The tropes that had defined modernist spectacularity—mirror images, mimesis and the copy—are no longer adequate categories to explain Erika Kohut's identity and gendering: perhaps a gallery of mirrors in a sideshow would be more to the point. In this sense, the book poses the problem of how to practice gender politics without a self-present subject. Erika's use, misuse, and abuse of clothes and ornaments merely grants her a hybrid and aggressive pose which culminates in her making a spectacle of herself in the book's grand finale. Under the conditions of late capitalism and its organization of vision, materiality and the body become mediated, mediatized, and abstracted; the book punctures this all-pervading logic by situating femininity at the nexus of fashion, pornography, and sadomasochism. In "Nausicaa" we saw how this space of mediated abstraction is used to reaffirm a synaesthetic perception of materiality through fantasy. The scenario of sadomasochism put in place by *The Piano Teacher*, as a particular fantasy configuration, is what defeats the anaesthetic power of the spectacle. The subject does not now, as Gerty could do in "Nausicaa," simply renounce her autotelic claims by acknowledging her own dependence upon her senses. Re-establishing the distinction between subject and object as a matter of role-playing and of a ritual scripted by the object, sadomasochism blurs the opposition between them. It invokes instead an impossible subject position, a self-inflicted simultaneous subjection and objectification. In the same way, Erika's unnatural use of clothes affirms an impossible notion of gender. Chafed by Jelinek's abrasive language, scarred by Erika's self-inflicted wounds, materiality in *The Piano Teacher* physically hurts. The brutally somatic materiality of the subject-turned-object cutting herself in front of the mirror suggests the price and the reality of sentient experience.

VI. Glum Glam

Clothes, fashion, adornment are the unmannerly objects threaded through *The Piano Teacher*. The novel opens with the purchase of a very flimsy and feminine dress, which Erika tries to hide from her mother by stuffing it among the sheet music in her briefcase, to create the strange intimacy of Beethoven and silk chiffon. This montage of Beethoven in silk drag—*pace* Loos—stands eloquently for how Erika is constructed as a subject. The violent fight that follows her mother's discovery of the dress sets the stage for the rest of the novel, and becomes Erika's way of reclaiming what is being forbidden by her mother's denial of fashion: femininity, consumption, sexuality, fantasy. Instead, the protagonist is situated by Mother herself (the capitalization of this name throughout bespeaks her power) in the position of the ascetic and productive masculinity of the artist, through an ideology of individual superiority which covers over Erika's powerlessness and Mother's claims to social advancement.

To grasp ornament's role in *The Piano Teacher* we need to turn to another illustrious figure of Viennese culture, the architect and critic Adolf Loos. In his excoriating 1908 analysis of ornament as the signature of "latent criminals or degenerate aristocrats,"[38] Loos makes clear his conservative masculine anxieties about social mobility, and the apparent collapse of social hierarchies:

We have our culture which has taken over from ornament. After a day's trouble and pain we go to hear Beethoven and Wagner. My cobbler cannot do that. I must not rob him of his pleasures as I have nothing else to replace them with. But he who goes to listen to the Ninth Symphony and who then sits down to draw up a wallpaper pattern, is either a rogue or a degenerate (36).

In its class panic, this anticipates Erika's and Klemmer's[39] spitefully snobbish attitude toward crowds who go to concerts for ornamental social reasons, without appreciating the music. Loos' anxiety appears unmotivated: he implies that because his cobbler does not possess the cultural capital to discriminate against the ornament, he remains inevitably condemned to his lower status. Loos' thesis is situated unabashedly in the realm of political economy; for him, ornament lies on the side of waste, against rational economics. In his words, "Ornament is wasted man power and therefore wasted health . . . . wasted material, wasted capital . . . it commits a crime" (33). Both Loos and Mother hang on to the bourgeois moralism of the useful, the principle that supports the utilitarian reinvestment of surplus value produced apparently for the good of all.[40] The value squandered in producing and consuming the ornament is posed as a dangerous obstacle to the circulation and accumulation of value. The purchase of the dress that opens *The Piano Teacher* immediately plunges us into the issues of utility, waste, pleasure, and productivity, through which the spectacle of femininity is complicated in the book. Jelinek shows how the desires circulated in the economy, whether it be capital's desire for profit or the consumer's desire for things, both put in place by the laws of circulation and surplus value,[41] can become a powerful antidote against a puritan notion of use. Made tangible in stuff, this desire becomes a weapon to tear through the doxa of the utilitarian common good.

Erika has no sovereignty as economic subject. In *The Piano Teacher* the common good which is hindered by Erika's vanity and expenditure is actually her mother's good.[42] Although cast as the masculine breadwinner, she lacks consuming power. This shift from control to submission produces the confusion of gender roles that defines her character. Erika is her mother's property, an object, and an exploited laborer, like other reified and marginal figures on whom the Austrian economy relies: women and immigrants. She owns nothing; there's no lock on her room door; worse, she sleeps in the same room, and bed, as Mother. She doesn't even own her own body: she doesn't, cannot touch herself, except through self-mutilation. As a substitute paternal presence for Mother, Erika embodies a "female virility" fully incorporating the feminine powerlessness of her father, whose wrong gendering is signaled by the madness which pushes him out of the scene and into an asylum. All that remains of him is an object, the razor blade, the talisman by means of which Erika tries to rewrite gender and sexuality on her body. Erika is all eyes and no touch. Trained into forgetting her sexuality since adolescence, her body becomes "the refrigerator of art"(98), and her cleanliness becomes an algid symbol of her artistic ascesis, to which she is not entitled insofar as she is a woman, but to which she nonetheless, at least nominally, devotes herself. Again, the ascetic impulse, to let the subject avoid matter as much as possible; when the subject is female, it appears that this Loosian inheritance is untenable.

If sexuality, femininity, and expenditure are forbidden to her, Erika's other everyday life, her "real" life, goes on in the realm of the Spectacle. If she cannot live life, she will then watch it, at the cinema, on television, or at the peepshow. Sex, pleasure, touch are taken back by Erika perversely, on the sly, through her pleasure as a *voyeuse*. Her outlaw and secret night escapades, performed as if by a gothically revisited and regendered Nietzschean beast of prey, take her roaming to Viennese porno theaters and lovers' lanes. In these locales she plays at practicing the male gaze, and watches for pleasure and for knowledge, spending money, as a male character at a peepshow points out, "to see what she could see for free at home" (55).

Vision as articulated in *The Piano Teacher* is complex and somehow contradictory; it is continually modulated according to the double register of the specular and the spectacular, both imbricated in fashion. Porn, sadomasochism, and television, the three venues of the gaze in the novel, are organized according to this double register: when absorbed into any of these visual activities, Erika neither gets lost in simulation, nor does she try to re-establish a baseline of the material real. As in "Nausicaa," so too in *The Piano Teacher* it is men who would maintain the distinction between real and fake. Rather, she works to reassert her power. In the story, Erika's unnatural use of clothes—either she buys them and doesn't wear them, or she "overwears" them, as Klemmer points out—produces a proliferation of signs, a form of signification out of control, where meaning and value have become compromised, an unorderly spinning away from function and official definitions of gender. Thus clothes, as an over-inscription of the body that sexualizes it and marks it socially, come to signify the inessentiality of gender. Clothes paradoxically become Erika's best shot at femininity and its disavowal at the same time.

Under the rubric of the spectacular Erika is an object who looks at herself through the very gaze with which her culture represents her as a woman. Through her book Jelinek casts a ruthless eye on the conditions of existence of women in contemporary Austrian society, and on the violence and humiliations to which they are subjected. Women are objects, whose fully measurable value diminishes with age: "Meanwhile, back on earth, men are trying to impress their girlfriends by shooting for kewpie dolls. They take their prizes home; and years later, the frustrated wives can see how valuable they used to be to their boyfriends" (131).[43] The novel presents them as powerless and thus full of self-hatred, wrapped in the cellophane of the bourgeois ideology of family, tirelessly teaching their own subjection to their daughters. Under the register of the specular, instead, Erika appropriates the position of the subject and steals his mastering gaze: this is what Klemmer means when he calls Erika "a woman who wants to rewrite Creation. A topic for humor magazines" (234). The peepshow, the porn flick, Klemmer's body during the scene of seduction that inaugurates their relationship, as well as her own self-mutilation before the mirror, are spectacles for *her own* gaze. Through them, vicariously, at a distance and alone, she enjoys the body and consumes sexuality, while trying to gain access to what seems to be so valued by patriarchy, what Klemmer calls "the enigma of woman." Porn and self-wounding before the mirror become for Erika ways of "seeing inside the female body" (108), to get a better look at something that is alien and invisible to her. The only access she is allowed to her own sexuality is filtered through patriarchal doxa about femininity: she is a body to be penetrated, specularly and physically. Thus porn here assumes a double function, anaesthetic *and* desublimating. Like television, it guarantees Erika a vicarious experience of second-hand reality, a way of watching reality at a distance that is both a defense against, and an index of, her cultural poverty as a woman. Yet it provides an entry point into the real that the bourgeois discourse of propriety and love would not allow her, what she calls "the banality of fleshliness" (255).

Porn and television, ironically, turn out to be moments of rehearsal of the tactility and intimacy that she cannot achieve with Klemmer. In her closed-circuit visual and televisual experience through peepshows and mirrors, Erika merely reprises what she experiences in the evening with her mother in front of the television. Television has a contradictory value in the book: it alienates living into the act of seeing, but also, as Erika sits with her mother, allows the only moment of togetherness in Erika's life, the only experience that approximates tactility and intimacy. This tactility is reached and becomes touch in the book's most baffling and disturbing scene, that of Erika's "parasexual attacks" (234) on Mother in bed, which occurs after a failed approach to Klemmer, who always remains an erotic decoy.[44] Allowing Erika to be close to her object of desire, her mother, television is at once both anaesthetic and shockingly somatic. If porn offers Erika-the-spectator a second-hand experience of reality, it also short-circuits the anaesthetic quality of tele-visuality by giving the lie to the cultural imperative of the body beautiful, presented by the plastified women on television. What porn makes visible for Erika are labor and pain:

> In porno flicks people work harder than in movies about the workaday world . . . These frazzled, amateur actors work a lot harder . . . They are defective. Their skin has spots, pimples, scars, wrinkles, scabs, cellulite, fat. Poorly dyed hair. Sweat. Dirty feet. In aesthetically demanding films at luxuriously upholstered cinemas, you mostly see the surfaces of men and women. Both genders are squeezed into nylon body stocking dirt-repellent, durable, acid-proof, heat resistant . . . Here . . . everything is reduced to outer appearances. (106–7)

Porn reveals what Klemmer doesn't want to see, that "banality of fleshliness" which he will be obliged to acknowledge through their relationship.

Before turning to the role of sadomasochism and of Erika's and Klemmer's love story, consider how Jelinek's cliché-spattered style inflects the spectacles of porn and television she presents. In *The Piano Teacher* this style reaches to the core of the problem of the spectacle. Designating the devalued *déjà vu* quality of the mechanically reproduced image, like the click of the camera, the cliché here points to a coded repertory of fixed meanings, ideological ready-mades through which knowledge is circulated and naturalized in a predigested form. The clichés through which all characters in *The Piano Teacher* approach reality stand as an extension of the sleep Benjamin says has come over the masses of modern consumers, this time with few chances for them to awaken from it: in the milieu of all-pervasive spectacle, both shock and aura generate numbness. Jelinek's style parodies this numbness through its use of cliché, so that, for example, the most atrocious moments of physical and psychological violence are announced in the cheerful language of sensible commonplace. Rather than naturalizing the violence, however, cliché-overload confronts the reader. If, in the world of *The Piano Teacher*, the spectacle works to normalize everyday violence and the prevarications the characters experience, the book wants to shake the reader out of her sleep, and puncture the mylar envelope of mediatized reality. Jelinek's aim is not to show the real "beneath the veil" which would be another return to the aura, but to make visible how and why this version of reality is naturalized into doxa. The book's *bravura* is its ability to jolt the reader awake by describing extreme and outlaw acts in the matter-of-fact, commonsensical language of the everyday. The book stridently opposes plain language and vividly violent acts.

The spectacle offers numbness when it shows pain, uses a narcotic language of health while it shows the wound. Underlined by Jelinek's use of the cliché, this matches the double meaning attributed to the televisual gaze.

It is at once highly anaesthetic—we are shown the numbness of Erika's domestic enclosure in the "amniotic liquid" of TV—yet its absenting of reality opens a space that can be scripted by the viewer's fantasy. Television alienates, but it also creates a space for Erika to rewrite reality, and, once she acts, to live her fantasies in the real world. In *The Piano Teacher*, televisual hyperreality and the way sadomasochism operates come to coincide. Neither works by the principle of reality, but by that of the script. Guy Debord castigates the society of the spectacle for creating a parallel world that trumps experience, yet such banal versions of that world, such as television, might also be used as a means of refusing reality-as-given. If you cannot change life, change the channel.

VII. Sadomasochism, Television, Script

The novel's turning point is Erika's affair with her student Walter Klemmer; this affair brings to the fore her "unnatural" use of clothing. Fashion for Erika is a form of seduction, but also of self-seduction. Like television and sadomasochism, fashion makes reality happen for her by allowing her to conjure it out of fantasy. A good example of this process of production of the real via fantasy is Erika's fantastically Austrian hiking outfit. It is the outfit that makes reality happen: "She's sporting a sporty checkered blouse, a loden jacket, knicker-bockers, and red woolen knee-stockings . . . Klemmer inspects the woman . . . Erika whimpers at him: She's been promised a hike today, and she's come to put in her claim" (239). All dressed up, wrapped in stuff, for the part in a play of her own making, she expects Klemmer to assume the supporting role she has destined for him in her highly filmic projection of reality.

One form of spectacle that turns fantasy into the foundation of reality is sadomasochism. Her sadism and masochism make Erika self-sufficient, capable of playing subject and object all by herself—to her students and to Mother, and at the peepshow and in front of the mirror. It's not love and reciprocity she looks for in Klemmer, but what she can obtain *through* him: he has only a supportive role in the staging of her fantasies, as a means to something else. The scene of seduction in the school bathroom immediately warns Klemmer that something is rotten in the state of Denmark: the male seducer is suddenly, and unexpectedly, positioned by Erika as the object of the female gaze. Next, Erika announces to Klemmer, in writing, how their relationship will proceed. Any sexual exchange between them will be mediated by her script: it's the letter, and thus the fantasy, that shapes reality and makes it happen. "Have you read my letter, Herr Klemmer?" (205) she prods him. "Why do we need letters?" he asks.

In the letters Erika orchestrates her own submission to Klemmer by telling him how to treat her: the paradox of sadomasochism is sharpened by Erika's written directives. The letter as text mediates the relation, a condition of what Erika calls love: "Erika Kohut is using her love to make this boy her master. The more power he attains over her, the more he will become Erika's pliant creature... Yet Klemmer will think of himself as Erika's master. This is the goal of Erika's love" (207). The textual mediation sharpens the angular paradoxes of her sadomasochism:

> He can take on Erika only under the condition of violence. He is to love Erika to the point of self-surrender; she will then love him to the point of self-denial. They will continually hand each other notarized evidence of their affection and devotion. Erika wants for Klemmer to abjure violence for the sake of love. Erika will refuse for the sake of love, and she will demand that he do to her what she has detailed in the letter, whereby she ardently hopes that she will be spared what is required in the letter (213).

Erika's script, besides sanctioning Klemmer's mastery as submission, makes fantasy a precondition of actual intimacy and vision. For her, the language of sadomasochism is not bent toward reality: the letter and its script are not even expected to materialize into staged theatrics. Thus sadomasochism in *The Piano Teacher* brings into focus the relation of the spectacle of porn and of television discussed earlier. Erika's masochistic bent, more than merely representing the internalization of her subaltern position as a woman, becomes her means of a mediated participation in the spectacle of porn she has so often only watched. Through masochism she welds the tactility of the spectacle of television to the "heaviness" of porn. In this sense, her sadomasochism repeats *and* twists the logic of television, and the way reality is constructed in the televisual spectacle, with a vengeance.

The Piano Teacher is no *Venus in Furs*: Erika's "unnatural clothing habit" makes her over-dressing a self-reflexive, narcissistic gesture that gives a visual dimension to her wound, to her solipsistic self-sufficiency, thus prefiguring her blurring of the subject and object positions.

In the novel sadomasochism is not articulated in the terms laid out by either Freud or Deleuze,[45] which begin with the male masochist's allegiance and submission to (respectively) either the Oedipal father or the pre-Oedipal Mother. As a *female* masochist, Erika is already usurping a place that is not hers. What's even more abnormal is her unsuccessful tampering with femininity, and her "parasexual" attachment to a phallic Mother who demands her subjection, not only at the expense of the Father, but also at the expense of Erika herself. In *The Piano Teacher* there's no space for the masochist's fixed, stable identification with either the maternal or the paternal figure, as Erika's continual gender oscillation shows. Erika is no Fanny Pistor, who is situated in the role of dominatrix by Severin, the protagonist of Leopold von Sacher-Masoch's novel *Venus in Furs*; in contrast, she turns the sadomasochistic theatrics into a one-woman show.[46] Playing the roles of subject and object at the same time, she actually doesn't need Klemmer, who is incidental to her routine (as he understands: "All she thinks is about herself"), but still needed: his function is to keep the level of fantasy high and untouched by reality. Contrary to Deleuze and Sacher-Masoch, we move in this novel from a masochism of masquerade and costuming, where the theatrically cathected and costumed female body gets fetishized and submitted, to a sadomasochism of the letter, where what gets cathected is textuality. The letter is a form of counter-abstraction that for Erika enhances rather than impoverishes experience. Throughout the book, the text of fantasy calls reality into existence, as we have seen in the case of the hiking outfit.

Through sadomasochism, the novel disrupts the spectacle with its own logic, the logic of the abstract textualization of reality. The script—of Erika's letters, of television, of sadomasochism—is not about simulation. Rather, it's another form of distance, implies not some feared end of meaning but rather the possibility of *choosing* different codes of signification to produce a new sense of the material. Erika converts the indirectness of watching, the mediation of voyeurism, into the indirectness of textuality, acting according to the letter. Both scenarios abolish touch: she hopes that "love" will stop Klemmer from doing what she has asked him to do. When at the end the materiality of the wound risks being produced by another—rather than by Erika herself—she thinks it is better to turn to the clichéd abstraction of "love according to Austrian standards" (226).

As a form of textuality without a material referent, sadomasochism does not do away with power: even when the material real is vacuumed out of Erika's letters, it makes a difference who is used by whom. Klemmer feels particularly disempowered by the "scriptural" apparatus Erika puts in place: "Reading isn't like the real thing" and the letter makes him impotent: "he cannot perform love, only talk about it" (244). That which gives Erika the power of mastery and control, paralyzes Klemmer into impotence and resentment. When she talks of submission, even when afraid of the violence it would imply, she would like her sadomasochistic relationship to Klemmer to work like television, through the suspension of reality and a distancing from action through narrative. The only action that the pseudo-tactile experience in front of the television allows, and, in turn, the only truly tactile scene of reciprocity that happens in the novel, is her exchange with her mother in bed. "She wants Mother per se, to go back into her" (233), the dictatorial and driven narrative voice claims, in a scene in which, at last, touch is directed toward what had long been the target of Erika's desire. Perhaps the adventure with Klemmer is both an anticipation of, and a substitution for this scene, and, at the same time, a detour from its taboo realization: a displacement and a replacement at the same time.

Erika's negotiation with abstraction and fantasy via the textuality of television and sadomasochism become particularly jarring in the two scenes of intimacy between Erika and Klemmer, the first when she shows him the toolbox containing the paraphernalia of sadomasochism, and the other when she gets raped by him:

> From beyond the door, the muffled thunder of the TV, in which a male is threatening a female. Today's soap installment cuts painfully into Erika's mind, which is open and receptive to it . . . Mother barks, the TV buzzes. The screen locks in tiny figures that one controls by arbitrarily switching them on and off. Big real life is pitted against tiny TV life, and real life wins because it has full control over the image. Life adjusts to television, and television is copied from life (221).

The darkly comic—and of course clichéd—interweaving of soap opera and sexual violence in the first scene turns into something more sinister in the second. This moment of violence, where the real of dominant culture and phallic masculinity takes over Erika's script, takes place after her "change of heart" toward love and normality. For a day she even gives up television. In so doing she renounces the letter, and thus the textuality of her perverse desire, in favor of the ultimate cliché of true love, which she has witnessed repeatedly in the soap operas she watches, and perhaps also in her fantasy of domesticity and maternal possession. In the absence of TV she gives up the separation of reality and fantasy that structures her relationship with Klemmer, and lets each category be sutured into the other under the aegis of "love" and its cliché affect, happiness. Her use of television, which stands in a continuum with pornography and sadomasochism, becomes naturalized into a hyperreal that substitutes reality. The narrator opines: "Now she wants the expanded attention and exaggerated affect that TV people enjoy" (260). So far the visuality of TV has been used by Erika as a fiction capable of unhinging and changing reality; now, like the masses she despises, she formats her reality to fit the television screen.

Through "love," of which she only knows the soap opera version, she hopes to get away from her own stipulations. At the end, the punishment she had wished for throughout comes not from Mother, who is, after all, "just" a woman, but from Klemmer. The scene of the rape paradoxically speaks the disillusionment of fulfillment, and makes Erika's dreams come true by anchoring her fantasy-approach to reality. This new reversal of reality and fiction, submission and power, masculinity and femininity which, in its sadomasochistic configuration, had reduced Klemmer to being a tool for Erika's desire, is redressed and violently shaken by his action. "This isn't how you had pictured it originally, is it?" "No, it isn't," she replies (266). The "banality of fleshliness," the desublimation of the body which Erika had taught Klemmer the hard way, becomes now her own experience. Yet once again, as happened when she mutilated herself in front of the mirror, under Klemmer's violence she feels nothing (272): reality disappoints her, and she irreducibly feels herself to be a victim of deception, as if her fantasy had been cheated by the real.

The Piano Teacher ends with a reminder of the danger and the precariousness of women's power. At the close it is Klemmer who turns the tables and reasserts the only possible reality in his culture, the patriarchal law, this time in its Cartesian version: "Kicking her, he demonstrates the simple equation: I am I. And I am not ashamed. I am behind me one hundred percent. He threatens the woman: she has to take him just as he is. I am as I am. Erika's nose is broken; so is one of her ribs. She buries her face in her hand" (270). Klemmer enjoys the power of a subject who has the prerogative to predicate himself at the expense of the other. He knows who he is because he can perform violence on a woman, a woman who tried to rewrite Creation, and to change the rules of the game. As Jelinek describes her in an interview, Erika is "a phallic woman who appropriates the male right to watch, and therefore pays for it with her life."[47] Erika is defeated because her fantasies really come true: from her playful, albeit powerful and dangerous, skipping rope between subject and object, and the theatrics of her masochistically scripted sexuality, she is brought back to the "heaviness" of the female material body as object, its labor and pain, its disappointment with sex, and a boring routine existence. She is defeated, but she doesn't give up her defiant attitude, and to signal it, she once again turns to fashion.

So what does a woman who wants to rewrite Creation wear? The book ends with another spectacular masquerade, through which Erika inscribes upon herself the signs of fantasy, along with the bruises of the body's materiality: "The new day finds Erika alone but covered with the bandages and poultices of maternal solicitude" (275); she leaves her house with a long kitchen knife in her bag. She's certainly dressed for the occasion: "Erika puts on an old dress in an outdated short style. The dress is not as short as other dresses were back then. The dress is too tight: it doesn't close in the back. It is completely outmoded. Mother doesn't like the dress either; it's too short and too tight for her taste. Erika is bursting out all over" (276). The mini-dress is a remnant from Erika's youth, the youth her mother did not let her have, but also of the youth that is slipping away from her now. This final outfit is as grotesque as the hiking attire, but this time her clothes make nothing happen. The hiking outfit, in which she demanded that Klemmer would take her to the mountains, is an example of fantasy that creates reality. Here instead, she's trying to chase after a reality that is escaping her—sexuality, desirability, youth. This "Baby Doll" picture of Erika is also mercilessly pitted against a group of laughing students, of which Klemmer is part, when she sees him in front of the Engineering School. The final note of this deranged finale is Erika's desire to be noticed: "Erika will walk through the streets, astonishing everyone" (276). This desire of the counter-*flâneuse* is disappointed—some passers-by look at her, others don't—and in the end, since Klemmer remains inaccessible, the knife she's carrying in the bag goes into her own shoulder. This scene is a *memento* of the wounds that she had inflicted upon herself, but more, a sign of her frustration at her inability to punish Klemmer.

At this point Erika has nowhere to go but home, back to the television and her mother, and this is perhaps the most transgressive and dangerous direction she can take. Her assault on the material world, on the cultural reality of conservative and patriarchal Austria, by deploying her material body as spectacle, has failed. Her exceptionality, even her horrific and wounded femininity is made once again part of a *déjà vu* visuality: the mylar of her cultural *milieu* is impenetrable, and goes unpunctured. Yet, from the viewpoint of a feminist reading, Erika goes out with a bang, carrying on her material body, amplified, all the signs of the practices that had helped articulate her transgression, and make corporeal materiality visible. She shows that the spectacle, which denies the tangibility of all material, embodied and otherwise, can be played against itself, and that learning from fantasy, of which both porn and TV are channels, can produce unregulated forms of femininity. For now, the oscillation of this femininity between the position of master and slave makes it monstrous. Erika's mini-dress, open in the back, pulling in all directions, her stuff worn as an image of her inappropriate and uncontrollable excess, demonstrates that patriarchal representation is always too short a garment to fully cover female desire, and that the spectacle, under its present management by capital, barely contains materiality and the body.

Notes

1   The similarities between commodity and woman are of course studied by Benjamin. For a classic reading of this homology see Luce Irigaray's seminal essay, "Women on the Market", *This Sex Which Is Not One*, trans. Catherine Porter with Carolyn Burke, Ithaca, Cornell University Press, 1985.

2 Abigail Solomon-Godeau sees this as the internalization of the male gaze, in "The Legs of the Countess" in Emily Apter and William Pietz (eds.), *Fetishism as Cultural Discourse*, Ithaca, Cornell University Press, 1993.

3 Susan Buck-Morss, *The Dialectics of Seeing: Walter Benjamin and the Arcades Project*, Cambridge, MIT Press, 1990; Martin Jay, *Downcast Eyes: The Denigration of Vision in Twentieth-Century French Thought*, Berkeley, University of California Press, 1990.

4 Feminists have revised this; see Stella Bruzzi and Pamela Church Gibson eds., *Fashion Cultures: Theories, Explorations, and Analysis*, London, Routledge, 2002. See also the important essay by Kaja Silverman, "Fragments of a Fashionable Discourse", Tanya Modleski ed., *Studies in Entertainment*, Bloomington, Indiana University Press, 1986.

5 Walter Benjamin, Konvolut B, "Fashion", B3, 4, of *The Arcades Project*, trans. Howard Eiland and Kevin McLaughlin, Cambridge, Harvard University Press, 1999.

6 Adolf Loos, "Ornament and Crime" (1908), in Bernie Miller and Melony Ward, *Crime and Ornament: The Arts and Popular Culture in the Shadow of Adolf Loos*, Toronto, YYZ Books, 2002.

7 Roland Barthes, *Le Système de la Mode*; Jean Baudrillard, *Le système des objets*.

8 J.C. Flugel, *Psychology of Clothes*, London, Hogarth Press, 1930.

9 Guy Debord, *La Societé du Spectacle*, Paris, Buchet-Castel, 1967.

10 Lutz Koepnick, "Aura Reconsidered: Benjamin and Contemporary Visual Culture", in Gerhard Richter ed., *Benjamin's Ghosts*, Stanford, Stanford University Press, 2002, p. 111.

11 "The senses maintain an uncivilized and uncivilizable trace, a core of resistance to cultural domestication." Susan Buck-Morss, "Walter Benjamin's Art Work Essay Reconsidered", *October* 62, Fall 1992, pp. 6–7. Terry Eagleton's text which Buck-Morss cites is *The Ideology of the Aesthetic*, London, Blackwell, 1990.

12 The synaesthetic system *par excellence*, as Buck-Morss explains, is the nervous system. Buck-Morss, "Walter Benjamin's Art Work Essay Reconsidered", *October* 62, Fall 1992, p. 12.

13 Jonathan Crary, *Techniques of the Observer: On Vision and Modernity in the Nineteenth Century*, Cambridge, MIT Press, 1994; see Ch. 2, "The *Camera Obscura* and its Subject."

14 This is Linda Williams' contention in "Corporealized Observers: Visual Pornographies and the 'Carnal Density of Vision'", where she provides a feminist critique of Crary's "disembodied" theory of vision in the nineteenth century. Patrice Petro ed., *Fugitive Images: From Photography to Video*, Bloomington, Indiana University Press, 1995, p. 7.

15 Crary, *Techniques of the Observer*, p. 93.

16 See Abigail Solomon-Godeau, "Reconsidering Erotic Photography: Notes for a Project of Historical Salvage", in *Photography at the Dock: Essays on*

Photographic History, Institutions and Practices, Minneapolis, University of Minnesota Press, 1991. This is the idea that Williams opposes in her essay.

17 "Touch ... though quite material and palpable, it is not a matter of feeling the absent object represented, but of the spectator-observer feeling his own or her own body." Williams, Corporealized Observers: Visual Pornographies and the 'Carnal Density of Vision'", Patrice Petro ed., *Fugitive Images: From Photography to Video,* p. 15.

18 Paul Virilio, "La troisieme fenêtre: Entretien avec Paul Virilio", quoted in Jonathan Crary, "Eclipse of the Spectacle", in Brian Wallis ed., *Art after Modernism,* Boston, Godine, 1984, p. 285. See also Anne Friedberg, *Window Shopping: Cinema and the Postmodern,* Berkeley, University of California Press, 1993.

19 Buck-Morss, in her article on Benjamin's Art Work Essay, talks about the "surface-unity" of the body as an illusionary effect of the subject's autogenesis, comparing *Art Nouveau* with Expressionism, which instead documented the loss of surface-unity. Buck-Morss, "Walter Benjamin's Art Work Essay Reconsidered", *October* 62, Fall 1992, pp. 33–4.

20 On masquerade, see Mary Ann Doane, "Film and Masquerade: Theorizing the Female Spectator" and "Masquerade Reconsidered: Further Thoughts on the Female Spectator", Chs. 2, 3, *Femmes Fatales,* New York, Routledge, 1991.

21 See Thomas Richards, *Commodity Culture of Victorian England: Advertising and Spectacle 1851–1914,* Stanford, Stanford University Press, 1990. Richards sees Gerty as passively responding to the call of consumerism. (222). See also Franco Moretti's reading of consumer culture in *Ulysses* in *Signs Taken for Wonders: Essays in the Sociology of Literary Forms,* London, Verso, 1983.

22 On "Nausicaa," femininity, and consumption see among others Peggy Ochoa, "Joyce's 'Nausicaa': The Paradox of Advertising Narcissism", in *James Joyce Quarterly,* 30, 4, and 31, 1; Suzette Henke, "Gerty MacDowell: Joyce's Sentimental Heroine", in *Women in Joyce,* Henke and Elaine Unkeless eds, Urbana, University of Illinois Press, 1982; Garry Leonard, "The Virgin Mary and the Urge in Gerty: Advertising and Desire in the "Nausicaa" Chapter of *Ulysses",* *University of Hartford Studies in Literature,* 21.1, 1991; Mark Wollaeger, "Bloom's Coronation and the Subjection of the Subject", in Bonnie Kime Scott ed, *The Gender of Modernism: A Critical Anthology,* Bloomington, Indiana University Press, 1990. For Joyce and consumer culture, or consumption in Joyce's times, see Jennifer Wicke, *Advertising Fictions: Literature, Advertising, and Social Reading,* New York, Columbia University Press, 1988, and "Modernity Must Advertise: Aura, Desire, and Decolonization in Joyce", *JJQ* vol. 30, 31; Cheryl Herr, *Joyce's Anatomy of Culture,* Urbana, University of Illinois Press, 1986.

23 See Enda Duffy, *The Subaltern Ulysses,* Minneapolis, University of Minnesota Press, 1994, and Jennifer Wicke's provocative "Who's She When She's at Home? Molly Bloom and the Work of Consumption", *JJQ* 28, 1991.

24 See Wicke, "Modernity Must Advertise: Aura, Desire, and Decolonization in Joyce", *JJQ* vol. 30, 31.

25 See Duffy, *Subaltern Ulysses*.

26 Rosa Luxemburg, *The Accumulation of Capital*, New Haven, Yale University Press, 1981; see also Derek Brewer, *Marxist Theories of Imperialism*, London, Routledge and Kegan Paul, 1980.

27 James Joyce, *Ulysses*, New York, the Modern Library, 1961, p. 348. Subsequent page numbers in the text.

28 Joan Copjec presents the opposition of the "law of psychoanalysis" and the law of utilitarianism thus: "What is crucial for psychoanalysis is not the reciprocity of individual subjects in their relations to a contingent realm of *things* but the non reciprocal relation between the subject and its sublime, inaccessible *Thing*; that is, that part of the subject that exceeds the subject, its repressed desire." "The Sartorial Superego", in *Read My Desire: Lacan against the Historicists*, Cambridge, MIT Press, 1994, p. 92.

29 The superego, for Freud in *Civilization and Its Discontents*, is the source of moral law. See Copjec, "The Sartorial Superego", in *Read My Desire*, p. 92.

30 Copjec on the decay of the aura in the nineteenth century lamented by Benjamin: "It was precisely this symbolic relation—this aura, or distance— that was in decline in the nineteenth century. Why? Because of the utilitarian definition of the subject which declared that the subject was indeed equal to its traces, that it could be fully grasped in its use or function. Not only did work democratize society, it also 'exposed simulation'", "The Sartorial Superego", in *Read My Desire*, p. 103.

31 "This boy with the arm outstretched, his radiant smile ... incarnates a kind of blissful eroticism; the photograph leads me to distinguish the 'heavy' desire of pornography from the 'light' (good) desire of eroticism." Roland Barthes, *Camera Lucida: Reflections on Photography*, trans. R. Howard, New York, Hill and Wang, 1981, p. 59.

32 Neil Hertz talks of Yeats in these terms. "Medusa's Head: Male Hysteria under Political Pressure", *Representations*, Fall 1983, no.4, pp. 31–2.

33 For a discussion of the "Seaside Girls" in historical and cultural terms, see Richards, *Commodity Culture*.

34 I use this term, "Spectacle," capitalized *à la* Debord, to signify the extreme form of abstraction achieved by the "vision" of capital. However I agree with Crary that this concept must be historicized. See Crary, "Spectacle, Attention, Memory", *Techniques of the Observer*, p. 97.

35 See David Harvey, *The Condition of Postmodernity: An Inquiry into the Origins of Cultural Change*, Oxford, Blackwell, 1989; on post-Fordist visuality see Victor Burgin, *In/Different Places: Place and Memory in Visual Culture*, Berkeley, University of California Press, 1996.

36 Burgin quoted in Koepnick, "Aura Reconsidered: Benjamin and Contemporary Visual Culture", in Gerhard Richter ed., *Benjamin's Ghosts*, p. 96.

37 On Jelinek's work see Matthias Konzett, *The Rhetoric of National Dissent in Thomas Berhnardt, Peter Handke, and Elfriede Jelinek*, Rochester, NY, Camden House, 2000; Allyson Fiddler, *Rewriting Reality: An Introduction to Elfriede Jelinek*, Berg, Oxford 1994; Jorum B. Johns and Katherine Arens, *Elfriede Jelinek: Framed by Language*, 1994; Ritchie Robertson and Edward Timms, *Theatre and Performance in Austria: From Mozart to Jelinek*, 1994.

38 Adolf Loos, "Ornament and Crime" (1908), in Bernie Miller and Melony Wards eds., *Crime and Ornament*, p. 29.

39 "for most of them the charm of art is to recognize something they think they recognize. A wealth of sensations overwhelms a butcher. He can't help it, even though he is used to his bloody profession. He is paralyzed with astonishment . . . Next to him his better half; she wanted to come along." Elfriede Jelinek, *The Piano Teacher*, p. 21.

40 See Jean-Joseph Goux, "General Economics and Postmodern Capitalism", *Yale French Studies*, no. 78, 1990.

41 "The capitalist economy is founded on a metaphysical uncertainty regarding the object of human desire. It must create this desire through the invention of the new, the production of the unpredictable." Goux, "General Economics and Postmodern Capitalism", *Yale French Studies*, no. 78, 1990, p. 212.

42 Elfriede Jelinek, *Die Klavierspielerin*, Reinbeck, Rowohlt Verlag GmbH, 1983; *The Piano Teacher*, trans. Joachim Neugroschel, New York, Weidenfeld and Nicolson, 1988. Subsequent page references given in the text.

43 "Ultimately, the only things that count are creases, wrinkles, cellulite, gray hair, bags under the eyes, large pores, artificial teeth, glasses, and loss of the figure." Jelinek, *Klavierspielerin*, p. 168.

44 However, this tactility is steered to vision: "Like a blind mole . . . . for a brief moment, Erika manages to see her mother's sparse pubic hair, which closes off the fat belly . . . Erika cunningly uncovered her mother . . ." Jelinek, *Klavierspielerin*, p. 234.

45 Sigmund Freud, "The Economic Problem of Masochism"; Gilles Deleuze, *Coldness and Cruelty/Venus in Furs*, Cambridge, MIT Press, 1993.

46 Erika plays the role of Severin, the male masochist, and feminizes Klemmer into the role of Fanny, while at the same time playing that role herself through her different costumes.

47 Quoted in http://kirjasto.sci.fi/jelinek.htm.

3

Paris circa 1968: Cool Space, Decoration, Revolution

This is a chapter about the fate of stuff in the post-World War II era of glass. With postwar consumer and work culture adopting minimalist functionalism as its house style, what was the fate of the object to be? In France after the war, for example, the minimalist clean lines and glass curtain walls of prewar modernist architecture became the approved and official style of the whole society. Cleanliness, smoothness, transparency, convenience, a complete lack of ornament: the white wall and the glass box became ubiquitous and characteristic of the new modernization. In this context, the object, even the stray commodity, became all the more excessive and out of place in a milieu shorn of ornament. In the interwar years, as a means to assert alternative subjectivities, different still-cluttered sites allowed for a certain manipulation of the stuff that had gone out of style or been cast aside. With postwar functionalism, the abstraction of all space, its rigorous organization into efficient spaces of traffic, circulation, work, and leisure, was matched by a new, smooth minimalism. In this starker world, stuff was utterly homeless and out of place, yet it persisted. Its recuperation as the details that interrupt the new gloss, the debris that makes the barricades of 1968, or the "inefficient" clutter of the home, declares the power of hybrid materiality over modern asepsis.

In the materialist critiques of the period we witness, first, a turn to the everyday as a temporal category where difference can still be negotiated, and second, a turn to the question of the organization of space. Henri Lefebvre is the French theorist of this period who made space his central preoccupation. Roland Barthes, Jean Baudrillard, and Guy Debord all wrote about things and commodities and their roles in modern French culture; for each, the tropes of space, surface, and transparency are key. In the first part of this chapter I show how their work, reacting to the new orthodoxy of minimalist style in postwar modernization, in a sense shares this minimalist impulse. Barthes, in his reading of some characteristic new commodities, searches for the "language-object" as the degree-zero of the object. Baudrillard announces the flatness of "simulation" as the modus of the new order. Debord turns the three-dimensionality of consumer culture into the two-dimensional image of the "spectacle." The effect of their moves, in each case, is to see the problem posed by the object in spatial terms. The question for these critics is this: if all lived space is now commodified, that is, fully managed for the smooth flow of consumers, goods, and money, then what possibilities exist to escape from or challenge this very system? If the whole environment is now commodified and controlled, how can the subject even imagine staging resistance, or reinstituting real contact with the material world? What are the stakes of imagining this contact as "real"?

The answer, it turns out, is by attending to the place of stuff, now more recalcitrant, embarrassing, and anomalous than ever, in relation to this new relentlessly smoothed-out spatial regime. To illuminate a new stage in the modern understanding of materiality, in this chapter we turn to postwar France. The post-World War II period in Europe was a sweeping moment of modernization, where a high Fordist reorganization of spaces accompanied an intensified level of production and consumption. This was sustained by an ideology that presented progress as inevitable and universal, and self-advertised by a vast new array of consumer objects, all presented in settings— the shopping center, the motorway, the modern home—that stressed smooth minimalist efficiency and the abstraction of space. The promise of happiness and pleasure through things that could be acquired accompanied the promise of leisure and freedom that modern functionalism claimed to champion. Hence the washing machine that does the work for you, the car that transports you . . . to work, and saves you time. The new commodity culture relies upon a full-scale rationalization of time and space, based on a scientific organization of life and labor modeled on American modes of corporate and social management. Yet in this smooth system, as we shall see, transparency was an illusion, an illusion which the clutter of stuff, a result of the new super-abundance of commodities, would expose. Europe during the 1950s and 1960s underwent the type of socio-economic transformation that the US had experienced earlier in the century, but the speed of Europe's modernization led to cultural changes which made the contradictions of capitalism's promises more visible.

While intensified production, consumption, and affluence characterized all the western European Marshall Plan countries after the war, in France the new conditions generated not only social change but an intense response in cultural analysis, film, and literature. The new realities of the boom became the preoccupation of an array of French intellectuals, writers, and film-makers: Henri Lefebvre, Roland Barthes, Cornelius Castoriadis, Alain Touraine, Jean Baudrillard, Jacques Tati, Jean-Luc Godard, Marcel Carné, Georges Perec, Simone de Beauvoir, and Elsa Triolet. After having been defined in phenomenological and existentialist terms in the 1940s and 1950s, the question of materiality and of the object is now articulated in historical materialist and structuralist terms, first as a critique aimed at producing social change, and second as a synchronic analysis of a system that seemed unchangeable, and yet whose functioning can produce its own pleasures, as Baudrillard and Barthes attest. In most cases, whether as signifying system or dialectical battlefield, the terrain of culture becomes the rallying point of an anti-bourgeois critique, the program, or the background noise of May 1968.

I concentrate on the period between 1958 and 1968, between De Gaulle's return to power and the May *événements*, to read the materiality and the consumer materialism of those years symptomatically, as speaking for the absences, the silences, the unsaid of the happiness promised by consumption and by a technologically enhanced life. The boom made postwar France the testing ground for a number of assumptions and hopes that had been developed in the previous generation by the modernist avant-garde, particularly those regarding the organization of social space and materiality. While the postwar commodity and its system proves over and over again that Benjamin's utopia of the object is definitely out, the negotiations between modern and unmodern, streamlined void and clutter, interior and street, show that in some cases the adversarial stance of the modernists can be reactivated, to suggest a form of collective resistance and critical dissent from the status quo, which takes place in the everyday.

In the array of voices which address changed conditions in postwar France, I chose those of Barthes, Baudrillard, and Debord, to show that while each focuses on the commodity-object, they all come to terms with the issue of the commodity in abstracted, smoothed-out space—the new efficient space of the modern state. From 1953, the year of publication of Barthes' *Mythologies*, to 1967, with the publication of Baudrillard's *The System of Objects* and of Debord's *Society of Spectacle*, their work spans the decade that leads to 1968 and its opposition to the democracy of consumption and efficiency as the newest form of bourgeois power. Barthes', Baudrillard's, and Debord's critique of stuff and of the myths of consumption complicates the matter-of-fact coolness of the commodity and the claimed transparency of its setting, to expose instead its imbrication in questions of class, privatization, and the social. This renegotiation of the relation of materiality and consumption is further elaborated by the cinema and the literature of the period. In the second section I turn to a film-maker and a novelist, Jacques Tati and Georges Perec, whose work highlights the unevenness of the miraculous happiness of modernity, as well as the pitfall of its functionalism; we examine Georges Perec's novel *Les Choses* (*Things*, 1965), and Jacques Tati's film *Playtime* (1969). On the set of *Playtime* Tati reconstructed the glass and steel architecture of the 1950s; replicating the building of La Défense with his "Tativille," he undercut modern urbanism's claims to transparency. Perec's provocation of the unmodern is at the center of his novel *Les Choses*, where *le vide* is filled with antiques and bric-à-brac as advertised in *Madame L'Express* magazine. For Perec the opposition of public and private, which makes social space disappear, becomes the occasion for a melancholic commentary on class inequality, youth, happiness, and the costs of technocratic modernization. Both Tati and Perec foreground unmodern stuff as the key to cracking the perfectly seamless glass surfaces of the spaces of consumption and modern workplace management. The transparency of glass, Tati's obsession in *Playtime*, is the perfect image for how a material is put to work for the apparent abstraction and derealization of space. This modern glass wants to prove that matter can disappear altogether—and with it history, and its hurt. In the work of Tati and Perec, however, matter's traces, as stuff, persist and strike back.

As Henri Lefebvre, Cornelius Castoriadis, and Rossanda Rossanda[1] theorized in these years, the revolution, when it can no longer be the proletariat's taking over the state and the means of production, implies the taking over of the everyday, and the reorganization of space and of materiality against the consumerist imperatives of the modern. In this sense the 1960s saw a resistance to the functionalism and technocracy of the previous decade, through a rejection of the claim of the modernist architectural avant-garde and its 1950s offshoots to have replaced nineteenth-century clutter with clean voids. The revolution's "right to the street," in Lefebvre's words, was made manifest in the rubble of the barricades, clutter, and bodily disorder. In contrast to the ascetic renunciation of stuff that becomes the sign of the revolutionary ethos of "traveling light," from Che Guevara to Mao Tze Tung,[2] in the First World the revolution would be signaled by a disruption of the order of public and private space, and by the disarray of objects. Bertolucci's film *The Dreamers* (2003), based on Gilbert Adair's 1988 novel, puts this potential of clutter into focus. Revisiting 1968, Bertolucci represents not so much the revolution, as the making of the bourgeois revolutionary as "homeless," renouncing privacy at the time when the street takes over the home. At the core of this implosion of the interior and its merging into the street, is the material body—now an emboldened sign of desire and transgression.

The 1950s and 1960s are the decades when the modernist avant-garde language of social change through a revolution is uttered for the last time in the west, in, for example, the fiery writing of Guy Debord and Claude Lefort, before the post-Fordism and poststructuralism of the recessionary 1970s and Thatcherite 1980s. It was a period when the revolution as reappropriation of the everyday, as labor and play, is still regarded as possible. It is also the time when the system of objects of modern capital, that is, commodification, the transformation of every object into a consumer product to be bought and sold, came to be applied to space. Space too was commodified—and the effect of this commodification on modern space was to make it seem smooth, abstracted, derealized. (Later, Marc Augé would call the new language "non-place": the featureless new worlds of airports, freeways, shopping centers, office blocks, chain hotels). To shatter this illusion of spatial transparency, French theorists and artists turned to stuff, the recalcitrant object interrupting the smooth new urban-scape, to envisage a resistance to the relentless smoothness of the everyday.

I. Paris Circa 1958

The fantasy of a total techno-environment where life is perfectly and efficiently run, while objects and machines guarantee the least expenditure of energy for the individual, a key effect of Fordism, was at the core of the Americanization of French life in the 1950s. The impact of American investment was also visible at the cultural level: now "lifestyle," centered on mobility and consumption at the shopping center, in the suburb, by car, took over, and being modern was measured against American standards. The productivist principles and technological advances imported with commodities and gadgets—Lefebvre's "cargo cult"[3]—structured social life on the American model. The principle of efficiency and function came to define the space of the factory, the office, the planned city and the home: the housewife becomes a "domestic engineer," while De Gaulle employs his *ministres techniciens*.

If "system" and "function" are the key economic and managerial categories, they also notably pervade the cultural and intellectual terrain of French life at the time. If factory automation was matched at home by the efficient kitchen of the 1950s, systematization also become the organizing principle of the philosophical discourse of structuralism, which, through Lévi-Strauss, and then Barthes, Lacan, and Althusser, overtake Sartrean existentialism with an anti-humanism that complements the technical aspect of Fordist efficiency. As Kristin Ross notes, "structural man takes the real, decomposes it, then recomposes it in the view of creating intelligibility underlying the *objet*; he creates the object's simulacrum … Subjectivity, consciousness, agency … are effaced to the profit of rules, codes, structures" (161). The system the structuralist studies can be explained, but not changed. This functionalist principle, economic as well as philosophic, is at the core of the ideology of modernization. It excludes history in the name of a perfect present. The citizen is invited to enjoy his "lifestyle," or, if he reads the theorists, to enjoy its contradictions as chilly ironies, certainly not to change the system. Politics and the public sphere, as well as theory, is in the hands of specialists, and the individual perceives himself as a cog in a mechanism of which he is part but which he cannot transform. This renunciation of history articulates the system's dominant ideology: one reads modernization as a tale either of happiness achieved, or of total bureaucratization that disables both collective and individual agency. The social ideal of Gaullist France is a classless nation predicated on modernity, efficiency, consumption, and centered upon the comforting space of home. Ross intelligently connects the privatization of life in the 1950s and 1960s to decolonization, and we can extend this to the rationalization of all space at the time. With the loss of Indochina after the battle of Dien Bien Phu in 1954 and Algerian independence in 1962, France abandoned the public, extraterritorial space of the Empire to retrench within its national borders. French colonial administration techniques could merge with the clockwork efficiency of the new French bureaucratic state, and the principles of modernity, function, and hygiene which had defined French identity in the colony could now help mold a post-imperial Frenchness: to be French is to be modern. What Lefebvre calls "the colonization of everyday life" becomes a temporal and spatial compartmentalization, now split between work and home, city and suburbs, home and shopping center, work and leisure.

This middle ground between the workers' labor and bourgeois free existence in consumption is the terrain of the *jeune cadre*, the young executive, a new social figure on whom is centered the mythology of modernization and efficiency. The young executive is of the class to which Perec's protagonists in *Les Choses* belong. As a new version of the clerk of the prewar era, he is the fantasy figure of the executive whose allegiance to the company makes him key to social stability, his potential *ressentiment* reabsorbed by his newly acquired power of consumption and newly formed taste, which his wife learns from women's magazines.[4] The *cadre* stands as a cipher of the claimed disappearance of labor and of the universal *embourgeoisement* promised by modernization: his identity is divided between the public sphere of his job, and the private sphere of consumption in the home, of which his access to credit gives him full use. Perec, as we will see, illustrates the (painful) contradiction of this "clean body in a fast car"; for our discussion, consider how the mystique of the *jeune cadre* is founded on an assumption of his activity as "clean" work, by which his office job is presented as a form of professionalism rather than labor, and is marked as smooth, efficient, and ultra-modern. The same cleaning up is at work at the time in the management of urban space.

It was only when the structuralist analysis of the contradictions inherent in any given object was allied to an analysis of the whole national space that a critique of the new phase of modernization could be articulated. The 1950s and 1960s witnessed a dramatic reorganization of Paris, the most famous example being the moving of Les Halles, *le ventre de Paris*, to Rungis. This reorganization contradicts the promise that modernization is universal, and exposes the unevenness of modernization at the time. The center of Paris is sanitized by pushing out to peripheral *banlieues* huge numbers of "unmodern" citizens, the poor, proletarians, and immigrants, who lose, in Lefebvre's words, "the right to the city." In contrast with the national rhetoric of inclusive modernization, this implies that those who cannot properly consume should leave. The critique of urbanism developed by both Lefebvre and the Situationists originates with this exclusion, focusing first on everyday experience and then on the organization of urban space. Attending to the quotidian in terms of space and materiality had been inaugurated with Lefebvre's *Everyday Life* (1947). Lefebvre's logic is that the new stage of modernization is managed by a penetration of capital in the most personal and apparently insignificant moments of one's lived experience, making it an everyday effect. However if the everyday is fully structured by capital, it is also the terrain of a possible attempt to resist its power. This becomes the project, and the meaning, of 1968: as Castoriadis wrote, "The project of the revolution is to reappropriate one's sovereignty over one's daily life, away from specialists and specializations, and use this sovereignty for a *projet* to live collectively and "totally"" (230). The aim is to change the modalities of social reproduction and eliminate the specialization and fragmentation of knowledge and practices, to understand "whatever remains", in Lefebvre's words, "after one has eliminated all specialized activities."[5] This everyday, in its ordinariness, manifests itself particularly in the spatial dimension, in the organization of space and structuring of time, the regimented and scheduled existence of masses of people in modernity. This is the rhythm, for Lefebvre, of "a carefully controlled passivity," which segregates life's activities and traps the individual in a spiral of consumption presented as pleasurable choice. Festivals and ruptures of this coercive organization cannot truly change it, and Lefebvre was only a hesitant supporter of the "festival" of 1968. The segregation and passivity that marks the everyday can be changed, he felt, only by changing how space itself is organized, and, through a critique of everyday life, changing critical thought, which he defined in *The Urban Revolution* as "the criticism of objects and subjects, sections and domains" (140). As we shall see, in this "criticism of objects," stuff, the marginal, outmoded and demoted object superfluous to the needs of modernization, could play a "minor" but vital role.

Lefebvre's words define the critical activity of the three theorists to whom I now turn. Notwithstanding their differences, Barthes the militant mythologist, Baudrillard the Maoist structuralist, and Debord the Dada and post-Surrealist Marxist, all take the everyday, its spaces, activities, objects, as their field of inquiry, aiming to transgress the system of segregated knowledge in a move that for Lefebvre is the aim of critical theory. Their work identifies a constellation of elements through which modern everyday materiality can possibly be redeemed. The object, in their rethinking of the spatial order of late modernity, shares a recognizable set of features. First, they all focus on its abstraction, discerning in the commodified object itself the abstraction that also characterizes the new modern spaces. They each then read the modern evaporation of the object in forms of consumption that are linguistic, ideological, and visual. In this abstraction of the object into a sign, they note a new intensification of its function as signifier of social distinction, its capability to produce cultural capital. Next, they attend to its way of ordering space into private versus public zones; the street becomes a crucial element for all three critics. Finally, each writes about the consumer object's intransitivity; the modern object, as Baudrillard points out, does not return the subject's gaze. Both Barthes and Debord, and to a lesser degree Baudrillard, who sees it as fully co-optable by capital, then foreground the importance of the dysfunctional and the "unmodern" object, that is, stuff, recalling Benjamin's interest in the dustier contents of the arcades but extending the scope of stuff as marker of dissonance in the newly smooth, clean, and efficient system. If Benjamin's stuff had found a kindred resting place in the backwaters of an earlier commerce, in the 1950s world of clean and shining modernity, stuff had nowhere to hide. In the face of the consumption of the new, in an environment that smooths over the mechanisms of capital's social relations, the old and unmodern can finally and more starkly become a spontaneous and adversarial conduit for experiencing life and reappropriating an affective and historicizing relation to materiality.

II. Materiality and Modernization I: Roland Barthes' Rib

Mythologies (1957), Barthes' most direct encounter with the objects of postwar French culture, collects his articles written from 1954 to 1956 for *Les Lettres Nouvelles* on objects from the housewife's net bag to the Eiffel Tower. These object-studies are capped with the essay "Myth Today," explaining his semiological method. The book bespeaks his wonder at objects and their magic, reminding one strongly of Benjamin; as Susan Sontag notes, this is the most political moment in the work of an aesthete, "one of the great refusers of history."[6]

If myth, as Barthes states in "Myth Today," is a form of speech, inevitably materiality gets abstracted into a system of signification which, as myth, further removes language from the real, and from people's material conditions of existence. Modern myth works by freezing the multiplicity, indeterminacy and drift of the signifier into one fixed signified, which for Barthes serves the purposes of doxa, "public opinion, the mind of the majority, petty bourgeois consciousness, the voice of Nature . . . arrogant ideology."[7] As "a language of robbery" (*Reader*, 118), myth essentializes history into nature, makes it disappear into an eternal present as an uninterrogated factuality, and makes bourgeois values appear universal. If myth is the all-encompassing *Weltanschaung* of the bourgeoisie, "the social class that does not want to be named", (126), and which has welded its particular interests to the discourse of humanism, and now nationalism, what constitutes resistance? Who can contest and attack the power of this class? Not the avant-garde, which is itself bourgeois,[8] and certainly not the petty bourgeoisie, immersed in the vulgarity of derivative language of consumer culture and the everyday (for Barthes sees nothing redemptive and redeemable in the everyday), through which the bourgeoisie stretches its *longa manus*. Only the working class, if it could only speak, and make its "monotonous", but "real" language be heard, could contest the bourgeoisie's power.

If myth is depoliticized speech which naturalizes historical intention and eternalizes contingency, its reifying charge must be opposed by a counter-language. Postulating a relationship between signifier and referent without the mediation of the myth, the language-object reaffirms the utopia of Adamic language, the zero degree of signification of the Barthesian "neutral," but rendered here in a more politicized perspective.[9]

The language-object is the concept through which Barthes attempts to re-establish the transference between a fully vibrant object and the eloquence that would fully comprehend its significance. The contemplative, passive spell of consumption, the key myth for modernity, must be replaced with the action of production, work, and the transformation of reality. This language, capable as it is of redressing "the loss of the historical quality of things . . . the memory that they were once made" (132) is what Barthes, referring to Marx in *The German Ideology*, calls the language-object. Inscribed by "the more or less memorable presence of the human act which has produced, or fitted up, used, subjected, or rejected it" (134), the language-object "speaks things". Barthes opposes the contemplation of the object in myth, which prepackages the consumer object, to an active relationship to materiality, in which language does not celebrate things but "acts them." This act is work, but it is also the object's subsequent use.[10] By granting the speaking subject an instrumental grasp of the world, the language-object, "the language of man as producer … [aims] to transform reality and no longer to preserve it as an image …."(135). Here the language-object is for Barthes the language of production, of the oppressed, and of the revolution, but is also accessible to the object's user. Barthes' invocation of working-class language is hagiographic but not a blind romanticism. It allows the subject to make the world rather than being acted upon by the world of commodities.

Barthes translates Marx's critical theory into the semiology of the signifier. The language-object is Barthes' dream of a perfect correspondence between "bare materiality" and a language degree zero. It would be a language divested of myth, just as the commodity might be divested of its fetish status. However, just in the same way that this cannot occur, and that once the object is a commodity its fetishistic quality is inevitable, Barthes' dream of a language-object is also the result of a degree of idealism on his part. This is evident, when he moves to speak, in an even more fully historical materialist key, of the oppressed. The opposition between oppressor and oppressed is posed by Barthes in terms of scarcity versus abundance, of poverty versus luxury, of use, which signifies the real, versus expenditure, cast as false. This places the bourgeoisie on the side of linguistic luxury, while "the speech of the oppressed is monotonous but real … This essential barrenness produces rare, threadbare myths" (135). In this romantic formulation, however, the oppressed subject's language, and his objects, are cast again in ascetic terms. Barthes recognizes that his own metalanguage is luxurious, so that he, as a self-confessed expert himself in the modern system, runs the risk of celebrating what he wants to critique: "For if we penetrate the object, we liberate it but destroy it; and if we acknowledge its full weight, we respect it, but we restore it to a state which is still mystified … we are condemned for some time yet to speak excessively about reality." The language-object, then, is a flawed weapon of critique, but it testifies to Barthes' desire for reality and materiality at the time when the object is being erased by being abstracted and made into a spectacle by myth. Barthes makes clear that there is a reality of the object that is not ontological but dialectical, that can only be spoken by its maker or possibly its user, not the expert. He finds himself, then, in the Faustian (or, given Barthes' aesthete-persona, the Dorian Grayish) predicament of the mythologist, prisoner of the structuralist-materialist desire to distinguish and separate the pure from the impure, frustrated at being forever condemned not to speak the object because he doesn't produce it. This materiality that, Barthes here suggests, can only be spoken by the person who worked on it, he will in his later work generalize into his notion of the irreducibility of the material—of the body, the neutral, and even the photographed object.[11]

When we turn to the individual essays of *Mythologies* and its array of objects, the contradictions of the mythologist as impossible producer are partially superseded by the sheer pleasure of criticism as a form at once of production and consumption, as Barthes fully displays the luxury of his own speech. The myths of French modern culture are unhinged from their mythic signifiers to meander into the paradoxical sphere of the almost language-object. Following Barthes among his celebrities, food, cars, toys, while dutifully critiquing the myths' complicity with consumerism, we cannot ignore his embracing of modern consumer objects' wondrous magic. His excitement, however, is not the pleasure of the commodity, but the pleasure of reading against the bourgeois grain. The essays have the quality of baroque conceits; they focus on the unexpected clash of semiotic codes. In "Operation Margarine", for example, Barthes shows how the advertisement for Astra margarine illustrates the way the Established Order affirms its power; in another, famously, he tells how the striptease, as "a meticulous exorcism of sex", de-eroticizes the female body. The shock of the defamiliarizing conceit should move the object from its context of the consumer's everyday into another code and reveal its actual meaning; two detergents are marketed as utterly different, obscuring the fact, as he laconically points out, that "there is a plane where Persil or Omo are one and the same: the plane of the Anglo-Dutch trust Unilever" (38). Barthes' pitch for the anti-mythical power of the producer is re-evoked in his lamenting the disappearance of wooden toys before the sterile chemistry of plastic, characterized by

> an appearance at once gross and hygienic [which] destroys all the pleasure, the sweetness, the humanity of touch ... [wood instead] is a familiar and poetic substance which does not sever the child from close contact with the tree, the table, the floor. Wood ... can last a long time, live with the child, alter little by little the relations between the object and the hand (54).

This is a celebration of an organic unmodern that, if it doesn't speak the object, nonetheless cites history, the history of gesture, of the touch that imprints the body into materiality. The battered wooden toy bonds subject and object, this time through play rather than labor. This dream of sensuous contact between subject and object is not without its nostalgia, a nostalgia which keeps alive a sense of the commodities' allure, even for a demythologizer such as Barthes. The seismologist's work of revealing the illusion behind its magic, in a switching operation, also works as a reverse tribute, which reveals the commodities' attraction. The commodity gets to be cleverly deceptive as well as glamorously itself.

The value of the imperfect object, here the wooden toy, capable of carrying the imprints of history, is pitted against the fetishism of the perfect surface that seamlessly slides the object into the circuit of the master-signifieds of modernity. Hence the pristine, always-made-new surface of the car, of the New Citroën as "the superlative object," or of the g-string of the striptease dancer, covered in diamonds: "This ultimate triangle, by its pure and geometrical shape, by its hard and shiny material, bars the way to the sexual parts [with] the irrefutable symbol of the absolute object; that which serves no purpose" (85). Against this fetishistic smoothing and cleansing of matter, Barthes, within the terms of his critique, wants to privilege the objects that suggest the instability and unconstrainable mobility of the signifier. In this mythic reading, the fake diamond refuses the dancer's movement any real contact with another subject, and thus, any change. In his search for the materiality of flow, he even praises the new material he had attacked in his essay on toys, plastic:

> So, more than a substance, plastic is the very idea of its infinite transformation . . . a miraculous substance: a miracle is always a sudden transformation of nature. Plastic remains impregnated throughout with this wonder: it is less a thing than a trace of a movement . . . This wonder, however, is re-absorbed into the prosaic uses to which it is converted, the necessary freezing of its movement of inexistent substance, into objects (99).

His own terms of reference, therefore, as in this case, do not allow for his admiration of flow and change to be followed: only critique of the fixed mythic object is possible. This undermines the radical potential of the critique, the admiration for the bare language-object of the worker notwithstanding. Despite the playful tone of the writing, this is high semiology, aimed at the readers of *Les Lettres Nouvelles* rather than those of *Paris Match*—who will never know what the detergents really mean. It is no surprise therefore that Barthes' brush with the politics of contemporary culture here is replaced later in his career with an impatience toward politics and any type of institution.[12] Once the revolution becomes coopted by institutional power, as happened, he felt, after 1968, the only possible revolution takes place in language. Literature as "speech outside the bonds of power," ("Lecture," 462) becomes the site of "the splendor of a permanent revolution in language," whose aim is no longer praxis but *jouissance*. Now the social reality that in *Mythologies* had been spoken by the language-object is abandoned: "the real is not representable, and it's because men ceaselessly try to represent it by words that there is a history of literature" (465). The drift of desire takes Barthes away from history and to the body, which now becomes *the* means through which materiality is reapproached. This time, in his "dream of a world which would be exempt from meaning (as one is from the military service)", (*Roland Barthes by Roland Barthes*, 87) he tries to affirm an absolute materiality wherein the distinction between subject and object, surface and depth, can no longer be upheld. In his analysis of Japan, *Empire of Signs*, he radicalizes materialism[13] to affirm matter as "insignificant," that is, beyond signification. As the example of the photograph in *Camera Lucida*, his last work, wants to show, the materiality of history is replaced for the subject by an overpowering presence of the Real in Lacan's psychoanalytic sense, where even fetishism, once the object as substitute fragment is gone, is also lost.

Even the body, in his late work, is similarly defetishized. A fragment of *Roland Barthes by Roland Barthes*, "*La Cotolette*" ("The Rib Chop"), playfully highlights the critic's dissociation from any fetishism of the body—a fetishism rampant at the time in consumer culture, as well as in the liberated sexuality of the 1960s. Here Barthes contemplates a part of his body literally made into an object, a fragment of his rib cut away in an operation years earlier, and given to him by his Swiss surgeon, as a part of himself, his own possession. The *cotolette* has lain for years among bric-à-brac in a drawer,

> And then one day, realizing that the function of any drawer is to ease, to acclimate the death of objects by causing them to pass through a sort of pious site, a dusty chapel where, in the guise of keeping them alive, we allow them a decent interval of dim agony, but not going so far as to dare cast this bit of myself into the common refuse bin of my building, I flung the rib chop and its gauze from my balcony, as if I were romantically scattering my own ashes, into the Rue Servandoni, where some dog would come and sniff them out" (*RB by RB*, 61).

Objects, in Barthes' anecdote, die like people, and people's bodies become objects, but not according to the rules of a fetishistic transformation of the human into the inanimate. Rather, the game of philosophical prestidigitation encoded in the anecdote makes the subject and the object co-participants and equals, their places repeatedly exchangeable in back and forth moves. The body is shown as disposable, but it gets a good send-off with a comically ritualistic gesture by a subject who uncannily contemplates a piece of himself as object, or better, as junk. Any possible fetishization of the body is preempted by Barthes' final gesture. The self and the body, the subject and matter are now even, their differences annulled in the name of that neutrality to which Barthes's theory of materiality aims.[14] The fetishistic desire to possess and preserve is disqualified; the body-as-object is returned to its negativity, a negativity faced through the comic inertia of Barthes' neutrality. This is a body that can be approached only in its drifting, in its flux from one state to another.

If in *Camera Lucida* materiality deprived of signification—the photograph as *punctum*—points to the silence of death, the material photograph is turned into a cipher of the Lacanian Real, which interrupts the signifying chain. In *"La Cotolette"*, disposing of his body part-turned-object is for Barthes a non-fetishistic way of exorcising death: not by preserving and accumulating, but by getting rid of stuff. With this act of throwing out, now that the subject and its object have been made equivalent and equivalently neutral, he also disposes of the self. Tossing the bone from his balcony, just as in the case of his desire for a minimalist "language-object," Barthes participates in the modernizing cult of clean minimalist spatial organization, getting rid of his stuff. Like Althusseur's fully-interpellated modern subject, who kneels even though he does not believe, Barthes is fully aware of the power of a totalizing commodification but finds it almost impossible to escape its power to structure even his own subjecthood.

III. Materiality and Modernization II: Jean Baudrillard

In *The System of Objects* (1968) and *Society of Consumption* (1970), Baudrillard too theorizes the cultural meaning of objects in consumer culture, and decides that materiality has become irrevocably alienated and abstracted into an all-encompassing system of signs. The first book studies the morphology of the system through which single objects enter the semiotic-libidinal order of capital,[15] the second focuses instead on the massive effect of consumption on 1960s French culture, judging that objects lose any material and historical weight by inevitably becoming the pure function of the prevailing semiotic system. Materiality, along with categories such as nature, the body, labor, the Symbolic, and death, is in Baudrillard's view now disqualified from producing subjective affect, in a new phase of consumer affectlessness which means that these categories are hardly experienced at all. We have seen how the arc of Barthes' analysis moves from having language as sign and the object as transparent materiality coincide in the language-object, to the suggestion that the body alone can be an anchor of the material in a full-scale empire of signs. In Baudrillard's work the question of what motivates the critique of the demise of tactile contact between subject and the material world is even more sharply posed. His apocalyptic claim is that now is the age of simulation, time of the wholesale death of affect. Here we see again, in terms more stark than those of Barthes, the claim that the material has given way to the semiotic register. He claims that the abstraction of the system is so intense that the immateriality of signs is now all that the subject apprehends. For Baudrillard, escape from the circuits of simulation is impossible. In "Towards a Definition of Consumption," which concludes *The System of Objects*, he insists on the limitless quality of consumption. "If it has any meaning at all," he claims, "Consumption means an activity consisting of the systematic manipulation of signs" (200). When Baudrillard turns to examples of this sign-system, his focus is on the spatial. To illustrate how commodity culture's regime of simulation invades social space and the privacy of interiors, for example, we will consider his analysis of functional "home furnishings," and of collecting as a counter-system of objects.

In the modern home, Baudrillard sees "symbolic values . . . supplanted by organizational value" (21), as he moves his critique from objects to the space that contains them. There taste, a form of "poetic discourse" in which objects responded to one another and communicate, is taken over by "an overall coherence" that deprives the object of the function it had had for millennia, that is, the task of "personifying human relations." Instead mass-produced furniture, systemic and modular, denies the "primordial function" of objects as "vessels of inwardness" in which matter is shaped by nature and becomes a reflection of it. In this logic, Baudrillard implies an almost organic ideal relation between the object and the individual, produced through the form that man imparts to it, in what he calls "a visceral intimacy". The modern culture of consumption and its system of objects has changed all this. What Barthes discerned as the object's carrying the trace of labor is for Baudrillard not simply silenced by myth, but actually lost. In the perfectly communicating system of signs that is the modern home everything has to be functional: "Everything has to intercommunicate, everything has to be functional—no more secrets, no more mysteries" (29). Amidst the kitchen's chrome and the plastic, as an after-effect of Taylorism, the human gesture, once the mark of "instinctual drives" and labor, becomes stylized, and any sign of the expenditure of energy suppressed "by *the great shift from a universal gestural system of labor to a universal gestural system of control*" (47).

Notwithstanding the nearly full saturation of the everyday by this system of objects as spatial control, Baudrillard tentatively sees ways of resisting it from within, with means the system itself provides. Antiques and collecting, which refuse pure functionality, are two examples of this oppositional logic. Antiques "symbolize an inward transcendence, that fantasy of that center-point in reality which nourishes all mythological consciousness"; collecting, because of the openness and the potential incompleteness of the collection, manages to compromise the closure of the system and its systematicity, affirming a certain transgressive imperfection. Collecting creates a parallel world where "passionate possession" replaces and defies function. When the subject becomes "master of a secret seraglio" (88) he chooses to passionately engage with objects and thus to fulfill his desire—or to embrace negativity by choosing never to complete the collection. Baudrillard admits that the collector's and consumer's relationship to the object is alienating for the subject, and makes the object "the recipient of a cathexis that 'ought' to have been invested in human relationships" (96). However, in his reading, the problem of alienation is recuperated as a means for the subject to exert control over his "singularity." "Once the authority of religion and ideology disappear," he contends, "there's nothing but objects through which the *Angst* and neuroses can be dissipated" (90). After speculating on the therapeutic qualities of collected objects he concludes:

> the object is that thing through which we construct our mourning: the object represents our own death, but that death is transcended (symbolically) by virtue of the fact that we *possess* the object; . . . Objects allow us to apply the work of mourning to ourselves right now, in everyday life, and this in turn allows us to live—to live regressively, no doubt, but at least to live (97).

The object helps us to cope with death once it has lost its anthropomorphic, political, and transcendent functions. Implicit in the image of Baudrillard's therapeutic object is a vision of stuff as dead matter (albeit magically resurrected by commodity fetishism), an inert surface upon which individual neurosis and anxieties can be inscribed and articulated. Because no transcendence is possible in the tightly organized, highly alienated, and utterly presentist system of signification that is consumption, objects help the individual to control and overcome his or her *Angst* about finitude.

At the end of *The System of Objects*, after a quote from Perec's *Les Choses*, Baudrillard writes: "there are no more projects, only objects. Not that the project has disappeared, exactly: it is just that its 'realization' as a sign embodied in the object is taken as satisfaction enough. The project of consumption is thus the precise form of the project of self-renunciation" (204). The project—of action, of social change, even of a volatile and affective relation of subject and vibrant object—is replaced once again by asceticism. The most Baudrillard can envision of this exchange between subject and object is a mirror function. The subject is capable of staging only an intransitive and claustrophobic relationship with the object. This foolproof system of identification, for the subject and the object alike, denies both any agency and meaning, except the tautology of their perfect identification. As he points out in *Society of Consumption*, the object is not the mirror, which still maintains a certain transitivity, but *la vitrine*, the shop window: "there's no more mirror . . ., where man faced his image . . .—but the shop window, geometric place of consumption, where the individual no longer sees his reflection, but gets absorbed in the contemplation of objects."[16]

Society of Consumption, where Baudrillard investigates the functioning of specific objects and locales—Le Drugstore, the planned community of Parly, Pop Art, kitsch and gadgets as Baroque emblems of post-industrial society— foregrounds not what materiality allows us to do, that is, our work of mourning, but what it disallows: *jouissance*. Contemporary abundance has, he claims, sanctioned the end of prodigality, a trait of premodern societies, that involved collective wasting rather than hoarding, using and abstracting materiality into economic or semiotic value. This end of prodigality as destruction of value points to consumer culture's denial of *jouissance* and of waste. Pleasure is replaced by "fun culture", which consists of trying out all the options offered by the system: "Thus the universal curiosity [spurred by advertisements] in cooking, cultural, scientific, religious, sexual matters. 'Try Jesus!' says an American slogan" (113). If stuff is hoarded rather than wasted or given as gifts, then *jouissance* is denied. The chief victim of the loss of *jouissance* is the body, "the most beautiful object of consumption" (109). Deprived of its negativity, as Baudrillard notes in *For a Political Economy of the Sign*,[17] placed at the center of a series of consumer preoccupations—hygiene, diet, beauty, elegance, youth—the body is treated as private property, and becomes instrumental, like every other object. Like any other object, "It can only emit signs", (203), which, in turn possess only the relational value conferred upon them by the system to which they belong. The transformation of the body into a sign of beauty or health is an act of sublimation aimed at containing the violence of desire, of negativity and of death. The ludic, which he explains as the manner in which we relate not only to objects, but more and more to all social practices and to people,[18] means merely playing with the combinatory possibilities offered by the system. This is what our fascination with gadgets simply expresses. The gadget has replaced unruly stuff.

Baudrillard, then, goes further than Barthes, whose minimalism only went as far as the "language-object," a pure coincidence of object and sign in which the worker or user of the object might name it, and who maintained a version of the body's exceptional materiality. For Baudrillard, in the dematerializing order of modernity, only signs are left. In this sweeping judgment, however, we might discern a theoretical version of the very same abstracting of space practiced by the newly modernizing consumerism itself. Like it, Baudrillard's own discourse also displays some pleasure in the totalizing seriality of the system: the society of consumption, the system of objects, appear as a given which simply exists in its present form. Like the system he describes, he too does not historicize, that is, discuss the present in historical terms. His brilliantly rendered vision of a total system dazzles the reader of his later works, making it difficult to decide whether the author's attitude to the culture of consumption is one of desperation or of ludic indifference. In these two texts of 1968 and 1970, written at the time of great social and cultural unrest, Baudrillard's present, curiously, has no past, and definitely no future.

IV. Materiality and Modernization III: Guy Debord

And yet ... by offering a theory which is as delirious and totalizing as the world it describes, Baudrillard's intervention offers a theoretical limit which only the improvisational, everyday, "minor" counter-tactics of artist-strategists such as the Situationists could think up. It's impossible to think of Debord, critic, film-maker, and *agent provocateur*, separately from the Situationist International (SI), a coterie of avant-garde critics, artists, and architects who, through their journals, art and politics, between 1957 and 1972 worked collectively on "situations," conferences and essays. The fluidity of the SI, their social and intellectual marginality, and the collective nature of their work are their most striking characteristics: the members joined, contributed, and left, often "dismissed" by Debord himself, in a transitoriness perfectly in step with the ideology they stood for. Significantly the title of Debord's 1959 film on the SI is *On the Passage of a Few People through a Rather Brief Unit of Time*: SI gatherings were ephemeral, its members there to carry out a project,[19] in an attitude of cultural disaffection and provocation, even sabotage. They wished to dismantle and reappropriate existing cultural forms, as is visible in their tactics: *la dérive, détournement*, and their refusal to work.

In a 1993 interview Debord points out that all his work is marked by "a taste for generalized negation" (Bracken, 35). The genealogy of this interest in negation takes us back to historical materialism and modernism. Debord's critical position merges Marxism as a modern critique of economic and cultural reality, Dada's iconoclastic desire to explode bourgeois order in a political use of art, Surrealism's interest in chance, the street, and *flânerie*, and, not least, the utopian social impulse of modern architecture and urbanism, taken from the Bauhaus. The Situationists proposed not only an analysis of life under modern capitalism, but a program to change it. At the time of an intensified standardization and abstraction of lived human relationships, predicated upon the principles of efficiency and consumption, Debord mounts an attack on alienation as it existed in both western bourgeois and Soviet forms. This is the basis of his analysis of what he calls "the society of the spectacle": the new form of capitalism, with new effects on people's lives, demands new types of resistance, to be articulated on the terrain of culture even more than on that of production. If capitalism is changing, went the logic of the SI, we need to change the revolution and its modalities.

The Situationist critique of capital centers on reification and its effect on social, specifically urban, spatial organization. Reification is the perversion of the Hegelian notion of *Verdingligung*, which in turn defines the Marxian notion of praxis—the human imprint on the material world, the materialization of human subjectivity and creativity into the object of labor. Under capitalism, this act is turned instead into *Versachlichung*, "thingification," the conversion of labor from an active human force into an object—that is, the transformation of labor, creativity, and human subjectivity into a thing that can be bought. At the social level, reification naturalizes an arrangement of social spaces that ensure the smooth functioning of the economic life of capitalism: these include the distinction between work time and leisure time, public and private life, office and home. In turn, reification manifests itself in the alienation of individuals from experience, in an intensified privatization of personal and social relations that makes it impossible to envision any form of real collectivity. The collective imaginary, to use Benjamin's term, is overtaken by the commodity, to the point where social life is imagined as a wide system of exchangeable commodities abstracted into signs. The pervasiveness of this system is the crux of Debord's *Society of the Spectacle* (1967), where, pre-Baudrillard, he theorizes that the commodity as sign has now been replaced by the commodity as image.

Published in November 1967 and sold out by May the following year, *Society of the Spectacle* is indeed a book of 1968. Widely read and translated, Debord's text was definitely on the 1960s reading list. The notion of spectacle pushes even further than did Barthes or even Baudrillard the idea that the abstraction of the material world and of every modality of the subject's encounter with it is the defining condition of capital's latest modernizing phase. The spectacle, note, is not myth; for Barthes in *Mythologies*, myth is a form of speech, so that its logic can be analyzed and dismantled by exposing the arbitrary coherence of signifier and signified. Nor is the system of images in which the spectacle manifests itself the same as the therapeutic sign-object that Baudrillard reads in psychoanalytical terms, which, as a means of mourning, still carries out a human function. With the spectacle, which sanctions the degradation of existence from "being" to "having," nothing is redeemable.

Written as a set of theses, and showing that Debord knows his Lukács, Korsch, and Lefebvre well, the book draws its force from its aphoristic mode. "The spectacle is not a collection of images," he writes, "but a social relation among people mediated by images. It is the self-portrayal of money in the epoch of its totalitarian management of the conditions of existence".[20] In the present cultural order, you can "see" experience, but not live it: "The spectacle in general, as the concrete inversion of life, is the autonomous movement of the non-living" (2). For Debord, the final abstraction of the commodity into spectacle has forever changed the nature of materiality since the only experience of it we can have is the experience of owning it. The material quality of reality has been superseded, and so have lived experience, human relations, time, and space. All that is left is the subject's contemplative absorption in the spectacle, which "is the nightmare of modern society that ultimately expresses nothing more than its desire to sleep." (29). It steals the subject's gestures: "the more he contemplates, the less he lives; the more he accepts recognizing himself in the dominant images of need, the less he understands his own experience and his own desires ... This is why the spectator feels at home nowhere, because the spectacle is everywhere" (29). This final abstraction of materiality had a further side effect which Debord terms the falsification of time and space. Going beyond Baudrillard, he points out what he considers the erasure of time: "On all ... fronts of the advertising onslaught, it is strictly forbidden to grow old." Unlike Baudrillard, Debord wants to reclaim social life and its spaces from spectacle's abstraction, and he does this by thinking spatially.

By developing a theory of the totalizing power of consumer culture, Debord paradoxically frees the Situationists to imagine local, improvised interventions in the spaces of everyday life. His theorization of urban space, always a Situationist concern, coincides with the work of Lefebvre, with whom Debord shared ideas from the late 1950s onwards.[21] In Debord's sweeping analysis, dominant culture, while valorizing the privacy of home, and fostering the false dislocation of tourism, immobilizes the individual in spaces where crowds are marshaled but collectivity is no longer possible. The system, he wrote, requires that individuals be "*isolated* together" in tourist resorts and factories. Modern urbanism's aim is "the suppression of the street ... the liquidation of the city" (172–6) in the name of the maximization of profit and of social control. Yet at the moment when the logic of reification, amplified by the spectacle, seems to have taken over all aspects of reality, he refuses to regard this order as perfectly sutured and calls for "the representation of negation" in the sphere of the everyday, where, he insisted, the artist-revolutionary, intervening in practices of spatial organization, can change reality.

How is Debord's notion of spectacle related to Benjamin's dialectical image? Key here is an understanding of the relation between image and space. When Debord, after Lefebvre, talks of unmaking the logic of capital by turning from the spectacle to space, that is, of transforming the flatness of the spectacle into the multidimensionality of social, urban, concrete space, he is invoking an act which Benjamin had already attempted in his work. From Benjamin to Debord the image, as a mental operation acting in and on time, turns into a practice situated in space. For Benjamin the object gets spatialized in the stereoscopic dimension of the dialectical image in order to reclaim time: as an unstable mental space, the dialectical image takes one back to the past, to the history that has not yet happened, to an anterior past of whose promise the object is the emblem and the frozen memento. Now that both image and consciousness have been fully colonized by the spectacle, the image needs to be externalized in the lived urban space, to make it dialectical—a sign of contradiction and of new possibilities. For Benjamin, as we saw in Chapter 1, when we see reality allegorically, the image materializes into a mental space that we enter "shamanistically," to use Taussig's term: the act of seeing conjures up a stereoscopic mental space. Debord turns Benjamin on his head, so that what happened in the subject's mind is now projected onto urban space, where the subject experiences, instead of the empty, abstract, and homogeneous space of capital, the unevenness of social contradiction. This is what the Situationists want to make visible in their interventions in the city.[22]

With Debord, Benjamin's visuality of the dialectical image as mental act of historical memory is turned into the practice of the situation: the situation, *contra* the spectacle, through its defamiliarizing juxtapositions and provocations, becomes a way of acting out in the urban everyday, the mental work of shock, recognition, and remembrance that the dialectical image had offered, and that the integrated circuit of the spectacle no longer allows. The situation is a strategy of exposure and resistance, of which the revolution, for Debord, is the ultimate instance. "Our central purpose", as we read in one Situationist manifesto, "is the construction of situations, the concrete construction of temporary settings of life and their transformation into a higher, passionate nature. We must develop an intervention directed by the complicated factors of two great components in perpetual interaction: the material setting of life and the behaviors that it incites and that overturn it."[23] In practice this meant a mobilization of public space through the creation of a provocative environment that makes the everyday space strange. There, the conscious and active role of the Situationist is counterbalanced by his desire to be "acted upon" by the environment itself, to recognize what kind of affective changes a specific street produces in the subject. Turning public space into a setting for a situation renders the environment fluid, open to new possibilities, which produces new behaviors and desires which refuse the depoliticization of the street and the abstraction of the urban environment.

Debord's "situation" is matched by *la dérive*, another characteristic Situationist street tactic. As "the pedestrian's speech act"[24] *la dérive* is an aimless drifting through different areas of the city, lasting one night, or as long as one week. Evoking Surrealist *flânerie*, it takes *le dériviste* as mid-twentieth-century bohemian to the margins to expose the contradictions of the modern gentrification and abstraction of space. As with the situation, *la dérive* is suspended between calculation and chance—"a calculated action determined by the absence of a proper locus." Situationist homelessness and nomadism—concepts soon to be taken up by Gilles Deleuze and Felix Guattari—are pitted against both the home's fixity and privacy, and hegemonic notions of movement. The passion that should characterize architecture, the city and everyday life is in open opposition to bourgeois happiness, which now merely means being pacified by commodities.[25] Beauty is reclaimed from dominant culture and its notions of public *grandeur*, in the name of anything capable of producing spontaneous reactions in the pedestrian. Unlike the *flâneur*, whose post-aristocratic posture and movement through the crowd relates him to the sociologist-urbanist and the dominant scopic regime of modernity, the *dériviste* wants to defamiliarize this scopic regime in the tactile real of the pedestrian's disorientation. For the Situationists, the hypervisibility of the city—which, like Barthes' myth, claims to be all there is to see—is replaced by the opacity of the pedestrian's step-by-step experience. The *dérive* is radically immersive participation in everyday space.

Détournement, a third Situationist tactic, refers to acts of illicit appropriation, plagiarism, misinterpretation, and the perversion of the intended use of a specific artifact. It is a deterritorialization and reterritorialization of an object or a space. Citing the act of stealing as its outlaw origin, it also evokes the Dada principle of montage, Brecht's notion of *Umfunktionierung*, and the tongue-in-cheek comedy evoked when the kitsch object is placed in an unlikely setting. *Détournement* had been an avant-garde practice from Hannah Hoch to Duchamp, to the flattening of its political impact in Pop Art, as in the case of Warhol. It aimed to cut the distance between art and the everyday, by bringing the everyday into art. Examples: the Situationist book with its sandpaper jacket meant to damage the neighboring volumes on the bookstore shelf;[26] the *Memoirs*, the book Debord constructed with Asger Jorn, entirely of gleaned elements; and, not least, the re-functioning of Parisian streets in May 1968.[27]

If the actual influence of the Situationists on the "facts of May" is a matter of contention,[28] their work (and play) certainly contributed to the cultural climate that produced them. Lefebvre's injunction to "decolonize life," in the wake of actual decolonization movements of this period, came to fruition in the 1960s. The Situationists' slogans—among which "*Sous le pavé la plage*" remains the most emblematic—became battle cries. In 1968 the street was reclaimed with street fighting, car burning, and the barricades, while the Sorbonne was "*détourné*" by the students' occupation, and declared an "Autonomous Popular University, open night and day to all workers." May 1968, *pace* Lefebvre, who in the end saw it as merely a carnival,[29] almost made visible the all-encompassing proletariat Debord had envisioned, bringing together Situationists, students, workers, and youths from the peripheries in the last Parisian Commune—to give to the Situationists' drifting a temporary point of arrival, and to remake spaces with which people would have real contact, amid the alienating spatial abstraction of consumption.

V. Modernism, Function, and the High Fordist Unmodern

The evolution of culture is synonymous with the removal of ornament from objects of daily use . . . Ornament . . . commits a crime itself by damaging national economy and therefore its national development.

Adolf Loos, Ornament and Crime, *1908*

Less privileged social strata (peasants, workers and "primitive" people) have no interest in what is old: they aspire to the functional.

Jean Baudrillard, The System of Objects, *1968.*

The French theories of materiality and consumption of the 1950s and 1960s I've examined here all look for means to oppose the abstraction, standardization, and "mythologies" of postwar modernization. They try to supersede what is made available in the culture of capital by turning to objects and then to spaces out of step with the rationalized efficiency of the era: habitual domestic objects for Barthes; old furniture and unfashionable antiques for Baudrillard; and the bohemian and marginal Paris for Debord. The same interest in the unmodern is written all over Jacques Tati's and Georges Perec's work, to which we now turn. To understand the specific power of stray objects in the art of each, however, we need to understand how the functionalist aesthetic of the machine had, by the 1950s, shed its modernist rebellious edge. Minimalist functionalism, especially in architecture, had signified for Loos and others a higher degree of civilization, and had been cultivated by the modernist avant-garde of Futurism, Constructivisn, Cubism, and Dada as a concrete means of achieving social change. By 1967, however, it had come to signify the opposite: petty bourgeois conformism and the uneducated taste of the lower classes, who only now aspire to the new once the cognoscenti have discarded it. Here we will briefly consider how the discourse of the new and functional was established in modernist design and architecture before World War II, focusing in particular on the role of class markers in this discourse. To understand how the idea of function changes from being a 1920s touchstone of the avant-garde to a 1950s petty bourgeois mythology (which is how Baudrillard reads the functional), consider the historical and cultural context in which modern rationalization and functionalism is born in the Bauhaus and Le Corbusier's work.

As Fernand Leger wrote in 1914, "The thing that is imagined does not stay as still, the object does not exhibit itself as it formerly did. When one crosses a landscape in an automobile or in an express train, the landscape loses its descriptive value, but gains a synthetic value."[30] The exacting aesthetic of the machine, with its geometric rationalism, and the rigor of montage, came to be shared by all the post-World War I avant-gardes: the Bauhaus, Constructivism, Dutch De Stijl, and Le Corbusier's villa design. Despite their differences, these movements shared a notion of function as use, purpose, efficiency, and "the value placed on the satisfying of material functions",[31] against the gratuitous quality of ornament. Function is valorized as a principle of social and individual utopia, capable of producing a new type of subject, as Walter Gropius believed: "Standardization of the practical processes of life does not mean new enslavement and mechanization of the individual, but rather frees life from the unnecessary ballast in order to let it develop all the more rich and unencumbered."[32] This utopianism found a fertile terrain in the Weimar Republic, where Fordism and Taylorization in industry, and *Amerikanismus*, an interest in all things American, inspired the technophilia of the *Neue Sachlichkeit*, the New Objectivity of the machine age. Yet the Bauhaus utopia of a classless mass design, addressing, in turn, a classless society, as in plans for workers' housing,[33] always had to struggle against the predominant bourgeois taste. The German bourgeoisie opted for *Vernugungsachlichkeit*, a "pleasure materiality" of decoration and décor, and the thirties saw a return to the ornamentation, albeit more streamlined, of Art Déco. Art Déco had been the style of the 1925 *Éxposition Internationale des Arts Décoratifs*, where the everyday object was made to seem functional with ornamentation which invoked the geometries of Cubism, the clear lines of Meso-American and Egyptian art, and even faux-neoclassicism, as in Paul Poiret's fashion. At that exhibition, in the midst of Ruhlman's furniture, Lalique's vases, Orrefor's glass and Eileen Gray's lacquered screens, stood Le Corbusier's pavilion, *L'Esprit Nouveau*. Rigorously minimalist, the pavilion reprised the cubes of *la maison blanche*, Le Corbusier's architectural signature.

In 1920 Le Corbusier had launched the review *L'Esprit Nouveau*, to publicize his at times contradictory theory of function. With Amedée Ozenfant he pursued a Darwinist theory of the object, which took him close to Loos' position about the ornament and the evolution of civilization. "Natural selection produces forms of natural simplicity," he would claim, in contrast to "the deadly germ of pretentious bric-à-brac." The "object-types" that furnished the 1925 pavillion evoked "the pure form of standardized objects" (wine bottle, flask, pipe) of Purist and Cubist paintings by Juan Gris, Fernand Leger and Le Corbusier himself. They affirm what he called "the heroic quality of the everyday object," ennobled by a classical severity and by function, which points to use. In "Vers une Architecture", spurred by his interest in Taylorization and the machine, Le Corbusier celebrates the power of cars, planes, and ocean liners: "We claim in the name of the steamship, of the airplane, and the motorcar, the right to health, logic, daring, harmony, perfection." Le Corbusier's understanding of function here welds a rationalism complicated by a cosmic notion of harmony taken from Plato onto his sense of the instrumental qualities of objects and spaces.[34] By the late 1920s, however, the dialectic of spirit and matter he described was hijacked as a style by a new generation of Bauhaus designers who wished to make it available to the masses, and by the American interpreters of modernism as the International Style.[35] In "La Defénse de l'Architecture" (1929) Le Corbusier points out[36] that while he shares the pre-World War I avant-garde idea that the machine aesthetic would lead to a more egalitarian society, the conditions of his practice, and his need to rely on private capital, lead him to acknowledge that " For the moment we build 'cheap houses' ... only for the aristocrats and the intellectuals." Before World War II the social utopia of modernism was not realized *en masse*, and modernism's social vision benefits instead the very class the avant-garde wanted to shock, but who alone could afford modernism. Apart from fifty-one units of low-cost housing outside Bordeaux, Le Corbusier's plans for the masses remained plans, while Villa La Roche was commissioned by a Swiss banker. When after World War II modernist tower blocks were built in the Paris suburbs, grim slab-like structures soon became the norm.

The utopian impulses of modernist minimalism were also compromised well before the war by the popularization of the style of Le Corbusier and the Bauhaus as the "International Style" in the United States. The 1931 exhibition by Henry-Russell Hitchcock and Philip Johnson at the Museum of Modern Art in New York brought modernist architecture to a wide audience and named it a style.[37] With this style soon industrially produced, the "mass modern" became, paradoxically, ornamental again, as in the Kodak camera design of Walter Dorwin Teague, or in streamlining, which transfers car design's stylization of movement onto home appliances,[38] repackaging the commodity under the aegis of speed and efficiency. With the war, and the syphoning of European modernist *emigrés* to the US, the International Style becomes the style of choice of corporate America, from Madison Ave. to the corporate cubes of every US downtown. Monolithic and functionalist space management became *the* symbol of the might of American corporate culture. Now, minimalist modernism had found its real terrain where form matched function, and both matched message.

When European modernism returns to Europe via the US, as part of postwar reconstruction and modernization, America and Americanism have a whole new meaning. It is this hegemonic might of American culture, its prestige as the harbinger of the new, that attracts Baudrillard's proletarians, and their choice of the functional against the less democratic bygone. This same style, now coded American and ultra-modern, becomes at once the approved style for urbanization and modernization, and provides the blueprint for the changes to its urban and suburban landscape of a modernized France, with the appearance of the *banlieus*, the *grandes ensembles* of La Défense, and the industrial city attacked by Lefebvre. Perhaps the most notorious example of this direction was Le Corbusier's Plan Voisin (not realized) for Paris, and, in 1955, the *Unité d'Habitation*, a complex (made of *béton*) that housed 1,600 people outside Marseille. "The culmination of Le Corbusier's research on housing and communal living", as Jencks defines it (248), was conceived as a high Fordist phalanstery, mediating between collective and individual life. All the same, as Jencks admits, shopping and exercising were the only social activities catered to, and any sense of a civic square where a communal, political life might be fostered was absent.

This homogenization and occlusion of the social is what Lefebvre vehemently critiques in his work, well aware that after *l'Unité* comes Lacq Mourenx.[39] In *The Urban Revolution* (1970), a post-1968 text that, with *Le Droit à la Ville* (1968), constitutes a manifesto for Lefebvre's ideas about social space, he accuses Le Corbusier of turning the city into a dormitory and extinguishing the street's life as space of information exchange, display, and human contact. Lefebvre looks at the street dialectically, as a site where, on the one hand, people are centrifugally pushed: "The rate of pedestrian circulation," he notes, "was determined and measured by the ability to perceive store windows and buy the objects displayed in them" (20). On the other, they are also centripetally pulled together by the desire for an "impassioned dialogue ... [of] the encounter, of simultaneity, of assembly" (21). This contradiction, which Lefebvre values in the urban, is present in the new cultural disorder put in place by 1968, which the critic reads approvingly as "a total phenomenon." The city as ocean liner, functioning as a model of the Taylorist organization that Le Corbusier admired, does not exist except as a capitalist fantasy, always already complicated by the urban, "a place of conflict and confrontation, a unity of contradictions ... where conflicts are *expressed*, reversing the separation of places where expression disappears, where silence reigns..." (176). The disordered abundance of urban space makes it a makeshift site of possibility, which allows people to reclaim "their condition in time, in space, and in objects" (179). In disordered space, they can re-establish a relationship to matter made obsolete by the Fordist regime of work and leisured consumerism.

Lefebvre's pedestrian and her desire, as much as Benjamin's *flâneur* and Debord's drifter, is a residual figure. Lefebvre valorizes the subject's improvised navigation of rationalized spaces, and the unmodern and the "dysfunctional" as oppositional tactics to obligatory efficiency. The unmodern here is not the antiquarian taste through which *Elle*'s "reader from Angoulême"[40] tries to attain social distinction; rather, it is an unregulated form of the old, closer to Benjamin's junk and the Surrealist *objet trouvé*, the outdated object in the period after it has lost the veneer of fashion, before consumerism reclaims it as "retro" or "vintage." In short, stuff. By the early 1960s, minimalism, which for the prewar avant-garde had a progressive and utopian edge, was fully recast as capitalism's house style. It characterized stark worker housing, sleek product design, and massive corporate power. A new minimalism was capital's spatial policy. This was a minimalism against which the commodity could stand out, and where stuff found no shelter. The apparent transparency promised by this new minimalist spatiality was however an illusion—and one which would be exposed by the drifting pedestrian in the everyday, interacting with lost and outré objects as unruly stuff. In the following sections I will show how the contradictions in urban everyday life highlighted by Lefebvre are rehearsed in key texts of the period. My discussion of unmodern stuff as a critique of postwar efficient, minimalist modernization will follow two axes. Regarding space, distinctions between interior and exterior, private and public, street and home are contested. Regarding materiality, distinctions between such categories as commodity and junk, new and old, the functional and the dysfunctional are put into play. In Jacques Tati's movies, the satiric display of clean modern space, and in it the representation of incongruous objects, brings a comedic eye to the new dangers of stuff. Stuff here blasts open the new smooth space of modernity. In Georges Perec's *Les Choses* it is the home as private space of the pseudo-bourgeois apartment dreamed of via the home-décor advertisements in a women's magazine, that becomes the fantasy site of objects out of bounds. This home excludes the street, while the new *flâneur*'s drifting turns into the wish for a shopping spree. Nonetheless, the protagonists' class and their social awkwardness makes their attachment to things more complex than commodity fetishism, and the novel is a melancholic reflection on happiness and youth in consumer culture. The caricature of hyperfunctional modernism in Tati's cinema is the other side of the fantasy of home-as-protective-nest in Perec's fiction. A different relation between inside and outside, private and public lives, is established in the film *The Dreamers*, Bernardo Bertolucci's evocation of May 1968 in Paris. Here, the faded upper bourgeois apartment leads to the labyrinthine space of the young people's quarters, where clutter and outlaw sexuality defy bourgeois propriety, while the body is a form of materiality that makes history, pushing the characters into the street. This return of clutter and bodily disorder points to what has been erased and apparently superseded by modern functionality. In that clean white world, outmoded stuff openly signifies political, social, and sexual transgression.

VI. Jacques Tati, the Door Handle, and the Film of Glass Architecture

Jacques Tati's cinema directly addresses the issue of the inexorable abstraction of space and the closing off of social possibilities for individuals posed by the advent of a more and more pervasive system of rationalized spaces and consumer objects. All the fixtures of the postwar culture of consumption reappear—with a vengeance—in his films: the car, the fully Taylorized factory, an impersonal and rationalized public space, the cool minimalism of post-Corbuserian architecture, now applied to the pretentious privacy of the suburban villa, and Le Drugstore as the immediate ancestor of the shopping center. Tati continually pits this sterile modern spatiality against the unmodern quality of an old-fashioned, residual culture, in turn represented by marginal figures (children, old people, even animals), spaces (the old town, the hamlet, the seaside village), and times (the vacation, the afterhours). He carefully and comically canvasses all the residual and interstitial locations of the modern in search of what dominant culture excludes, but also for elements *of* dominant culture that can be used differently, for a utopian reconstruction of social space and social interaction. Tati's satire of modern reality in his later films often appears to echo aspects of Lefebvre's theory: the desire to study reality in order to change it, by pinpointing the weak points of the system, and exploring how they could come loose. At the center of this universe is Monsieur Hulot, invented and played by Tati, who describes him as "a completely independent character, ... and, because of his *étourderie*, which is indeed his worst defect in our functional epoch, an unadjusted individual, *un inadapté*."[41] Through Hulot's inability to "adapt," which marks his unmodern resistance, Tati explores the potential aberrations of modern functionalism: excesses, often involving stuff, that can be twisted into scenarios of local resistance.

Hulot in the films is in fact notably passive and flexible vis-à-vis his material environment, particularly when he is compared to Charlie Chaplin's Charlot. While Charlot dominates his surroundings by taking the initiative and making things happen, Hulot characteristically will suffer a situation and flexibly adapt to it. This comic adaptability of an *inadapté* suggests not Chaplin but Buster Keaton, whom Tati admired, and who in turn admired Tati, as his homage to the French comic actor in an issue of *Les Cahiers du Cinema* demonstrates.[42] Striking too is Hulot's limber self-effacement in the world of things, both modern and not. This hints on the one hand at the oppressive pervasiveness of consumer materiality, but it also implies a dispossession, a collapse of the subject into the object—which characterizes the hybrid. Charlot makes us laugh at himself and his actions; Hulot makes us laugh at the circumstances to which he reacts. Tati's films downplay the plot and even their hero—*Vacances* and *Playtime* could easily sustain their narrative without a protagonist. The hero is shown subjecting himself to this order of things not only, the implication is, to make visible their nefarious power, but also to explore their playful, and potentially redemptive, quality. What Hulot's gags illuminate most, therefore, is the play of things. This play, again and again, dramatizes a surreal and unexpected transfiguration of materiality that signals the transformative, unstable, and poetic quality of the real *qua* modern. For example, the flat tire becomes a funeral wreath in *Vacances*; labor, as in the case of the worker carrying a sheet of glass in *Playtime*, turns into an improvised ballet for a street audience. This play of things points to an excess ingrained in the logic of modernity, to a mystery that the prevailing system of reality can never contain. Sleek modern systems, in Tati's films, continually threaten to erupt, often spurred by Hulot himself.

In Tati's films, the material is more than meets the eye, and it's the capacity to re-envision that turns the modern subject-as-spectator of a Taylorized real into an actor herself. The viewer becomes active agent; the objects in the movies have agency too. This agency of materiality in Tati's cinema is reminiscent of the magic of things in Dziga Vertov's 1929 film *Man with the Movie Camera*, when, at the beginning, the viewers are invited to "sit" in a movie theater shown on the screen by the chairs which magically open for them. However, the automation of the object in the work of Vertov and Tati corresponds to two different moments in the cultural spectrum of modern technophilia: while Vertov's opening chairs and doors testify, at the moment of high modernism, to an earlier wonder at the machine's automatism, the magic of Tati's object is produced as resistance to a modernity that has betrayed and lost its utopian charge.[43] Tati's objects show the instability of the captions they have been granted by capital, and their dysfunction makes them uncontained and uncontainable by its system of value.

Ultra-modern, rationalized space is similarly threatened and muddled by the unmodern it marginalizes. Tati's films expose the technocratic logic of modern urban space: the massed skyscrapers *à la* Mies van der Rohe and the glass interiors of *Playtime* show the end of modern functionalism as social utopia, to show how modern glass architecture's attempt to abolish privacy only eliminates the potential social space of the street. Against the smoothing out of social difference and conflict, as promised by modernist utopianism, Tati proposes an interaction of the ordinary subject with glass architecture. Under the destructive aegis of Hulot, the subject manages to reconquer sociality again, *within*, and not outside of, the impersonal and disorienting spaces of modernity. Like Barthes' *Mythologies*, Tati's 1950s films do express a certain wonder at postwar modernization, but Hulot's defamiliarized eye makes visible the often inhuman and exploitative contradictions of the new to expose modernization as myth. His gags become the perfect *locus* for a politics of the situation, where the *debris* of functionalism folds into what Baudrillard called Hulot's Baroque inventiveness. To understand how this works, we will now examine forms of resistance and invention in Tati's *Playtime* (1967).

In *Playtime* the contrast between technological efficiency and Hulot's bumbling explores the interaction of human subject, objects and the futuristically homogeneous space of Paris. Here the new-suburb versus old-city distinction of *Mon Oncle* is invalidated: the old city is now Paris itself, reduced to a few postcard clichés, and the lived-in city is the totalized glass-slab high-rise world represented by Tativille. Tati famously built for this movie a gigantic set of skyscrapers which became known as Tativille. The set of *Playtime*, built on leased land south-west of the city,[44] covered 15,000 square meters where skyscrapers of glass, plastic, and concrete were erected, some with functioning escalators and heating. Around a number of fixed buildings, surrounded by streets with real traffic lights, others were set on rails, to be moved according to Tati's directions. The film took almost three years to complete, and bankrupted Tati.

Playtime belongs, if in unorthodox fashion, to the genre of "one day in the life of a city," of which the most famous example is Walter Ruttman's "New Objectivity" 1927 film *Berlin Symphony of a City*. A group of American tourists arrive in the morning in the futurist Paris, visit the city during the day, during which they repeatedly cross paths with Hulot, and spend the night in a restaurant-club, to have breakfast the next morning in the novelty space of Le Drugstore, site of American-style consumerism in the city. More than in any other Tati film, the plot, as well as the figure of the protagonist, recedes, to give scope to situations that are themselves connected only by a character, a space, or an object. Hulot acts as ludic catalyst, letting us see through his eyes unnoticed elements in the regimented traffic of the city.

The first image on the screen is of a parade of modern angular glass skyscrapers lined up along an avenue. Then the camera cuts to various figures: a cleaner who looks like a surgeon, a woman pushing what seems to be a wheelchair, a nurse with a baby, a person carrying flowers, all in a sterile space that might be a hospital. The announcement of a "speakerine," whose smiling intonation is the merest sign of human warmth, reveals that it is in fact an airport, which turns out to be Orly. In this characteristic space of modern efficiency, we then begin, through the eye of the camera, to follow a series of characters, most of whom, apart from the American tourists, we never see again in the film. This first sequence establishes the key themes: the disorienting homogeneity and sameness of the spaces, which, blurring into one another as in the case of hospital and airport, lose any specificity; the apparently American quality of this uniformity; the emergence of play in the middle of this disorienting rationality, often erupting in the form of dance, for example the exhilarating ballet of the travel agent's feet behind the counter, pushing himself on the revolving chair from one customer to another, which we enjoy through the behind-the-scenes gaze of Monsieur Hulot. The chief image of this modernity remains, however, glass, which appears in virtually every scene of the film.

The omnipresence of glass is crucial in Tati's critique of the modern. Glass straddles two spheres, that of a disciplining modernity, invisibility limiting the individual freedom, spontaneity, and sociality through its invisible wall, and that of the unmodern, always already ingrained in the rationalized and functional everyday.

Playtime is a film about glass architecture and its changed cultural meaning, from modernist utopia to emblem of systematic abstraction and

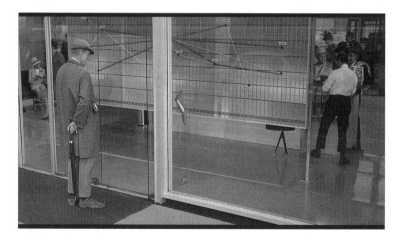

Figure 3.1 Playtime
Jacques Tati, *Playtime* (screenshot) Hulot contemplates the glass wall.

social separation. It could be said that by 1967 reality has become entirely mediated by glass, that of the skyscraper, the shop window and television screen. The transparency of glass means it has an insidious claim not to be there, and rather purports to enhance and assure a transparent access to the real. Glass, then, is the perfect material for a functionalist modernity which claims to abstract matter. The sheets of glass that are everywhere and often invisible in this film are the brilliant exemplars of the abstraction of the material real which Barthes had railed against as mythology, Baudrillard had described as the hyperreal, and Debord called the spectacle. Glass in this film is also the equivalent of the Barthesian "myth," the Baudrillardian simulation, and the Situationist spectacle: each of these conceptual categories, for the critics who named them, represent the ultimate degree of the modern system's power to abstract materiality—and the point at which that abstraction, named, could be seized and turned back on itself. *Playtime*, filming glass, also wants to define in the sharpest terms possible the dream of the functionalist abstraction of space, and therefore of all materiality, into a smooth nothingness, into absolute degree-zero minimalism. Yet its running gag is built on the actual materiality of the glass, and glass' strange off-kilter powers of reflection and deception. The comedy of this bending and distortion shows up the possibilities of refusing glass's dream of total abstraction and its promise of transparency. Tati, with his brilliant film, affirms that this simulative and circular space can actually be reclaimed and rehumanized.

After the opening image of Miesian skyscrapers, glass in *Playtime* becomes a more and more imperceptibly pervasive element of the modern. On the way from Orly to Paris, while the tourists marvel at how similar Europe is to America, ("Look! [at the lamps] They are the same as at home!" says a voice), only after the aluminum frame of the bus window appears in the cinematic frame do we realize that we have been watching the freeway and sky through a window; until then the mediating function of glass had been naturalized. Next Hulot enters one of the skyscrapers, looking for somebody. The concierge, an old man, a residual element inefficiently smoking during work time, activates a futuristic panel and parks Hulot in a waiting room, a glass cage where the only sounds are the noises of things—the puffing air-exhaling armchairs, the rasp of the briefcase zipper. In the space of absolute abstraction suggested by the glass, things seem most alive since they emit noise. It is the human subjects, emitting lesser sounds, who appear anthropomorphic. The lack of communication denoted by the glass box becomes amplified in the huge room of cubicles which Hulot next surveys. Seen from above, the ultra-modern space of the offices shows a crowd at work, organized by productive isolation and surveillance. But once Hulot gives up his bird's eye view and enters the room, it becomes, with its grid-plan, a maze where he gets lost. Finally he sees the *fonctionnaire* doorman, but we realize that they are merely seeing each other's reflection on a glass wall, and cannot communicate. The man is in fact behind Hulot, who sees the man's reflection as a figure facing him in the next room, across more glass. Hulot runs away from the real man while chasing his phantasm through the glass door. They will connect and communicate only after hours, in a chance encounter on the street.

In *Playtime*, Tati's analysis of modernity through the trope of glass marks a fascinating critique of the long association of glass architecture and modernity. The glass conservatory, housing tropical plants in cold climates, was the model for Joseph Paxton's Crystal Palace, "one of the world's first modern buildings."⁴⁵ Built in 1851 for the Great Exhibition in London, to display a vast sea of commodities, it was the precursor of much nineteenth-century public architecture, especially, as Benjamin notes, buildings that served "transitory purposes: covered markets, railroad stations, exhibitions" (F2, 9, F, "Iron Constructions"). The transparency of glass in the work of Le Corbusier, which Benjamin celebrates via the writing of Siegfried Giedeon, makes for the total visibility of the subject, who, in his glass abode, abdicates his primacy to become like a commodity in a shop window. In such conditions dwelling, that sign of bourgeois retreat from history and the public scene, is no longer possible, and neither is interiority as a psychological dimension. With no more dark corners in which to withdraw into privacy, the individual can finally become the "machinic" and innervated subject of modernity.

Glass architecture has a similar utopian charge in the discourses of the early twentieth-century avant-gardes. The *Deutsche Werkbunde* saw glass as the material symbolizing the architecture of the future; celebrated prototypes were the model factory by Walter Gropius in the 1914 *Werkbunde* Exhibition, the Fagus factory in Alfeld, and Bruno Taut's Glass Pavillion. Also in 1914, Paul Scheerbart in his book *Glasarchitektur* proposed to change culture by changing architecture: "We can only do that by introducing glass architecture, which lets in the light of the sun, the moon, and the stars, . . . through every possible wall, which will be made entirely of glass— . . . The new glass environment will completely transform mankind." In 1925 Gropius designed free-form glass walls for the Bauhaus building in Dessau. Le Corbusier used Scheerbart's ideas in his design for the Salvation Army City of Refuge in Paris, but the building was an environmental failure, since the glass curtain wall made the un-airconditioned building extremely hot. Pierre Chereau in his *Maison d'Alsace* (1931), also in Paris, wanted, through the use of glass, to represent a vision of social equality, as did Hans Meyer in his League of Nations Building (1926–27) where, as he wrote, there were "No pillared reception rooms for weary monarchs, but hygienic work rooms for the busy representatives of their nations. No backrooms for backstairs diplomacy, but open glassed rooms for public negotiations of honest men" (58).

However, when glass architecture, after the vicissitudes of European modernism, gets first successfully exported to America, and then reimported to Europe as part of modern functionalism, its social and visionary impulse gets erased by its adoption as corporate style. Glass, iron and concrete produce no new man, only the post-bourgeois subject as bureaucrat or employee, and the clinical ambiance of managerial culture. This is what the setting of *Playtime* represents. As Tati himself explains, he is making a film about an epoch: "Glass, nothing but glass: we belong to a civilization which experiences the need to put itself in the (shop) window ... Our universe becomes more homogeneous and uniform day by day" (Cauliez, 106). While the clinical aspect of modernity is written all over *Playtime*, its glass architecture also echoes its modern origins in the Crystal Palace and the Paris Universal Exposition (1900): the Strand, the economic center of Tativille, is hosting an international fair, to celebrate the kitsch novelties of French gadgetry: the garbage can shaped like a Greek column, the eyeglasses whose lenses lift to allow ladies to apply makeup (another glass). The hyperfunctionality of the gadgets makes them actually useless: the door that doesn't make noise when it closes becomes comically dysfunctional when the salesman, angry with Hulot, slams it: since it cannot make noise, it cannot express the salesman's anger.

In this immaterial world, derealized into a series of glass planes, place, as in "Paris," can only exist as tourist view and postcard cliché. Carried along by the crowd, Hulot finds himself at the fair, caught in the midst of a group of Japanese tourists. To catch his breath, he steps out of the building onto a balcony to look at Paris, Eiffel Tower in the distance. This is the only time that the city is perceived by Hulot and the film audience directly, without the mediation of glass—and it's a postcard image. Paris in *Playtime* appears in two forms: cited by its famous monuments the Arc de Triomphe, the Sacré Coeur, and the Eiffel Tower, all momentary reflections in glass doors, lost as soon as the door closes; or symbolized by residual and out-of-place, and also stereotypically French, figures on the street, such as the flower seller or the male shopper with *beret* and *baguette*. Both figures are, significantly, elderly people, representatives of a world made old by modernity, and effigies of a lost street life, reduced by the glass world of fairs and mass tourism to stereotypes. Paris has become a picturesque postcard for tourists, available only as cliché to the eye of the camera—itself another image of glass.

It is in the night city that the film's signal event occurs: the breaking of the glass. While Hulot and Barbara—Hulot's American sweetheart—exchange glances through the windows of their respective buses, as she goes back to her hotel, the night descends upon Paris, and the windows of the skyscrapers light up, looking like Las Vegas or at least New York. In the after hours, glass offices close and street life resumes. Yet this becomes the stage for the most ominous aspect of modern glass architecture, whereby the individuals in the lighted spaces behind it become like specimens or shop-window commodities, and private life turns into a spectacle of which those living it seem unaware. The film's key action and one of Hulot's most spectacular feats, the glass breaking, is anticipated by the comic image of the German salesman's broken eyeglasses. This moment is an indication of the fragility of function, and a reminder that "function" is born of the subject's need. It is also, however, a dramatic smashing, literally, of the system of signs, looks, and spectacles that sustain modern culture and its order of things. First, however, there is the night scene before the glass curtain wall, when Hulot, visiting a friend's apartment, can see all the occupants of the building in their private spaces, as in a cross-section of a doll's house. Here the space of home gets blurred with that of the office and the shop window, and privacy is reduced merely to what cannot be heard. We cannot hear what the people inside the apartments say, but we can see all of their moves. There's nothing "transitory" in Tati's rendering of glass architecture: this is not the end of privacy and the beginning of a new experimental spatiality, but rather the ludic reification of both, offered as voyeuristic pleasure to the passer-by.

The "Royal Gardens" instead are the setting for the dramatic scene of the breaking of the glass. While Hulot eats prepackaged food at the counter of Le Drugstore, his friend Marcel, the concierge at the Royal Gardens, invites Hulot to join him. The sleek look of the restaurant, decorated in office grey and furnished with uncomfortable chairs that leave a mark on their users' backs, contrasts with the messy atmosphere of the kitchen. Here, instead of the pristine and perfect space, we are shown the work behind it: not only is food cooked, but the restaurant itself is still under construction, while the waiters seize every chance to smoke and drink wine. The upper bourgeois clientele is perfectly used to the rules of such a space, rules soon violated by a loud American customer, who arrogantly takes a reserved table, by a band of black musicians playing jazz, and by the backstage disorder of the workers. The contrast of minimalist propriety and hints of raucousness sets the scene for the smashing of the glass.

At the entrance of the club, Hulot and Marcel, each on either side of the glass door, pull the handle in two different directions, in a convoluted game of compliments ("Please come in!", "Oh no, I couldn't possibly . . .") until Hulot accidentally breaks half of the glass door with his head. Too scared to tell his boss, Marcel, in one of the great comic moments of postwar cinema, keeps holding the handle, making the gesture of opening and closing the door as if the sheet of glass were still there. This is more than a comic gag. If glass, throughout the film, points to simulation, to the disorienting impossibility of distinguishing between different spaces, and at the same time represents the barrier through which we experience a mediated and alienated relation to reality and other people, the handle is a fully philosophic object signifying the re-materialization of what has been abstracted. If, in the hands of Marcel, the handle supports a function, it is a newly engineered one, over which both Hulot and Marcel now have control. The system of signs, or of myths, through which capitalism works and which glass symbolizes, gets smashed to show its man-made, unnatural quality. To prove all this, the object that supported function, the handle, then gets repurposed again to show the reality of the social relations of production: when a customer forgets the tip, Marcel follows him, tilting the handle to convert it into a little plate, demanding to be recompensed for his labor.

In this scenario, passive observer no longer, Hulot becomes, albeit accidentally, an agent of destruction. After smashing the glass door, while trying to help the loud American he causes the ceiling of the restaurant to collapse, inaugurating the playtime of the title in full carnivalesque mode. The restaurant gets re-zoned on the spot, its spatial order disorganized: across the fallen ceiling, the American invites the customers into his "private bistrot." The private bistrot becomes a sort of "court of miracles," a convulsed scene where everybody is out of his or her prescribed place, dancing to a frenetic rhythm. When the musicians leave, Barbara at the piano accompanies a woman singing French *chansons*, showing that a dash of the stereotyped unmodern can be the background music to a riotous remaking of the space of human relations.

The French music carries into Le Drugstore, where the crowd moves to have breakfast at the end of the *soirée*. Dawn is announced by a rooster, symbol of rural France, inexplicably crowing in the midst of the glass, iron, and cement landscape of the city, and a *bal musette* music rings in Le Drugstore, where, in the daylight, everybody stands at the counter eating and talking. The signs of alienation and Americanization are still there: "How do you say "drugstore" in French?" asks an American tourist, while a French woman, looking at a display of *fromage* labeled in English, asks "What does "cheese" mean?" Yet Tati, at the end of the film, in a tone that echoes Lefebvre, chooses to stress the power of festival and of play that invades the geometrical space of the city. Public space, even the empty post-Le Corbusier space of the modern metropolis, can be transformed, and even a hint of utopia can be achieved by the very means that had so far caused its demise—the car. We could say that utopia here is figured through an event, a way of coming together through play, for all the inhabitants of Tativille.

In the final scene, the village and its communal life emerge in the middle of Tativille, in a series of dislocated gestures which the smooth and transparent featureless city cannot stifle: the clowning of the little boy in the black raincoat, in the ice cream cart, and in the motorcycle which lifts the woman rider up and down as if on a merry-go-round. In the final scene, the traffic circling the roundabout does become, almost magically, a merry-go-round, where people enjoy themselves together and objects dance. This utopian scene of communal pleasure will no longer be possible in 1970: at the end of *Trafic*, Tati's next film, Hulot and the girl are lost in the grid of a crowded parking lot, a maze that isolates them, in a rainy landscape. Yet in 1967, before the events of the following May, reality is a roundabout, and the techno-object—the car—can still be turned into a means of enjoyment, a playful toy with some power to bring people together.

VII. "Tiny Little Things, Tiny Little Bits of Happiness": Décor and Desire in Georges Perec's *Les Choses*

Georges Perec's *Les Choses* (1965), set in 1960s Paris, foregrounds the home as a space made of carefully chosen pieces of furniture and knick-knacks. Instead of representing family and sociality, the apartment of Jerome and Sylvie, the protagonists of *Les Choses*, is for the couple a shelter from the tensions of public life. In the world depicted in *Les Choses*, objects work as they do in the new décor magazines, that is, as components of a setting, a space, which bespeaks the social distinctions of which Pierre Bourdieu wrote. Spaces, that is, complete environments, as well as objects are now commodified. The novel thus charts a new phase of immersive consumerism in which the horizon of consumer desire is a personal space of consumption and status display, a "lifestyle." Home in *Les Choses* is the locus not of privatization but of consumption, integral to the spatial logic of modernization.[46]

Jerome and Sylvie, in their twenties, quit "the studies they had never begun" around the time of the Algerian war. Their highest aspiration is to be affluent and live in a *haut-bourgeois* apartment, which they fully furnish in their fantasies. Here they would live an aesthetic life without worries, and without having to work. Instead they need to support their dreams and desire for objects as signs of social distinction through their jobs as "psychosociolinguists"—interviewers for market research. But even this untaxing work impinges on their freedom, the freedom to enjoy life and buy objects they cannot afford. So they leave for Tunisia, where Sylvie takes a teaching job. After living in the scarcity of a place without objects, and, therefore, for them, without meaning, they return to Paris. Finally they move to Bordeaux, where they will advance their careers and be able to afford the things and apartment they had always desired.

Les Choses, which belongs to Perec's early, "sociological" period, and which made his name,[47] treats the central issues of the era's cultural critique: the value of the everyday, play, and leisure as potential means of resistance against the standardization of life, the mythic quality of the language of advertisements. All of these are read as components of the abstraction and reorganization of real, material space. Probing the new French culture of the 1960s, Perec takes to task the chief claim of consumerism: that commodities will make you happy. This is a new kind of happiness, as he noted in an interview: "You could call it Orly-joy, a joy of ... fitted carpets."[48] No longer "an inner value", modern happiness "is more like an almost technical relationship to your environment, to the world." Regulated by the commensurability of desires and the means to realize them, this new order of happiness concerns one's environment and the spatial disposition of the self. Happiness in the novel is a problem, complicated by the class status of the protagonists and by lack of an actual correspondence between their means and desires. This incommensurability of desire and means can help us solve the ambiguity of the novel's ending—"A happy ending, and the saddest conclusion," said Perec himself (18)—and decide whether the protagonists are dupes of consumption blind to the reality of the commodity, or conscious agents who appropriate consumerist logic for their own ends. In exploring the *promesse de bonheur* of the commodity and its settings, the narrator oscillates between two positions. On the one hand, "they lived in a strange, iridescent world, the shimmering universe of a mercantile civilization, the prisons of abundance, the fascinating snares of happiness" (*LC*, 72). On the other, things and the spaces to put them in also leave Jerome and Sylvie vaguely aware that their aspirations to everlasting youth and a higher social status are no more than consumerist fantasy.

Happiness for the couple is the attainment of a class position, which the objects they consume and the spaces they hope to live in signify. Yet it is also presented as freedom from work and responsibility, an idea signaled by the two characters' unproductive loitering. This is the couple's form of aimless mobility, expressing the desire "not to be there," and not to be caught in a system of production, but rather to simply pass the time. However, their loitering differs from both Baudelairean *flânerie* and Lefebvre's notion of play. In *Les Choses* loitering shows how happiness is imbricated in the category of youth, which at this same historical moment was recast as another reified object of mass consumption. The book, then, can be seen as a post-Benjaminian story of *flânerie*, where the *flâneur*'s "death by the commodity" turns into the wish not to grow up, and into the desire for the city—the desire to live in Paris and be absorbed by its phantasmagoria of places, images, and commodities. By rejecting work, Jerome and Sylvie appear to be the perfect apprentice Situationists. But instead of turning their refusal into a means of social protest, they take shelter in the privacy of their fantasy home, in the pleasure of objects and of beautiful interiors. Their *acedia* sets them in opposition to the active and cheerfully productive young executive, but in the end imprisons the protagonists in a self-made cage of melancholia, a melancholia shot through with nostalgia for the yet to be lived life they had in their twenties, which may be the chief pleasure of consumption Jerome and Sylvie are after. *Les Choses* can also be read either as a melancholic novel about the passing of youth—that is, youth as a well-spent consumer product— or as the attempt to postpone this passing by getting caught in the endless logic of the latest system of objects.

Perec's investigation of modern happiness is not a humanist lament about the alienation produced by consumer culture, but rather a sincere speculation on the new meaning of objects for the individual. He wants to establish not the specific meaning of a single encounter of subject and consumer object, but the effect on the subject when this becomes a continuous process—that is, what living in and negotiating one's identity in a commodity-saturated spatial order means for a life. *Les Choses'* two protagonists are absorbed in the ideology of progress and abundance brought by postwar reconstruction. The generation of the 1960s was born to this abundance, a world that now starts showing its first cracks: the abundance was not available to all, nor did the commodity deliver the happiness it had promised. Whether unsure or seduced, the generation of Jerome and Sylvie is however fully caught in the mythology of modernity, that is, in its objects as signs and myths. In writing a book "about the language of advertisement and how it works through us" (*Interview*, 18), Perec declares his debt to Barthes: "the book was in the beginning two different plans: first an exercise on Barthes' *Mythologies*, . . . on advertising language as it is reflected within us; then a barely heightened description of a particular social set, that happens to be my own." In another interview he explained that "I wrote *Les Choses* with a pile of *Madame Express* beside me, and to wash my mouth after having read too much *Madame Express* I would read some Roland Barthes."[49] Thus, as Andrew Leak notes, Sylvie and Jerome inhabit a world of myth. Yet their particular version of the consumer's fantasy and failed relation to the real—while they repeat fetishism's old adage ("it's not true but I believe it"), they also loiter and continually defer—complicates any simple version of consumer desire by exploring how it is worked out not just in relation to things, but to the spaces things inhabit. This is their "spatial fix" of modern subject–object relations. The "spatial fix" is a term used by the geographer David Harvey to describe how economic expansion into ever new global spaces is a strategy for overcoming crises in rich nations. Harvey's term, however, can also be applied locally. *Les Choses*, in its depiction of objects and spaces, shows the spatial fix operating at the everyday level in modern consumer culture.

While the protagonists' relationship to things and spaces in *Les Choses* is "vertical," an index of their desire for social status, space in the book also pulls them along the horizontal axis of the street as the location of intense happiness. As it is for Lefebvre, the street in *Les Choses* is the place of the spectacle of commodities, but also of a certain youthful expenditure, which, after Perec, we may call "loitering." The Parisian street, in contrast to the apartment, to Sfax as postcolonial city, and to the provinces, is where the danger of becoming adult and settled is contested and opposed, and where the protagonists feel most free and happy. Paris comes to stand, therefore, for a spatial and temporal limbo, representing both the volatility of youth, and the impossibility of their achieving class mobility. The same volatility and movement is reflected in Jerome's and Sylvie's work and in their uncertain class status. In interviews and in the novel, Perec defines his characters as intellectuals: they qualify as such because of the non-manual, non-physical quality of their labor (they are "psychosociolinguists"). Yet, although they are able to reflect on their predicament, they never have any clear awareness of their position in the system to which they contribute.[50] On the one hand their profession evokes the cleanliness and prestige of the new white-collar employee; on the other, Sylvie and Jerome have none of the corporate spirit of the *cadre*: they take on their work not as a vocation, but in order to live better.

If being an intellectual means being able to reflect on one's role, Perec's calling Jerome and Sylvie intellectuals is ironic. However, their story also elucidates the condition of a new class of white-collar service workers, who, not fully professionalized and therefore "homeless" in the emerging order, get domiciled in the makeshift privacy of consumer fantasy. "Dislocation" names their status, a desire to escape, their psychological stance. Thus only a dreamed-of home, a space for their status-objects, becomes an imaginary space in which to locate their subjecthood. Their uncertain class definition, cast as dislocation, is compensated for by dreams of their own self-made space, stage for their new status. Since the object's status as a sign of distinction has changed since the 1950s, and the modernist faith in technology and function has become massified and no longer guarantees any social distinction,[51] Sylvie and Jerome don't dream of the modern kitchen-as-laboratory, advertised at the time as the acme of modernity home, but of the Chesterfield settee. They desire the antiques and knick-knacks they have seen in the windows of antiquarians in Rue Jacob, things that would demonstrate their taste: "fake Épinal prints, English-style engravings, agates, spun-glass tumblers, neobarbarian knicks-knacks, parascientific bric-à-brac" (*LC*, 24). The blank space of streamlined modernity now demands the antique, redolent of a strange pastness and certainly not organically related to any acknowledged historical sense, as the force that will neutralize it. They desire not grand or monumental objects, but the bric-à-brac that only the connoisseur recognizes as valuable, that is, that conveys an absolute, idiosyncratic individuality germane simply to the aesthete.

The *fin-de-siècle* aesthete had signaled his exceptionalism (in terms of class and sexuality) and his anti-bourgeois stance through overconsumption and the collecting of precious objects, as in the lavish home décor of Huysmans', Wilde's, and D'Annunzio's characters. When this figure and his mode of consumption are again mobilized, indirectly, in the promised "life style" of 1960s abundance, his adversarial quality gets domesticated into a mere sign of class distinction. "Lifestyle" then becomes imitation and approximation between reality and an unapproachable ideal, that allows Jerome to be somebody by simply wearing second-hand English shoes. Jerome's and Sylvie's aesthetization of life through objects relies on a double paradox. First, the residual aristocratic life style of the aesthete is now achieved by means of the new bourgeois culture of consumption, through which the protagonists try to distance themselves from their class of origin. Second, through things, Jerome and Sylvie also try to imitate the life of the *cadre*, and yet they resolutely refuse to work. Their dilettantism—and whatever trace of the oppositional is contained in it—is continued in their refusal to take up full-time jobs. This refusal puts into focus their dilemma of having to choose between freedom and wealth. This suspicion of work is shared, for similar reasons, by Debord, who, when asked by Lefebvre what did he live on, "very proudly answered '*Je vis d'expédients*' ('I live off my wits')."[52] In Sylvie's and Jerome's case, the suspicion of work is fueled by their desire for what they see as the real magic of capitalism—a reality from which any sign of production has been erased. To renovate the house according to their taste, for example, they simply wish for a miracle; they would like to come back from a vacation to find the apartment transformed. This is where Perec's characters part company with Debord, whose refusal to be productive turns into the practice of communal play. Sylvie and Jerome, instead, want leisure time as organized by the work schedule to take over the entire day, so that they can spend every day of the week as if it were Sunday enjoying the *luxe et volupté* of their stuff. The objects they buy create an aestheticized environment as fantasy, which allows them not to *play* as Debord does, but to *play the role* of an aristocratic version of the *cadre*. Work, in their mind, is not the opposite of play, but of leisure and consumption, and their role-playing is something they learn and are trained into by the media—in particular by *L'Express*, bearer to a mass audience of the mid-century modernization in France, and which all their friends read, even as they disagree with its political line: "Where could have they found a truer reflection of their tastes, of their desires? Were they not moderately rich? *L'Express* offered them all the signs of well-being: thick dressing-gowns, brilliant exposés, beaches that were in." *L'Express* offered them a map of modernized middle-class experiences, self-definition, and taste. "They dreamed, in half-whispers, of Chesterfield settees: *L'Express* dreamed with them." "Lifestyle" here is a mode of commodity-centered life, in which the commodities need a setting, and inhabiting the setting needs the style.

Sylvie's and Jerome's role-playing affords them only a seemingly "effortless Bohemia,"[53] at which they in fact work hard, chasing the right porcelain and the right brand of second-hand shirt all over Paris. However, if the ideal remains elusive and can be approximated only by the unavailable objects that signify it, when their dilettantism is consumed on the street, in cinemas, or in cafés, their happiness becomes tangible. It's the feeling of being on the street, on their walks, that most signifies freedom and pleasure:

> Just being there in the street, warmly dressed in a cold, dry, blustering day at nightfall, walking without hurrying but at a good quick pace, toward a friend's place, was enough to make their slightest gesture—lighting a cigarette, buying a cone of hot chestnuts, threading their way through the crowd at a railroad station exit—seem to them like the evident, immediate expression of a boundless happiness (*LC*, 51).

Now happiness is not a new fridge or a new car, but loitering in the city streets and cafés—their desires and fantasies scattered around, rather than actually lived. In the end this loitering, their improvised use of city space, is also only deferral.

"Youth," that is the split between childhood and adulthood put in place by the new phase of consumerism, turns out to be key to how this spatialized consumption is negotiated by the protagonists. In a world where becoming an adult is presented as working, entering the world of production and of the everyday, the couple refuse to subject themselves to what they think of as imprisonment in "glassed in offices ... installment buying, primary and secondary residences and educating the children" (*LC*, 58). These "offices that have two telephones, one Dyctaphone, a built-in refrigerator, and sometimes even a painting by Bernard Buffet" (*LC*, 85), don't measure up, in Jerome's and Sylvie's eyes, to the freedom of youth. Work too is thought of spatially, as imprisonment behind glass. In this world, to be a consumer is to be forever young. In this sense their "poor choice" in terms of class is in fact the right one. Lacking the financial capital to live in luxury, they are destined to fail, so that they can live exactly the way they want, and get what they want: an improvised life in Paris, signified as youth. Their means do not allow Jerome and Sylvie to become the ideal prescribed by *L'Express*. Their depoliticized consciousness makes it necessary that things fill a void. This prosthetic meaning of objects becomes even sharper in Tunisia, where they move for a year. The *void* is significant: a deficiency of happiness imagined as empty space, or rather space abstracted to an uncanny nothingness.

In Sfax the scarcities and poverty of postcolonial Tunisia make both face up only to their emptiness and lack of identity in the absence of the phantasmagoria of commodities: "They would glance vaguely at the hideous shop windows: frail furniture, iron work candelabra, electric blankets, notebooks for schoolboys, street dresses, ladies' shoes, bottles of butane gas— it was only the world, the real world" (*LC*, 102). Cut off from their western "system of objects" (*LC*, 115), the scarcity of commodities in Tunisia produces in Jerome and Sylvie a kind of cathartic lethargy, so that they feel like "dispossessed persons ... sleepwalkers." The question for these particular postcolonials, then, is how to escape their history, which for them has nothing to do with postcoloniality, but merely the history of the western subject as consumer. They return to France, and soon abjure bohemian youth culture, moving to provincial Bordeaux to "take over an agency" (123). At the fateful age of thirty, according to the age-scheduling of modernity, there's only one thing worse than losing their youthful freedom: that of becoming "overage Bohemians, in turtleneck and velvet pants, at the same cafés in Saint Germain and Montparnasse each night, eking out an existence through rare strokes of luck, shabby to the very ends of their black fingernails" (93). This evokes the Situationists, who didn't give up the street and freedom, and kept loitering and playing for the revolution. While their unavailable objects allow Sylvie and Jerome to remain in the limbo of youth-as-unsatisfied desire, when confronted with the dilemma of the young intellectual ("For a young intellectual there are only two solutions, each as desperate as the other—to become a bourgeois or not to" (18)), they will choose a certain mediocre well-being: "To be well-housed, well fed, well dressed ... [with] money for smoke-tanned peccari gloves" (*LC*, 124). They settle down, and buy the Chesterfield settee. But in the novel's final ambiguity, getting the house with the settee means the realization *and* the end of their dreams at the same time. Reality comes, and with it the end of life as unfulfilled possibility, figured by the street and by their unrealized fantasies.

The end of the novel sees the protagonists in the restaurant car of the train that is taking them to Bordeaux, enjoying the anticipation of their future wealth in "the starched linen ... the thick plates with the coat of arms" (125) while eating a tasteless meal. This situation uncannily evokes the disappointment they had experienced when, eating an elaborate "egg in aspic", about which they had long fantasized, they discovered that it tasted just like a boiled egg (47). However, just as the disappointing egg doesn't deter them from fantasizing, they will get over the insipid meal on the train, and learn to repackage loss into the kitsch pleasure of nostalgia ("'Remember?' Jerome will say, and they will remember time gone by" (124)). They will loiter now with the only slightly less kitsch pleasure of melancholia, possibly the only tangible pleasure of consumer culture, once the gesture at *jouissance* and play is gone. In their memories, the loss of something they never had, and which modernity has carved out of working time and space and called youth, survives as a remembered fantasmatic plenitude, itself another object of desire.

Is the conclusion of *Les Choses* a happy ending or, as Perec claimed, "The saddest conclusion you could imagine?" To answer, we need to go back to the issue of means and desire. The novel is contained, almost parenthetically, between two epigraphs, one at the beginning by the British novelist Malcom Lowry, and the other at the end by Karl Marx. While Lowry points out that capitalist development, and the progress and happiness it promises all, is in fact uneven,[54] Marx is more enigmatic: "The means are part of the truth, as well as the result. The search for truth must itself be true; true research is truth spread out before us, the scattered members of which are reunited in the result." He foregrounds the importance of means as always already part of the result. In the context of *Les Choses* Marx's words might refer to the importance of fantasy, and, by inference, to the objects and their spaces that are the matter of that fantasy that guarantees happiness. But Marx talks of truth, one might remark, not of happiness. This disjunction between truth and happiness, the choice of concluding a book on happiness by having Marx talk of truth, is perhaps Perec's ironic—not to say sarcastic—comment on the quest of the two characters. The means through which one searches for truth or happiness are not superseded and forgotten in the final result, but they fully inform it; that is, the blind and naive materialism of the hero and heroine produces a fully deserved insipid meal, which has nothing disappointing in it, but is, in fact, what was expected in this context.

There's a third epigraph that would have further illuminated the dialectic of means and result: a passage by the sociologist Raymond Aron, mentioned in another novel by Perec, *Un Homme Qui Dort* (*A Man Asleep*, 1967), a sort of anti-*Les Choses*, in its rejection of commodities and consumption. Alone in his garret, the protagonist sits on his bed with a book on his knees, *Eighteen Lessons on Industrial Society*, open at page 112.[55] This page, not quoted in *A Man Asleep*, has been tracked down by Andrew Leak; it comes from the first edition of a book born as a series of lectures by Aron given at La Sorbonne in 1955–56. The page begins: "It is poverty, that humanity as a whole, still suffers from today. Poverty, defined simply by the lack of common measure between the desires of individuals, and the means to satisfy them."[56] Aron describes a novel concept of poverty based on the incommensurability of the desire for an endless consumption, and individuals' actual means to realize them. Capital creates a new definition of happiness—relying on things—and at the same time a new notion of poverty as the inability to consume and realize one's personal space of consumerist distinctiveness. Jerome and Sylvie, who "wanted to be rich simply because they were not poor" (18), are caught in this new idea of poverty that, to all intents, tries to erase and make invisible real, material indigence: "Millions of men once fought, and still fight, for bread. Sylvie and Jerome hardly thought that they could fight for a Chesterfield settee. But that would have been the slogan most likely to have mobilized them" (72), the novel informs us. Nonetheless, they are poor in the midst of a culture of abundance. This is the "poverty" of the consumer of luxury items, incited by the society of consumption.

Les Choses is a novel about the happiness and the affluence, dreamed of or not, that things can give, and the contradictions produced in consumer culture by the gap between means and desires, dreams and reality, between the signs and the materiality of objects. If the novel were simply denouncing consumer culture, which, as Perec makes clear, it is not,[57] what value can be attributed to the incommensurability of means and desire, means and result? Lowry and Aron talk of the uneven development of capitalism and a new notion of poverty recast in terms of unhappiness, thus saddling happiness with the utilitarian logic that subjects the means to the ends to stress the importance of the result. Marx, however, asks us to focus on the means, on the object as itself already signifying, already part of the measure of how truth and happiness coincide. Marx's materialism is supposed to defeat consumer culture's appeal to ephemeral idealism: the forever-postponed pleasure of consumption, the futility of the commodity, are defeated by the present time of the now of the object, and by the suspended present of Jerome and Sylvie. Reality, truth, happiness, are already present in the object, in the materiality which we experience daily, and which capital repackages and marks up for profit. Marx the materialist philosopher asks us to lower our eyes to the immediate materiality of things, in opposition to the abstraction of myth and consumer idealism. Through Marx, Perec ironically provides a more enabling reading of Jerome's and Sylvie's desire: while consumer culture and its idealism tell them that the object cannot be had, that perhaps its doesn't exist *qua* materiality but only as simulacrum, Perec's Marx re-materializes the object by stressing the power of means *as* result, and by pointing out that means are always present in the result, as much as the result always bears the traces of the means. Another interpretation of the book, however, is possible, one that turns Marx on his head, and ironically downsizes his words to a sort of consumer existentialism: their "poverty" and their disappointment with the real allow Sylvie and Jerome to linger in the realm of the signifier, and suspend reality, the reality of becoming adults and entering the sphere of production and its regimented everyday. Beyond the context of Perec's novel, such lingering in the realm of the signifier, to maintain the mirage of the consumer space of the dream apartment, is the distinctive signature of the postmodern. At that point, the fetishized accomplishment of consumption and end of desire is not simply disappointing, in a way that might still propel a return to materiality, but has disappeared. In this (I believe perverse) reading of Marx's quote, the invitation to focus on means would be an injunction to "enjoy the symptom," because the real can now be sensed only as simulation, as we have seen Baudrillard claim. Read in this sense, perversely (but the logic of capital is perverse, and Perec in his book is, ultimately, trying to expose and illuminate this very logic), Marx's words would be a prophetic anticipation of Perec's dissection of the predicament of post-Fordism, in which disembodied, de-signified objects threatening to fade into virtuality behind the glass, appear lit up by a certain Nietzschean joy, or a postmodern dizziness. In other words, the décor is always a mirage, the consumer's private space impossible. The tone of *Les Choses*, however, is melancholic, and its conclusion speaks of loss. Youth is gone—which wouldn't have made Nietzsche happy either—and a reality that doesn't match up to the consumer's fantasies is still there, part of the game. The point, however, is not to retrench into a dialectic of materiality and fakery, in which the pleasures of consumption can be dismissed as inauthentic, but to return to Marx's *hic et nunc* of materiality announced in the epigraph. Here we get a clue from Perec himself, when he says: "But that happiness [the happiness of things], is always potential. In our capitalist society what is promised isn't delivered ... advertising entices us toward everything, and we have nothing, or we have just tiny little things, tiny little bits of happiness" ("Interview," 17). If Sylvie and Jerome are blind to the implications of their desires, the choice to inhabit, to loiter in the space between desire and reality, situates them in the proto-materialist space of means. The unfaithful commodity, that delivers only "tiny little things," is therefore the appropriate means for satisfying their willingness not to get to the point of arrival, not to grow up. Instead of being a means to the supposed happiness of the *cadre*, things become their point of arrival. The novel, then, has a happy ending, and at the same time talks about the shortcomings of happiness in the age of consumption. The atmosphere is very much that of

David Hockney's painting of 1970–71, "Mr. and Mrs. Clark and Percy," in which the dreamlike bliss of the couple portrayed is shown in tandem with five featured objects—all of which are "décor," accessories of a "lifestyle," and which seem to float in a defined domestic space.

As representatives of the generation of the 1960s, Jerome and Sylvie occupy an anomalous position. Potential *saboteurs*, destined by their class of origin and by their wages to enjoy only the crumbs of modern affluence, they do not however end on the barricades of 1968. Neither is their entrance into the contingent of French modern technocracy particularly enthusiastic or motivated. Jerome and Sylvie, consciously or unconsciously, are *bricoleurs* of myth, but having read too much *Madame Express* and not enough Barthes, they never recognize their identity, which can only be mirrored back to them by the things and settings they desire. This mirroring makes of their spaces a funhouse mirror-world of consumerism. This blindness makes them nothing more than the organic intellectuals of capital.

The novel dramatizes the gap between desire and the inability to fulfill it by buying objects in consumer culture. This effect is imagined and represented socially. The rhythm of deferred desire is dramatized as a set of spatial movements that get enacted in a series of spaces—the café where the characters loiter, the Parisian street where they stroll, and centrally, the rented apartment where they survey their décor, their collection of "little" objects. The effect of consumer culture, therefore, is not experienced as an encounter with the objects themselves, but as an effect of inhabiting the space that the objects occupy. Consumerism has by now not only commodified objects, but has wholly colonized spaces both public and private, and, through the insidiousness of advertising, subjective affective life as well. Thus Sylvie and Jerome are being ideal consumers when they encounter commodification at the level of the spatial. *Flânerie*, as an earlier subjective response to the commodification of daily life and urban space, may be thought of as an earlier symptom of this spatialization, and even read positively as an unconscious attempt to escape while it was still being put in place. By the postwar era private spaces too had been wholly colonized, so that the apartment, emptied now of its Empire paraphernalia, got refilled with faux antiques, bric-à-brac and mementoes of the couple's artful consumerism. Or rather, not quite filled—and this incompleteness becomes the index of the couple's perpetual unfulfillment as consumers. It is this unfulfillment, however, which keeps alive their consumer desire. What Perec gives us in the novel is an anatomy of the never-ending rhythms of consumer desire experienced as one kind of inhabiting of urban spaces. In *Playtime*, the new kind of abstracted space is still fearfully and comically unfamiliar, and only the play of its little objects, torn away from the smooth and transparent false promise of its glass walls, provides any opening, literally into an ordinary, everyday (and unmodern) counterlife. In *Les Choses*, a more insidious kind of satire, the inhabitants are drawn into the space of consumption by the little objects with which they fill it. The book satirizes that dangerous moment when minor things—once again, stuff—are in danger of losing any real resistant charge.

VIII. Clutter, Sex, and Revolution: Unhomely Objects in Bertolucci's *The Dreamers*

Yet even Rue Jacob antiques become clutter, overwhelm, and, in aggregate as stuff, can signal a disorder countering the smooth modern. I want to conclude my discussion of objects and spaces as they relate to notions of identity and social change in postwar France, by turning to a text that is a meditation on those years, Bernardo Bertolucci's 2003 film *The Dreamers*. The film is based on Gilbert Adair's 1988 novel *The Holy Innocents*, which, influenced by Alain Fournier's *Le Grand Meaulnes* and Jean Cocteau's *Les Enfants Terribles*, satirizes, as one critic put it, "the responses of self-absorbed radical-chic middle class folk to the disturbances of May 1968."[58] In Bertolucci's text the satire has disappeared, as the plot follows the trajectory of many of his films— the relation between the bourgeois individual and politics, history, mass movements. From *Last Tango in Paris* (1972) to *Besieged* (1998), this relation gets articulated between the opposite spaces of a cluttered interior, an apartment, and the exterior, the street.[59]

The film is not about the events of May 1968 as such; rather, Bertolucci presents that time by focusing on what comes "before the revolution" (the title of another of his films, of 1964), through an idealized look at the cultural elements that fueled its sense of possibility and hope for change: cinema, music, the body, political activism, drugs, and philosophic debate. The film eschews nostalgia;[60] this is not 1968, but the dream of 1968 from the perspective of over three decades later. This retrospection is managed with flashbacks using real footage. For example, we see the actor Jean Pierre Leaud playing himself reading a tract by Godard to the protestors in front of the Cinématèque Française; suddenly the scene is intercut by images of the same actor reading the same tract on the same spot thirty-five years earlier. Leaud's now aged face exposes any temporal artifice; when the film recreates the scene, the contrast suggests that while the possibility of what existed "before the revolution" has been betrayed, it is not exhausted. This refusal of cynicism, shown in its very form, is what saves the film from being a mere period piece; Bertolucci gives us what was there before the revolution, and what was left after, unvanquished, that can potentially happen again. This refusal to not dream, then, shapes the film's specific organization of spaces and objects, which are cast in opposition to the configuration they received in the bourgeois order of the early 1960s. Bertolucci's film focuses on a set of issues about the meaning of bourgeois life that would get sharpened by the *événements*: sexuality and the body as a means of dissent, transgression, generational rebellion, the desire for, and fear of, adulthood, the possibility of political action. The film focuses on the character's attempt to make the possible real through a specific reorganization of space and materiality. In the protagonists' apartment, itself a kind of character in the film, the *projet*, to use Baudrillard's words, takes over the *objet*. There, clutter sets the scene for the explosion of middle-class privacy, which, at the end, will bring the three chief characters into the street.

The revolution that came to Paris in May 1968 was reminiscent of the Commune of 1871: barricades set up in the streets of the Latin Quarter and the boulevards, burned cars, shops looted, and police charges confronted with the launch of cobblestones. Before May, however, came January '68 and *les enragés* of Nanterre, where Lefebvre and Baudrillard taught, when Daniel Cohn-Bendit led a large protest. When in March *les enragés* occupied an administration building the March 22 Movement was born, and the insurrection soon reached Paris. May 6 saw scenes of street fighting against the police in Paris; La Sorbonne and the Theatre de l'Odeon were occupied; on May 13 the unions and the student movement called for a general strike.[61] May '68 produced a non-party-led movement of students and workers, bent on attacking the authority of the state; this protest accompanied other 1960s uprisings, by anticolonial, revolutionary, and students' groups from Warsaw, Prague, Cuba, and Algeria, to Berkeley, Berlin, and Rio de Janeiro.[62]

One event that stirred the anger of Parisian students was the closing, in February 1968, of the Cinématèque Française by the minister of culture, André Malraux. The Cinématèque Française, a cinema and museum, had been founded by Henry Langlois to save old film stock, and had a significant impact on such New Wave directors as Truffaut, Godard, Chabrol, and Resnais. As *The Dreamers* opens, the three protagonists meet in front of the Cinématèque Française, during the protest following its closure. Here Matthew, an exchange student from California and film fan, meets the twins Isabelle and Theo; after escaping the police attacks, they start a friendship, cemented by their love of cinema and their youth. Matthew moves into the raffish, high-bourgeois apartment where the twins live with their parents (who are away) and becomes part of a transgressive *ménage à trois*, where he functions as a medium for Theo's and Isabelle's incestuous desires. The mutual attraction and the sexual games spurred by the re-enactment of scenes from famous films (of which we are shown clips), isolate them from the external world. Yet the events of '68 inexorably seep into the apartment: we can hear sirens; a stone smashes a window. Once the money left by the parents is spent, the three regress to a wilder state: they don't dress anymore or go out, and they scavenge in the garbage for food. When Isabelle, finding a new check on the table, realizes that her parents have returned and seen the trashed apartment and the three of them asleep together, she attempts to stage a collective suicide with the kitchen gas. But a brick breaks a window and wakes Theo and Matthew from their—literal and metaphorical—sleep, so that at last they join the fighting in the street below.

The Dreamers proposes the image of the revolution as an expression of the body, connected to sexual transgression and fantasy, especially the "dream" cinematic fantasy to which the film's title partly refers. What is new is how Bertolucci imagines the events of 1968 in terms of space, and represents its political violence as a rejection of the privacy and claustrophobia of the bourgeois interior. The revolution is here preconfigured by a specific interaction of space and body: the space of Isabelle and Theo's apartment is immediately made transgressive and heterotopic by their incestuous desire, and by their careless trashing of the place. This trashing is analogous to the disorder of the characters' sexuality; the world outside, with its violence and conflict, is no longer counterposed to the *luxe et volupté* of the bourgeois order, signified by the décor of the bourgeois apartment, as happens in Perec. The illusion of privacy is exposed and reversed in Bertolucci's film, which flaunts two motifs to underline it: the dis-ordering of the topography of the apartment, and the cluttered presence in it of things.

Here, as in Tati's work, subversion is not associated with the new and functional, but with the old. Theo and Isabelle's home is Jerome and Sylvie's dream house: a *grand-bourgeois* apartment on Boulevard Raspail, furnished with antiques; one wall even has an enormous tapestry. From the front rooms we move to the non-functional and antiquated kitchen, where the signs of labor are counterposed with the bohemian chic of a Louis XVI couch and settees used as kitchen chairs. We then recede into the night zone, in the innermost part of the house, where the bedrooms are situated. This apartment replicates the traditional arrangement of bourgeois domestic space, guarding the secret spaces of interiority, privacy, feelings, and sexuality. The bedrooms represent what is not supposed to be seen, and are encased in the carapace of bourgeois propriety. Here, the drawing room provides a muffled silence around the liberal poet-father, while the kitchen, part of the public sphere of home, but anticipating the tattered disorder of the bedrooms, becomes the stage of the generational conflict between father and son. The dialectic between inside and outside, by which these moments of "philosophy in the kitchen" are fueled, is key to the rest of the film, and is repeated in a series of oppositions between apartment and street, fantasy and reality.

Through a smaller door beyond the kitchen the three characters enter a labyrinthine corridor filled with books, which leads to the spare room the American guest will occupy and to a vast old-fashioned bathroom. If the drawing room is elegant and grand, if a little faded, this space is run down, hung with peeling wallpaper and cluttered with a jumble of discarded furniture. The ascetic "traveling light" of the revolutionary, whose virtue and power was predicated on giving up the unnecessary,[63] is replaced here by the disorderly clutter of useless objects of décor, returning us to the hodge-podge of old commodities in Benjamin's and the Surrealists' arcades.

The mismatch of stuff in these rooms is a corruption of both the modern and the traditional bourgeois order, where everything has its place, in an *ambiance* of function and beauty. This is, instead, the home décor of the revolution at the time when the functionalism of the avant-garde has been coopted and domesticated by modernization. Its obtrusiveness in the film establishes the adversarial quality of clutter and stuff. In the film's set design, the cultural tropes of the epoch are self-consciously cited through the material ones: see Theo's poster of Godard's *La chinoise*, the lava lamps, the record player, the half-bust statuettes of Mao and Lenin—while on the telephone table, in the foyer of the apartment, there's a bust of Dante Alighieri. (This stuff is displayed against a busy soundtrack of Jimi Hendrix, the Doors, Françoise Hardy—and film references from *Shock Corridor* to *Queen Christina*, from *Johnny Guitar* to *À Bout de Souffle*).

Cinema and cinephilia filters everything that happens within the private space of the night zone: politics, sexuality, and revolt are accessed through the images and cinematic situations the characters have seen in films. Cinema and the Debordian spectacle are counterposed here. Rather than being a form of escapism, film is cast as a way of rehearsing life and of playing out the characters' fantasies. The three act out movie scenes, not as a way of living vicariously, but living for real what they have watched. This is the logic of Bertolucci's use of film clips: Theo, Isabelle, and Matthew's discussions or games are continually intercut by film images, on which the characters model their reality here and now, without sentimentality. Thus the re-enactment of a scene of Godard's 1966 film *Bande à Part*, where its three stars race through the Louvre, sanctions Theo, Isabelle, and Matthew's friendship, announced with a line from another film, *Freaks*, that "we accept him as one of us."

The film charades they play provoke two of the movie's most transgressive scenes: the spectacle of Theo masturbating in front of a Marlene Dietrich poster, and before the eyes of his sister and his friend, after failing to guess the title of the film Isabelle is acting out (*Blonde Venus*), and Matthew, missing another, having sex with Isabelle while Theo watches. While this second scene is supposed to take place in the spare room, "under the Delacroix"—the famous painting of the revolution, whose leading female figure has been "collaged" with the face of Marilyn Monroe—in the film it occurs in the kitchen, while Theo makes an omelette. Beyond its shock-value, the scene sanctions the moment when sexuality, cinema-as-fantasy, and transgression move away from their designated part of the apartment, and begin to percolate through the entire place, leaving a trail of junk and disorder behind. This disorder stands as a sign of the degradation of the three "holy innocents," who leave the bourgeois conventions of their parents' life behind: "We didn't leave the apartment anymore", says Matthew's voiceover, "we didn't care if it was day or night, drifting out to sea, leaving the world behind." There follows a scene of the three falling asleep in the steaming bathtub; the final reterritorialization of the night zone takes place when the characters move to sleep in the drawing room, under the tent that Isabelle constructs with chairs, garments, and rags. A memento of their childhood, here orientalized by a confusion of fabrics, the tent is a fantastic dream space and object of interior décor, a home away from, and against, home. In the Bohemia and innocent transgression of the tent, privacy is pushed into the public arena of the house, and from there it finds its way onto the street, its final displacement and first signified.

Theo, Matthew, and Isabelle do not join the uprising that has for days gone on on the street, but they respond to it in an uncalculated, joyous way when a thrown brick breaks their window—when, as Isabelle explains in a line worthy of Giacomo Balla, "The street came flying into the room." With this osmosis between inside and outside, private and public, the three launch themselves onto the street. The camera pans around the now empty house: it's as if all the junk the three left behind might have gone into making the barricades of the '68 events. The high pile of lost objects in the street barricade matches the tent and the accumulated clutter of the apartment backrooms. The stylized image of the Revolution that ends the film, while the credits roll and Edith Piaf sings *"Je ne regrette rien,"* is a violent turn that disrupts an already compromised domesticity. For the three characters, their joining the uprising is not so much a way of reclaiming the street, in Lefebvre's sense, but of letting themselves be transported there by their transgressiveness, *ennui*, and energy. There's a continuity between inside and outside that the notion, and practice, of bourgeois privacy doesn't manage to contain: the disorder of the house, produced by the disorder of sexuality, and by the fantasy that cinema represents, finally rejoins the chaos of the street, where it began.

Tati, presenting modernity as the Potemkin city Tativille, shows us that behind the glass there is nothing. Nevertheless *Playtime* insists that through the communal sociality built around the jetsam of unmodern stuff, a sense of the social, and perhaps even a tactile relation to materiality in its poetic and political sense, might still be possible. The social and the tactile survive at least as melancholic carnival. Perec constructs the narrative of *Les Choses* around a dream apartment whose image testifies to the colonization of the unconscious by consumer culture and its myths. As a fantasy, Perec's home could be, like the nineteenth-century Louis Philippe interior studied by Benjamin, a modern consumer's "dream house," where something different from bourgeois reality could be envisioned. However its occupants do not recognize this potential, as they fail to see the reality, and the meaning of their tiny apartment in Rue des Quatre Fages. Instead they fill both spaces—the imagined and real one—with objects prescribed by the fashion and décor magazines they read, giving in to the "cerebral pleasure," as it is called in the novel, of consumption, which gives up the body and its more material and social pleasures. Both of these texts against the consumer-driven state consider space the issue; all of smooth modernized space, rather than simply specific commodity-objects, is what has been commodified.

In *The Dreamers* Bertolucci affirms that we must make space for the Symbolic at all costs, and he does so by focusing on the transgressive quality of sexuality. In the film it is the body, not as a naively natural power, but as always mediated by cultural discourses and values, that destroys and transforms the objects and spaces that more usually contain it. The sense of play, of angry and joyous festival, is preeminently *ce qui reste* of 1968, a kind of defiant euphoria that Bertolucci does not undermine either with melancholia or with a retrospective notion of history. The film's sense of "future posterity," the traffic of past and future in the present mediated by the image world of the cinema, suggests to us that cinema can be a screen that, unlike the glass wall, can reanimate the actual materiality of our bodies and lives. Such a play of the cinematic and the actual is evoked, for example, by Isabelle when she says to Matthew (now in 1968): "I was born in September 1959, on the Avenue des Champs Elysées, and my first words were: 'New York Herald Tribune, New York Herald Tribune!'" In this exchange, she is not just re-evoking, but living Godard's *À Bout de Souffle*, to which the director cuts to show us the famous scene with Jean Seberg and Jean-Paul Belmondo. Yet Bertolucci rejects history, cinematic or otherwise, as an inevitable progress by choosing to stay with the immediacy and the materiality of the now, signaled by the bodies that, in the age of virtuality, have become anachronistic. His suspension of time is not escapism but a way of naming the possible, and of celebrating utopia in the time before the revolution. By staging his movie scenario as a languid choreography of escape from the cluttered, stultifying apartment that guards the privacy and the confidence of the middle class, he makes the issue of space and the transgression of its protocols the signal issue of the revolutionary change that may be happening in the apartment or in the street.

Notes

1 Rossana Rossanda, *La Ragazza del Secolo Scorso*, Torino, Einaudi, 2006.
2 Kristin Ross, *Fast Cars, Clean Bodies: Decolonization and the Reordering of French Culture*, Cambridge, MIT Press, 1995, p. 174.
3 Henri Lefebvre, *The Critique of Everyday Life* vol. 1, trans. John Moore, London, Verso, 1991.
4 For a discussion of the importance of *Elle* and *L'Express*, in the formation of a 'modern' middle class consciousness in postwar France, see Ch. 3, "Couples", in Ross, *Fast Cars, Clean Bodies*.
5 "[The critique of everyday life] . . . is not merely a detail of sociology, an 'object' that can be studied critically, or a 'subject'; it has no clearly circumscribed domain. It makes use of economy and economic analysis, just as it does of sociology, psychology, and linguistics. Yet it does not fall into any of those categories." Henri Lefebvre, *La Révolution Urbaine*, Paris, Gallimard, 1970; trans. Robert Bononno, *The Urban Revolution*, Minneapolis, University of Minnesota Press, 2003, pp. 139–40.
6 Susan Sontag *A Roland Barthes Reader*, New York, Hill and Wang, 1982, xxii.
7 Roland Barthes, *Roland Barthes par Roland Barthes*, Paris, Editions du Seuil, 1975; trans. Richard Howard, *Roland Barthes by Roland Barthes*, New York, Farrar, Straus, and Giroux, 1977, p. 47.
8 See "Myth Today", *A Roland Barthes Reader*, New York, Hill and Wang, 1982, p. 126.
9 "Figures of the Neutral: Adamic language—delectable insignificance—the smooth—the empty, the seamless—. . . the vacancy of 'the person'". See *Roland Barthes by Roland Barthes*, p. 132.
10 "Political language: it represents 'Nature' for me only inasmuch as I am going to transform it . . . the language thanks to which I act the object . . . But if I am not a woodcutter I can no longer 'speak the tree'", *Roland Barthes Reader*, New York, Hill and Wang, 1982, p. 135.
11 Roland Barthes, *Mythologies*, Paris, Editions du Seuil, 1957; London, Granada, 1972, p. 86.
12 "Inaugural Lecture, College de France", in *Roland Barthes Reader*, 1982, p. 459.
13 See Michael Moriarty, *Roland Barthes*, London, Polity Press, 1991, p. 181.
14 Another image of "the neutral" is presented at the end of Barthes' "autobiography": "Nothing stirs, neither desire nor aggression; only the task is there, the work before me, like a kind of universal being: everything is full. Then what would be Nature? . . . Totality?" *Roland Barthes by Roland Barthes*, p. 179.

15 In 1967 Baudrillard was an assistant (with Alain Touraine) to Lefebvre at the University of Nanterre, where he was also very involved in the politics of that time and place (see Len Bracken, *Guy Debord, Revolutionary: A Critical Biography*, Venice, CA, Feral House, 1997, p. 228).

16 Jean Baudrillard, *La Société de Consommation*, Paris, Gallimard, 1983, p. 309 (my translation).

17 Jean Baudrillard, *For a Political Economy of the Sign*, St. Louis, MO, Telos Press, 1981; see in particular Ch. 3, "Fetishism and Ideology: the Semiological Reduction".

18 "The ludic corresponds to a very particular type of cathexis: not economic (useless objects), non symbolic (the gadget has no 'soul'), that concerns the play with combinations, . . . [of the system]." Baudrillard, *Le Société de Consommation*, Paris, Gallimard, 1970 p. 172.

19 Edward Ball, "The Great Sideshow of the Situationist International", special issue of *Everyday Life*, Alice Kaplan and Kristin Ross eds, *Yale French Studies* 73, 1987.

20 Guy Debord, *La Société du Spectacle*, Paris, Buchet-Chastel, 1967; *Society of the Spectacle*, Detroit, Black and Red, 1983, p. 4.

21 On Debord's and Lefebvre's friendship see Bracken, *Guy Debord*; on Lefebvre's critical thinking and his relationship with the Situationists see Mary McLeod, "Henri Lefebvre's Critique of Everyday Life: An Introduction", in Steven Harris and Deborah Berke eds., *Architecture of the Everyday*, New York, Princeton Architectural Press, 1997.

22 "The Situationist International realized and practiced a critique of reification that previously had lived only at the level of discourse", Edward Ball, "The Great Sideshow of the Situationist International", *Yale French Studies* 73, p. 31.

23 "Toward a Situationist International", presented by Guy Debord at the SI conference of Corsio d'Arroscia, 1957. All the Situationist documents I refer to are collected in *Guy Debord and the Situationist International: Texts and Documents*, Tom McDonough ed., Cambridge, MIT Press, 2003, p. 44.

24 Tom McDonough, "Situationist Space", in McDonough, *Debord and the Situationist International*, p. 259.

25 In "Our Immediate Tasks", in "Report on the Construction of Situations" (1957), Debord writes: "to concretely contrast, at every opportunity, other desirable ways of life with the reflection of the capitalist way of life; to destroy, by all hyperpolitical means,the bourgeois idea of happiness." McDonough, *Debord and the Situationist International*, p. 50.

26 Edward Ball, "The Great Sideshow of the Situationist International", p. 32. This cover has been reproduced in a recent book on Situationism, *An Endless Passion . . . An Endless Banquet: A Situationist Scrapbook*, Iwona Blazwick ed., London, ICA Verso, 1989.

27 We can think, with Debord, of all the facts of May 1968 as forms of *détournement*, particularly the occupation. Kristin Ross reads (after Lefebvre) 1968 as a "return" of 1871. *Yale French Studies* 73, 1987, p. 116.

Stuff Theory

28 Among the Situationists' detractors are Peter Wollen, ("The Situationist International", *New Left Review* 174, 1989), and the critics who contributed to *Telos* 86 (Winter 1990), edited by Russell Berman, David Pan, and Paul Picone "The Society of the Spectacle 20 Years Later". Lefebvre, after his break with Debord, became more skeptical about the the Situationists (see Ross, "Lefebvre on the Situationists: An Interview", in McDonough, *Debord and the Situationist International*).

29 In Ross, "Lefebvre and the Situationists: An Interview", in McDonough, *Debord and the Situationist International*, p. 283.

30 Quoted in Bevis Hillier, *The Style of the Century*, New York, Watson-Guptill, 1998, p. 69.

31 This, as Tim Benton explains, has been the zero degree of the notion of function since Vitruvius. See Tim Benton, "The Myth of Function", in Paul Greenhalgh, *Modernism in Design*, p. 42. For a complete discussion of the history of function see Larry L. Ligo, *The Concept of Function in Twentieth-Century Architectural Criticism*, New York, 1984.

32 Quoted in Hans Wingler, *Bauhaus*, Cambridge, Harvard University Press, 1986, p. 410.

33 Their plans were realized in the *Weissenhof Siedlung*, built in the outskirts of Stuttgart, 1927. See Michael Horsham, *20's and 30's Style*, London, Grange Books, 1989.

34 See also the essays collected in Russell Walden ed. *The Open Hand: Essays on Le Corbusier*, Cambridge, MIT Press, 1977, particularly Jencks, "Le Corbusier and the Tightrope of Functionalism".

35 See *Livable Modernism*, and Klaus-Jurgen Sembach, *Into the Thirties*, trans. Judith Wilson, New York, Thames and Hudson, 1972.

36 Le Corbusier, *The Radiant City*, New York, George Braziller, 1967, p. 146.

37 What made the *esprit nouveau* widespread on both the sides of the Atlantic was the participation of American designers in the 1925 Parisian *Exposition des Arts Décoratifs*, and the CIAM International Conference that in 1928 brought together all the major modern architects and designers. See Horsham, *20's and 30's Style*, London, Grange Books, 1989, p. 46.

38 In 1935 the Super-Six Cold Spot refrigerator, designed by Raymond Loewy, Geddes, and Lurelle Guild, was advertised as "Stunning in Its Streamlined Beauty", Hillier, *Style of the Century*, p. 10.

39 Lacq-Mourenx was a company town in the petrochemical complex of Lacq, whose utilitarian birth took place in 1957. In their "Critique of Urbanism" the Situationists comment on the photograph of the super-modern city thus: "The town of Mourenx. Its 12,000 inhabitants live in the horizontal blocks if they are married, in the towers if single." (1961) in McDonough, *Debord and the Situationist International*, p. 107. See also Mary McLeod: "He [Lefebvre] was also deeply affected by the construction of a new town, Lacq-Mourenx (1957–60), near his birthplace in southwestern France, and decried its desertlike spaces that killed any quality of public spontaneity or play."

McLeod, "Henri Lefebvre's Critique of Everyday Life: An Introduction", in Harris and Berke eds., *Architecture of Everyday*, 15.

40 "The reader envisioned by the staff at *Elle* was most likely young, between twenty-five and thirty-five, tired of wartime deprivation, in need of frivolity, and she lived in Angoulême. Why Angoulême? I don't know, says Giroud. Perhaps because of Rastignac." Kristin Ross, *Fast Cars, Clean Bodies*, p. 1.

41 Armand J. Cauliez, *Jacques Tati*, Paris, Editions Seghers, 1968, p. 9.

42 *Les Cahiers du Cinéma*, no. 130, April 1960, in Cauliez, *Jacques Tati*, p. 13.

43 "Hulot, in all his awkwardness, makes the object dance. While he picks up the falling sugar-paste (in *Les vacances*) he resembles a minor Sysiphus, friend of all things." Cauliez, *Jacques Tati*, p. 29.

44 See Stuart Klawans, *Film Follies: The Cinema out of Order*, London, New York, Cassell, 1999; and Cauliez, "Document: Tativille", in *Jacques Tati*, p. 77.

45 Michael Wigginton, *Glass in Architecture*, London, Phaidon Press, 1996, p. 38.

46 This is the more 'canonical' reading of Perec's novel, proposed by Baudrillard, who comments on *Les Choses* in *The System of Objects*, and by Kristin Ross, in her excellent analysis of the book in *Fast Cars, Clean Bodies*.

47 The book was awarded the prestigious Renaudot Prize in 1967. See Jacques Neefs and Hans Hartjie, *Georges Perec Images*, Paris, Editions du Seuil, 1993, p. 73.

48 "Georges Perec Owns Up: An Interview with Marcel Bernabou and Bruno Marcenac", *The Review of Contemporary Fiction*, vol. 13, no. 1, Spring 1993, p. 17.

49 Quoted in Andrew Leak, "Phago-citations: Barthes, Perec, and the Transformation of Literature", in *Review of Contemporary Fiction*, vol. 13, no. 1, Spring 1993, p. 64.

50 "They never fully realize what is at stake ideologically in the values they believe to be truly theirs." Leak, "Phago-citations: Barthes, Perec, and the Transformation of Literature", in *Review of Contemporary Fiction*, vol. 13, no.1, Spring 1993, p. 68.

51 "Things fold and unfold, are concealed, appear only when needed. Naturally such innovations are not due to free experiment: for the most part, the greater mobility, flexibility and convenience they afford are the result of an involuntary adaptation to a shortage of space." Jean Baudrillard, *The System of Objects*, trans. James Benedict, London, Verso, 1996, p. 17.

52 In Ross, "Lefebvre on the Situationists: An Interview", *Fast Cars, Clean Bodies*.

53 The line is Hanif Kureishi's, in his novel *The Buddha of Suburbia*.

54 "Incalculable are the benefits civilization has brought to us, incommensurable the productive power of all classes of riches originated by the inventions and discoveries of science. Inconceivable the marvelous creations of the human sex in order to make men more happy, more free, and more perfect." Malcom Lowry quoted in *Les Choses*.

184   *Stuff Theory*

55 Georges Perec, *Un Homme Qui Dort*, Paris, Editions Denoel, 1967; *A Man Asleep*, my translation, p. 21.
56 "The *18 Lectures*, published in 1963, consists of actual lectures for ... sociology students at La Sorbonne delivered in 1955–56. The first "edition" was a cyclostyled volume ("polycop") distributed by the *Centre de Documentation Universitaire*, on page 112 of which the eye is caught by the isolated middle paragraph that concludes with the statement (...) That is where *Les Choses* begins." Leak, "Phago-citations: Barthes, Perec, and the Transformation of Literature", in *Review of Contemporary Fiction*, vol. 13, no. 1, Spring 1993, p. 64.
57 "People who think that I have denounced consumer culture have understood absolutely nothing of my book." Perec, "Interview", op. cit., p. 17.
58 Philip French, *The Observer*, Sunday February 8, 2004.
59 For a discussion of Bertolucci's cinema see Claretta Tonetti, *Bernardo Bertolucci: The Cinema of Ambiguity*, New York, Twayne, 1995; Millicent Marcus, *Italian Film in the Light of Neorealism*, Princeton, Princeton University Press, 1986; Fabien Gerard, T. Jefferson Kline, and Bruce Sklarew (eds) *Bernardo Bertolucci: Interviews*, Jackson, University Press of Mississippi, 2000; Donald Ranvaud and Enzo Ungari eds., *Bertolucci by Bertolucci*, trans. D. Ranvaud, London, Plexus, 1987; Robert Philip Kolker, *Bernardo Bertolucci*, New York, Oxford University Press, 1985.
60 J. Hoberman, in his scathing review of the film, disagrees, see "60s-Something", *The Village Voice*, Feb. 4, 2004.
61 On Paris, May 1968, see Hervé Hamon and Patrick Rotman, *Generation: Les Années de Rêve*, Paris, Editions du Seuil, 1987. Henri Lefebvre gives a history in the interview with Ross. See also René Vienet, *Enragés et Situationistes dans le Mouvement des Occupations*, Paris, Gallimard, 1968, trans. L. Goldner and P. Sieveking, *The Enragés and the Situationists in the Occupation Movements, May–June, 1968*, New York, Semiotext(e), 1990.
62 For a world history of 1968 see Mark Kurlansky, *1968: The Year that Rocked the World*, New York, Ballantine, 2004; David Kaute, *The Year of the Barricade: A Journey through 1968*, New York, Harper and Row, 1988; and *The 60's without Apology*, Sohnya Sayres, Anders Stephanson, Stanley Aronowitz, Frederic Jameson eds, Minneapolis, University of Minnesota Press, 1984.
63 Ross compares the identity of the *jeune cadre* with that of the revolutionary *cadre* in the last chapter of *Fast Cars, Clean Bodies*, where she discusses "The lifestyle of the revolutionary ... is necessarily ascetic, stripped down, and unencumbered ... The loss of possessions is compensated for by a gain in physical strength." Ross, *Fast Cars, Clean Bodies*, p. 1. See also Rossanda, *Ragazza del Secolo Scorso*.

4

"You Must Remember This": Memory Objects in the Age of Erasable Memory

For the reader of stuff, there is another event, besides Virginia Woolf's well known dictum, which establishes the year 1910 as crucial for modernism[1]: the publication of the Italian poet Guido Gozzano's collection *I Colloqui*. Gozzano's poetry rails against a present he considers vulgar and the middle class he detests.[2] In one of his best poems, "L'Amica di Nonna Speranza," ("Grandmother Speranza's Friend"), he attacks bourgeois kitsch:

> The embalmed parrot, Alfieri's and Napoleon's busts
> the flowers in a frame (all things in terrible taste)
> The dismal fireplace, empty bonbon boxes
>   the marble fruit under bell jars
> A rare toy, the containers made of seashells
> the objects inscribed with "greetings", "souvenir of . . ."
> Venice portrayed in mosaics, the faded watercolors
> the prints, the small trunks, albums painted with archaic jonquilles
> . . . the daguerrotypes; . . . The cuckoo clock singing, the chairs
>   upholstered in crimson damask . . .[3]

The dating of this scene of nineteenth-century clutter, where the most disparate bibelots mingle in a dusty intimacy, tells us that the souvenir, so prominent among Gozzano's *buone cose di pessimo gusto*, is no longer functional. Gathering dust in the unused drawing room, already destined for the attic, the souvenir is unable to anchor memory and is degraded to kitsch.

As Susan Stewart notes, the souvenir tries to articulate a "lived relationship to the body and to the phenomenological world,"[4] which, in a modern exchange economy where experience itself has withered, is felt to be lost and therefore possibly authentic. The souvenir borrows the compensatory logic of the fetish. It substitutes a part, the tactile and sensual quality of the personal memento, for the lost whole, and speaks nostalgically about origins while miniaturizing history into private time.[5] Thus it puts in place a specific modality of remembrance, what Marita Sturken, in describing how cultural memory is recast in post-9/11 souvenirs, calls "historical tourism."[6] For Sturken, the teddy bears and the snow globes with the Twin Towers both acknowledge and disavow historical truth; they create a culture of comfort that reassures by deflecting anger. As she notes, "The teddy bear doesn't promise to make things better, but makes us feel better about things as they are" (7). These souvenirs, like all souvenirs, allow people to remember but foreclose political engagement, occluding the history that produced the traumatic event in the first place.

The early twentieth-century crisis of the souvenir as memory object indicates an impatience with its fetishistic claim to be a prepackaged fraction of the past, guaranteeing access to an unproblematically consumable memory. With the failure of the souvenir a whole modality of remembrance enters a crisis. At the precise moment when the object as commodity was coming into its full power with the hegemony of consumer culture, the object as *bibelot*, paradoxically, was being shorn of some of its most reputed powers. This incapability of the object to represent the past for the subject could be read as another sign of the crisis of realism and the beginning of a form of abstraction that, through and after modernist experimentation, culminates in the immateriality of the spectacle. For the post-Lukácsian critic, the crisis of a coherent mimetic representational language is nothing less than the possibility of history and collectivity, or at least a concept of historical time capable of defying the isolating power of the image in contemporary culture. I suggest however that this modernist crisis is not immediately and *tout court* a prelude to the abstraction and depoliticization of the past, but rather might offer the possibility for a new notion of memory to be elaborated. Between the time when the souvenir's relation to the past becomes perfunctory and that of the post-World War II era of the all-encompassing presence of the image, there is an important interval, when the modernist is offered the chance provided by the dehiscence of the object (and of the subject) of memory to tear a breach in the amnesia-inducing tendencies of modernity. No longer talismanically contained in an object, now memory might be made part of the body sensationally. This idea of a corporeal memory allows no spectatorial or dominating relation to the object, and instead envisions the subject itself "subjected" and acted upon by memory. A new tactile relationship to remembered reality and experience is possible. A somatic discernment of the past in the stuff which remains in the present, a new experience of temporality in the unruly object: these are the stakes of the early twentieth-century crisis of representation in its bearing upon the notion of history. Here we investigate this new relationship between materiality and memory in the aftermath of the souvenir by attending to the power of different memory objects. After exploring Walter Benjamin's reading of Marcel Proust's famous *madeleine*, we turn to the forgotten clothes in Virginia Woolf's *To the Lighthouse* and to the waste left on World War I battlefields in Bertrand Tavernier's 1989 film *La Vie et Rien d'Autre* (*Life and Nothing But*).

Yet if high culture was suffering a crisis of representation of the past and witnessing the modernist outlawing of the souvenir, mass culture at the same moment witnessed a rearguard return to materiality and to "solid" memory objects which claimed once again to guarantee the presence of the past "as it really was." This drive is evident in the time capsule, where objects are hoarded by official culture to signify time's passing, usually in the service of monumental notions of history. We will explore the contradiction between the high-modernist disqualification of the memory object and its pop-cultural return in this impulse to memorialize with a hoard of bibelots. Both the high-modernist object-project in relation to history and the time capsule are experiments in developing new relations between objects and the subject's experience of time. Each questions what kind of materiality is needed to reclaim memory as a component of experience. If we are not to yield to an amnesia that knows nothing more than present and future, what kind of materiality, we must ask, would undo such a sense of time?

I. Modern Amnesia

Modern commodity culture tends to the narcotic and therefore to the amnesiac. Adorno and Horkheimer, in *Dialectic of Enlightenment*, formulate a theorem on this amnesia as follows: "Every reification is a forgetting." Reification, as the cultural and existential condition of capitalism, is founded like the commodity itself on an act of amnesia: the history of the commodity as the product of social relations between human beings and matter is erased by its smooth and beguiling surface.[7] For many critics, the rise of presentism and forgetfulness follows from the late nineteenth-century increase in technological acceleration: from the first use of radio signals to the mass-produced automobile, as Stephen Kern has shown, emerges a new experience of time and place centered on simultaneity and speed. This, in turn, led to a crisis in representation;[8] acceleration, simultaneity, and synchronicity translated into the experimentations of Balla, Marinetti, and Robert Delauney, and later into the full-blown modernisms of the 1920s. This version of the rise of modernist innovation as reaction to technological change clearly owes a certain debt to materialism; at the same time it begs to be read in the context of a western crisis of over-accumulation brought on by the second industrial revolution, which in turn led to new forms of credit and increased circulation of money and goods. In this context, the various modernisms' new versions of corporeal time and disjointed space often seemed to collude with the amnesiac tendency of consumption; texts that immerse the reader in the present, such as Joyce's *Ulysses* and Tati's *Playtime* a half-century later, both of which show the life of a city in a single day, may seem to wish away past time. Yet the past resurfaces, so that every modernism produces a formal architecture of memory, and hence a new understanding of it.

The theorist who has offered the most sustained reflection on how modernist amnesia relates to the real world is Fredric Jameson, who opened his most important work with the injunction to "Always historicize!" and for whom the failure of memory is the precursor to the tragic end of politics in culture. In his approach to time, Jameson follows Lefebvre's idea about space: that capitalism will invariably abstract it, smooth it out, make it "homogenous and empty." Extrapolating from theories of uneven development of global space, he develops Nietzsche's critique of the western narrative of irresistible historical progress[9] by underscoring how the loss of a sense of the past also developed unevenly. Given the incomplete and uneven modernization of the early twentieth century, the various modernisms, in his reading, produce different temporalities and suggest contradictions capable of troubling the homogenous time of capital. Thus a sense of the temporal is still possible in modernism; its interest in time has both a past and a future dimension. On the one hand time moves toward what Andreas Huyssen terms "the new as utopian and irreducible other,"[10] and on the other toward a past that, once it is no longer understood in mimetic and fetishistic terms, seems to be always on the verge of disappearing.[11]

Having allowed that an intuited project to recuperate memory is possible in modernist art, and suggested that the defamiliarizing shocks of modernist representation can be read as indices of this project, Jameson then goes on to paint a picture of almost universal amnesiac presentism as the condition of post-modernity. For him, the end of temporality is paralleled by a late twentieth-century shift to the predominance of finance capital, which functions at a level of abstraction beyond that of its monopoly stage. Now, "money sublimates into sheer number, and a new value emerges that has little to do with the old fashioned value of . . . products and their marketability . . . . a novel and more universal microtemporality . . . condenses the rhythms of quantity profit making" (703). Abstraction intensifies, and time is compressed. In culture, this new abstraction translates into the flatness of the image. It is reflected in contemporary culture not in estranging modernist obscurities, but in the smooth surfaces of popular forms. Warning us to beware of the smoothness of this new easily digested art, Jameson insists upon a distinction between the image, in Debord's sense of the spectacle, and the object, as materiality itself. Postmodernism, he notes, is perhaps a realism of the image, certainly not of the object.

For Jameson the "realism of the object" demands a certain solid quality of materiality, and individual access to it as a prerequisite for the making of a representation with the power to evoke history. Yet this may be a restrictive demand; a mimetic logic of representation is not necessarily needed to connect subject and object. It follows that Jameson's chronological division between modernism and postmodernism must also be interrogated. First, the disappearance of memory was already a modernist phenomenon; second, we may wish to recuperate the site of materiality he now sees as its last redoubt—the subject's body. "When you have nothing left but your temporal present, it follows that you have nothing left but your own body," he insists,[12] and despite his qualms, we can seize this statement as a point of departure. Modernist experiments in recasting the subject–object encounter could be either dangerous or promising: the choreographed aesthetic effect that tied the crowd to the fascist leader in an "oceanic feeling" contrasts with the modernist evocation of the somatic and synaesthetic body whose carnivalesque solidity was potentially liberating. Proust's subject in *À la Recherche du Temps Perdu* is highly synaesthetic, open to sensations, centered on and decentered by its sensorium, *and* at the same time solipsistically fixated on his private space and memory. This synaesthetic incorporation, focused on the subject's nervous system, can therefore reveal the body as dependent on its social context.

It is to the body, social and individual, and its sensorium that modernist experiment entrusts memory once the materiality and the logic of the souvenir are no longer viable. This corporeality is not the anaesthetized "exquisite corpse" of capitalist spectacle, but an open, permeable, fragmented and living matter that calls into question bourgeois subjectivity and its armored unity of surface. The dissolution of the split between subject and object via a plastic (in Malabou's sense) understanding of the body repeatedly appears in different registers in the long modernist era, in texts from Darwin's *The Expression of the Emotions in Man and Animals* of 1872 to Jean Rhys' *Good Morning Midnight* of 1939. Our task is to gauge the implications of this dissolution, rather than to declare its oppositional power *tout court*. This body and its synaesthetic openness, as articulated by Benjamin, Proust, and Woolf, suggest new notions of subjectivity, memory, even history. Later twentieth-century commodity culture repeatedly tries to close the gap between subject and object, what Jameson calls the "realism of the image." That this gap needs to be closed means that the commodity's forgetting is never fully accomplished: instead, as lived and embodied in the social, memory is not simply lost,[13] cast in the "dustbin of history," or immured in the archive.[14] Although the conditions that produced this notion of lived memory in the early twentieth century have changed, it persists as embodied desire.

For Benjamin the function of memory and materiality is to reactivate something that has never been fully disabled and concluded. The fading of the messianic image of the past, which in the *Theses on the Philosophy of History* he names as the tragic danger, is instead saluted and recycled by the culture of capital as optimistic farce, the farce of futurity. Capitalism happily revels in the positivity of ignoring the present by trundling a cryogenic past-into-the-future, *à la* Walt Disney. The past, in this conjuncture, is presented as futuristic taxidermy, where memory is in fact not needed, because the past and the future will be exactly the same, as in the case of the cryogenically preserved corpse. However, even when the past is allowed to show its face in culture and the everyday as souvenir or memorial monument, it will not interrupt or question the continuum of history because such memory can be neutered by propriety. In contrast to these approved memory sites and their remembrance etiquette, it is around ephemeral and chance objects, appearing unexpectedly, that a struggle is staged between a culture of certainty and positivity that looks at the object as repository of a dead past, and an embodied "lived memory" which looks at materiality as still living history. In Proust's and Benjamin's individual and historical memory, the past, rather than existing as facts to be "reconquered," remains out of focus and instead approaches us through the senses; when it flashes as an image (which is not Benjamin's dialectical image), what matters is what is not there, what is not visible but inferable from outside the frame. This flickering memory, marking an uncertainty about the past, is ingrained in Proust's work; if *À la Recherche* sanctions the demise of the souvenir, it celebrates the body and its sensations for a somatic and sensory encounter with the past. Part II of Virginia Woolf's 1927 novel *To the Lighthouse* goes further, to show that memory can be supported by objects as tokens of the subject's body. Her objects keep memory in their forms in the absence of a perceiving subject. The same elements of Proust's memory kit reappear in Woolf, yet the body, the past, materiality, and art in Woolf combine to reverse and complicate the Proustian articulation of time. While in *À la Recherche* memory can be understood as an act or matter of bodies without objects, in "Time Passes," the key section of *To the Lighthouse*, it becomes a matter of objects without the body, where materiality and nature take over the functions of the subject. In both Proust's and Woolf's scenarios of memory the subject renounces its narcissistic selfhood to approach moments of temporal suspension, where representation and referentiality cease, ceding ground to the timelessness of the material real. Woolf's clothes literally keep time within themselves by maintaining a physical memory of absent bodies, whose parenthetical disappearance reintroduces history in the form of physical decay, illness, and war.

In Bertrand Tavernier's 1989 film *Life and Nothing But*, which centers on the objects left by the dead soldiers of the Great War, memory and the subject's identity again depend on the object. The residue left on the battlefield, which the soldiers' relatives pick through to identify bodies, are no souvenirs, but objects which themselves cite the idea of a differential history, the victor's and the victim's. War residue, what is left of persons, marks the moment when history, or better, History, is silenced and memory speaks once again a tale of objects without bodies. This history in discarded objects speaks against the lies of the war memorial's nationalist rhetoric. Tavernier's film underlines the importance of even the personal object to sustain memory. None of these objects can be kept as mementoes, and their referents, the dead soldiers' identities, are tentative and equally ephemeral. The subject here is literally an unstable trace. Years after the Great War, when it has seeped out of personal memories and found a (small) place in collective ones, this film is a moving meditation on the power of things—lost and cast-off things, stuff—to speak eloquently of the subject who should be remembered and to the subject about how to remember.

The time capsule as memory object has its own pathos; as official memory object, it strives to return materiality, memory, and history to the fetishistic status which the modern culture of capital attributes to things. In the capsule, official memory is frozen into a number of artifacts endowed with the power again to "represent" western civilization and its cutting-edge technological discoveries. It is this confident representationalism and its claims that Peter Greenaway mocks in the museum exhibit and prop-opera *One Hundred Objects to Represent the World* (1992), where the referentiality of the time capsule is hollowed out—to open a carnival space for wild and untethered allegories, in which stuff, in a super-ensemble of bits and pieces, stands for an unstable emblem-status to multiply the stakes of memory.

II. Bodies without Objects: Benjamin's Proust (or Teatime in the Land of the Real)

"Proustian temporality", writes Julia Kristeva, "has remained steadfastly modern."[15] Here I will not provide a full-scale reading of Proust's textual memory palace, but rather a reading of Benjamin's reflection on Proust, to show how the latter's negotiations with the past influenced Benjamin's thinking on experience and history, and his remaking of the relationship between the object, memory, and the body.

Proust offers Benjamin the means to respond to what he considered the modern crisis of experience. Benjamin's understanding of this crisis is, as Buck-Morss notes, neurological, founded on Freud's insights into trauma and memory in the minds of soldier survivors of World War I. Confronted by the shocks of modernity, consciousness does not register experience, but rather acts as a shield against excessive stimuli; painful and anxiety-producing experiences, therefore, often never enter consciousness. "Put in Proustian terms," writes Benjamin, "this means that only what has not been experienced explicitly and consciously, what has not happened to the subject as experience, can become a component of the *memoire involontaire*."[16] Before explaining how involuntary memory works, consider the crucial relation that both Proust and Benjamin posit between experience and the past: for both, to be able to experience reality is a matter of remembering it. Experience for Benjamin is deeply imbricated in the past, in a dialectical relationship between past and present. Hence his notion of tradition: "Experience is indeed a matter of tradition, in collective existence as well as private life. It's less the product of facts firmly anchored in memory, than a convergence in memory of accumulated and often unconscious data" (*CB*, 110). Facts anchored in memory are here opposed to "a convergence of accumulated and unconscious data," which is how he defines tradition. In Latin, *tradere* means "to pass on"; this "passing on," which for Benjamin takes place through ritual, implies an unceasing movement of experience, knowledge and affect from one generation, group, or individual to another. The fixity of "facts firmly anchored in memory," on the contrary, defines modern amnesia and the atrophy of experience. "Perhaps the special achievement of shock defense," noted Benjamin, "is exactly this function of assigning to an incident a precise point in time, in consciousness, at the cost of the integrity of its contents … The intellect would turn the incident into a moment that has been lived (*Erlebnis*)" (*CB*, 116). This regimen of "firmly anchored facts" is precisely the notion of temporality that both Proust and Benjamin oppose. To unblock such fixity is to let the subject's body experience the facts despite the push-back of self-defense. *Erfahrung*, what both writer and critic are after, cannot be contained in a causal, teleological notion of time, in which each event belongs to a precise and concluded moment of the past. Such precision and closure characterizes the temporality that the souvenir claims to automatically bring back to us. Strictly speaking, Proust does not want to resurrect the past, but to experience what has been accumulated in the unconscious. The unordered and tactile mode of this accumulation is well captured in Benjamin's "The Image of Proust," where Benjamin compares the "contents" of involuntary memory to a fisherman's catch; in the bottommost stratum of involuntary memory, he writes,

> … the materials of memory no longer appear simply, as images, but tell us about a whole, amorphously, and formlessly, indefinitely and weightily, in the same way as the weight of his net tells a fisherman about his catch.

Smell—that is, the sense of weight of someone who casts his nets into the sea of the *temps perdu*. And his sentences are the entire muscular activity of the intelligible body; they contain the whole enormous effort to raise this catch.[17]

Here he makes clear that experience is located in the body, and that time for Proust, as Kristeva also noted, is time embodied. Moreover, what spurs this experiential-mnemonic act is materiality, and Proust's fidelity to it.[18]

For Proust, following Bergson, while voluntary memory remains in the domain of the intellect and of the empirical experience of reality, involuntary memory is sparked by a chance encounter with an object which dissolves into bodily sensations. "Objects begin to have meaning," writes Kristeva on this corporeal memory in Proust,

> once I discover the sensations associated with them. Such objects always come in groups of two or more (the *madeleine* mamma offers me and that that Aunt Leonie gives me, the paving stones of the Guermantes' courtyard and those of the Baptistery at Saint Mark's in Venice). Time, then, is the association between two sensations that spring from signs and make their presence known (169).

Memory is set in motion, and the past "opened up" by an object and by the sensations produced on the body of the subject of remembrance. The subject is no longer the spectator of a past scene that he recalled contemplatively as an image; instead, the past happens to the present-day subject as tactile experience. The Proustian *objet trouvé* activates involuntary memory, through which "an individual forms an image of himself . . . [and] can take hold of his experience" (*CB*, 112). Bergson, in his notion of *memoire pure*,[19] claims that "turning to the contemplative actualization of the stream of life is a matter of free choice"; the encounter with one's *madeleine*, however, is for Benjamin as well as Proust entirely a matter of chance, and might not even happen during one's lifetime.[20] This constellation of memory, object, and body through which Proust refigures not the past per se, but a new relation to the past, is the basis for Benjamin's theorization of experience and history. At the same time, the conditions in which involuntary memory comes into being, and the notion of time it produces, reveal elements which signal that the stakes of Benjamin's thought about history and experience extend beyond those of Proust.

Involuntary memory depends upon the body as the material space onto which the object is grafted via sensations, so that the blocked *experience* of the past event becomes available for the first time. Proust's doing away with the object in favor of the experience of it destabilizes the perceiving subject-of-reason, and with it the notion of perception and temporality that it supports. Proust's subject is synaesthetic, receptive to the object's radiant secret which narcotic modernity has striven to negate. This subject is always already made part of the world via its nervous system. It is also Benjamin's innervated subject, incorporating the object (reality), and being incorporated by it—a subject made post-bourgeois by its receptivity to its own sensations, and by its prosthetic affinity with technology.[21] At the same time, paradoxically, this neurologically open-ended subject becomes aware of his surroundings and of the past in social isolation: if the Proustian subject of remembrance is part of a sociality, his mnemonic efforts do not bond him to a collectivity. For Benjamin as well as Proust the situation that gave rise to involuntary memory

> is part of the inventory of the individual that is isolated in many ways. When there is experience in the strict sense of the word, certain contents of the individual past combine with materials of the collective past. The rituals (ceremonies, festivals, quite probably nowhere recalled in Proust's work) kept producing the amalgamation of these two elements of memory over and over again . . . (*CB*, 113).

Collective dimensions of experience and of memory, key for Benjamin, are missing in Proust. Yet Benjamin forgives this gap, given the conditions of modernity: "*À la recherche* can be considered as an attempt to produce experience synthetically, as Bergson imagines it, under today's conditions; for there is less and less hope that it will come into being naturally" (*CB*, 11). In the Benjamin–Proust experience project, the point when they part company is on the question of the collective, and thus properly historical, past.

Proust provides Benjamin with the tools for redeeming experience and attacking nineteenth-century teleological ideas of history: past and present intersect through the object of involuntary memory, rather than being articulated sequentially. The reminiscences of voluntary memory, however, are—as in the case of Baudelaire's *correspondences*—data of remembrance, not historical data, but data of prehistory. That is, they belong to the sphere of ritual and of the auratic connection between individual and collectivity. For Benjamin, like the time of spleen, the time of involuntary memory is "outside history" (*CB*, 143). The *memoire involontaire*, then, is the index of a non-historical time, home to the aura. Insofar as involuntary memory allows the subject to experience the past for the first time, it stands outside history, but not outside time. Its imbrication in tradition, the passing of knowledge through time from one generation to another, and ritual, repetition through time, shows that its temporality is not metaphysical, but contingent and historical. It acknowledges death. In this sense, both Benjamin and Proust, in their search for experience, go well beyond Bergson's metaphysics; in Benjamin's terms, "If Baudelaire of 'Spleen'... holds in his hands the scattered fragments of genuine historical experience, Bergson in his concept of the *durée*, isolates it effectively from historical (as well as prehistorical) order.... The *durée* from which death has been eliminated has the miserable endlessness of a scroll. Tradition is excluded from it" (*CB*, 145). This question of death, of (historical) finitude, *vis-à-vis* the metaphysics of Bergson's *durée* or of any metaphysics, represents a crucial moment in Benjamin's thinking about experience and the past. Benjamin is anxious to show that Proust and his work are free from any metaphysical quality: "In Proust ... we are guests who enter through a door underneath a suspended sign that sways in the breeze, a door behind which eternity and rapture awaits us."[22] The Proustian rapture, which involuntary memory produces, allows and stands for several of Benjamin's concepts: the monad as dialectical image, the *nunc stans* of the *Jetztzeit*, a messianic time that cuts and explodes history, an ecstasy that produces rupture. Benjamin makes clear that Proust's work is steeped in time, in finite time, bound by change and death: "The element that Proust opens to view is convoluted time, not boundless time. His true interest lies in the passage of time in its most real, that is space-bound form—and this passage is most visible in remembrance within and aging without" ("Image," 24). Involuntary memory becomes a means of rejuvenation that connects two moments in time by bringing one to fruition in the other.

This is Benjamin's "theory of the second chance," the idea of the unexperienced past intervening in one's life to change it, to make actual what could have been possible but did not happen. (It anticipates his ideas in the *Theses* of an incomplete history). Benjamin wants to see the past actualized in the present, because "A historical materialist cannot do without the notion of the present which is not a transition, but in which time stands still, and it has come to a stop. For this notion describes the present "in which he himself is writing history" ("Thesis XVI", 262). In the *Theses*, Benjamin's difference from Proust becomes clear on two issues: first, the question of the subject of experience or of history, and, second, the question of the "completion" of history, of convoluted rather than boundless history—and of death. I want first to address the second issue, to show how in the end they hold quite opposing views on the relation between materiality and subjectivity.

"There is a Proustian vision of the world," writes Gilles Deleuze. "It is defined initially by what it excludes: crude matter, mental deliberation, physics, and philosophy."[23] Deleuze reads *À la Recherche* as an "apprenticeship" to truth via art, and via the interpretation of signs that by the violence of their encounter force us to interpret them.[24] Proust deals only in ever-equivocal signs; to properly interpret them, Deleuze develops a concept of "involuntary intelligence" to accompany the Proustian "involuntary memory." In his terms, "Thinking happens not by an abstract and voluntary intelligence which claims to find logical truth by itself, to have its own order and to anticipate pressures from the outside world," but by involuntary intelligence, which "undergoes the pressure of signs ... to exorcise the void" of threatened illegibility (96). In this anti-humanist, post-Proustian, and anti-Oedipal reorganization of the subject–object relation, Deleuze posits materiality as emitting signs that "assault" the philosopher into thinking. Signs make the individual into a subject insofar as they call him to interpret. Deleuze's perspective on Proust here differs from Benjamin's: its brand of "Platonism" turns the sensuous quality of the object encountered, that which spurs involuntary memory, into "the sign of an altogether different object that we must try to decipher" (11). The perception of the sensuous quality of an object, and the joy it produces, turn into an imperative for the subject: he must interpret it, so that its "objective sensation" can be disclosed and recognized. The happy epistemological convergence between subject and object via the signs the one reads and which the other emits can be taken as the other side of the violence which, for Deleuze, defines their encounter. But what if this communication breaks down? What if involuntary, as well as voluntary, memory fails, and with it "the sign's meaning ... yielding to us the concealed object—Combray for the *madeleine*, young girls for the steeples, Venice for the cobblestones ..." (11–12)? The rhythm of *À la Recherche*, Deleuze admits, is made of "disappointments and revelations .... We are disappointed when the object does not give us the secret we are expecting" (34), where sensuous signs are incapable of giving us an essence. What of the times when the object does not seem to emit signs, and "crude matter," which Deleuze excludes from the Proustian landscape as the void that has been exorcised and excised by the Proustian work of art, reappears?

This is the scenario Jameson depicts in his discussion of the automatization and depersonalization of language in the writing of Proust and Joyce, which he regards as moments of contact with the Real. In Proust one such moment is the narrator's much anticipated and final visit to Venice. Venice is re-experienced by the narrator when he stumbles on the uneven paving stones in the Hotel de Guermantes courtyard. In Richard Terdiman's account, "His body memory recollects a similar posture, remembers the same posture in the Baptistry of San Marco. The experience rematerializes Venice."[25] Venice is where the narrator situates his fantasies of escape during his love affair with Albertine, and where he goes with his mother after Albertine's death. Jameson comments on the moment when the narrator looks at Venice and remains disappointed:

> The town that I saw before me had ceased to be Venice ... I saw the palaces reduced to their constituent parts, lifeless heaps of marble with nothing to choose between them, and the water as a combination of

hydrogen and oxygen, eternal, blind, anterior and exterior to Venice, unconscious of the Doges or of Turner ... I could not tell it anything more about myself, I could leave nothing of myself imprinted upon it, it left me diminished, I was nothing more than a heart that throbbed, and an attention strained.[26]

This materiality that refuses to emit signs, this "negative sublime" is for Jameson nothing less than the closest literature can even come to the Real:

We reach some ultimate point ... of the stripping away of the surface of appearances to reveal a kind of dead extension beneath, a kind of zero degree of being of the world and of reality itself, a fabulous place-name from which the name and the image, the very "place" itself, have vanished away leaving nothing behind them but pure matter.[27]

For Lacan, the Real had been what resists symbolization absolutely, that which falls outside the symbolic order and the categories that organize meanings, outside language and history, with no space for the subject. This "dead extension beneath" about which Proust writes, points to a lifeless quiescence, a form of being as non-existence, which Jameson reads as a totality unavailable to us while we live, for it exists only in death. This is the space where the subject can only be matter in the midst of matter, where no relationship (auratic or not) can be articulated between subject and object.

Is this encounter with the Real the point of arrival of Proustian temporality? Is remembrance, which always struggles against its failure, invariably on the side of paralysis and death? And how can this presence of the Real in *À la Recherche* be reconciled with what Benjamin learns from Proust, the will to experience historical change? In *The Arcades Project*, Konvolut S, Benjamin acknowledges Proust's *penchant* for the Real: "I grant that Proust, in the deepest sense, perhaps ranges himself on the side of death. His cosmos has its sun, perhaps, in death, around which orbit the lived moments, the gathered things .... his subject is the obverse, *le reverse*, not so much of the world but of life itself" (Benjamin, *Arcades*, S2, 3, 547). It is upon the image of a materiality that exists autonomously from the perceiving subject that Benjamin and Proust part company, as Benjamin's thought about experience and the past has a historical dimension. The "rapturous eternity" shared by both Benjamin's and Proust's idea of temporality takes us either in the direction of the Real or that of the incomplete temporality of history. For Proust, the subject's disappointment can always be "remedied" by art, or, if it is not, as in the case of Venice, *tant pis*. In Benjamin this same disappointment acquires a dangerous edge, as the *Theses on the Philosophy of History* show.

"For every image of the past that is not recognized by the present as one of its own concerns, threatens to disappear irretrievably," we read in *Thesis V*. While Proust's subject can enjoy the luxury of failing at remembering, and then, as in the Venice episode, can contemplate his own demise at the hands of the Real, Benjamin's historical materialist critic lives at a time of historical and political emergency. Thus his demise would be definitive, and so would be the demise of those for whom he speaks, the oppressed. In the history of the victors (and history, notes Benjamin, is always the domain of the victors), being forgotten means to be dead twice: "In every era the attempt must be made to wrest tradition away from a conformism that is about to overpower it . . . even the dead will not be safe from the enemy if he wins" (*Illuminations*, *Thesis VI*, 255). Given this sense of historical emergency, Benjamin does not hesitate to enlist the powers of theology;[28] for him, remembrance and theology have the power to open history as a time filled "with the presence of the now" (*Thesis* XIV, 261). The moment of the Proustian "disappointment," in contrast to the politically urgent temporality of the *Theses*, risks colluding with "the homogeneous empty time" of bourgeois history and might end up fostering amnesia rather than memory. The historical materialist instead wants to make visible what the "unity of surface" of the past has made invisible: the presence of the oppressed, so that "he recognizes . . . a revolutionary chance in the fight for the oppressed past" (*Thesis* XVII, 263). This last phrase would certainly never have been written by Proust. The unactualized past cannot be understood and reclaimed just in personal and aesthetic terms, but must also be reclaimed in historical and collective ones. The body without objects, through which Proustian memory is articulated, opens for Benjamin a new way of thinking about temporality: it shows him that "happiness," redemption, the revolution, historical change, is not, so to speak, at the end of the road, safely waiting for us, but must be actively grasped.

When Proust looks at Venice unsymbolized, he looks at the same panorama at which both Benjamin's allegorist and his Angel of History look: a space filled with ruins that exclude and alienate the subject. Proust contemplates this panorama of rubble with a dismal and disaffected look: if Venice rejects him and doesn't let him inscribe himself upon its stones, he will have to find another object that might allow that puncturing of the flow of time that constitutes Proustian memory. Benjamin, like the Angel of History, would like to stay and redeem the rubble, because he knows that the series of objects that might strike the messianic time into being is finite, and that, if they are not remembered, the dead will be really dead.

III. Objects without Bodies: Your Clothes When You Are Not There

Could the materiality that Proust finds disappointing, the materiality that refuses to emit signs to be interpreted by the subject, be something more than an encounter with the Real? How can Proust's unsubjected objects be used to defeat the fetishism of the souvenir and discern a differential notion of history, a memory without monumentality?

Virginia Woolf, like Proust and Benjamin, recognizes temporality as ephemeral and unstable, always at its vanishing point. Her very style strikes the reader as an index of her sense of the insubstantiality of materiality, and of its inability, whether as souvenir or monument, to capture the past or represent the flow of time. Like Proust and Benjamin, she looks for the means to strike this flow into a temporary arrest. *To the Lighthouse* is perhaps the novel in which she most starkly juxtaposes temporality, space, and stuff. Here Woolf wants to bring an unfulfilled past to completion, first in the gesture of the trip to the lighthouse, and second in the art object that is Lily Briscoe's unfinished painting. The aim is to overcome the past, to let go of what is truly lost; the book is in part an autobiographical work of mourning. On the other hand, Woolf strives to mark the instability and openness of time. This openness can be captured by the artists—here, Lily and Mrs. Ramsey—in the moment, a full experiential instant that cannot be inscribed anywhere but upon the body, to last the duration of corporeal, physical existence.

The same constellation of object, body, and memory sketched in the work of both Proust and Benjamin reappears in *To the Lighthouse,* but in a different configuration. Here, the perceiving subject is ultimately excluded from the act of remembering, and materiality itself is instead shown to maintain memory. Woolf implicitly turns to Proust's notion of memory, but mostly to illuminate its shortcomings; rather, through an alternative reworking of the subject–object relation, she points us in the direction of Benjamin and his differential notion of history. As for Proust and Benjamin, for Woolf too the body is crucial for reclaiming experience and memory. By means of the body, temporality is momentarily fixed in art. However, while in Proust the memory of the past is activated by what I called a body without objects, for Woolf memory is maintained by objects in the absence of the body. Woolf, particularly in Part II of the novel, pushes to the extreme an impetus evident in most modernist writing, the disintegration of the subject, whose "grip" upon materiality through language and reason is undone.

In a diary entry of 1925, Woolf describes *To the Lighthouse* as an elegy, a means to end her mourning over the death of her parents, her mother in 1895 and her father in 1904.[29] Pursuing this autobiographical lead, the novel may be read as Woolf's means of working out her relationship with her father, and his faith in the subject-of-reason. Like Leslie Stephen, Mr. Ramsey in *To the Lighthouse* is a philosopher steeped in British empiricism. Woolf knew of her father's interest in David Hume (and read Hume herself in 1920), philosopher of subjectivity and perception. When Andrew Ramsey explains "Subject and object and the nature of reality" to Lily, who "... said Heavens, she had no notion what that meant. 'Think of a kitchen table then,' he told her, 'when you are not there.'"[30] This famous passage takes us to the core of the novel's ontological and epistemological problematic and its challenge to the principles of empiricism; it also opens the path to a new understanding of memory. Woolf confronts the same questions as Proust: what is the past, how is time unraveling, how does one suspend its course to get hold of experience and make the moment permanent? She does not just look at time as "time past," but focuses on time, and reality, after the subject is gone. She asks what endures in the absence of the subject.

To the Lighthouse dismisses the idea of memory as fame, attached to the deeds of a "great man" as a rational subject who wills his permanence into being with his intellect. This leads not to a turn to involuntary memory, but to the possibility of an alternative version of memory, independent of the perceiver and rather consigned to materiality, whether that of the body or of objects themselves. This image of unsubjected objects then becomes the foundation of a new understanding of art, imbricated in the ordinariness of the body and of materiality, and yet non-referential, shorn of what Gillian Beer calls "the burdened authority of the symbolic object."[31] To theorize and write this innovative version of materiality in the novel, Woolf challenges the discourse of empiricism and, given her father's predilection for Hume, the paternal affective and intellectual trace. The preoccupations of British empiricism—the skepticism about substance, the status of materiality and of the perceiving subject, the nature of identity and non-entity—assume a particular relevance for Woolf's discussion of materiality and time. Abjuring this philosophical discourse, Woolf elaborates her notion of subject and object. For Hume, the subject is made by his perceptions, which succeed one another in a continuous flux. Materiality is contingent upon the presence of a perceiving subject, and reality is established through this act of perception, so much so that, as Hume describes it, substance and its ontological status remains alien and unknowable to the subject. In *A Treatise of Human Nature* he writes that "A substance is entirely different from a perception. We have, therefore, no idea of a substance." If subject and object are related only through perception, the existence of each when they are not connected is not guaranteed.[32] Woolf instead makes it one of the goals of her novel to entertain the possibility of their existence beyond this connection. Hume insists that we know nothing of substantiality outside of perception. Woolf works to recuperate the idea of the substantiality of matter as a prerequisite of both memory and art.

The novel proposes two different answers to the question of what constitutes the past, and what survives after the subject disappears: one associated with the character of Mr. Ramsey as the man of reason and Hume's version of perception, and the other connected with Mrs. Ramsey as the mother-housewife-female artist figure. In Mr. Ramsey's empiricist view, the subject of experience is crucial in supporting an ordered notion of reality. That reality is stabilized by Mr. Ramsey's "logic of facts": "He was incapable of untruth; never tampered with a fact; never altered a disagreeable word to suit the pleasure or convenience of any human being" (*TTL*, 4). This factual logic is shunned by Woolf as gendered and sexist; if Mr. Ramsey is on the side of facts, Mrs. Ramsey is on that of desire, pleasure, and aesthetics. He writes and reads philosophy, while she reads poetry (without, her husband claims, understanding it) and tells fairy tales to her children. Nonetheless, notwithstanding his empiricist faith in the certainty of facts, Mr. Ramsey is anxiously aware that materiality will outlast him: "The very stone one kicks with one's boot will outlast Shakespeare" (*TTL*, 35). His peevish solution to this problem is to do away with Shakespeare and all art as ornamental (therefore feminine) and inessential to the progress of civilization. By the same stroke he also dismisses a phenomenon he deems merely distasteful to the liberal intellectual with a social conscience,[33] "the existence of a slave class." Here Benjamin's dictum in the *Theses*, "There is no document of civilization that is not, at the same time, a document of barbarism," is turned on its head and made moot:

> If Shakespeare had never existed, he asked, would the world have differed much from what is today? ... Possibly the greater good requires the existence of a slave class. The liftman in the Tube is an eternal necessity. The thought was distasteful to him ... To avoid it he would find some way of snubbing the predominance of the arts ... the arts are merely a decoration imposed on the top of human life; they do not express it; nor is Shakespeare necessary to it. (*TTL*, 42–43).

Woolf's irony brings the Aesopian fable of the fox and the grapes to mind here. The class of workers, those who, as we have seen, Barthes acknowledged as the group who have concrete physical dealings with matter, will return as arbiters of the power of matter and memory in Woolf's text.

Although he disapproves of art, Mr. Ramsey does not give up the symbol, neither in a Lacanian or aesthetic sense, as his quoting poetry demonstrates.

Symbolizing for Mr. Ramsey constitutes a double move of displacing the materiality confronting him, and renaming it, making it manageable through a codified language. He turns to the aesthetic to make reality controllable; in poetry he finds a prosthetic, ready-made repertoire of symbolizing language he uses to stave off the dangers of the Real, of which negativity, death, and the unsubjected object are the building stones. Mrs. Ramsey, instead, is placed in a continuum with untranscended materiality and the aesthetic. In her case the aesthetic is understood neither simply as art, in which she has no stake, as seen in her lack of interest in Lily's painting, nor in whether she herself is seen as an object of beauty. Rather, the aesthetic for her is a form of plasticity, her ability to create pleasure and memorable sensations in her guests. She is delighted by the communal eating of the *Boeuf en Daube*, which she serves and for which she provides the recipe (but does not cook), and the connections that food and conversation create among the guests. Eating and the materiality of food offer the synaesthetic experience and open-ended tactility that Lily tries for in her painting. Lily's attempt to connect different elements of "pictorial" reality—"It was a question, she remembered, how to connect this mass on the right hand, with that on the left" (*TTL*, 53)—evokes the connection of people at the dinner table, as well as the flavors in the dish itself. For Mrs. Ramsey, the materiality of the body and of food have no symbolic dimension; rather, bodily experience allows an immediate relationship between subject and object, which in turn produces memory via sensation. This memory will not be eternal or monumental, but, after "[it] struck everything into stability," will last through her guests' lives. This projective retrospection is achieved through subjective sensation. Mr. Ramsey, with his *penchant* for symbol, would do away with the object by representing it, thus keeping it at a distance. Woolf places Mrs. Ramsey, on the contrary, on the side of the object's creative plasticitity. Mr. Ramsey's positivist understanding of life and matter clashes not only with his wife's "lies" and loving fictions, but also with her negative ontology. From the start, Mrs. Ramsey perceives herself as part of the material world. Significantly, and ominously, she identifies with nature and the inanimate, for instance with the stroke of the lighthouse:

> Often she found herself sitting and looking, with her work in her hands, until she became the thing she was looking at—that light, for example. . . . It was odd, she thought, how if one was alone, one leant to inanimate things: trees, stream, flowers; felt they expressed one; felt they became one; felt they knew one, in a sense were one; felt an irrational tenderness thus (she looked at that long steady light) as for oneself (*TTL*63–64).

In this passage the human contiguity with materiality and nature upends the traditional Hegelian relationship of subject to object.

This identification of subject and object, associated with Mrs. Ramsey in Part I, takes center stage in Part II, "Time Passes," the section which registers the events which take place over ten years. "The Stephen family (the 'real' Ramseys)," as Gayatri Spivak notes, "had visited Talland House in St. Ives (the 'real' location of *To the Lighthouse*) for the last time in 1894. Julia Stephen (the 'real' Mrs. Ramsey, Woolf's mother) dies in 1895. In a certain sense, 'Time Passes' compresses 1894–1918—from Mrs. Stephen's death to the end of the war."[34] Spivak, who reads the novel as "a search for a language to predicate Mrs. Ramsey," one split between Mr. Ramsey philosophy and Lily's art, proposes that "Time Passes" "narrates the production of a discourse of madness within this autobiographical *roman à clef*. In the ... hinge in the book, a story of unhinging is told" (35). The first intimation of this unhinging is the darkness that descends upon the house, the traditional locus of reason, domesticity, and order, once its inhabitants leave it. Emptied of human agency—"Not only was furniture confounded; there was hardly anything left of body or mind by which one could say 'This is he,' or 'This is she'" (*TTL*, 126)—the house becomes a site of Benjamin's *nunc stans* without messianism, without the possibility of redemption: it becomes the sphere of the Real and its negativity as total materiality. Woolf valiantly tries to represent this absolute materiality through an anthropomorphized language of things and an unstable and shifting impersonal narrative voice. Finally, "the kitchen table when you are not there" exists in the absence of a perceiving subject, but is at the same time made ephemeral by the work of nature which now takes over the space of the house: "Only through the rusty hinges and swollen sea-moistened woodwork certain airs, detached from the body of the wind, (the house was ramshackle after all) crept around corners and ventured indoors ..."[35] Refusing to play dead matter upon which the subject can project his desires and anxieties, now nature indulges in its own narcissism, becomes mirror to itself: "Now day after day, light turned, like a flower reflected in water. Only the shadows of the trees, flourishing in the wind, made obeisance on the wall, and for a moment darkened the pool in which light reflected itself" (*TTL*, 129). In this flux, materiality remains, but its permanence is not presented as eternal stillness. The objects of "Time Passes" decay under the effect of nature *and* keep memory. With the perceiving subjects gone, two alternate temporalities emerge to run parallel through Part II: the historical time of human death and war, which speaks parenthetically to announce the disappearance of Mrs. Ramsey, Andrew, and Prue, and the other time of the compromised permanence of things, running its course at a pace other than human time.

"Time Passes" does not allow any suspension of time or any auratic idealism of permanence, no contiguous running of a world of contingency along with an eternal sphere of Ideas. Here the relations implied by Benjamin's aura are reversed, and it's rather the object that endorses the subject with the power of returning its gaze. There is a moment, however, when these two temporalities, the historical-human time of death, and that of the natural decay of materiality, intersect in the image of the clothes and other effects left behind by the house's occupants. We read:

> What people had shed and left—a pair of shoes, a shooting cap, some faded skirts and coats in wardrobes—those alone kept the human shape and in the emptiness indicated where once they were filled and animated; how once hands were busy with hooks and buttons; how once the looking glass had held a face; had held a world hollowed out in which a figure turned, a hand flashed, the door opened, in came children rushing and tumbling, and went out again (*TTL*, 129).

In a world devoid of human presence, where nobody is there to perceive and represent, the inanimate is attributed agency: the clothes "when you are not there" are the only thing that holds the memory of the people who once had used them. In this scenario memory has no monumental or intellectual quality, but rather it is the imprint of the body upon one's clothes. Differently from Proust, here the object does not "melt" into the bodily sensation that give rise to involuntary memory: in the absence of the subject of experience the memory of the missing body is supported directly by the object. If for Benjamin "eternity is more like the ruffle in a dress," for Woolf the past is like a wrinkle in a faded coat. While Proust's silent materiality, refusing to emit signs for the subject, marks the ahistorical temporality of the Real, Woolf's unsubjected objects acknowledge the passing of time yet manage to arrest it, by keeping the presence of the body and giving temporality a shape.

The chaotic reality of "Time Passes" reverses the reflective relationship between subject and object, almost making the object more active and powerful than the subject. However, there *is* a human presence in "Time Passes": the only subject allowed to witness the disorder and decay of the house, and the historical disorder of the war, is Mrs. McNab, the caretaker. Mrs. McNab's ability to save "an ontology on the brink of disaster," in Spivak's phrase, is connected to "a force working; something not highly conscious" (*TTL*, 139), which is presented by Woolf in anthropomorphic but impersonal terms. What does it mean that the only subject allowed to perceive the chaos following the breaking of the mirror of western ontology and of the subject–object relationship is a subaltern—and so by definition lacking subjectivity, a non-subject? Mrs. McNab's alignement with the world of things in "Time Passes" is underlined by the fact that she, like the clothes, is another, *the* other, keeper of memory, the subject of a memory without symbol. The objects of the past present themselves to her, as the images do to Lily. Mrs. McNab has *her* vision of Mrs. Ramsey, immediately produced by an object: "Why, the dressing table drawers were full of things (she pulled them open), handkerchief, bits of ribbon. Yes, she could see Mrs. Ramsey as she came up the drive with the washing" (*TTL*, 136). To be aligned with objects is no natural privilege or prerogative of the humble. This representation of the subaltern is the product of Woolf's ambivalence toward "the servants," the ambivalence, similar to that of Mr. Ramsey, of the socially minded upper-class liberal intellectual. Mrs. McNab's presence, and, above all, labor, proves again that civilization is sustained by the work of the subaltern. The negative potential of "the thing itself," for which Mrs. Ramsey stands, its traffic with the Real, reaches its culmination in the moment of unhinged, unsubjected, and destructive expenditure of "Time Passes." The end of this chaos, the restoration of order of bourgeois domesticity and reason, is willed by the Ramseys, but carried out by Mrs. McNab, in the same way as Mrs. Ramsey had provided the recipe for the *Boeuf en Daube*, but the actual dish was cooked by Mildred. When, after ten years have gone by, Mrs. McNab sets the house in order for the Ramseys, the split temporality of "Time Passes" is sutured by gendered human labor.

The plot of *To the Lighthouse* poses a classed shift from one notion of production to another: while the female subaltern is handed the productivity of manual labor, the female artists—Lily and Mrs. Ramsey—are handed the conceptual, aesthetic, and affective productivity of the work of art. The value of this art, in turn, in the novel proceeds from a synaesthetic view of the body as the space of pleasurable sensations. If Lily and Mrs. Ramsey produce analogous works of art in different media (painting and food), what does Mrs. McNab's aching body produce, except the conditions that enable her employer's and Lily's work? The prosaic reality of Mrs. McNab, the materiality she helps produce through her labor, is not occluded by Woolf, yet it does not amount to anything; it doesn't produce any development in the novel, and after Part II it disappears. The evanescence of time and experience that characterizes Woolf's narrative signals, but then erases, the presence of the time of manual production and of its subject.

In *To the Lighthouse* Woolf seeks to place before us a truly asymbolic, radically untranscended materiality, which might point to new concepts of memory and art. However, the total materiality of the object in "Time Passes" gets caught into the objectivity of the servant, in her subaltern status and in the materiality of her labor. The unstable temporality of the products of manual labor always clashes with the stasis of the real, of which Mrs. Ramsey is the harbinger. Woolf tries to weld together these two temporalities, that of manual labor and that of the real, through Lily's aesthetics of "ecstatic ordinariness," as we will see. Woolf acknowledges the subaltern and her labor, her adjacency to objects, but at the same time wants to downplay, if not transcend, both. This is the reason why the materiality of production is displaced by the production of art in Part III, and the suffering, burdened body of Mrs. McNab ("It was beyond one person's strength to get it straight now. . . . Her legs pained her" (*TTL*, 135)), turns into the joyous substantiality of Lily's body, producing the sensations that flow into art.[36]

At the same time Mrs. McNab and Lily share the same "power of vision" and of memory: Mrs. Ramsey seems to appear to both in their memories of the past. This unacknowledged symmetry between Lily and the subaltern culminates, paradoxically, in the moment when the artist, acknowledging the disinterestedness of her work, and her disinterest in fame, anticipates the future of her picture: "It would be hung in the servants' bedrooms. It would be rolled up and stuffed under a sofa" (*TTL*, 158). The text that Lily claims has no audience, no addressee, is in fact directed to, if not meant for, Mrs. McNab. The work of a dilettante (who produces for her *dilectus*, her pleasure), Lily's picture declares the lack of any artistic and economic value, and rather is cast as the artist's private experiential and memorial act. Through this act Lily, and, through her, Woolf, wants to bring to closure the mourning for the loss of the center upon which her affective-aesthetic world hinges, and for which the permanence of Mrs. Ramsey stood. She wants to elaborate a new aesthetics unburdened by symbolization, a way of inscribing upon the canvas not only reality on its own terms, but also the corporeal process through which her own artistic production takes place. The text is clear: "What she wished to get hold of was that very jar on the nerves, the thing itself before it had been made anything" (*TL*, 63). Lily vacillates between the materiality of the product of labor and that predicated by Mrs. Ramsey, another embodiment of "the thing itself." In this perspective, Mrs. McNab would be the perfect audience for Lily's picture of untranscendent, non-figural materiality: the picture and the subaltern, insofar as they are both outside symbolization in that one refuses it and the other would be incapable of it, appear to share an existential and ontological common ground. In fact, it's the charwoman's supposed proximity to the object that could teach the artist a thing or two about materiality and the radical aesthetics that it might inform. This, of course, is the dream of the modernist avant-garde, and also the reason for its failure. For here Woolf's radical theory of materiality cracks, and gets caught in a contradiction: the texture of Lily's picture, whose origin lies in the process of labor, like the laboring materiality of Mrs. McNab's hands, gets stripped of any symbolic quality—but, in the process, it gets turned into a baser kind of ornament (kitsch again) for an addressee who, if she inspired this art, will not be able to understand it.

Thus while the novel establishes a contiguity between the female avant-garde artist and the servant in terms of their refusal to symbolize, it does not acknowledge how differently their distance from representative language and transcendence is produced. This comes about by choice in the case of Lily, but through exclusion, because of class and education, in that of Mrs. McNab. At the very moment when the novel seems to become aware of this situation, the analogy between the artist and the servant can no longer be sustained. After Part II Mrs. McNab disappears, and with her any hint of the materiality of labor. The *Boeuf en Daube*, and the house cleaned and reorganized after ten years, are silently replaced by Lily's "attempt at something," her artistic work. After the labor of which Woolf allows us a glimpse is excised from the text, the only materiality left is that of the embodied feelings and emotions of the artist, in her effort to capture what the novel terms a sense of plenitude and connection. "She was not inventing; she was only trying to smooth out something she had been given years ago folded up; something she had seen" (*TTL*, 199), we are told. This "something" is the unity that the presence of Mrs. Ramsey had guaranteed.

In Part III "the thing itself" and its promise of plenitude in the image of Mrs. Ramsey is reintroduced, after its disappearance in Part II, in order to suture the tear that Mrs. McNab had produced in Woolf's narrative of the object. Only when this suturing is accomplished can *To the Lighthouse* become what Spivak terms "the elaborate story of the acquisition of a vision of art" (39). This vision takes place outside language: "Words fluttered sideways and struck the object inches too low" (*TTL*, 178). It is eased by the mysterious appearance—or apparition—of Mrs. Ramsey, who, not clearly willed into presence by Lily's memory, is "simply" there: "Mrs. Ramsey—it was part of her immense goodness—sat there quite simply, in the chair, flicked her needles to and fro, knitted her reddish-brown stocking, cast her shadow on the step. There she sat" (*TTL*, 202). Any point of origin or reason for this presence is missing, and, as Beer puts it, "Absence and substance momentarily resolve"[37] by magic. This resolution to the problem of loss and absence through the vision of Mrs. Ramsey makes possible Lily's aesthetics of "ordinariness and ecstasy": "One wanted, she thought, dipping the brush deliberately, to be on a level with ordinary experience, to feel simply that's a chair, that's a table, and yet at the same time, It's a miracle, it's an ecstasy" (*TTL*, 202). At the end of the novel "the kitchen table when you are not there" and the clothes forgotten for ten years in the closet, can exist in their ordinariness; further, in the way they conjure up memory as presence, they can become the occasion for the subject's ecstasy, which transfigures and replaces the laboring body with a consuming body-in-pleasure.

At the beginning of this section I proposed that Woolf's work refers to Proust's theory of memory and experience, both in its "disappointments" and successes, to point, tentatively, in the direction of Benjamin. Indeed Woolf's idea of an unsymbolizable materiality, of an irreducible power of the object— the clothes—to maintain memory independently of a perceiving subject, appears to be more radical than that of Proust, who ultimately never relinquishes the individual subject and his primacy over the object. But Benjamin? Can Lily's art be considered a means for a kind of reawakening of the dead, for recalling their memory so as to blast open the continuum of history, or at least of time? "I have had my vision" are the words that close the novel. Her vision is ephemeral, a flash-like experience apparently in assonance with Benjamin's flashing of the "now time" of history. Yet as a means to resolve and bring to completion both Lily's and Woolf's work of mourning, this vision simply wishes to bring the past to a closure. Benjamin's conception of the past, instead, is essentially melancholic, and rather than letting go he wants the past to keep haunting the present by any means—material, historical, and theological alike.

If the dead in Woolf's novel are not being forgotten, the effect of their presence is not to arrest time and remake history, but to enable the creation of art. Furthermore the subaltern, whom Benjamin wants to rescue from the forgetfulness of the victors' articulation of memory, is only for a moment acknowledged by Woolf, and then made invisible again. Similarly art has less a political than a compensatory value: in "Time Passes" we learn that Mr. Carmichael has become a prominent literary figure in the aftermath of World War I, since "the war, people said, had revived their interest in poetry" (*TTL*, 134). The symbolic language of poetry seeks to unmake the destruction of the war, and compensate for the losses it caused. One has the impression that, no matter how close to the bone Woolf's own work may be, even in its achieved balance between "ecstasy" and "ordinariness," it still runs the risk of "hitting the object too low," or perhaps of hitting it just (too) right, so that, while managing to reclaim materiality, art for this writer remains consolatory, and not quite a practice which alters people's relations to matter in the real world. Reading between Woolf's deft and brilliantly sustained ironies, however, we as readers might be incited to such change.

IV. War Memorabilia

Proust's and Woolf's subtle post-Bergsonian engagement with materiality and memory under the aegis of art marks a radical moment in the modern understanding of how subjectivity, temporality, and materiality commingle and converge. Their aesthetic practice prepares the ground for such theoretical interventions as Benjamin's redemptive notion of time, and his hopes for a renewed tactility in the encounter of materiality and of the body, in contrast to the calculated contact of consumerism. Nonetheless, if we compare Proust's and then Woolf's theorization of experience and memory with Benjamin's, it is evident that his notion of the past and of history possesses a further collective and political edge. It is as if high modernism could not escape the binds of its elite position in the dominant culture that privileged monumentality while fostering forgetting. Modernism's attack upon both the traditional souvenir and spectatorial subject occurred at the same time as a new impetus to monumentality in dominant culture, which reached its acme in the monumentality of the various totalitarianisms.

The antagonism between a monumental history and a more intimate, but not less historical, form of memory, is at the center of Bertrand Tavernier's 1989 film of the post-World War I moment *Life and Nothing But*.[38] With this film Tavernier broke a taboo of French culture: the official silence about the 350,000 French soldiers "missing" in World War I, whose disappearance has been erased from collective memory since. Tavernier's film is set immediately after the conflict, to show what the bombastics of nation, heroism, and sacrifice cannot acknowledge: the reality of the war, which in the film is represented through destroyed space, dead bodies, and waste. The constellation of body, materiality, and memory through which the past resurfaces in Proust, Benjamin, and Woolf reappears in this contemporary text about a quite recent past, but it poses different questions from the ones we have encountered so far. How are memory and materiality articulated when the time past is that of historical trauma, and the body is missing—so that a sleight-of-hand resolution between absence and substantiality ("Mrs. Ramsey simply sat there"), cannot take place?

Life and Nothing But begins in October 1920, in Verdun. An aristocratic lady, Irene Descourtier, travels from Paris to the military hospital of Vezille, in search of her husband, missing in the war. Here she meets Delaplane, the officer with the impossible task of keeping count of the nameless, and often body-less, dead soldiers. As the daughter-in-law of a rich industrialist and senator, Irene arrogantly demands that Delaplane pay full attention to her husband's case. The officer instead shows his integrity by refusing to give up his work of making a census of the dead. A true bureaucrat, Delaplane keeps in his archives photos and drawings of unidentified bodies left on the battlefields. The plain of Verdun after the war is still crowded: amnesiacs wander through the site, while a mini-army of military rescuers work in a railway tunnel full of corpses, victims of a blast by the Germans before they withdrew. A second woman, Alice, also searches for her missing lover;

Delaplane will discover that he is in fact Irene's husband. Finally the fields are also scoured by a number of artists searching for inspiration for war monuments to dedicate to the French victory, which will stand in every village to the memory of the war heroes. Delaplane's work of cataloguing the dead is interrupted by the State's demand for the body of the Unknown Soldier, to be honored at the military parade of November 10 and buried in the Pantheon. Delaplane refuses: his task is to identify corpses, not to leave them unknown so that they can be celebrated in Paris. He is declared a subversive and his job is taken over by Captain Perrier, who searches frantically for a body which might not be that of an Englishman, or a German, or, even worse, "a black." When the Descourtier case is not resolved, Irene remains in Verdun, where she makes friends with Alice and pursues a relationship with Delaplane. Irene insists that Delaplane declare his love for her, as the condition upon which she will follow him anywhere, "without a past." The officer will declare his love only three years later, once Irene is in New York, when he tells her that he is ready to love her "for one hundred years." In his last letter he includes his final maniacal computation of the missing: it took three hours for the French army, at the November 10th parade, to march down the Champs Elysees; if all the 350,000 French dead of the war had been there, it would have taken eleven days and eleven nights. Delaplane's words give a grotesque tinge to the pieties by which the dead soldiers are remembered by the State. The absurdist tone of the film leaves the viewer uncomfortable, uncertain of how to read the story: confronting him with a de-anaesthetized image of a vast mass of wasted lives and lost things, it asks the viewer to reflect on the war through the stuff that remains, but is not yet a memory object.[39]

The film's most striking moment occurs when the relatives of the victims of the train explosion examine the objects found in the bomb-blasted tunnel, now laid out on tables in order to help them identify the dead: playing cards, books, photos, medals, watch-chains, and keepsakes are examined as clues to direct them to the body of a soldier. These objects will not, like souvenirs, release the comfort of memory and of the past at a distance; on the contrary, they produce the immediate discomfort of loss in the present. Similarly, through these formal fragments of "war memorabilia" no symbolization of the facts of war is made possible; Tavernier uses the prosaic and matter-of-fact device of the catalog, a means to impose order upon chaos, as a path to a name and identity. The objects on the tables are not fetishes but detective clues, traces that might help a relative to attach a name to a body, or, in the absence of the body, to direct them to a name. The attribution of a name is all that needs to and can be said about the dead. The film, in this regard, stands as a literalization of Benjamin's intent of redeeming the dead, this time without any messianism—in fact in a world where messianism, both in its theological and lay version (as, for example, in the case of Mrs. Ramsey's apparition), is no longer possible.

Delaplane's work is impossible and incomplete: he manages to identify a mere 51,000 bodies. This irony too signals a refusal of the logic of remembrance as completion and closure. The difficulty of identification demonstrates the past's unmanageability, in contrast to the State's desire to bring it to closure in the monumental anonymity of the war memorial—an amnesiac architecture that perfectly dramatizes Adorno's idea of reification as forgetting. Fetishistically congealed in the monument, the past is reified exactly because of the monument's lack of individuality, its refusal to name. This anonymity allows for the metonymical representativeness of the Unknown Soldier: the carapace of the monument freezes both body and the passing of time into eternity, positioning the body and its wounded temporality in History, but outside time. In the monument the past is truly overcome, finally put behind our backs. This is the significance of Delaplane's silence to Irene's demand that he declares his love to her, so that they can begin a life together "without a past"; his silence insists that the past cannot, should not be given up.

If we understand memory only in the ways it is articulated between the two extremes of the *madeleine* and of the monument, or between the Proustian disappointment in contemplating the mere materiality of Venice and, on the other side of the spectrum of mnemonic experience we have traced in this chapter so far, the perfect pleasure the substantiality of Mrs. Ramsey gives Lily, we are missing an important quality of the memory object in a culture deeply centered upon forgetfulness. In *Life and Nothing But*, on the table where the visitors look for traces of a missing body, the object is reinstated in its solid, substantial materiality, but it is no longer a souvenir, or even a relic, something that lasts, that could be kept to sustain memory. Instead, it's the fetishistic emptiness of the war memorial that claims to produce presence, while taming the past in a reconciled form. The past of the object found on the battlefields gives no guarantees; its temporality is unsteady and incomplete, and points neither to a messianic futurity (*à la* Benjamin), nor to a fulfilled present (*à la* Woolf). Rather, it signals the ephemeral temporality of the moment when the body is found, and, even more, when a name is given to it. Delaplane's war memorabilia, in open opposition to official remembrance, point to an unresolvable form of memory which exceeds how both the monument and every archive, including Delaplane's own, try to contain it.

Official history, the triumphant narrative of national heroism and sacrifice, is silenced in Tavernier's film by the mnemonic performance of materiality.

This performance is extremely fragile, and somehow, like the moment of felt presence in Woolf, volatile. But while Mrs. Ramsey, as the harbinger of total materiality makes a kind of ghost-appearance in Woolf's text, the body of the soldier in Tavernier's film, brought for a moment to visibility on the radar screen of history by the object, vanishes. What remains, in contrast to the official panegyric, is a zero degree of language, the name. Important also for both Proust and Benjamin, the name here affirms the individuality of the dead, not History, but the dead's own story. Finally, Tavernier's film underlines the persistence of objects as means to memory—objects whose immediate connection to the body and lack of permanence leaves no space for fetishism. Under these conditions, in order to maintain the memory of the dead, both the object and the subject are necessary: the image of the people examining the objects on the tables at Verdun reintroduces both the object and the body into the sphere of affect and sociability, making clear that the survival of the past is never for oneself only, and that the past is always a matter of a lived connection between the individual and the collectivity.

V. The Present as Future Past: Time Capsules

Proust in Benjamin's reading, Woolf's forgotten clothes, and Tavernier's war waste all directly connect stuff to the decaying and unstable temporality of the body, to produce a synaesthetic, plastic and radically embodied form of memory born of an intense contact of subject and object. This modernist recasting of how memory is awakened by materiality, however, remains an exception in the modern and postmodern culture of capital, where the tendency to abstraction is still compensated for by the souvenir's logic of nostalgia. Consider "war memorabilia," for example: the detritus of war on the battlefields of Verdun may be intensely evocative in Tavernier's film, but becomes a priced collection of impersonal memory-toys in a flea-market sale. The object in consumer culture, apart from a few intermittent flash-like moments, remains a fetish, a *tchotchke* which remembers and signifies *for* you, presenting one with a ready-made version of the past, affect, and meaning.

Despite its demolition by the avant-gardes, souvenir culture therefore persists. The culture of official commemoration and remembering has proliferated and grown more complex, and capital's resourcefulness with the object has been harnessed as one part of this. The complexity of the memory work of official culture is suggested by at least one intriguing modern memory object, the time capsule. The time capsule diverts thought of the past and of a relation to it to another relation, that between the present and the future. It is a form of communication between a sender and a recipient; whether in its millennial, centennial, or cinquantenarian versions, it intends to preserve the present in all its greatness for future human—and at times non-human, outer-space—generations. It aims to install the present in the future, as a history in advance. Cultural historians[40] have presented the phenomenon as transhistorical, in a continuum that stretches from the Egyptian tombs to foundation deposits "interred" at the White House by Teddy Roosevelt, Harry Truman, and George H.W. Bush. In fact, the first modern centennial time capsule was assembled at the International Centennial Exposition at Fairmount Park, Philadelphia, in 1876. Renamed "The Centennial Safe" when it was opened in 1976 before President Ford, revealed among its contents were "photographs, autographs of civic personages and prominent civil and military officers . . . a tea service and a watch" (105).

It is appropriate that time capsules were centerpieces of late nineteenth- and early twentieth-century world's fairs, integral to their phantasmagoria of technological progress and futurity. The first Westinghouse Time Capsule was buried at the New York's World Fair on September 23, 1938, and became an attraction in its own right both at the 1939 Fair—themed "The World of Tomorrow"—and at that of 1940—"Peace and Freedom." The "Cupaloy Capsule," as it was known, consisted of a sealed vessel of specially treated glass inserted into a metal tube; shaped like a torpedo, it was actually called "a time bomb" (173). As the time capsule was buried at the fair's site, "male spectators impulsively removed their hats, while those present at the 1940 sealing up ceremony solemnly bowed their heads."[41] Scheduled to be opened in 5,000 years, the capsule, but not its contents, was visible between 1938 an 1940 through a periscope. Intending to give posterity "an authentic 1930s experience," G.E. Pendray, the engineer who designed it, divided its contents in categories from the mundane ("nail file, set of alphabet blocks, deck of cards, keys, toothbrush . . . and Lilly Dache brand designer hat from the Autumn fashions of 1938"), to the scientific ("a microfilm essay" of 1930s knowledge, a small microscope with instructions on how to construct a larger one). Examples of art and entertainment, "everything from applied chemistry descriptions to the Sears-Roebuck catalog, and samples from the Encyclopedia Britannica" were included, along with "samples of U.S. money, seeds . . . a specially produced newsreel . . . to give an authentic 1930s experience [of] Franklin Delano Roosevelt, the billionaire Howard Hughes . . . famed American athlete Jesse Owens running the 100 meters at the 1936 Berlin Olympics, the bombing of Canton, China, in June 1938, and an April 1938 Miami fashion show" (152). World's fairs were not the only sites for time capsules: as an exercise in cultural memory they were also assembled in universities. Scheduled to be opened in 6970 AD, the Oglethorpe Vault, or "The Crypt of Civilization" at Oglethorpe University in Georgia, was also assembled in the 1930's and sealed in 1940. At issue here, rather than the futuristic wonder of a technological utopia, was the question of history and of civilization. In 1940, the year of the publication of *Theses on the Philosophy of History* and of Benjamin's suicide, when France fell to Nazi Germany, Thornwell Jacobs, the mind behind the Oglethorpe Vault, explained its rationale thus: "The world is now engaged in burying our civilization forever and here in this crypt we leave it to you."[42] Futurity, in the example of each of these time capsules, is addressed through the language of death and war: the Cupaloy capsule resembles a bomb and gets "buried"; the Oglethorpe memory objects are buried in a crypt. If the slightly gothic secrecy of the time capsule can be read as an index of the secret of the commodity, bearing the always already scripted future of time's homogeneous progress, the most direct inspiration for the capsule's funerary logic was the 1922 rediscovery of Tutankhamen's tomb, which gave rise to the "King Tut" craze. When Jacobs, president of Oglethorpe, discussed with Orson Munn, editor of *Scientific American*, the possibility of building a long-term repository of scientific knowledge and information on "human civilization" for future millennia, he modeled the time capsule on an Egyptian tomb: its chamber is made of granite blocks "embedded in pitch, built around a steel hull itself lined with vitreous porcelain enamel" (173). Still, the list of the contents assumes a Surrealist tone:

> a model electric train, an aluminum foil sample, male and female mannequins in glass cases, a pair of binoculars, an Emerson radio receiver, glass refrigerator dish and cover, electric toaster … a pair of ladies' stockings, dentures (upper), plastic flute, glass rolling pin, a quart of beer, lighted make-up mirror, life-size cut-away model of a pregnant woman, phonograph records of music.

There were also larger technological objects:

> a motion picture projector, a small windmill to generate electricity for the projector … and a "Language Integrator" … When the hand-crank of this penny arcade-like device is turned, a metal page will flip up, displaying the picture of an object with its name printed as a caption. At the same time, a recorded voice on a phonograph record will speak the pictured object's name (in English) so that eighty-second century linguists could hear the pronunciation and read the name, and see an image of the object simultaneously.

The time capsule craze, with future memory objects celebratory of human (i.e. American) civilization, continued after World War II; there were 1960s

Westinghouse Capsules, and Voyager I, launched in 1977, was equipped with a set of discs which claimed to represent Earth culture, so that "When and if those phonographic audiovisual discs are played, they will reveal a multimedia show of photos, text, human voices, music, and other Earth noises" (127).

Situated half-way between curio-cabinet, trunk, the junkyard, the carefully catalogued museum, and the souvenir shop, the time capsule looks at the future with optimism and at the same time acknowledges the dangers of amnesia. It wants to insure that the present will be remembered, and the experience of the past maintained as computable and recognizable in its materiality. The time capsule's will to memory, its faith in mimetic representation, relies on a specific, convoluted notion of temporality. While time is empirically rendered as the irresistible march of techno-scientific progress, the time capsule's temporality posits archeology in reverse: we are asked to look at the present as a past which people in the future will see. Through this clash of past and future, which both foregrounds and makes the present disappear, the western subject celebrates himself in the midst of his artifacts, to which he consigns his desire for permanence. The contents of the time capsule, the more mundane and trivial the better, claim to represent the past for future generations, anticipating a sci-fi futuristic and possibly apocalyptic scenario when people will no longer know what a safety-pin was. In its claim to both representation and representativeness the time capsule speaks the language of both an encyclopedic inclusion, and of a "scientific," disinterested objectivity. The Earth is represented mimetically, through a captioned object that moves from the hands of a sender to those of a future addressee.

The modern time capsule as memory object wants to close the lid of history and turn history itself into a museumized, catalogued, and packaged memory for future generations. No change takes place in the objects housed in the time capsule, and their permanence becomes immediately a form of obsolescence. They will be perfectly preserved to show how life "really was" in the past: they fetishistically deny death by embodying its very stillness; in this sense, the language of vaults, crypts, and burials associated with time capsules is the most appropriate. The time capsule and its contents allow no chance encounter with time in its address to the rational, disembodied subject of voluntary memory. Its materiality, so carefully labeled and scripted, has nothing excessive. Its future is not imagined as utopia, merely as the time when the buried objects of the past will be received. Caught in a static relationship of past and future, the present shrinks, but not into some contracted "now time." The time capsule produces no break in time as it celebrates the continuity of historical progress. It makes an hypothetical past out of the present for the future: implying, thereby, that the past and the future might be the same, while the present, the time of historical change, disappears. The subject–object opposition is reaffirmed, and with it a notion of representation that claims to be realist, therefore objective, while it's deeply ideological without admitting it. Thus the time capsule's temporality and claim to representation is apotropaic: from its insulated chamber the memory object denies decay and the passing of time, as well as the impossibility of a stable, foolproof memory. This denial, and the unreliability of this automatically signifying materiality is taken to task by another modern genre, which might be termed the anti-time capsule. An outstanding example is Peter Greenaway's 1992 prop-opera *One Hundred Objects to Represent the World*, to which I turn now.

VI. *One Hundred Objects to Represent the World*

Although Peter Greenaway is best known as the director of controversial films *The Draughtsman's Contract* (1982), *A Zed and Two Noughts* (1986), *Drowning by Numbers* (1988), *The Cook, the Thief, His Wife and Her Lover* (1989) and *The Pillow Book* (1996), he also produced "metacinematic projects"[43]—exhibitions, operas, and websites. His cinema has always been multimedial and generically hybrid, with writing, painting, and musical forms that break the soundtrack's bounds. Trained as a painter, Greenaway uses one medium to test the limits of others. As "moving images" (see the reproduction of scenes from Vermeer in *A Zed and Two Noughts*), Greenaway's films illuminate the limits of cinematic narrative,[44] in a systematic search for different principles to organize reality. Thus his work is well positioned to investigate new ways of thinking about materiality, which he presents as a premodern, "Baroque" overpresence of both stuff and the naked body.[45] The overpresence of corporeality, particularly as aged and imperfect bodies which do not display the fetishistic signs of youth, beauty, and fitness, suggests the reclaiming of both materiality and history in all its density.

History for Greenaway is first of all natural history: "I doubt whether cinema has any real history in the world. The passage of history effects inevitable material changes in an artifact," he has said.[46] This density of materiality, affirmed, and yet at the same time shortcircuited in its representation in images, is recuperated in his installations. One of the most striking, *One Hundred Objects to Represent the World*, is not only a multimedia event that blurs and hybridizes different genres, but is also multiform, existing in different versions. When it opened in Vienna in 1992, *One Hundred Objects* was an exhibition. In 1997 it debuted in Salzburg as a prop-opera, before traveling to other European and South American cities.[47] In the opera actors share the stage with lots of objects, and objects and people are introduced by voice-overs, with music playing and cinematic images projected on screens. Before and after the opera the props are displayed for the audience. The opera and exhibition catalog is yet another version of the same work, a book which does not simply "reproduce" either text: the script is accompanied by a collage of stills from Greenaway's films and photos of his paintings. In this genre bending, *One Hundred Objects* as action-text-opera evolves in an open, looping circularity.

In the introduction to the book Greenaway explains that *One Hundred Objects* is his direct answer to NASA's decision to include a number of artifacts "to represent life on earth" in the 1977 spaceship Voyager:

> In 1977 Cape Kennedy launched into outer space two Voyager spacecrafts containing material to represent life on Earth. In its payload it held description of the earth's characteristics, its flora, and fauna, and human life ... This was a project with great responsibilities. Necessarily the choice of material was subjective to an American, scientifically educated 1970s community with perhaps arrogant democratic ideals and possible paternalistic attitudes to the rest of the world. In the end it could only contain a small spectrum of reference when the diversity of the Earth and its communities are considered. But even so, you and I, as Earth representatives, were not consulted.... How could our planet be represented without our permission or consultation? We should endeavour to put this right. So, ... I have prepared a subjective shopping list of my own, of what I consider, with a mixture of due irony and due seriousness, can represent the world ...[48]

For Greenaway the representative universality of the Voyager's time capsule is replaced by the ironic particularity of the subjective shopping list: not representative, but still representational. In *One Hundred Objects*, the dubious universality of the memory object in the Voyager is challenged with a mock-historical prop-fable, given voice by a "child cataloguer" and commented upon by "Thrope," that is, the Misanthrope, and the (biblical) Serpent, who set out to educate Adam and Eve. In the opera the uncritical and apparently neutral objectivity of the objects in the time capsule is taken to task both by Greenaway's ironic-serious hijinks, and by his characters' often conflicting readings of an object:

> Thrope's purpose is to educate these two innocents in what the earth, and humankind upon the earth, have achieved in the last millennium ... Thrope conducts them through the comforts of domesticity and sentiment, through the delights and torments of sex, power and money,

to the tragedies of war, disease, loss and death. Initially pupils of Thrope's didacticism, Adam and Eve gradually gain confidence to make demands which increase beyond reasonability, eventually bringing about their own demise.

Setting his prop-opera at the dawn of biblical time, Greenaway gets to imagine the contents of a time capsule of objects from the future opened in the past; he plays loose with the time capsule's time-line logic.

One Hundred Objects is Greenaway's time capsule as Pandora's box. Rather than its being used to memorialize the past, the very act of remembering becomes enmeshed in the question of representation and its stakes. In his commentary to Item Number 6, "The Catalogue," Thrope affirms the successfully encyclopedic power of Greenaway's list: "Nothing has been left out. Everything is represented. Everything alive and dead. Every material. Every technique. Every science. Every idea. Every discipline, construct, illusion, trick and type, and every type of every type." Serpent: "It has been said that all the world exists to be put in a book." Thrope: "This is the book." The notion that every thing in the world can be fitted in a book, and of the perfect coherence between world and book, reminds us of Foucault's view that taxonomy and representation are historically produced ordering strategies.[49] Greenaway's comic cataloging upends the teleological narrative that anchors the organization of materiality and events into a grid, to expose its arbitrariness. What Foucault calls the *tabula*, "that which enables thought to operate upon the entities of the world, to put them in order, to divide them into classes," (xvii), is *de facto* eliminated in Greenaway's work. This use of a taxonomy without the *tabula* recalls Borges' classification of animals "from a certain Chinese encyclopedia" which inspired Foucault's archeological project in *The Order of Things*.[50] Without the *tabula*, representation, understood as the perfect coincidence of the order of being and the order of the book, crumbles; if "the entities of the world" are established by the logic of the grid, their disenfranchisement from the *tabula* frees them into history, materiality, and a new notion of representation.[51]

This is what the props in *One Hundred Objects* achieve. Greenaway's operatic time capsule comes to speak this history via a specific narrative— that of Judeo-Christian tradition; however, as one of the items on the list makes clear, this is only *one* way of organizing meaning. More, the objects that support this narrative continually exceed any fixed epistemic grid. Despite the apparently empirical enunciation of the names of the catalogued objects, the matter-of-fact tone is dispelled by the overpresence of each object itself, doubled by the image and further multiplied by the character's different interpretations of them. These objects become the focus of a comic and polyphonic commentary on the achievements of millennia of history, that history which the conventional time capsule invariably celebrated.

With Greenaway, memory as scientific taxonomy is transformed into memory as contingently arrayed art. The contained space of the time capsule and of the vault opens onto the more flexible space of the stage and installation space. The materiality of his objects, also, is dense, but not fixed: some items, centered on the solidity of an object, morph into events. This is the aesthetic power of the sorcerer-Greenaway's "celestial toyshop":

> But the objects presented in this opera . . . are not to be inanimate, they are to be presented akin to the exhibition of ideas in a Machiavellian, celestial toyshop crossed with a Faustian wonder-room. When we call forth the object "Fire" there will be flames; when we summon "Snow," it will snow; when we call forth the object called "God," then God will be truly God-like.

On other occasions, the immaterial is made material and the inanimate is animated through Thrope's and the Serpent's words, by the unexpected scenarios they conjure up. No longer fixed to the part of the *tabula* that gave it meaning, the prop object fends for itself. In Greenaway's object performance piece, there are no guarantees: the grid is loosened, its table cracked, and the objects are no longer contained in a bounded epistemic territory.

In *One Hundred Objects* the only narrative ordering comes from the choice to catalog between Item Number 1, "The Sun," and Item Number 100, "Ice." However, all the objects are interconnected: repeatedly one item fades into the next, often by the physical or acoustic reoccurrence of the same word, with which a new idea is now associated. For example, Number 7, "The Wind," ends with an image of the sky in movement ("Windmills . . . sails; sailing . . . and blowing away") and thus takes us to Item Number 8, "Cloud" ("A cloud demonstrates the diaphanous made whole. . . . The beginnings of precipitation"), "performed" in the exhibition, by an artificial cloud pouring water on one hundred open umbrellas. From Item Number 9, "Water," we move to Number 10, "Umbrella" ("A small, discreet personalized shelter. A protector. Much like God."), followed by Item Number 11, "God." Here God is evoked as a character in response to the existential questions of the child cataloguer ("Who are we? Why are we here? Where are we going? What is it all about?"), but all He says, in a line that keeps punctuating the text every time the work "God" is uttered, is "I am God": the perfect affirmation of God's absolute being according to Judeo-Christian tradition, turns into a mechanical repetition of a script, in an almost Beckettian vein. Moreover God, absurdly following the umbrella, is actually presented as a mechanism: "God is an umbrella ... a machine for permitting and forbidding ... God is made of convincing words. Words are nicely ambiguous. Capable of infinite meanings which should keep everyone happy." Keeping everyone happy, one could argue, is what the commentary on each item does. But in *One Hundred Objects* the mystifying ambiguity of language is exposed by the montage of word, projected images, and music, and anchored in each case to the materiality of the object used to demonstrate any given item. Repetition and transformation propel the catalog: the "Fallen Tree" (Number 52), leads to the "Column," (53): "from the fallen tree cut by the chainsaw, you can make, A column, which demonstrates an ubiquitous image, Of architectural structure." Or, in a darker mode, see Number 49, "Classical Fragments," which take us directly to Number 50, "Rubble": "To demonstrate sexual refinement. To demonstrate classicism. The Mediterranean cultures, History. Reverence. Academicism. Legitimate nudity and voyeurism." Serpent: "Just broken plaster rubble."

In this catalog without classification western tradition and its history is put on show in its minutiae, sometimes as linguistic *divertissement* (Number 58, "The Alphabet," names an alcoholic drink for each letter; or see Number 84, "Red Books": "Red Books, read Books. I have red books. I have read books."), without leaving out the less complimenting aspects of this tradition, such as "Death," "Imprisonment," "The Law," "The Gibbet." Finally, throughout, *One Hundred Objects* demonstrates a keen awareness of the connection between power and knowledge, power and art. Item Number 83, "Ink" reads: "Thrope: "You think sometimes that ink and blood could be interchangeable, for it might seem that as much ink has been spilt over blood, as blood over ink." The Serpent: "At the Nurnberg trials there were over 15 million documents of ink-written evidence to settle the blood-accounts of over 57 million killings to occupy a library of over a million books." The chilling image of a library of books written in blood (demonstrated, at the Vienna exhibition, by a mass of IV bottles spilling a red liquid onto a white scroll on the floor) makes the memory of twentieth-century history tactile. It makes the object act, and act passionately: it precipitates an event. It does this by turning the metaphor material and materiality metaphorical, in a way that no object in a time capsule could ever do.

One Hundred Objects catalogs without classifying, and demonstrates by performing, without truly representing. Greenaway's multitextual prop-opera questions and exposes the principles of mimesis. It breaks open the time capsule's memorialization of the present. It undercuts the claim to objectivity and transparency proposed by its objects. Thrope's and the Serpent's comments are always interested, and ideologically informed, no less than the objects in the Oglethorpe Vault. By cracking the *tabula* with the active objects and the multivocal commentaries on them as they transform themselves, Greenaway shows how the representativeness of memory is informed by power. The multivocal commentaries show the lack of objectivity of any representation, and the complicity of power in organizing its plot. The great story of technological progress told by the Voyager's time capsule is retold as the rickety history after the Garden of Eden, with irony and seriousness. In the time capsule a particular and partial historical memory is posed as universal; Greenaway instead insists on its particularity and partiality, by idiosyncratically making representative the marginal and the everyday. Notice, however, that he does not give up either the impulse to systematize or the chance to represent.

The contents of the time capsule are selected to celebrate the greatness of humankind, while Greenaway provides us with a different memory kit, in this "unnaturally" assembled menagerie of past and present. His private *abecedaire* of the past two millennia doesn't last, doesn't guarantee any permanence: the installations were dismantled at the closing of the exhibitions and of the opera, and the audio recording for sale only records the sound of the performance. In this postmodern reenactment, whatever truth that matter might reveal is, as modernism teaches, a phenomenon of flashes, of Joyce's and Woolf's striking of the match, an always short-lived illumination. The ephemerality of the past and of the present we live in is again a matter of the moment and of aesthetic performance. What kind of temporality is this? The object in the time capsule cites the abstraction of the fetish, its reification and forgetfulness: the homogeneous empty time of the capitalist present is translated into the clinical, and equally empty, time of science, or claims to do so. Greenaway, mocking any scientific system of classification in which the time capsule participates, disqualifies that particular type of referentiality, but does not give up the possibility of representing differently, critically or historically.

One Hundred Objects to Represent the World speaks of the crisis of mimetic representation and of the *tabula*, the space where signs organize reality and materiality into the knowable, but not of meaning and representation *tout court*. Perhaps this is not the creation of a new language "in any meaningful realist sense," as Jameson says, capable of defeating the postmodern "realism of the image" or of the logo. Yet, in the urgent cultural panorama of the present, when memory is more and more entrusted to the archive, electronic or otherwise, and the experience of time risks being erased by the abstraction and amnesia of consumerism, Greenaway's iconoclasm, or better, icono-hypertrophism, and his multimedia explorations, may provide at least the tool for a critique. The mimetic cataloguing of the past, as Greenaway's opus implies, or the sidereal objectivity of the archive or of the time capsule, will not do: memory remains a collective and lived practice, a form of traffic between past and present, tactility and materiality. Memory is not articulated through objects, but *with* objects, in the same way that Benjamin thinks of history as an experiencing *with* the past. At the time of what Andreas Huyssen calls "a return to the promise of the future as articulated today in neoliberal discourses of economic and technological globalization,"[52] both memory and the past must be understood as tactile and thereby political categories, and reclaimed, as the examples in this chapter imply, as a knowledge to help us understand our power in a time when amnesiac forgetting or approved memorializing is being sold to us as enough.

Notes

1   See David Harvey, *The Condition of Postmodernity* (London: Blackwell, 1993), p. 266.
2   Lina Angioletti, *Invito alla Lettura di Guido Gozzano*, Milano, Mursia, 1975, p. 42.
3   My translation. See Pier Vincenzo Mengaldi ed., from Guido Gozzano, *I colloqui*, p. 118, Milano, Mondadori, 1978. "Loreto impagliato e il busto d'Alfieri, di Napoleone/ i fiori in cornice (le cose di pessimo gusto),// il caminetto un po' tetro, le scatole senza confetti/I frutti di marmo protetti dalle campane di vetro, . . ."
4   Susan Stewart, *On Longing: Narratives of the Miniature, the Gigantic, the Souvenir, the Collection*, Baltimore, the Johns Hopkins University Press, 1984, p. 133.
5   Stewart, *On Longing* p. 150.
6   Marita Sturken, *Tourists of History: Memory, Kitsch, and Consumerism from Oklahoma City to Ground Zero*, Durham, Duke University Press, 2007, p. 12.
7   See Susan Buck-Morss, "Aesthetics and Anaesthetics: Walter Benjamin's Artwork Essay Reconsidered", *October* 36, 1996, p. 35.
8   Stephen Kern, *The Culture of Time and Space*, Cambridge, Harvard University Press, 1993, p. 24.
9   See Andreas Huyssen, *Twilight Memories*, London, Routledge, 1995, p. 6.
10 Huyssen, *Twilight Memories*, p. 6.
11 "Modernism has to be grasped as a culture of incomplete modernization . . . When the pre-modern vanishes, . . . then the very sense of an alternate temporality disappears as well." Jameson, "The End of Temporality", *Critical Inquiry* 29, Summer 2003, University of Chicago Press, p. 706. Subsequent page numbers in text.
12 "When you have nothing left but your temporal present, it follows that you have nothing left but your own body." Jameson, "The End of Temporality", *Critical Inquiry*, p. 713.

13 Andreas Huyssen, *Present Pasts*, Stanford, Stanford University Press, 2003, p. 28.

14 "Memory is always transitory, notoriously unreliable and haunted by forgetting. In brief, human and social." Andreas Huyssen, *Present Pasts*.

15 Julia Kristeva, *Time and Sense: Proust and the Experience of Literature*, trans. Robert Grussman, New York, Columbia University Press, 1996, p. 168.

16 Walter Benjamin, *Charles Baudelaire: A Lyric Poet in the Era of High Capitalism*, London, Verso, 1983, p. 115.

17 Walter Benjamin, *Illuminations*, New York, Schocken Books, 1969, p. 214.

18 "With a passion unknown to any writer before him, he took as his subject the fidelity to things that have crossed our path in life. Fidelity to an afternoon, to a tree, a spot of sun on the carpet; fidelity to garments, pieces of furniture . . ." Walter Benjamin, *The Arcades Project*, Cambridge, Harvard University Press, 1999, S, 23, p. 547.

19 Quoted in Benjamin, *Charles Baudelaire: A Lyric Poet in the Era of High Capitalism*, London, Verso, 1983, p. 111.

20 "The past is beyond the reach of the intellect, and unmistakably present in some material effect (or in the sensation that such an object arouses in us), though we have no idea which one it is." Marcel Proust, *Du Côté de Chez Swann*, quoted in Benjamin, *Charles Baudelaire*, p. 112.

21 Walter Benjamin, "Surrealism, or the Last Snapshot of the European Intelligentsia" (1929). On incorporation in Benjamin, see Miriam Hansen, "Benjamin and Cinema: Not a One-Way Street", *Critical Inquiry* 25, Winter 1999.

22 Walter Benjamin, "The Image of Proust", *Critical Inquiry* 25, Winter 1999, p. 211.

23 Gilles Deleuze, *Proust and Signs*, trans. Richard Howard, Minneapolis, University of Minnesota Press, 2000, p. 92.

24 Deleuze, *Proust and Signs*, p. 95.

25 Richard Terdiman, *Modernity and the Memory Crisis*, Ithaca, Cornell University Press, 1993, p. 220. See also Christie McDonald, *The Proustian Fabric Associations of Memory*, Lincoln: University of Nebraska Press, 1991. On Proustian matter see Francesco Orlando, *Gli Oggetti Desueti nelle Immagini della Letteratura*, Torino, Einaudi, 1994.

26 Marcel Proust, *Remembrance of Things Past*, trans. Scott Moncrieff, New York, 1932, II, 837–38, quoted in Jameson, "Joyce or Proust?", *The Modernist Papers*, London, Verso, 2007, p. 200.

27 Fredric Jameson, "Joyce or Proust?", *The Modernist Papers*, pp. 198, 200.

28 On the question of the incompleteness of history, see Horkheimer's letter of March 16, 1937: "Past injustice has occurred and is completed. The slain are really slain" (*Arcades Project*, N8, 1, 471).

29 "Father's birthday. He would have been 96, 96, yes, today; and could have been 96, like other people one has known; but mercifully was not. His life would have entirely ended mine." 28 November 1928, Virginia Woolf, *The Diary of Virginia Woolf*, Anne Olivier Bell ed., London, 1980, vol. III, p. 208.

30 Virginia Woolf, *To the Lighthouse*, 1927; New York, Harvest Books, 1981, p. 23.

31 Gillian Beer, "Hume, Stephen, and Elegy in *To the Lighthouse*," *Virginia Woolf: The Common Ground*, Ann Arbor, University of Michigan Press, 1996, p. 38.

32 David Hume, *A Treatise on Human Nature*, (1736), T.H. Green and T.H. Gross (London, 1874), vol. I, p. 534; quoted in Beer, "Hume, Stephen, and Elegy in *To the Lighthouse*," *Virginia Woolf* , p. 29.

33 See Raymond Williams, "The Bloomsbury Fraction", in Francis Mulhern ed. *Contemporary Marxist Literary Criticism*, London, Longman, 1996, p. 130.

34 Gayatri Spivak, "Unmaking and Making in *To the Lighthouse*," *In Other Worlds*, New York, Methuen, 1987, p. 30.

35 *To The Lighthouse*, 1927; New York, Harvest Books, 1981, p. 128.

36 "For how could one express in words these emotions of the body?", 1927; New York, Harvest Books, 1981, p. 178.

37 Beer, "Hume, Stephen, and Elegy in *To the Lighthouse*," *Virginia Woolf*, p. 39.

38 On Tavernier see Stephen Hay, *Bertrand Tavernier: The Film-Maker of Lyon*, London, I.B. Tauris Publs., 2000.

39 "Michelet wrote a sublime line: 'To deal with history one must be disrespectful.' . . . The aim is to raise doubts in the viewer regarding the official version of history." "Interview with Bertrand Tavernier", Sergio Arecco, *Bertrand Tavernier*, Pavia, Il Castoro, 1992, p. 7.

40 William E. Jarvis, *Time Capsules: A Cultural History*, Jefferson, N. C., MacFarland and Co., 2003, p. 165.

41 D.S. Youngholm, "The Time Capsule", *Science,* October 4, 1940, 92.

42 E.D. Brewer, "Oglethorpe Crypt Sealed amid Gloomy Forecast", *Atlanta Journal*, May 26, 1940; in Jarvis, *Time Capsules: A Cultural History*, Jefferson, N. C., MacFarland and Co., 2003, p. 148.

43 John De Stefano, "Peter Greenaway and the Failure of Cinema", in Paula Willoquet-Maricondi and Mary Alemany-Galway, *Peter Greenaway's Postmodern/Poststructuralist Cinema*, Lanham, Scarecrow Press, 2001, p. 38.

44 See Peter Greenaway, *The Stairs/Geneva: Location*, London, Merrell Holberton, 1994, pp. 22–3.

45 See Cristina degli Esposti-Reinert, "New-Baroque Imaging in Peter Greenaway's Cinema", in Willoquet-Maricondi and Alemany-Galway, *Peter Greenaway's Postmodern/Poststructuralist Cinema*; Timothy Murray, "You Are How You Read: Baroque Chaos-Errancy in Greenaway and Deleuze", *Iris*, 23 (Spring 1997).

46 Greenaway, "Interview," *Stairs/Geneva*, p. 3.

47 I saw the prop-opera at the Theatre Bobigny in Paris the same year, 1997.

48 Peter Greenaway, *One Hundred Objects to Represent the World*, Milano, Change Performing Arts, 1997.

49 Michel Foucault, *The Order of Things: An Archeology of The Human Sciences*, New York, Random House, 1970.

50 "Animals are divided into : a) belonging to the Emperor, b) embalmed, c) tame, d) sucking pigs, e) sirens, f) fabulous, g) stray dogs, h) included in this present classification, i) frenzied, j) innumerable, k) drawn with a fine camelhair brush, l) etcetera, m) having just broken the water pitcher, n) that from a long way off look like flies." Michel Foucault, *Order of Things*, xv.
51 See Bart Testa, "*Tabula* for a Catastrophe: Peter Greenaway's *The Falls*, and Foucault's *Heterotopia*", in Willoquet-Mariondi and Alemany-Galway, *Peter Greenaway's Postmodern/Poststructuralist Cinema*, p. 102.
52 Andreas Huyssen, *Present Pasts*, p. 6.

5

Garbage in Theory: Waste Aesthetics

Garbage, a full affront to ordered materiality, is stuff at its most uncertain, vulnerable, and wild. To contemplate for a moment stuff's fragile status, and the ease with which it is exposed, consider the photographs from Peter Menzel's 1994 book *Material World: A Global Family Portrait*.[1] Menzel photographed families before their houses, in each case with the entire contents of the house, objects and people, carried outside and displayed for the eye of the camera. Menzel repeats this image over and over as he travels the world: the British family with their stuff strewn on a village green, the Italian family with their beds and tables on the stones of a Tuscan street, the American middle-class family with their furniture in their yard, all the possessions of a family from Bhutan, including a set of spades proudly displayed, the sparse furniture of a rural Somali family. With its global reach, the book implies the utter difference and the utter sameness of "home" once it is stripped to a degree zero of domestic materiality. Your home, these photos repeatedly say, is your stuff, no matter where you live or what culture you come from. They also witness the moment when the absolutely valuable seems exposed as valueless. Each home's stuff, it is implied, becomes junk outside its domestic shelter: outside, each object appears disposable and vulnerable, its presence, permanence, and meaning suddenly uncertain. (The homes seem vulnerable too, as the photos disquietingly recall evictions.) This uncertainty and liminality is what waste illuminates, and what makes the discarded, on the borders of stuff, key to this inquiry.

This book has already dealt obliquely with stuff's penchant for becoming rubbish, from Benjamin's disused arcade wares, trash-fashion in Jelinek's *The Piano Teacher* and the 1968 barricade-debris in Bertolucci's *The Dreamers*, to Monsieur Hulot's bric-à-brac in Tati's films. In the modernizing 1950s and 1960s, junk appears in art—consider the uncanny installations of Ed Keinholtz—as an echo of modernist utopianism; by the century's end, junk as such, now more efficiently hidden, surfaces with surprising effects.[2] The rise of the economy of services and affective labor,[3] outsourcing of production to the global south, and the "end of work"[4] as the manufacture of things in the west, all meant that consumption would assume new forms. In brief, consumption grew ever more abstract, pervasive—and trash-producing. Further, the regime of "programmed obsolescence"[5] inaugurated in the 1950s, and the invention of new disposable objects such as the plastic bottle, styrofoam cup, and plastic bag,[6] advertised as aids to convenience and hygiene, made trash proliferate in previously unimagined quantities.

In this chapter I study the symbolic value of junk and its relevance for a new politics of materiality and the social in a hyper-consumer culture gone awry. Western culture has only recently started to change its practices and its penchant for waste. The cultural syndromes surrounding the trashed object track the shifting meaning of materiality in societies organized according to garbage's own chief characteristic—the fluidity and instability described both by Zygmunt Bauman's idea of "liquid modernity" and Rem Koolhaas's term "junkspace."[7] Garbage's fluidity may be seen as a threat to be contained, or as a force synonymous with the fluid enticements of consumerism itself. Garbage is the most characteristic object-hoard of consumer culture, and its outlaw underside. Thus it occupies a dangerous, potentially disruptive position. Stuff is always on the verge of becoming trash; composed of commodities destined to be trash, it is trash's natural ally. Garbage is stuff in its most extreme form. The unruliness of stuff becomes trash's revolting quality. Our task is to attend to thinkers, artists, and filmmakers who are formulating a cultural politics out of trash's disruptive power.

By now the analysis of junk and garbage has become a field of study in its own right, with its own disciplinary discourses, whether ecological-environmental, historical, anthropological, aesthetic, literary, or psychoanalytic.[8] Synonyms for garbage proliferate: "Semantically trash belongs with garbage, junk, rubbish, refuse, debris and waste. Trash is more like junk than garbage. Garbage is organic. It's formless and stinks. . . . Trash, like junk, is often clean, a matter of well-made paper, plastic, or metal. Like junk, trash includes the malfunctioning, failed, burned out and obsolete. . . ."[9] Even this typology signals trash's chief characteristic: its undifferentiation and loss of value, which makes the dumpster, in Taussig's words, "a playroom, or the cemetery for lost objects that never made it to the world of categories."[10] Such lost objects are by definition materialities ex-*tabula*, anomalously hybrid, the most dangerous version of the stuff that is this book's concern. Dropped from the networks that give it economic and affective significance, it points beyond official taxonomies of value. This is a condition of materiality which for some critics might just be a temporary stage in the social life of things, as Arjun Appadurai points out,[11] or, for Michael Thompson, a moment in the circulation, distinction, and recirculation of value.[12] For others, the changes which waste incurs are more definitive, and result in an entropic formlessness that, even before Georges Bataille, has occupied the imaginary of the early twentieth-century avant-garde and is now being rethought in such forms as environmentalist vitalism. The obverse of this formlessness is the quality that has come to define another view of junk: a *quidditas* of the object, an "essence" of the material that comes into being only through disuse, and which may produce a more ethical and empathetic relationship to the object. As Gay Hawkins, following Bill Brown's treatment of materiality, notes in her reading of Bill Keaggy's installation "Fifty Sad Chairs," we see the "thinginess" of an object only when it stops working for us. This breakdown reveals "the recalcitrance of trash, its lingering presence, its refusal to go away."[13]

Here, sympathetic to but parting ways with thinkers who want to reclaim trash as a bedrock of materiality, let us propose again the example of Benjamin's ex-commodities in the arcades. These may be as close as forgotten consumer products can be to what Bruno Latour calls "quasi-objects." Both the ex-commodity and the quasi-object imply an arrested circulation, a clogging of the sleek flows along the approved routes of capital, those vectors of an assured subjectivity, economic order, and affective propriety. This arrest matters, not because it helps us reach any essence of the dysfunctional object, or simply observe how the matter in question, now somehow freed, acts upon us. We should not be tempted to poetically imagine that the thing in all its reconquered thinginess inspires us to connect ethically or empathetically with the abandoned object's ontological essence or empirical existence. Rather, the hybridity and liminality of junk allows one to rethink relationally, in a way which situates the object *and* myself in a multiplicity of relations— perceptual, bodily, affective, economic, individual, collective—with other materialities, people, discourses, events. This multiplicity of subject–object relations is what produces the subject, that thing I call "I." The encounter with the discarded object makes visible how much both subject and object are co-implicated in the networks that produce each of them. Reading the encounter allows one to think, in Deleuze's phrase, rhizomatically, in collective, political, and structural terms, not about who I *am*, and what the object *is*, but about our compromised position in the networks of reality and power to which we both belong. This allows me to interrogate how I am produced as part of materiality and vice versa, and thus to intervene differently in the conjunctures of subject and objects in which I participate.

The elegiac ontology of the object alone, and the empathy it might inspire, is not the type of affect produced by junk in its current status. The empathy for the chair and the trash ontology proposed by Hawkins is a form of aestheticization as purification of materiality, where the afterlife of the commodity is used to once again fetishize it. I propose instead to look at garbage in its less aesthetic and aestheticizable form, to turn to a different aspect of the recalcitrance of the material: to consider its disturbing vicinity to people, the disturbing extension of its characteristics to human beings when they have themselves become disposable. Let us foreground junk as a limit to categorizing, and thus focus on its capacity to signify the redundant, the wasted, the irredeemably out of place. This is a way of considering junk that disallows empathy, sadness, melancholy, or ecstasy to open a path to the more political affects of anger, passion, and disgust.[14]

As "matter charged with more radical alterity" (123), junk starkly presents itself as an image of full-on negativity. Junk shocks because it refuses to be hypostatized in a recognizable ontological position. It confronts us by remaining unavailable to existing representational languages and to the dualist logic of subject and object. From this place of overt negativity, junk allows a radical critique of the myths of pleasure and progress of industrial and consumer society, and of the mechanisms of separation and exclusion through which subjective and collective political identities are produced. Current discourses and analyses of waste, whether environmental, economic, cultural, or even psychoanalytic, share a view of garbage as potentially threatening and contaminating, a form of materiality that needs to be controlled, managed, and reined in. By separating ourselves from garbage we draw a boundary that establishes order, value, and identity.[15] Mary Douglas' anthropological analysis of dirt and purity and Julia Kristeva's discourse of the abject, for example, both hinge on the necessity of this separation. Douglas' famous definition of dirt as "matter out of place" points both to the transgressive spatiality of garbage and to its normative reaffirmation of the law: "Where there is dirt there is system. Dirt is the by-product of a systematic ordering and classification of matter, insofar as ordering involves rejecting inappropriate elements."[16] Disorder for Douglas is not excluded, but remains the necessary, albeit dangerous, limit that helps culture establish its order: "This is why, though we seek to create order, we do not simply condemn disorder. We recognize that it is destructive to existing patterns: also that it has potentialities. It symbolizes both danger and power" (114).[17]

Similarly, in psychoanalytical terms, it is through an act of separation from the maternal body that order—the Law of the Father, language, identity—can be established. In *Powers of Horror* Kristeva presents the abject as a state of dangerous viscosity, which must be overcome for the individual to become a subject.[18] Neither subject nor object, the abject "has only one quality of the object—that of being opposite to the 'I' . . . what is abject . . . the jettisoned object, is radically excluded and draws me toward the place where meaning collapses" (1–2). As dirt was for Douglas, the abject is important for its power to prompt the drawing of boundaries, and defend the moral and social order: key here is the man-made, rather than natural, process through which culture affirms itself via a series of separations, reinscribing the order of inside and outside. In political terms, this produces what Zygmunt Bauman calls "wasted lives," redundant human beings who must be cordoned off and disposed of for order to be maintained. For Bauman this logic lies at the core of modernity and its economic progress, always associated with anxiety about security and safety, particularly now, at the time of global flows of mass emigration. Just as the figure of the unassimilated immigrant opens the issue of possible change in the host culture, trash, refusing to give up its foreignness and otherness, becomes a threat, for it suspends any opposition between a classificatory order and the chaos of hybridity. The spaces and time scales of waste are disturbing because they seem to collapse in the *métissage* of a new category. Disused or decaying matter, in its liminality, plasticity, and abjection, occupies space in new, unexpected ways. Its ephemerality makes it impossible for the subject to own it as she owns every other type of object,[19] or to consume it. Only by reinforcing this liminal status and assigning trash to the negative *tout court* can order be reestablished. However, as Bauman notes regarding the task of the rubbish collectors, the fact is that the boundary between "the admitted and the rejected, the included and the excluded, inside and outside" (28) signals the instability of the boundary itself and the order that supports it. Junk as a particular instance of stuff implies a negativity that radiates beyond the object, signified by the plasticity (in Malabou's term) of the object itself. The junk object teaches us to think of negativity as a plastic and mobile category.

The impermanence of certain types of waste runs side by side with the durability and indestructibility of others.[20] Both the permanence and impermanence, the mobility and unchangeable quality of waste contribute to its problematic and ungovernable nature, its refusal to stay in its assigned place, to be confined, to use a phrase from Žižek, to the role of "undivisible remainder."[21] In theoretical terms the liminality and inexhausted multiplicity of junk points toward the notion of hybridity that both Bruno Latour and Donna Haraway elaborate, and which Catherine Malabou develops through the trope of plasticity. Waste invokes the radical materiality of Latour's quasi-object quasi-subject; it partakes also of the hybridity of Haraway's cyborg. Both quasi-object quasi-subject and cyborg are examples of anti-modern monstrosity: each actively and vociferously works to upset the epistemological and representational orders which since early modernity have defined what is normal, thinkable, and representable.

For Latour, the pre-modern moment was one when the networks of what later would be established as subject and object were still visible. At the onset of western modernity, with the birth of the empirical method of scientific inquiry with Boyle and of modern political theory with Hobbes, the hybrid is still visible and recognizable. Through progressive mediations, however, these hybrids get translated into the categories and knowledges of the modern grid, and become invisible, "merely a residue"[22]:

> Here on the left are the things themselves; there on the right is the free society of speaking, thinking subjects, values, and of signs. Everything passes in the middle, everything happens between the two, everything happens by the way of mediation, translation, and networks, but the space does not exist, it has no place, it is the unthinkable, the unconscious of the moderns (37).

Only when we stop being modern, which, according to Latour, we have never been, because the modernity of the subject–object opposition has always relied on the invisible existence of the networked quasi-object and quasi-subject, can the latter become representable. Haraway's cyborg, itself the "refuse" of western humanism, is another figuration of Latour's (and before Latour, Michel Serres') quasi-object, a figuration founded on a logic at odds with the epistemological claims of modernity's *tabula*. The theoretical understanding of garbage as that which refuses representation contributes to this figuration. Following its cyborgian logic, the materiality indexed by trash is not that of the object *vs.* the subject, but that of the hybrid and its plasticity. Trash theory implies that materiality is not simply a question of individual ethics, but of a politics of the subject–object relation. This might be a politics after representation: given that representation always smacks of mimesis and of the autotelic fantasies of reality and self, perhaps we should follow Haraway and talk instead of "figuration."

To constellate a figure: what would this mean as the critic considers the contemporary encounter with materiality? In the first place, it should not be merely a mental operation, but a corporeal one. Tim Edensor, in his study of industrial ruins, centers this encounter with junk on the body, invoking an imaginative and sensual relation to things that have escaped their assigned meanings, so that "the human body is connected with unfamiliar sensations which disrupt habitual ways of embodiment" (123–4). Recuperating corporeal freedom through connections with a materiality outside the expectations of capital, Edensor, following the Situationists' *dérive*, aims for a perceptual connection that could jumpstart experience again, against the spell of narcotic modernity. To affirm this experience of "the contact zone," as Haraway calls it, would mean to yield to the dangers of waste, embrace its hybridity, renounce the will to transcendence, and abdicate the illusion of human exceptionalism. Instead, in modernity, this potentially dramatic tear in the apparently seamless fabric of dominant culture is circumvented by techniques of containment: garbage and what it figures is alternatively made invisible, sanitized, destroyed, or, with a perverse move that mimics its newly found perceptual potential, aestheticized, made beautiful, useful, and divested of its confrontational quality.

To manage junk either through its disposal or its return as art is to affirm the anxious dream of a world without a residue. This dreamworld is a space of pure modern efficiency in which the cycle of production, exchange, consumption, and recycling runs in an absolutely smooth flow without interruptions. We need to mediate between this dystopic fantasy, where nothing is potentially redundant because everything is similarly expendable, disposable, and capable of losing its solidity, and the neocolonialist fantasy of the "other space," where junk can be dumped and disappear. Geopolitics has taught us that there is no "other space" to be invoked; in the integrated circuit of the global economy all peoples live their different levels of exploitation in closer proximity. More broadly, a world without residue is a world without negativity. Garbage invokes the theoretical problem of how to talk of negativity, how to figure it without falling into the trap of the language of the dialectic, where negativity exists only in order to be superseded, ultimately to be incorporated and recycled into the positivity of the subject. What are the potentialities of the negative once it is no longer harnessed to the dialectic? How does this concept change through a radical understanding of garbage as a no-man's-land, a space out of bounds capable of questioning the reassuring seamlessness of the material and symbolic circulation of capital? To figure negativity via waste, we must confront the aestheticization of garbage. Rendering trash beautiful is a double-edged move: trash-as-art can work either as an anaesthetic, to produce more narcotic seamlessness, or it can foreground waste as the sign of the inadequacy of the distinctions that patrol the western system of objects.

An aesthetics of trash has existed at least from the early twentieth century.[23] By turning to trash the modernist avant-garde produced a textuality of adversarial dissonance against what avant-garde artists saw as the complacent hypocrisy of bourgeois art. Today, when the aesthetic seems to have left the work of art behind to seep into everyday reality, thus realizing the dream of the avant-garde with a vengeance and a twist,[24] the avant-garde's "junkification" of art can easily turn into the aestheticization of junk. While the aestheticization of waste and garbage's traffic with the beautiful is one concern of this chapter, my chief interest lies in the spaces and materialities where the alterity of the discarded remains visible, unrecuperated by aesthetics. First, we will read three trash-texts: Rem Koolhaas' essay "Junkspace," to show how aestheticization and junkification go hand in hand to reshape public life into the activity of shopping; José Luis Pardo's vitriolic irony in "Never Was Trash So Beautiful . . ."; and Italo Calvino's redemptive reading of trash in "La poubelle agrée." We then turn to two films centered on the question and the image of waste: Sam Mendes' *American Beauty* of 1999, and Agnés Varda's *The Gleaners and I* of 2000. In *American Beauty* both trash and reality are dealt with in terms of transcendence, but the only way of transcending the meaningless life of the suburban consumer is through an aesthetic recycling of garbage, as with the plastic bag in a key scene. In Varda's film, centered on the politics of gleaning rather than recycling, a different aesthetic strategy allows not short-circuiting but tactility, proximity, and shock. Each of these negotiations of trash and aesthetics are staged against the early twentieth-century trashing of aesthetic proprieties by the various modernisms, which delighted in using and showing up trash while they invoked it at the level of style. Thus a brief look at the stakes of modernist trash culture is where we turn now.

I. The Beauty of Trash

Trash, for the most profound reasons, was a modernist obsession, from the junk on a café table in a Braque painting to the sawdust and oyster shells in Eliot's "The Wasteland." If modernism is understood, as Sanford Kwinter puts it, as a further "untimely break with an . . . expansive tradition, metaphysic, or world view,"[25] then what intermittently emerges at these moments is the philosophical counter-tradition of immanence, from Lucretius to Bruno, to Vico, to Spinoza and Nietzsche, which challenges the hegemony of the metaphysical thought of transcendence. The work of Bergson and Benjamin belongs to this counter-tradition, especially in its claims regarding perception and aesthetics. The various modernist avant-gardes thought of this philosophical rupture in terms of styles that would blur the distinction between art and life drawn by bourgeois aesthetics. Incorporating refuse into art played a central role in this project. From Cubist collage to Kurt Schwitters' assemblages, the use of lost objects in Dada's installations and photomontages, Arman's *poubelles* exhibited in art galleries in 1960s Paris, the crowded boxes of Joseph Cornell, to more recent full-frontal confrontations of art and trash by Robert Rauschenberg, Ed Kienholz, Kiki Smith, and Cindy Sherman, not to mention the Museum of Garbage launched in Sweden in the mid-1990s,[26] in the twentieth century garbage stridently entered the frame of the artwork, marking the artists' intransigent resistance to the *status quo*. This is the same irrecuperable negativity that Adorno attributes to modernist writing, which mimics the horror of bourgeois "administered" life to expose it, and does so by digging out its dirt—as in Kafka's insects or the contents of Beckett's *Endgame* trash cans. (Eliot's "I will show you fear in a handful of dust" sums up this literary modernist attitude). Modernism's interest in trash and in the *minutiae* of the everyday is invariably an attack on the dominant ordering-systems of modernity. As with the fetish, however, the negativity of junk under the spell of capitalism turns out to be reversible: just as the iconoclastic aesthetics of modernism itself can become, in pop-culture's sleight-of-hand, the cool shock-tactics of advertising,[27] waste likewise can quickly be accepted as no longer opposed to, but often happily and successfully integrated into, culture. It can be aestheticized, made unremarkable, deprived of its critical bite.

On this danger, Walter Benjamin, in "The Author as Producer" (1937), makes an interesting detour on Dada's aesthetic practice. He notes that Dadaist montage lets reality and, more poignantly, junk, into the frame of the picture, so that the shock might jolt both audience and author into recognizing their positions in the existing relations of production. Yet for him the author's attitude is not enough to make a work of art political, and make the author a producer; rather, the "literary tendency" (257), the style in which a subject is presented, is key. Dada is indeed revolutionary, he claims, when it punctures the smooth surface of the artwork with objects he calls "pieces of reality": "Still lives put together from tickets, spools of thread, cigarette butts were linked with artistic elements. They put the whole thing in a frame. And they thereby show the public: look how your picture frame ruptures the age; the tiniest authentic fragment of daily life says more than paintings" (262). Accepting Dadaism as properly political, he balks at German "New Matter of Factness," despite its claims to social consciousness, because it makes reality beautiful and narcotic again. In its cool modernism, "It can no longer photograph a tenement block or a refuse heap without transfiguring it. For it has succeeded in making even abject poverty,... into an object of enjoyment" (262). In attacking the aestheticization of poverty, Benjamin foregrounds the problem that making art out of junk poses today: now negativity itself can become an object of consumption and passive contemplation for the audience. Real critique is neutralized; poverty and waste are felt not through critical alienation, but merely by the apparent proximity of an anaestheticized perception,[28] simply as art.

Taking his cue from Brecht, as the antidote to this aestheticization, Benjamin proposes that the photograph be captioned. If the shock value of reality is reabsorbed by aesthetics, to affix a caption to the image becomes the artist's task. When the *techne* is not enough because liable to being made to work against itself, the caption, the author's voice, will reclaim its tendentious meaning. Along with Latour, vouching to represent the quasi-object, and Taussig, who recognizes in the aesthetic strategies of modernism the most appropriate means to represent the Nervous System— one of the spatializations of postmodernity—Benjamin regards adequate forms of captioned representation as a way of exposing the subterfuges of power, subterfuges from which even trash itself is not safe. Taking as my departure-point his prescription for the author as producer—"To the dramatic total art work he opposes the dramatic laboratory" (267)—I want to draw a line from how Koolhaas extracts the image of reality as *Gesamtkunstwerk* in "Junkspace" all the way to Varda's art laboratory in her documentary on waste and poverty.

II. The Opposite of Junk: Rem Koolhaas' Viscous Modernity

The visibility of junk makes it possible to approach materiality in a way that contests the primacy of the subject of reason, the subject of perception, and the subject–object distinction itself. Further, as we have seen, an apt stylistics of garbage would prevent us from immediately assigning negativity a fixed role in the circulation of value and meaning. Garbage's rawness makes it a prime materiality to precipitate the tactilities, the encounters, and the intimacies and rhizomatic connections capable of propelling unpredictable flows of people, things, language, value. But this might seem to be the very logic, economic and cultural, according to which capital itself operates. The problem in the 1980s heyday of postmodernism appeared to be that of becoming dizzy and disoriented in the funhouse of simulation; by now, the strategies of capital appear more complex. First, ever-increasing deregulation, both economic and political, makes easier the flows of capital, people, and cheap labor. Contrary to this is the tendency of the system to control economic deregulation's chaos by corralling any type of disposable excess, whether garbage or people, in the name of a security regime that professes to keep contamination at bay. The language of safety reinstates a system of exclusion-inclusion intended to contain and stabilize what the economic moment has set in motion: a nomadic displacement of people and manufactured goods from poor to wealthier countries, and, in the opposite direction, the global transport of garbage, dispatched to Africa or Asia to be recycled or in most cases, dumped.

The perfect reversibility of regulation and deregulation, inside and outside, toxicity and decontamination is at the core of today's culture of capital as total work of art. It is also at work in consumption and its twin behavior, recycling. As anything is consumable, and as we consume too much, anything is similarly disposable and potentially recyclable, recuperable, made beautiful and valuable again. Recycling, as the master verb of the twenty-first century, speaks of plasticity, and of the dematerialization and rematerialization of the object into a different form. The utopia of the perfect recirculation of junk speaks of the myth of materiality's eternal life (or of eternal life in general), that excludes decay, loss, and excess. The implied indestructibility of waste, and with it the denial of timed matter and memory, is situated somewhere between what Paul Virilio calls "the aesthetics of disappearance," and the neutralizing aestheticization, the recasting as art and beauty, of the negative. Recycling also brings to the fore the circular temporality of capital and its "eternity," in which the idea of time as progress gets spatialized into the image of a world without a residue, a space devoid of any element that might disturb its flows. Or even more ominously, this is a world where difference is produced *because* we are made aware that it is perfectly reabsorbable at the same time.

This reversibility—of value, of space, of time—characterizes that particular configuration of everyday experience for millions of people, that the Dutch architect Rem Koolhaas calls "Junkspace." "Junkspace" is the title of an essay published in the Harvard School of Design *Project on the City, Guide to Shopping* in 2002.[29] As star-architect modeling postmodern urbanism, Koolhaas is a controversial figure; yet his glitz, on par with the aestheticization of reality championed by corporate culture, works to counter the corporatization of resources.[30] "Junkspace" matters to any discussion of waste and materiality because it presents the full panorama of postmodern viscosity and elaborates ways it might be confronted. *Le visqueux*, the slimy, is a concept Jean-Paul Sartre uses in *Being and Nothingness* to designate a state very close to Kristeva's abjection : "a condition of matter that Sartre analyzes as neither liquid nor solid, but somewhere midway between the two," as Rosalind Krauss explains. Sartre's viscosity maintains a paradoxical quality as overpowering *and* docile, which marks both the alienated nearness of the contemporary culture of capital and the plasticity of contemporary materiality. In other words we cannot simply oppose the viscosity of junk to the frozen stasis of the well-ordered capitalist system of consumption, since that system has already adopted a kind of viscosity as its own strength.

The impossibility of drawing boundaries and distinctions between different categories, and the idea that difference melts entropically into its opposite, has been implicit in most discussions of postmodernity, starting with Baudrillard's notion of simulation. Versions of this scenario of postmodern undecidability which center on the dissolving of clear oppositions, are Debord's category of the Spectacle and Taussig's notion of the Nervous System, discussed in Chapter 3; both present the image of an all-enveloping reality with no exit in sight, in which the subject is trapped and unable to "read" herself and her position. To compare these versions of contemporary experience with "Junkspace" illuminates a crucial issue: the possibility of difference, of dissent, of the caption—that is to say, of a counter-consciousness that is political and might ignite resistance. Junkspace, the Spectacle, the Nervous System as images of the capitalist real: if the latter excludes even the fantasy of an outside, what cognitive mapping can each allow? What caption?

Their difference is mostly a matter of language and style. Debord's language in *Society of the Spectacle* (1967) is Marxist and Hegelian, founded on the distinction between appearance and reality, false consciousness and truth. For Debord the image is the utmost form of capitalism's abstraction and has colonized every space and experience, so that "Everything that was directly lived has moved away into a representation." The image lives the autonomous life that had been the commodity's prerogative, and "the Spectacle in general, as the concrete inversion of life, is the autonomous movement of the non-living." In this context people's relations become unavoidably mediated by the Spectacle, and lived reality is overtaken by the individual's contemplative relation to the image. The Spectacle is a façade imposed to permeate reality and human experience, "beneath" which life exists—the life around which May 1968 rallied.

Taussig's Nervous System, as a figure of the contemporary corporeal, political, and cultural system put in place by capital, is as far-reaching as the Spectacle, but it no longer allows the critic to take up a position of distance outside it. Taussig makes clear that "[the Nervous System] passes through us and makes us who we are" (3). Thus the landscape of the Nervous System is much closer, as we will see, to that of Junkspace, and similarly refuses to speak, either openly or implicitly, any language of transcendence or authenticity, but rather tries to outsmart and make manageable a system of which we are always already part. Without mentioning either critic, Taussig echoes Foucault's and Latour's critique of the *tabula*; countering it, the Nervous System is modeled on the irrepressible mobility and power of the fetish as live matter, continuously shuttling between the utterly material and the utterly spiritual. No institution, be it state, academy, or corporation, manages to fully contain and fix this mobility. Taussig uses the hybrid quality of the Nervous System—its systematicity *and* its "nervousness"—to illuminate the irrationality of reason in, for example, the mythical mentality of the Enlightenment *ratio* and the claim to objectivity of all western knowledge. The flip-flopping of matter from commodity to fetish and back again, whether at work in the Putumayo healing nights or in the *maleficium* of State terror, allows him to recognize the reversibility of the Nervous System, its continuous need for a fix that establishes it, at once whole and fragile. The point is not to fight it, to find a place outside it or a way to represent it mimetically, but rather to find a suitable way to mimic it, to adjust to its style; this mimicry echoes what both Benjamin and the modernist avant-garde attempted to do with their experiments. Again, the point is not to take one's distance from the Nervous System, to consider it as an object to represent and dominate, but rather to "ride" with it, like surfing a wave, by giving yourself to the phenomenon, as Adorno suggests in another context.

Instability, and loss of clear boundaries are at work in different ways in the Spectacle, the Nervous System, and Junkspace. This is the theoretical direction toward which waste moves and what gives it the preeminence I attributed to it among the different forms of materiality I have examined so far. Garbage, as junk, as viscous, as protean, may then be the most appropriate figure for understanding the cultural condition of the present and the status of materiality within it. Not only does junk stand for the potentially emancipatory paradox of the Nervous System, but also for the plasticity and formlessness of capital itself. Junk shares in the hybridity of the artefactual and of the quasi-object, and moves along their same lines of flight. To be able to situate oneself within this matter-space is particularly difficult when the rhizomatic proliferation of garbage, matter, and events comes to coincide with the circulatory flows of capital. For Koolhaas this is the challenge that Junkspace, as a new all-pervading type of space, poses: at stake is the possibility of making any other form of social and individual experience visible and thinkable.

Like junkmail and junkfood (mail that doesn't communicate anything of value; food that does not nourish), Junkspace is space that doesn't function the way it is supposed to, and that should be discarded. Given the reversibility and transvaluation of categories that contemporary culture allows, the valuable and the valueless exchange places and collapse into each other in a landscape that Marc Augé calls non-place,[31] which is now the only place.[32] By "non-place" Augé means all of those dull, equal spaces that retain no trace of the local—airports, malls, chain-hotels, offices—which might be anywhere and bear only the bland imprint of corporate culture. Worked-upon materiality, following the wave of mid-twentieth-century minimalism explored in Chapter 3, is now undergoing a process of homogeneization which leaves nothing untouched—the everyday, the private, the public, affect, culture, language. This system is not only minimal and bland, but plastic: the full plasticity and flow of this system is capable of incorporating every form of heterogeneity. Dissonance is preempted and recuperated by the perverse move of attributing to the discarded marginal the centrality of the norm.

As Koolhaas makes clear, Junkspace is first of all corporate, a space of consumption modeled on the mall—a space designed for the maximal consumption of commodities. Its key feature is our inability to position ourselves outside it. If the mall is the model of Junkspace, its many locales include the airport, the duty-free shop, the hotel, the nightclub, the freeway, the bachelor pad, the hospital, the golf course, the office. The osmotic transformation of these spaces into each other was anticipated in Tati's *Playtime*, where what we first take to be a hospital reveals itself to be an airport. However Junkspace is no longer the same as Tati's and Augé's non-places, for the *Playtime* moment when Hulot can contemplate from above the grid of ultra-modern office cubicles has passed. That position and viewpoint is still modern: it allows the viewer a vision unavailable to the contemporary critic. From Hulot's position we could laugh at the ruthless inhumanity of this organization of space; now we are either inside or outside the cubicle itself, inexorably within the grid of Junkspace.

Consider the morphology of Junkspace: urban and modular, it can endlessly proliferate. Its infinite malleability and liquidity make it non-architectural, "a kingdom of morphing" (177), with "the fortuitous configuration of a snowflake." Its continual mobility, its "fuzzy quality … empire of blur" (180), expresses "zero tolerance to configuration … no original architecture, only conversion and restoration, no history" (183). As architecture is replaced by modularity, touch has been replaced by a defused tactility which targets the senses but excludes contact, as the act of walking through an airport, in one of "our enforced *dérives*" shows: "We merely submit to grotesque journeys past perfumes, asylum-seekers, building sites, underwear, oysters, pornography, call-phones—incredible adventures for the brain, the eye, the nose, the tongue, the womb, the testicles" (181). Interpellating the subject's soma by the encounter with objects and their sensuousness may seem to repeat Benjamin's act of grasping experientially the jumble of objects in the arcades. Whereas for him, however, the unpredictable intimacy of these objects among themselves and with their consumers worked as a form of tactility that produced *Erfahrung*, and allowed the subject to experience materiality outside the protocols which consumer culture prescribed, in Junkspace perception *is* the experience, an end in itself, producing only self-reflexive isolation. "Transparency only reveals everything in which you cannot partake" (177) as Koolhaas puts it. Touch and connection are replaced by a wide-angle and thinly spread spectacularity, individually gratifying only, destined to remain incommunicable.

As a culture of leisure and comfort, driven by the imperative of safety, and dedicated to instant gratification, Junkspace's most important affect is sedation: in this sense Junkspace is the culmination of the narcosis of modernity, a post-Wagnerian total work of art which has managed to fully aestheticize reality. Its temporality is that of the vacation, of "corpotainment": it implies the eradication of work, and with it of the divide between work and leisure. The impact of a reality where there's only leisure time is blandness. Here the aesthetic (the bland lack of detail of a style blending "Mayan, Disney, and Art Déco" (176)), and the affective are perfectly commensurate. Against this commensurability Koolhaas rebels, in an effort to break the spell of Junkspace: "On popular demand organized beauty has become warm, inclusivist, arbitrary, poetic, and unthreatening ... No canned laughter but canned euphoria ... Why can't we tolerate strong sensations? Dissonance? Awkwardness? Genius? Anarchy?" (184). Dissonance, the unpredictable, laughter, are eliminated from Junkspace so that its balanced and air-conditioned *Geist* can be maintained.

Junkspace's viscous embrace of every event and object doesn't blind Koolhaas to its authoritarianism ("Junkspace is authorless yet surprisingly authoritarian" (185)), which, in turn, makes politics impossible. But this impossibility is nonetheless itself political. At the highpoint of his analysis Koolhaas declares: "Junkspace is political: it depends on the central removal of the critical faculty in the name of comfort and pleasure" (183). This is the point when the author's stylistic mimicry of the euphoria of Junkspace, the mimicry that Jameson has praised as Koolhaas's essay's adversarial power, becomes critique. Here Koolhaas builds upon Benjamin, Tati, and many others as critics of the derealization of the material in consumer modernity.

What is to be done when the critic speaks from inside Junkspace and the caption is no longer really possible, preemptively provided as it is by the space itself? Koolhaas' delirious performance of style is only one half of the deal; he also bemoans the waning of the critical faculty before Junkspace's viscous and comforting blandness, and implicitly calls us to be alert to possible points of rupture in the system. If the critic is no longer allowed to append his own caption to the cultural and political reality he is analyzing, he is still able to single out possible points of attrition in the system, both in specific structural conditions and in individual bodies. These are, for instance, the "unloyal" cleaners who appear at night: "between two and five a.m. yet another population, this one heartlessly casual and considerably darker, is sweeping ... Junkspace does not inspire loyalty in its cleaners" (179)—these are the paid servants who remove the actual trash, so that the blandness of junkspace can be maintained, and its viscous borders be rendered invisible. There are the occasional subaltern subjects, the mother and the refugee, aliens capable of "destabilizing an entire Junkspace" (180), and the system's own flows, which can become disabled by their functioning ... too well, as in the case of "the department store at the beginning of sales; the stampedes triggered by warring compartments of soccer fans; dead bodies piling up in front of the locked emergency doors of a disco—evidence of the awkward fit between the portals of Junkspace and the narrow calibrations of the old world" (180).

These images suggest that Koolhaas' *agon* with Junkspace is less a matter of representation and stylistic mimicry than of being alert to the points at which it might "come unstuck."[33] He knows that it is capable of inadvertently generating possible points of disruption, for instance through the figure of displaced people, whose nomadism implies a possibility of resistance. The model for Junkspace is immanence, but instead of the productivity of the Spinozian encounter and of the Deleuzian rhizome, instead of the activity we can see in Haraway's "contact zones" of "natureculture," or in the artefactuality of waste, Junkspace offers an entropy that culminates in a nightmarish vision of immanence in reverse. "Junkspace" says Koolhaas, "is often described as a space of flows, but that is a misnomer; flows depend on disciplined movement, bodies that cohere. Junkspace is a web without a spider ... Its anarchy is one of the last tangible ways in which we experience freedom." (179). Here Koolhaas adds a usefully skeptical gloss to the tendency in post-Deleuzian critiques to valorize flows for their own sake.

At the center of this web without a spider is the experiential and cultural project of capitalist abstraction, now presented as a fully realized form of self-referential materiality. Koolhaas' example is the foods covering the buffet tables of hotels: "... assemblies of caffeine and calories—cottage cheese, muffins, unripe grapes—notional representations of plenty, without horn and without plenty" (179), where objects only manage to be indexes of what they are. In this image of healthy junkfood, or non-food, the object finally evaporates. In Junkspace, the most complete abstraction of solid materiality happens again and again before our eyes, yet we don't feel deprived or experience a loss of unmediated reality, as was the case with Debord's society of the spectacle, since the disembodiment of matter is experienced as the most somatic of events. Yet at the end of it all, the immateriality of Junkspace is still a matter of discomfort rather than comfort, stress rather than reconciled sedation. For Koolhaas the distinction evidently still holds: this is why one can call him, paradoxically, a modernist. Junk, as a form of scandalous materiality that has reclaimed its disturbing quality, might be the right—and odorous—stuff with which to counter the trademark fragrances that pervade every corner of Junkspace.

For the time being shopping, in Jameson's formulation, spreads like a virus through Junkspace. From Marx to Debord to Koolhaas the commodity becomes more and more abstract and immaterial, and its fetishism changes from a fact of false consciousness, to a behavior, to an addiction. At last, consumption, Jameson asserts, has become spiritual: "Materiality is here a mere pretext for an exercise of the mental pleasures" (77). By now consumption has less to do with objects, merely working as incitement to desire around the planet. In Baudrillard's "society of consumption" the object had been entirely abstracted into the sign; now, however, consumption means we pay for "both the meaninglessness of life and the impossibility of satisfaction" (78). The perfect circularity of this new stage of affective consumption is fully in synch with the new emphasis on recycling: as we recycle object-parts and specific materials from the dump, we are finally consuming the unconsumable, the very meaningless of life, and the impossibility of finding satisfaction in the commodity. As in the case of the insipid foods in the hotel buffet, by buying objects now we consume both their immateriality and our recognition of their ineffectuality as commodity fetishes. We consume the acknowledgment that we see through them. This is no longer a desire for the commodity as image in the society of the spectacle; now the object of consumption is desire fueling itself, as the waste of waste. In this circuit, through the desire to consume, loss and negativity are at the same time entirely dispelled and yet maintained in effigy.

Faced with the neutralization of junk, how can we recall its negativity as a way of acknowledging difference, materiality, decay, and change as parts of the integrated circuit that is our habitat? How can we do this without going back to the dialectic and its skirmishes between subject and object, its temporality of progress and its foolproof affirmation of an outside? At the same time, how can we make sure never to forget that this protean world of plasticity, hybridity, and possibility, exemplified by the very recycling of junk, where events and encounters take place in the realm of creativity and freedom, *is* the integrated circuit of capitalism, in which quasi objects and quasi subjects exist, live, labor, and are, in various degrees, exploited? How do we bring to fruition the ruptures that Junkspace itself may produce, so that the reversibility and recuperability of materiality as disposable waste may hinder, rather than ease, the possibility of its recirculation? Can we come face to face with junk's unmanaged and unmanageable residue and its abject liminality? These are our questions as we examine the constellation of waste, aestheticization, narcosis, and style in culture. The films discussed here foreground the semiotic and libidinal charge of the discarded to make its unruliness visible, reaffirming the weight of materiality as antidote to the empty circularity of desire and the abstraction of consumption-without-an-object.

III. Extreme Recycling: The Plastic Bag as Portent

Contemporary consumer culture is founded on a paradox concerning its excess. On the one hand it breezily implies the impossibility of junk in the dream of a world without a residue, where negativity is constantly denied and converted into its opposite. On the other, there is an obsession with garbage and its management, the repeatedly announced need to dispose, born of the fear that the residue might overwhelm us. Both positions similarly invoke recycling, alternatively as the panacea and nemesis of post-industrial society, but certainly as the practice that can reinstate the sanitized and pleasing scenario of consumer culture. This world can then be thought of as "empty, serene, free of commercial debris," like the golf course Koolhaas describes. With recycling, waste is cast in relation to beauty, garbage in relation to aesthetics. As these are relations central to both films studied here, we need first to consider the implications of recycling, the chief model of contemporary waste management. To do so I turn briefly to two essays, one by the Spanish philosopher José Luis Pardo, the other by the Italian writer Italo Calvino. Both offer points of departure for a critique of the garbarge-aesthetic of Mendes' and Varda's films.

Its representation of the residual situates Sam Mendes' film *American Beauty* at the core of my discussion. In the film, the vision of blasé suburban Junkspace is mediated through the voyeuristic gaze of one of the characters, Ricky, who obsessively films the text's most arresting image of garbage, the plastic bag twirling in the wind. This image portentously reiterates the numbing power of aestheticization: the plastic bag becomes an allegory of metaphysics colluding with consumption to produce a new type of intransitive aestheticism, a one-way image of beauty which precludes any form of critique. This bag, emblem of how the film deals with waste, directly points to Pardo's critique of recycling in his essay "Never Was Trash So Beautiful."[34] For Pardo, whose analysis echoes those of Augé (whom he mentions) and Koolhaas (whom he doesn't), trash is directly connected to the issue of spatiality, no longer, as Mary Douglas affirmed, as "dirt out of place," but as "trash that does not have a place, that which is misplaced, and therefore, that which has to be moved to another place to make progress" (Pardo, 1). Recycling implies the hope to make trash "beautiful again" (2), reintegrated into the circulation of commodities and normalized. But this perfect scenario of checks and balances is no longer possible. For Pardo, the waning of the idea of the world without a residue—as he says, simultaneously the dream of the engineer, the accountant, and the businessman—sanctions the crisis of modernity and of its ideology of perfect rationality which leaves no waste, except for its marginal figures: "monsters, prodigies, exceptions without destiny, future, or purpose" (2). When, with the increased consumption levels of advanced capitalism, we start feeling besieged by our own trash, this delirious model of perfect re-circulability is no longer tenable. It is replaced, as Pardo sardonically suggests, by a new one, in which we learn to experience trash as something already and immediately positive. Therefore

> Never was trash so beautiful. I don't know who got the idea first, but it was a very clever one ... What if what we call trash was not really so? Then we would not have to worry about it devouring us, we would not feel suffocated by waste if we would stop experiencing it as waste and make a new urban landscape out of it. (3).

In this world there are no losses or regrets: we eat no-food, we work in no-companies under conditions of no-employment, shopping centers feature no-shops; Koolhaas' Junkspace becomes the everyday. Places, the experienced, affect- and memory-filled locales of Augé, have been taken over by Junkspace: "We have learned to experience junk as luxury ... we have managed to start not to see and not to feel the trash that suffocates us" (5). Pardo, suggesting it is a form of self-defence against the potential onslaught of excessive refuse, delineates a form of numbness and a waning of experience inaugurated by the modern system of things.

Ultimately this self-defence is reduced to a paroxysm of recycling in a world where recuperation, whether in material or metaphorical terms, is merely a wish, never to be fulfilled. Recycling then becomes the label under which more and more trash can be created, the act which grants permission to create more waste. In Pardo's words: "Something which is conceived for recycling from its origin is something that is from its origin conceived as trash. And this, being originally conceived for recycling, is what distinguished both objectivity and subjectivity ... The process of becoming trash is a process of disqualification in which things are reduced to that de-individualizing 'thinginess'—fluid and without attributes." Recycling is supposed to reinvest materiality with its lost properties and value. However, since it is not possible to recycle at the speed we waste, all of these things that lack properties from the moment of their origin, as they are imagined as recyclable from the start, are therefore "part of the fluid and disqualified 'thinginess' which is what we now—according to the junk strategy of the new paradigm—have to experience." The guarantee of their recyclability means that we experience them in this bland fluidity, "Not as a degraded and 'dirty' type of thinginess, belonging to the tip and the dump, but rather as a superior form of objectivity, the quintessential luxury and clean thing, because it is immediately recyclable" (5). Pardo's paradoxical thinking underlines the formless blandness of Junkspace. Contemporary materiality is born recyclable; it is recyclable insofar as it is already junk. Its plasticity means no more than the effect of its disposability. The same relation between plasticity and disposability returns, perhaps with pathos, in *American Beauty*. Mendes' film, instead of surrendering to the viscosity of Junkspace, which recycling only magnifies and enhances, resists it by seeking transcendence through the aesthetic. In so doing it only manages to fetishize garbage, and to deprive it of its antagonistic power.

Lester Burnham, the protagonist of *American Beauty*, lives his mid-life crisis as a desire to escape the constrictions of his suburban life and job in middle- management. He resigns, takes a job at a fast-food diner, and falls in love with Angela, his teenage daughter's best friend, to the chagrin of his wife Carolyn, a real estate agent cast as emasculating career woman. Lester reconquers a clichéd juvenile freedom by living the fantasies of a younger man, even to buying a red sports car. Ricky Fitts, his daughter's boyfriend, son of the authoritarian, abusive Colonel Fitts, collector of Nazi memorabilia, plays midwife to Lester's escapism by supplying him with drugs and convincing him that Angela might be conquered. Through the film Ricky wins Lester to his vision of reality—that is, to the "world of beauty behind things" that he, Ricky, sees when filming with his video camera. By the end, when he gives up Angela, Lester seems to embrace the norm and reconquer his adult masculinity by submitting to the paternal role. At this point the Colonel, suspecting a homosexual relationship between Ricky and Lester, approaches Lester, now reconciled to the joys of family life, and when Lester rejects him, shoots him dead. The film, narrated by Lester's voiceover speaking from high above, ends with Ricky looking at Lester's corpse as yet another example of the "beauty behind things," and Lester's memories of what had really been important in his life.

While the gender politics[35] being canvassed in *American Beauty* have generated striking feminist[36] and queer[37] readings, especially of the incest motif and masculine desire, here we will read the film as a narrative about consumption and aesthetics—about the protagonist's attempt to reanimate desire, to come to life again, and to transcend his present conditions of existence by becoming "young" again. This is a film about beauty, consumption—and recycling: it is, literally, about the subject's hope to recycle himself. Lester's desire is rooted in tenets of the American cultural imaginary, long ago taken over by consumerism: youth, and the fantasy of an unfettered masculinity in the wilderness. Following this cultural script, Lester's desire is destined to be contained and in the end punished. His transgression is not the film's only sign of Americanness: what makes the "beauty" in the film American is its inbuilt recyclability, its continual traffic with the commodity and the discarded object. If Ricky's videotaping captures the intimations of "a world behind things," as he insists, the "American beauty" of the title is an intimation of the reified, Henry James-goes-to-Hollywood use of aesthetics that the film contests but doesn't manage to avoid. Here, "American Gothic" becomes "American Beauty" in a milieu where recycling can work as the final frontier even of subjectivity.

The suburbs are an appropriate locale for this kind of beauty. Cradle of über-domesticity, suburban life is centered on a fantasy of safety and cleanliness, with trash left rigorously out of sight. This is a place of harmony and manicured nature, of Carolyn's roses and the eternal cheerfulness of the gay couple next door. At the same time, the suburbs have a more dangerous underside, made of the false-bottom drawers where Ricky hides the cocaine he deals, the porn and voyeurism, extra-marital affairs, incestuous desire, and a stupefying materialism. Two levels of reality coexist uneasily in the film, even to the end. There's no severed ear abandoned on the ground here, as in the full-on suburban gothic of David Lynch's *Blue Velvet*, to plunge us into a perverse world; in *American Beauty*'s satire this world is miniaturized and contained both in Lester's unrealized fantasies (for instance in the merely envisioned moment where Angela bathes among the red rose petals, while he stands by, barely touching her), or by Ricky's own hunting for *meta ta physika* with his camera, intermittently fishing for a world beyond, as unreachable as Angela.

Beauty here is articulated according to the same narrative model of surface and depth, and represented as the search for transcendence that is both desired and feared. "Under the surface" of a life made pleasant rather than pleasurable, and presented as an experience of inevitable happiness, via staged dinners with muzak and flowers, lurks a world of transgressive sexuality. This is the world that Ricky's camera, as a means of voyeuristic pleasure *and* surveillance, reveals and controls. It is also the world of meaningless materialism which so infuriates Lester that he embarks on his homegrown version of Bataillean *dépense* by breaking china and upsetting Carolyn's decorous domesticity. Here Lester is not (yet) the happy consumer of Junkspace; with his rebellion he actually pursues a world beyond the surface of things, a beauty deeper than that of the Italian couch, which upsets him when Carolyn refuses to dally on it, for fear of damaging the upholstery. "It's only a couch!" shouts Lester, insulting her things.

To the easy-listening beauty of the designer couch, the film counterposes the only apparently different images of authentically and ominously beautiful objects: Colonel Fitts' collection of military memorabilia, through which he anchors his identity into a fantasy of fascist hypermasculinity; Angela as an object of beauty in Lester's eyes; and last but not least, Ricky's video images of waste. These latter include the plastic bag dancing in the wind, a dead bird, a beggar woman frozen to death in the street, Lester's body after he has been shot by the Colonel. We note at once the peculiarity of Ricky's choice of subjects: in order for reality to reveal its hidden beauty and become an object of contemplation, the inanimate object must become "alive," and the animate must have died. What makes Ricky's subjects beautiful, therefore, is exactly this exchange of qualities between the animate and the inanimate, the very death-in-life that defines the commodity. Second, the divide is not stable between the two versions of beauty with which the film deals, the "American Beauty" of the commodity fetish and the possible beauty—perhaps not less American, given Transcendentalism's importance in the American philosophic tradition—of metaphysical reality. Carolyn's couch and the Colonel's Nazi plate subscribe to a similar identificatory and fetishistic logic: both characters identify with and are given an identity by these objects. The same is true of the red roses that surround Angela in Lester's fantasy of transcendence, which in turn take us back to the world he would escape, that of red roses in manicured gardens and on dinner tables. Lester's means for his leap into freedom and a more authentic existence, sexual desire, is shaped by a recurring ready-made image in which *Playboy* encounters Hallmark cards (but this time not on Lautreaumont's operating table). Even more striking is how Mendes' cinematography suggests a connection between the Nazi plate, dark symbol of authoritarianism, and its supposed opposite, the floating plastic bag as an image of "otherwordly" freedom. When Ricky breaks into his father's cabinet to show Jane the plate imprinted with the swastika, embarrassedly claiming that this is "one thing" his father has, so that he is not really part "of the whole subculture that collects this Nazi shit," Mendes swiftly cuts to the image of the plastic bag, "the most beautiful thing" Ricky has ever seen.

The encounter with the discarded object through the eye of the video camera affords Ricky, he claims, a momentary contact with the divine. It allows a sacred, rather than profane, illumination: as Ricky says about one of his video subjects, the homeless woman frozen to death on the street, "When you see something like that, it's like God is looking right at you for a second, and if you are careful, you can look right back . . . and see beauty. . . ." If beauty must be deeper than that of the designer couch, its authenticity can be guaranteed only by the continual reversibility of opposite categories. This recyclability flips the inanimate into the animate and vice versa, and seeing into being seen, without stopping or without a point of arrival. To be beautiful a living subject needs to be dead, or if it's an object that is in question, it needs to be alive. And to see beauty and make eye contact with God you need a video camera.

At the end of the film, both notions of beauty, the superficial beauty that needs to be transcended and the "real" one, collapse into the image of Lester dead in the garage. Blood oozes from his head onto a table; the shadow of a smirk parts his lips. The visual clue of the red roses returns as the red of the blood, a loud nuance of color, almost Tarantinoesque. In this final image he appears to be punished and redeemed, happy and himself, via the color red, the marker of beauty the film had played with throughout. At last, after looking for beauty, he has become an object of beauty himself. Dead, he lies, like all objects in consumer culture, in an infinite chain of equivalence and exchange with all other objects. Framed by Ricky's gaze, this time without the mediation of his camera, he himself becomes the thing of beauty Angela had been for him, and yet another connection with an elsewhere for Ricky. In a world where touch and human relationships are impossible—as they have been either commodified or turned into forms of destructive violence (both the Colonel and Carolyn at the end approach Lester with a gun)—it is only when dead that Lester can become transitive and permeable to others.

The plastic bag, once we see it in a continuum with the series of objects of Ricky's video gaze, does not recuperate the thingness of things (which never was). Neither does it suggest a different way of relating to garbage in the name of pleasure rather than guilt, as some critics claim.[38] Rather it celebrates the immediate recyclability of materiality of which Pardo speaks. In Mendes' film the beauty becomes Beauty, because aesthetics here does not produce tactility and relationality, but only reifies both subject and object into the dead quality of the image. Aesthetics here renounces its power to produce a shock capable of jumpstarting a new type of perception and experience; art remains instead yet another means of consumption and acquiescence for the subject. *L'art pour l'art* now yields to trash for trash's sake, and "never was trash so beautiful." Its negativity is recouped under the aegis of aestheticism.

Should a film about transcendence in Junkspace, about piercing the veil of appearances at the time when both metaphysics and the dialectic appear to have lost their prestige, be read as an ironic statement or as speaking in earnest? Mendes' identification with Ricky, declared in an interview,[39] makes it even more difficult to answer this question. At the end, dead in his garage, staring emptily, Lester seems to have had his vision. But what has he seen? To where has he managed to escape? For all its utopian and metaphysical claims, *American Beauty* says that there is nowhere to go but to die, and that only the past matters. Lester's transcendence comes in the form of memories, of memories of objects and materiality at that.

In *American Beauty*, after Lester's death, his disembodied voiceover reflects on his past life (in the "fabulous fifties" world of Coppola's *Peggy Sue Got Married*) from the "elsewhere" he has finally reached. From this other dimension "the truth" comes to him as the memory of objects. As he speaks, we see them in Lester's own view from above, while he reminisces about his life's important things: "My ball, my pedal car . . . my grandmother's hands . . ." Mendes' camera shows us these objects displayed on a lawn—very much as if they are the massed "homeless" objects taken out of homes in Peter Menzel's photographs. Lester's ball and pedal car have outgrown their status as commodities, but are not less fetishistic; they still occupy a middle ground between the plastic bag and the Italian couch. Notwithstanding its vaguely Proustian echo, their image reduces memory to a flat spectacle of things that change nothing, touch nobody, and ultimately produce only a voyeuristic pleasure for the film viewer, while infantilizing the protagonist in the position of an innocent child. From this position he can now be happy—experience no desire, no lack—but it's a passive happiness that dangerously resembles that promised by the commodity. The objects he reminisces about are presented as if displayed for their (recycling) yard sale. Ultimately the beauty of the plastic bag precisely denies it the tactility and the experience that the encounter with junk might promise. Lester's attempted line of flight is reabsorbed into the metaphysical reading of reality that Ricky's camera eye imparts to the world.

Both the "other world" Ricky sees in his videos and which Lester experiences with death bring no shock, no illumination. The things that truly mattered in Lester's life were things, and stubbornly remain such. That glimpse of God through the beauty of trash is yet another glimpse of the capitalist divine, where everything can be enjoyed at a distance, and things per se matter more than relationships and people. In the film all human relationships are either abusive and exploitative, or mediated by objects: for example, the relationship between Lester and Ricky, which starts Lester's search for a different life, suggests a connection between father and son, but is structured as an economic transaction around buying drugs. Even after Lester's "redemption" through his acceptance of the paternal role, the film is relentless in not allowing any form of human immediacy that might be experienced in earnest. Just before being shot, Lester is shown looking at an old photo of his family. Although the photo portrays the immediacy of family relationships, the director doesn't let you forget that this is an *image*, and not the real thing; an image of the most embattled unit of American society, to whose dysfunctionality Lester has contributed as ineffectual father and husband. What he looks at is the photographic equivalent of the plastic bag: the effigy of an elsewhere that remains unreachable, or perhaps has been reached and is meaningless.

American Beauty's desire for transcendence reifies the aesthetic into serving, again, the purposes of commodity fetishism. Lester's search for happiness reaches only a remembered well-being always mediated by images of things. Mendes' film implies that in Junkspace, where there is no future and the present is disappointing, all that can be experienced is the self-referentiality of the past. This is not the past as history, but the past as "the way we were." And as we know from Marx, when history repeats itself (even the privatized history of Mendes' characters), it returns as farce. Worse, when history is only an image of second-hand reality, it returns as trash.

IV. Of Sprouted Potatoes and Other *Trouvailles*: The Politics of Gleaning

In the essay "La Poubelle Agrée"[40] Italo Calvino's understanding of garbage seems diametrically opposed to the scenarios offered by Koolhaas, Pardo, and Mendes. While these all take their distance from the materiality of trash to reflect in structural terms upon its disposability, Calvino stays close to garbage itself, analyzing his personal relation to it. In "La Poubelle Agrée" he focuses on what happens before recycling, even before the garbage truck arrives. He writes from the viewpoint of the people who actually handle garbage, himself and the *ébouers*, the garbage collectors. Each contributes to a process that he senses is somehow outside his full control, a machinery larger than himself, part of the circulation of matter in modernity. Calvino is aware of this industrial level of circulation; in this essay, however, he sets out to understand his own role in the process he describes.

The daily ritual of taking out the garbage has the effect of placing the writer in a liminal position between inside and outside the house, the kitchen, and the street: in this act he is made part of a social whole, and thinks of himself as part of a collective. The adjective "*agrée*," speculates Calvino, implies complying with the law: "It's the English verb "to agree" that intervenes: it's in order to respect an agreement, an agreed upon pact between two parts, that I am putting this object on the sidewalk" (5). This agreed-upon pact makes him also think of this process "in personal, sociological, and philosophical terms," and leads him to reflect upon the production of his own subjectivity. He experiences the *enlèvement des ordures* as a purifying rite:

> in this daily gesture of mine I affirm the necessity to separate myself from a part of what was mine, the remains, or the chrysalis, or the squeezed lemon of living, so that the substance of it may remain, so that tomorrow I may identify entirely with what I am and have. By the gesture of throwing out I can be assured that something of me has not yet been thrown away, and perhaps it's not, and will not be thrown away (7).

The miser and the constipated, instead, are failed subjects, exactly because they resort to an image of the self as fixed, and inclusive: "Curse of the constipated (and the miser) who, fearing to lose something of themselves, cannot separate from anything, accumulate what they do not expel, and end up by identifying themselves with their own excrements, and lose themselves in them" (8). Yet to despise the miser's abjection is not quite enough to sustain the fantasy of a stable self; Calvino knows that this stability is temporary. "La Poubelle Agrée" leaves no space for this fantasy, crucial to western thought and its subject: the author is fully aware of this process as one through which the self is repeatedly remade, and thus can easily become unmade. Neither does Calvino forget about one's finitude: "As an offer to the underworld, to the gods of disappearance and loss," taking out the garbage is a way of exorcising death, of postponing metaphorically the moment when we ourselves will become waste. "This daily representation of a descent to the underworld, this domestic and municipal funeral of garbage is meant first of all to postpone the person's own funeral, even if just of a little, so that I know that for another day I have been the producer of waste, and not waste myself" (7). From Calvino's philosophy of garbage we learn not of the subject's power over the object, nor of his shrewd taking advantage of matter's plasticity through recycling. Instead garbage teaches the subject about his own limitations: that he is "like garbage" himself, or that he is soon to become garbage, part of a process of circulation he does not control.

Calvino makes a point of the difference between the person who takes the garbage out into the street, and those who collect it with their truck: the satisfied consumer on one side, "while the man who unloads the *poubelles* in the rotating crater of the truck, gets the idea of the quantity of goods from which he is excluded, which reach him only as unusable leftovers" (10). While consumer and sanitation worker participate unequally in the elimination of waste, both are similarly ineffectual in stopping the process of overproduction and disposing:

> To no avail do I and the trash collectors pour our obscure cornucopia in the track; the recycling of the residues can be only an accessory practice which does not modify the substance of the process. The pleasure to make finite materiality reborn remains the privilege of god-capital, which commodifies the soul of things and, at best, leaves us to consume their material remains (10).

In the alienated panorama of late capitalism matter takes center stage, while humans, filling and emptying the garbage truck, perform an act whose rationale is established elsewhere.

Calvino refuses to aestheticize the contents of his *poubelle*, or to forget them once they are out of sight. At the end of the essay he reflects on his work as a writer and on the creative process by pointing out that art is produced by the same mechanism through which both order and self are maintained: an act of separation from waste and debris. Even the essay worth publishing is the result of a form of "self-dispossession," the result of loss, what remains after throwing away "a pile of crumpled sheets of paper and a pile of pages written over till the last line, both no longer mine, disposed of, expelled" (13). Finally, in a gesture which testifies to his belief in the dangers of garbage, and to his refusal of the delusional fantasy of a world without a residue, Calvino refuses to perform this act of separation, and instead in this case publishes the "garbage" of his essay, the drafts and notes that preceded the final version. With this Brechtian choice to make visible each and every phase of the aesthetic process, the author demonstrates his impatience with the smooth surface and sutured perfection of some art objects, which, like commodities, claim to have come into existence magically by themselves. The work of art, like the self, like social and personal order, depends on its traffic with waste and negativity. As Calvino makes clear, this exchange is never resolved.

I premise my discussion of Agnés Varda's documentary on Calvino's ideas because his understanding of garbage is at the core of Varda's work. Each sees interaction with waste as a moment when ordinary individuals participate in the collective. Each thinks of the interaction with waste as a chance to become aware of one's role in a process definitely not of one's own making. Each, looking garbage and decay in the face, identifies a positive plasticity in the encounter between waste and the human subject, a plasticity that is destructive and productive at the same time. *The Gleaners and I* (*Les glaneuses et la glaneuse*), Varda's documentary film made in 2000, attends almost lovingly to waste and marginality, but goes far beyond Mendes' film to delineate the interaction between marginal subjects and objects where one works upon the other. Varda shows no interest in transcending reality, no matter how grim, via the solipsistic aestheticization of garbage. Instead her film-making takes her on the road, connecting her to a great number of people, whom she films, interviews, and gets to know. Making visible what the audience doesn't know and doesn't want to know about waste and poverty, Varda's narrative in the film is a form of critique, while her aesthetic choices are the perfect stage for a "captioning" of the reality she films. While Benjamin's captions always run the risk of Brechtian didacticism, Varda's use of montage, and of words such as "pleasure" and "delight" in her comments and interviews, manage to integrate aesthetics and politics, critique and the personal in a document both tough-minded and poetic.

Presented at the Cannes Film Festival in 2000 and then broadcast on French television, Varda's documentary enjoyed an immense success; a sequel followed in 2002. *The Gleaners and I* opens with three images emblematic of Varda's interests: a Larousse dictionary (with her cat sitting on it), out of which she reads the meaning of "gleaning"; two famous French paintings of women gleaning in the fields, Jean François Millet's *Les Glaneuses* (1857), and Jules Breton's *La Glaneuse*, (1877); and an actual *glaneuse*, a countrywoman, Varda's first interviewee. These images point to three central elements in the film and its sequel: the dictionary to the voice of the law and of doxa, the paintings to art, and the countrywoman to real people and their bodies. By focusing on gleaning, a practice with a very long history of picking up what's left on the ground after the harvest, now extended to trash-diving for food and junk, Varda critiques contemporary western culture's vast overconsumption and waste, and reveals a submerged network of gleaners who daily improvise a more honest and intimate relation to the material. In her travels through urban and rural France, driving around with her troupe, she meets a variety of gleaners for whom an improvised materiality of making-do is their livelihood.

The film first focuses on gleaners of food, walking through harvest fields for leftover potatoes, apples, and grapes, as it establishes the cultural understanding of gleaning. People in cafés reminisce about their own experience of gleaning during and after World War II and look upon it as a practice long disappeared. At these words Varda cuts to a contemporary image of gleaning, highlighting the continued reality of poverty. From the sequel, *Deux Ans Après*, we gather that this aspect of the film shocked viewers. Yet the interviewees agree that gleaning grants a person a dignity that neither begging nor stealing would: "To bend is not to beg," says one man. Not all of Varda's interviewees, however, are so resigned: Ghislaine, a woman the director meets at a gypsy campsite, protests vociferously against her living conditions as she forages through trash. While the calm resignation of some of the interviewees recalls the gleaners of Millet's painting, Ghislaine strikes the defiant attitude of Breton's *glaneuse*, carrying herself proudly and fiercely accusing her society.

Early in the film Varda establishes herself too as a *glaneuse*; in the Museum of Arras she is filmed against Breton's painting, carrying, like his peasant woman, a bundle of wheat. "I put down the wheat and pick up the camera," she says. The documentary is thus a form of gleaning, a collection of art-scraps from literature, film, photography, painting, and music, that the director takes up and incorporates in her work. The film follows a collection of the people Varda encounters and the things she finds; here the Surrealist notions of *rencontre* and *trouvaille* are recast as the creative labor of survival.

At the same time the documentary is an encounter with Varda's own "laying to waste" through aging. Her reflections on gleaning and encounters with waste become occasions for reckoning with her own aging and finitude. By turning the camera on herself, as she says at the end of *Deux Ans Après*, she wants to be "as honest as the gleaners had been." In the face of her own demise no protest or anger is possible, only acceptance: "It's not 'O rage, O despair' . . . My hair and my hand tell me that the end is near."

Along with impoverished gleaners, Varda encounters people who glean by choice, for personal and at times artistic reasons; she also interviews those whose fields are being gleaned, such as the wine-maker, psychoanalyst, and theorist Jean Laplanche. Among the interviewees are "artists of *la recoup*," for instance Louis Pons, who looks at "a cluster of junk as a cluster of possibilities," and makes "sentences of things," or Litnianski, the retired Russian stonemason who makes monumental towers out of discarded objects and dolls; or the artist who picks up objects off the street at night, and keeps them in his house, while trying to "move toward lessness." Aware of the life of discarded things— "They have a past, they've already had a life and they are still very much alive"—this nameless artist feels a "call" to pick them up: "The objects beckon me from the street." The director herself feels the same call, when, during a stop at a *brocante* she discovers a painting crudely combining Millet's and Breton's *glaneuses*, which she considers a real "find": "The painting had beckoned me because it belonged in the film." Thus the documentary is also a metacommentary on its own gleaning as art-making, and shows that the chance involved in this gleaning intervenes in the director's plans. Her editing—a true work of montage—and the voiceover commentary which captions her images are crosscut by chance, which features again and again in the narrative, and by which Varda lets herself be guided. In this way gleaning, chance, and art-making are shown in the film as natural allies. But Varda is quick to recognize how easily the radical potential of gleaning for art can be transformed into recycling with a price-tag. After showing a children's workshop where art is made out of recycled materials, she peruses "grown up" art similarly made from trash. Exhibited in a gallery, the pieces she admires are as playful as the children's work, and highly commodified. "But junk," she says, "is highly priced art, now."

Varda's gleaners glean for survival, for choice, for pleasure, and only occasionally for money. Solomon, an African immigrant, picks up appliances from the street, repairs them, and gives them to his friend Charlie Plusquellec, an elderly Vietnamese man who now owns "four fridges and two freezers," as he says, smiling, as he cooks the food Solomon salvages from dumpsters. From Solomon and Charlie, Varda cuts to the studio of an artist who creates dioramas inside discarded refrigerators: one is of a mini-rally made with

Lego figurines, and from this Lego rally we move to a real street rally. Such sequencing compliments the chance element in gleaning itself; it also foregrounds a key element of Varda's work, the connection between art, everyday life, and politics.

The film closes with the director's own highlight: her meeting Alain, an ex-university biologist, who for the last eight years has lived in a shelter in the *banlieues*, where at night he teaches immigrants how to read and write. At the closing of the market where she does her own shopping, Varda meets him picking vegetables from the ground, carefully choosing what to eat for its nutritional value. Alain's life and activity as a teacher shows that marginality is not passivity or parasitism, but a refusal to play by what he sees as unjust rules of the game of consumer culture. What sprouts from this marginality and waste, like the sprouted heart-shaped potatoes Varda gleans in the potato field, films and brings home, can be very productive, but not according to the logic of productivity prescribed by capital. The other remarkable experience for Varda is the recuperation of Edmond Hedouin's painting *Les glaneuses fuyant l'orage* (*Gleaners Running Away from a Storm*, 1852), from the basement of the Museum of Villefranche sur Saône, as the result of her film. In *Deux Ans Après* she will say: "I feel I participate in the history of Hedouin's painting."

In *Deux Ans Après*, Varda meets new interviewees and some we already know, including Ghislaine, whom Varda spots by mere chance on the street. Ghislaine is still homeless, sleeps in a park shed, and makes a spectacle of herself drunk. When asked by Varda the reason for her behavior she answers: "I want a lot of people to see that and understand. Then they'll see what it is like to live in poverty, in the street and all, and why they drink." Both gleaners, the marginal Ghislaine and Varda, are absorbed in the same activity: making visible, revealing, denouncing. For Varda this is an act that passes through aesthetics and its pleasure. One scandalous moment in the second documentary is Varda's response to the word of *l'homme aux artichaux*, the "artichoke man," another destitute homeless figure, a squatter, rummaging through the leftovers of a market. "Wasting shows no respect for the worker who made it. That's one of the many reasons I salvage," he says, "I've recycled myself into non-consumerism." To which Varda replies: "I enjoyed filming him. I also enjoy filming potatoes, life going by, and cats." Rather than a demonstration of Varda's shallow social consciousness or callow aestheticism,[41] her answer foregrounds a nexus of the political, the personal, and pleasure. Varda stages a synergy of these apparently disparate and clashing elements—art, materiality, social consciousness, pleasure, critique, beauty, resistance—into a new ecology of stuff. Her two documentaries are eloquent texts with which to conclude a discussion of unruly materiality, because they set out to show the scandalous uses to which stuff can be put by people whose lives are as marginalized as the used trash they appropriate.

The Gleaners and I is a critique of wasting and a denunciation of the effects of overconsumption and overproduction. This is a materialism with a critical edge. At the heart of this critique, as its counterpunch, is a valorization of the improvisational practice of gleaning. This implies a specific understanding of materiality. There is no fetishism of the object here and no search for *quidditas*. Rather, Varda gleans and assembles a political film about plasticity, power, and interconnectedness that defies and gives the lie to the model of smooth circulation of flows and networks. She situates the always marginal, "wasted lives" (Bauman's phrase) at the center of her narration, and presents junk as a process and opportunity, rather than merely a problem to solve or to overlook and deny. The documentary implies that there is an unfinished materiality of the things and foods wasted which can still be recuperated, rather than merely destroyed or recycled, in a way that might actually help people to connect and come together. The stakes of the scenario illustrated by Varda are high: in proposing a different way of looking at materiality, the film invites us to challenge the ways everyday human relations and public space are organized. The selfish indifference of the "haves" is vividly shown, for instance, when the Burgundian wine-makers forbid gleaning in their vineyards ("It's for the protection of our profession, of our capital"), so that grapes are left to rot on the ground, lost to everybody. In the universe of recuperation, transformation, and chance *The Gleaners* depicts, two key issues contribute to a new critique of objectivity: first, the difference between gleaning and recycling, and, second, the relation between aesthetics and waste, discernible in the role that art, artfulness, and pleasure play in the documentary.

Gleaning is not recycling. Each activity is based on a different economic vision and on a different understanding of stuff. As Pardo pointed out, recyclability always implies the disposability of an object. The recyclable is recuperated only insofar it has no identity as an object, and this lack of identity is predicated on the plastic quality of its material. Recyclable matter leaves one circuit of commodification and consumption only to be inserted into another; what is visible in the recyclable object, at least to the entrepreneur, is not its unfinished life, but its profitability. Those who work in a recycling plant are like workers in a factory, or in any other space of production: they work at the transformation of the object but they will soon be alienated from it. More often than not, the recycled object goes to appease the "green" conscience of another consumer. Recycling supports the modern ideal of a self-sufficient world, in which any excess is reabsorbed and made useful again thanks to the calculations of scientific knowledge. The recirculation of matter, of objects made unrecognizable and incapable of carrying any imprint of either their former producers or consumers, curtails memory. All we know is that the object we buy is "made of recycled material." Finally, recycling tends toward another form of fetishization of materiality: it always suggests the suspicion that in its unceasing transformability the object might harbor still another level of substantiality. The process of industrial recycling continues to alienate the object from its temporal and human context, its political economy, and its past.

The way Varda portrays gleaning, on the contrary, renders it a political activity, a transformative practice through which excess is repurposed in ways that defy established economic and legal rules of property. Gleaning is both legal and outlaw at the same time. As the two lawyers she interviews, the first standing in a field of cabbages and the second by a trash bin, agree, it has been sanctioned by centuries of French law. One reads from the legal code: "The poor, the wretched, the deprived have the right to glean." Still, as the other notes, "the property of gleaned objects is strange: it comes from nobody, so it cannot be stealing, because the things gleaned are the result of renounced property." Thus gleaning intervenes in a rare zone of non-ownership of matter, and while it speaks of poverty and need, it also implies active resistance to consumer culture. It's not the anonymous collectivity of society that benefits from it, but the *hic et nunc* individual, who can eat discarded foods or collect and reuse stuff for herself. Although gleaned objects can become commodities again, as when, for example, gleaners recuperate copper out of old televisions, their recirculation remains marginal as an economic circuit. The ephemerality of gleaning is matched by its logistical inconsistency: although one gleaner, the artist trying "to move toward lessness," shows Varda a map of all the spots in town where refuse can be found, another claims that "people don't know where to go." While food will presumably be found behind a restaurant or a supermarket, which fields to go to, or where to find good pieces of junk which can be used in everyday life or in art, is more often than not a matter of chance.

Varda, the artist as producer and gleaner, subjects herself to the same chance. She acknowledges that what one finds and where, how it's going to intervene in and shape the work you are doing, or nourish you, is not completely in one's hands. Choosing to become dispossessed of her authorial power, she repeatedly surrenders to chance rather than insisting on a fully controlled organization of her material. Through her surrender she bows to the silent work of the unconscious ("We work without knowing," she says in *Deux Ans Après*), implying an "agency of the object" similar to that of the Surrealist *trouvaille*. For example when, in the second-hand shop by the freeway, she finds the painting of the gleaners "which wanted to be in the film," she recognizes the power of this lost object, its call to her to be discovered and dug out of its dusty burial ground. At once she renounces her machinery of control over her material, and lets herself be questioned and led by it. This image of matter, instead of the director, directing the action, shows that the conditions of chance and contingency by which the gleaner relates to stuff are a lesson for everybody.

When, as Varda does, we reverse the relationship of power and agency, and of intentionality and chance between subject and object, we are in for surprises. Take the burst of an actual thunderstorm at the moment when Hedouin's painting *Les glaneuses fuyant l'orage* is finally brought to light, out of the basement and into a little courtyard of the museum of Villefranche sur Sâone: "You organize things, people are kind, competent … Then this marvelous gust of wind comes along, and no filmmaker can order and obtain that," notes Varda. When the raindrops hit the canvas, it's no longer a matter of art imitating life or life imitating art, according to the same old charade of mimesis, but of either and both intervening, cutting through the other, like the locomotive of the 1895 Lumière brothers film appearing to leap from the screen. This two-way, open, unresolved interpenetration of art and the everyday is what Varda is after in her work. She uses her *techne* to illuminate a reality that never lets you forget its own artistry, so that the artificial and the artefactual are never once and for all assigned to either "art" or "reality." With her approach to aesthetics and chance she wants to show that art does not live in its own sphere, separated from real life; she sees the aesthetic as a force that shapes the everyday and that, in turn, is a force that everyday materiality is capable of putting forth. This is why she attends to the moments when this aesthetic aspect of reality sneaks into one's life, and one's film, by chance.

Aesthetics and garbage intersect at different levels in the film, in the first instance economic ones: the potatoes left behind in the field are "non-commercial" because outsized and misshapen. Twenty-five thousand tons of potatoes are dumped in France every year, we learn, because they don't conform to certain formal standards: in other words, garbage is created in the name of the beautiful and "normal," that is, in the name of aesthetics. In the field Varda notices knobbly potatoes shaped like hearts and, delighted, picks them up, takes them home, and films them with a caressing close-up that sensuously reveals every detail of their texture. For her this is a chance encounter with beauty, and with form where form is, by definition, absent, at least according to western philosophic norms. Under the eye of her camera, what is excluded from the grid of scientific-consumer normality—and can survive only as the monstrous, the curiosity—assumes another value. The heart-shaped potatoes evoke the world of Baudelairean *correspondances* in reverse, so that timeless nature returns in this form whose beauty implies the artificiality of the nature we eat when we buy our perfectly shaped supermarket potatoes. They taunt the unnatural nature we are called to consume.

The *trouvaille* of the heart-shaped potatoes is only one of the many moments of chance encounter, gratuitousness, and play in the film. In *Deux Ans Après* a woman explains: "Life is about learning to adapt to it." There is no tinge of resignation, however, in the way the documentary appropriates this line. "Adapting to life" for Varda means living *with*, rather than passively subjecting oneself to what one encounters, or what one is encountered by. Gleaning the possibilities and the surprises that are offered, Varda surrenders to them and at the same time artfully uses them to produce meaning, or to make visible something or someone who otherwise would disappear. Examples of these gratuitous moments: the man seen one morning looking at the river Rhône in Arles, unaware of Varda's camera— "I half felt like talking to him," says the director, and, although she doesn't, she still includes him in her text; the camera panning, without any voiceover, on stranded animals after a flood in the Jura; finding the painting at the *brocante*; Varda playing with her hand, curving her fingers to represent the lens of a camera, and filming with the other; filming the big trucks that she remembers delighted her as a child. The most striking of all these moments comes when, walking through a vineyard, she forgets to turn off the camera and to cover its eye; later she decides to include these "wasted," involuntary, chance images—the film's waste—in her text, images that show the lid of the camera hanging down, the ground and her own feet: Varda captions this scene as "*la danse du bouchon de l'objective*," and sets it to a jazz score. Chance, as it did for Calvino, lets her recuperate and include, rather than separate. Here the artist as producer is the gleaner who lets herself be acted upon by the things the camera sees when she forgets to switch it off. This gleaning, and her choice to include it, also becomes a courageous gesture of acceptance. She abdicates her agency and recognizes that no separation is possible from the processes that waste and gleaning signify—marginalization, decay, and death, but also a disjointed rhythm of survival and life. Her friend François finds an empty clock without hands, and the director takes it home: "A clock without hands is my thing. You don't see time passing."

Chance encounters imply a quotient of unfinalized gratuitousness, which for Varda relates both to art and waste, and, in turn, to play and pleasure. "Where does play end and art start?" she asks, looking at art made out of repurposed material. Art for her is never a world of abstract beauty separated from the everyday: on the contrary, for her pleasure and surprise occur when these two realms, which bourgeois aesthetics keep apart, collude. Delight, pleasure and surprise at this interpenetration of art and reality punctuate the film, designating its rhythm. They also shock, when associated with poverty. But Varda's is aesthetics without aestheticism. The attention with which she films certain objects—books, potatoes, her own body, the clock without hands—gives the images a haptic quality. Her close-ups, which allow the viewer to see what could not be seen with the naked eye, also lets her see what one often does not want to see, and that no aestheticism can recuperate. Unpacking her suitcase after a trip to Japan, for example, she notices that the stain of dampness on her living-room ceiling has grown deeper and has spread: there follows a lingering shot of the stain, inviting the viewer to see its beauty, the painterly quality that transfigures it into something else. "I am used to it. It looks like a landscape, a painting," she says, and somehow redeems it.

The stain on the ceiling also shows that there's nothing affluent in Varda's own domestic whereabouts, and the camera shows that among her possessions are a host of gleaned objects. Next the director extracts a few souvenirs of Japan from her suitcase, postcards of Rembrandt portraits whose originals she has seen on the top floor of a department store in Tokyo. These tokens of the souvenir world of beauty, however, are complicated and questioned by the image of herself, portrayed by her camera with the same technique she uses for the postcards: an inquisitive close-up. As the camera edges closer, we hear her voice: "Saskia [Rembrandt's wife] in detail. My hand in detail—to film my hand with the other hand. To enter the horror of it. I find it extraordinary. I feel as if I am an animal, worse, an animal I don't know." Varda's technique, the close-up with which she portrays both Rembrandt's paintings and her own hand, does not have the effect of aestheticizing aging, but rather has a defamiliarizing effect both on Varda and the viewer: moving from the magnified texture of Rembrandt's brushstrokes to that of her own flesh, she doesn't recognize herself, and she doesn't identify with her image. Both the heart-shaped potatoes and her hands will never be fetishes, objects of gratifying identification and desire; they are a precariously unstable materiality which changes and shows its deterioration. The close-up that reveals the beautiful details of Rembrandt's art also prompts us to appreciate the same detailed view of Varda's hand. But her own caption doesn't let us: art is not just a matter of appreciating beauty and form per se. There is no per se in Varda's aesthetics, just as there is nothing portentous or fetishistic in how she shoots aspects of reality. Perhaps, finally, in her cinema we are in a non-Junkspace zone: the close-up of her hand, time and again reappearing in the film, does not elicit the type of affect of which Koolhaas writes. Euphoria and blandness, the state of contented sedation pervading Junkspace, is here replaced by the shock of the director's, and viewer's, fascination *and* horror at what she sees.

In a very political move, *The Gleaners and I* shows that aesthetics, instead of being self-indulgent and ornamental, must rename and restructure materiality, whether human, corporeal, or objectual. In this perspective, the most important moment of the entire film comes when Varda is shown gleaning fruit in an orchard. While commenting on the selfishness of the owners, who don't allow gleaning, she approaches a fig tree: "You are beautiful, and I eat you!" she says to the fig before tasting it with gusto. The beauty Varda sees in the fig is not the spectacular perfection we expect from supermarket fruit. Here the aesthetic quality of the fig seems tactile: with this simple gesture of "eating beauty," rather than simply admiring it, Varda accomplishes a Copernican reversal of modern bourgeois aesthetic theory, and the distant contemplation of the auratic museum object is replaced by proximity, use, multisensual incorporation, and pleasure. Just as the potato in the field, for Varda, can be eaten *and* filmed, so can the fig be eaten because of its beauty. Both filming and eating are productive: the pleasure of the *trouvaille* produces both the materiality of corporeal and aesthetic gratification.

Nonetheless Varda knows that, although put in place by the same desire, these materialities are not the same. This political understanding of art, the affirmation of pleasure by a recuperation of the aesthetic as corporeal, and the awareness of their difference, is expressed in Varda's words at the end of *The Gleaners*, when she says: "I like to film rot, leftovers, debris. But I never forget those who stay in the leftovers and trash after the market is over." This statement again invokes the split between pleasure and need, choice and necessity. It's the figure of "the most impressive" person Varda encounters, Alain, the ex-university assistant, that helps suture this split and allows Varda to rethink the notion of need. We never learn the circumstances that took Alain from a profession to the street, but his words and tone convey the sense that he might have chosen this life in the name of a truly militant activism *and* of pleasure. This might be the life he *likes* to live. In *Deux Ans Après* we are given a hint of this: even though after Varda's film he enjoys a temporary celebrity, he carries on with his life selling papers on the street. Incomprehensible as it may seem to those who feel there's no other satisfaction outside the affluence of consumer culture, Alain's life is his choice and pleasure. Yet often this choice is interpreted as a sign of near-insanity. This is also the case of another gleaner, "*l'homme aux bottes in Aix*," the man with the big rubber boots Varda meets in Aix: neither homeless nor unemployed, the man gleans from the street because he hates how people throw out so much. He ends up "under psychiatric observation" at the request of his neighbors who are annoyed by all the stuff he hoards. For them, one becomes a gleaner for necessity, not for choice, and even less for pleasure.

Varda's mixing of the categories of need and pleasure in her depiction of gleaning is the film's most scandalous element. This scandal is made fully visible in *The Gleaners* when the lawyer who she plants among the cabbages reads from the civil code: "The poor, wretched, deprived, have the right to glean." The declaration that it's people who are in need who glean is intercut by the image of the woman who, when asked by Varda, answers that she gleans "for fun." To which the lawyer, in Varda's montage, responds, thus establishing the legitimacy of this other type of gleaning: "She needs fun." Soon the woman "who gleans for fun" becomes Varda herself: "I walk with my little camera among colored cabbages and other vegetables that I like." In her documentary gleaning has the effect of bringing the concepts of need and fun closer to each other, and of attributing a degree of agency to everybody who does so. That gleaning can be a pleasure doesn't change the fact that it almost always implies social and economic inequality—"I don't forget those who stay behind at the end of the market," as she says. However, the proximity of need and pleasure in the way the film treats gleaning also makes pleasure available to those definitively excluded from it in a culture where the chief pleasure is owning and buying. Varda implies that pleasure is a necessity of life for everybody: bread alone, although it might be all one gets, is not enough. No doubt some viewers were offended, as she herself suggests, when the homeless alcoholic woman Ghislaine confesses that she is in love with an immigrant from the Caribbean eighteen years her junior. Such offense is based on the assumption that even falling in love, if you are poor, is something excessive and accessory. The film says that there shouldn't be any utilitarian order of importance between her gleaning for food and gleaning for fun, for love: as a human being she is entitled to both, as is everyone else.

Centered on issues of recuperation, transformation, and chance discovery, Varda's film is articulated as a network of traces and criss-crossing paths where people and things encounter one another and in turn produce more connections. Thus the documentary is an occasion for outlining a different politics of consumption and of representation, both hinging on the practice of gleaning, and committed to a politics of style as transformative. This style is a means of plasticity, an improvised practice in which subaltern, marginal subject and discarded, minor and "improper" object help and transform each other in an encounter of mutual respect. Varda's cinematic technique, especially with her favorite medium, the digital camera, jolts the viewer, in contrast to the spectatorial comfort the use of the same camera by Ricky creates in *American Beauty*. Through the same technique she instead questions the opposition of subject and object, and shows how both can become disposable: the expiration date printed on discarded foods serves to remind her of her own limited "shelf-life," particularly as a woman. Her choice to be filmed against one of the paintings she likes, Breton's "Gleaner," is not a claim to permanence, or a flattening of life into art, but rather a way of acknowledging the ephemerality, and yet the productivity of both art and waste. At the end of *Deux Ans Après* Varda's prized heart-shaped potatoes have withered—like her hands—and sprouted. This image is sobering *and* flamboyantly, rather than melancholically, significant at the same time. For one thing, this matter is alive. With it, Varda recuperates the excess of the aesthetic, that which in dominant culture gets tamed into the ornament, as both horrible and delightful. This double register of materiality is here expressed as tactility, corporeality, the pleasure of form and at the same time the delight at its dissolution. If the withered, sprouting potatoes represent the most disturbing and intense image in the film, it is because here it foregrounds a rough-skinned sensuousness and an organic, living materiality as always already part of the perceiving subject—in this case, the counterpart to Varda's own living creativity, even as her skin withers too. This encounter of the living object and the living person is offered as a contrast to the utilitarian ethos of beauty that bourgeois culture has always preached, and which it now spreads through the saturation of experience accomplished by Junkspace.

Through her political reappropriation of aesthetics Varda also recuperates (rather than recycles) the disturbing aspect of the materiality of junk, in which we all partake along with our stuff: the finitude and decay she sees in aging and death. Her position partly recalls John Scanlan's at the end of his book *On Garbage*: "No criticism . . . only the sobering reminder that might counter reason's hubris, and that is, man is nothing but a bit of mud" (183). Varda, however, like Calvino, manages to rewrite and in part change the death sentence that trash utters by turning to the aesthetic. Calvino achieves something similar by attending to the less threatening realm of the private, to expose the process of exclusion through which the self and the text are made. Varda moves into the realm of the social and of history, and proposes an understanding of aesthetics closer to Benjamin's: against the impulse on the part of contemporary culture, to aestheticize politics, she politicizes the aesthetic into a project of reaching tactility and social consciousness. This *The Gleaners and I* achieves by weaving together the threads of the social (gleaning and the critique of waste), art (the film itself and the paintings and other works of art that appear in it), and the director's personal reflection on aging and decay. In turn, these three elements prompt her plea for the need for critique *and* pleasure.

The narration grows more melancholic when Varda reflects upon her own end, or when she reports the death of Charlie Plusquellec and the solitary grief of his friend Solomon. The same melancholia is audible in the voice of the artist Masha Mekeieff, the "collector of inconsolable things" in *Deux Ans Après*, whose words provide a very appropriate epigraph for a book on stuff, while also aptly describing the activity of the critic as a connector of things and ideas: "It is as if gleaning is my mission. I pick up things to tell our story. I think that objects contain part of us." "Tell our story," intervenes Varda. "Contain us," explains Mekeieff,

> I am not a collector. I don't look at an object for itself. There's a huge transfer of things that are lost, found, picked up. There's this trade in all things. Connections, things that circulate. They leave wonderful traces of … I imagine … the relationships people had with these objects. It's a rather indirect, modest way of meeting these people. It's as if they gave me a sign.

Then, examining a group of gleaned wedding cake figurines she continues: "An inert object tells of life and celebrates it. That's what an exhibition is: a celebration of life. There is something painful in all of this. The order seeks to ease that pain. At the same time, there's an attempt at humor." Varda comments: "She's a sentimental gleaner, undoubtedly; a gleaner of yore, perhaps."

This melancholic tone is dispelled at the end of the second film, where, as had happened at the beginning of *The Gleaners and I,* the three threads that Varda interweaves in the narratives of her two documentaries are spliced again. The film shooting ends on the first of May, Labor Day; the director includes images of lilies of the valley, springtime flowers; she then closes with the image of a rally against the right-wing, xenophobic movement the *Front Populaire.* A film on injustice, poverty, exclusion, ends with a final incitement to recuperate the social marginality of immigrants, and this time with anger, as the chanting of political slogans and the inscriptions on the banner—"We are all immigrants' children"—say. The film ends with an image of connection, with people coming together to protest and add their own caption to their own history and to the conditions in which they live.

What we look at in contemporary forms of materiality, what we should see when we look at objects, is neither the dead matter of the commodity fetish nor plasticity for plasticity's sake. We should see instead what Varda shows with the images that conclude her film, the images with which she asks us to look at reality again, and with which I choose to conclude this book. This is the capability to look at objects as stuff, as *Wunschbilder,* whose unfinished quality, its pointing at the process of materiality, at materiality as historical and experiential process, at how things get made, happen, and encounter each other and us, can only be read as a step toward changing them.

Notes

1 Peter Menzel, *Material World: A Global Family Portrait*, text, Charles Mann, San Francisco, Sierra Club, 1994.

2 See Perry Anderson, "Jottings on the Conjuncture", *New Left Review* 48, Nov.–Dec. 2007; Naomi Klein, *No Logo*, New York, Picador, 2000; Antonio Negri and Michael Hardt, *Empire*; Helga Leitner, Jamie Peck, Eric S. Sheppard eds., *Contesting Neoliberalism: Urban Frontiers*, New York, Guildford Press, 2007; Nigel Thrift, *Knowing Capitalism*, London, Sage, 2004; Antonio Negri, *The Porcelain Workshop: For a New Grammar of Politics*, trans. Noura Weddell, Los Angeles, Semiotext(e), 2008.

3 Paolo Virno, "The Ambivalence of Disenchantment", in Paolo Virno and Michael Hardt eds., *Radical Thought in Italy: A Potential Politics*, Minneapolis, University of Minnesota Press, 1996.

4 Jeremy Rifkin, *The End of Work: The Decline of the Global Labor Force and the Dawn of the Post-Market Era*, New York, Putnam Books, 1995.

5 See Walter Moser, "The Acculturation of Waste", in Brian Neville and Johanne Villeneuve eds., *Waste-Site Memory and the Recycling of the Past*, Albany, State University of New York Press, p. 85.

6 See Heather Rogers, "Message in a Bottle", in John Knechtel ed., *TRASH*, Cambridge, MIT Press and Alphabet City, 2007; A. Clark, *Tupperware*, Washington, D.C., Smithsonian Institution Press, 1999.

7 Zygmunt Bauman, *Liquid Modernity*, Cambridge, Polity Press, 2000.

8 Selected references: William Rathje and Cullen Murphy, *Rubbish!*, Tucson, Univ. of Arizona Press, 2001; Michael Thompson, *Rubbish Theory: The Creation and Destruction of Value*, Oxford, Oxford University Press, 1979; John Scanlan, *On Garbage*, London, Reaktion Books, 2005; Susan Strasser, *Waste and Want: A Social Theory of Trash*, New York, Henry Holt, 1999; Thomas Tierney, *The Value of Convenience*, New York, State University of New York, 1993; Daniel Miller, *A Theory of Shopping*, Cambridge, Polity Press, 1998; Elizabeth V. Spelman, *Repair: The Impulse to Restore in a Fragile World*, Boston, Beacon, 2002; Greg Kennedy, *An Ontology of Trash: The Disposable and Its Problematic Nature*, Albany, State University of New York Press, 2007; William Cohen and Ryan Johnson eds., *Filth: Dirt, Disgust, and Modern Life*, Minneapolis, University of Minnesota Press, 2005; Kevin Lynch, *Wasting Away*, San Francisco, Sierra Club, 1990.

9 Barry Allen, "The Ethical Artefact: On Junk", in Knechtel, *TRASH*, Cambridge, MIT Press and Alphabet City, 2007, p. 202.

10 Michael Taussig, "Miasma", in Gay Hawkins and S. Muecke eds., *Culture and Waste: The Creation and Destruction of Value*, Lanham, MD, Rowman and Littlefield, 2003, p. 17.

11 Arjun Appadurai ed., *The Social Life of Things: Commodities in Cultural Perspective*, Cambridge, Cambridge University Press, 1986.

12 Michael Thompson, *Rubbish Theory*.

13 "For me the most powerful effect of '50 Sad Chairs' . . . it's the way it captures the recalcitrance of trash, its lingering presence. Bill Brown describes this aspect of materiality as thinginess . . . we glimpse thinginess in irregularities in exchange circuits, in moments when objects stop working for us, and when we are not sure how to identify them." Gay Hawkins, "Sad Chairs", in *TRASH* p. 54.

14 Tim Edensor, *Industrial Ruins: Spaces, Aesthetics and Materiality*, New York, Berg, 2005.

15 Thompson, *Rubbish Theory,* pp. 11–12; also Zygmunt Bauman, "Rubbish Collectors Are the Unsung Heroes of Modernity", *Wasted Lives: Modernity and Its Outcasts*, Cambridge, Polity Press, 2004, p. 28.

16 Mary Douglas, *Purity and Danger*, New York, Lord, 1966, p. 36.

17 As Walter Moser points out, Douglas' approach to dirt is more ambivalent and flexible than Jonathan Culler concedes; see Culler, *Framing the Sign: Criticism and Its Institutions*, Norman, University of Oklahoma Press, 1988, pp. 168–82, in Brian Neville and Johanne Villeneuve eds., *Waste-Site Memory* p. 92.

18 Julia Kristeva, *Powers of Horror: An Essay on Abjection*, trans. Leon Rudiez, New York, Columbia University Press, 1982, and Rosalind Krauss, "'*Informe*' without Conclusion", *OCTOBER* 78, 1996, 89–105.

19 Scanlan, *On Garbage*, London, Reaktion Books, 2005, p. 34.

20 Anthropologists of the University of Arizona are involved in a contemporary archeology of garbage, digging landfills for preserved garbage and junk, including 1950s cars. See Rathje and Murphy, *Rubbish!*, Tucson, Univ. of Arizona Press, 2001.

21 Slavoj Žižek, *The Indivisible Remainder*, London, Verso, 1996.

22 Bruno Latour, *We Have Never Been Modern*, trans. Catherine Porter, Cambridge, Harvard University Press, 1993, p. 47.

23 It could be argued that this aesthetic of garbage formed as middle-brow sentimentality in the nineteenth century, and congealed around the figure of the prostitute. See D.G. Rossetti's poem "Jenny," for instance.

24 "No works of art, but aesthetics is everywhere," notes Bauman in *Wasted Lives: Modernity and Its Outcasts*, Cambridge, Polity Press, 2004, p. 39, referring to Yves Michaud, *L'Art à l'Etat Gazeux: Essai sur le Triomphe de l'Esthetique*, Paris, Stock, 2003.

25 Sanford Kwinter, *Architectures of Modernity: Toward a Theory of the Event in Modernist Culture*, Cambridge, MIT Press, 2001, p. 34.

26 The viewer experienced the exhibits in a tactile manner: "a broken refrigerator handle, a diaper, a headless, one-legged Barbie doll, carefully selected." Susan Hauser, "Waste Into Heritage: Remarks on Materiality in the Arts, or Memories and the Museum", in Brian Neville and Johanne Villeneuve eds., *Waste-Site Memory*, p. 50. M. Gara and G. Bandolin, "Das Mull Museum", Schweden, *Topos*, 14 (1996: 66–71), quoted in Hauser.

27 This is the case with photography; see the work of André Kertész and, Ch. 1, *Albert Renger-Patzsch. Photographer of Objectivity*, Ann and Jürgen Wilde and Thomas Weski eds., with an introductory text by Thomas Janzen Cambridge, MIT Press,1998.

28 Benjamin, "The Author as Producer", 1937, p. 236.

29 The Harvard School of Design *Project on the City*, Chuihua Judy Chung, Jeffrey Inaba, Rem Koolhaas, and Sze Tsung Leong eds., 2 vols: *Great Leap Forward* and *Guide to Shopping*, Cologne, 2002.

30 Fredric Jameson, "Future City", *New Left Review*, 21, May–June 2003.

31 "If a place can be defined as relational, historical, and concerned with identity, then a space that cannot be defined as relational, or historical, or concerned with identity will be a non-place." Marc Augé, *Non-Places: Introduction to an Anthropology of Supermodernity*, trans. John Howe, London, Verso, 1997, 78–9.

32 Rem Koolhaas, "Junkspace", *OCTOBER* 100, Spring 2002, p. 186.

33 "A single citizen . . .—a refugee, a mother—can destabilize an entire Junkspace." Koolhaas, "Junkspace", *OCTOBER* 100, Spring 2002, p. 180.

34 José Luis Pardo, "Never Was Trash So Beautiful", in *Distorsiones Urbanas*, Madrid, Basurama, 2006. Web, April 2008 (http://www.basurama.org/b06_distorsiones_urbanas_pardo_ehtm).

35 Kathleen Rowe Karlyn, "Too Close for Comfort: *American Beauty* and the Incest Motif", *Cinema Journal*, 44, 1, Fall 2004.

36 Judith Feher Gurewich, "Masculine Mystique, Feminine Mistake, and the Desire of the Analyst", January 2001, available at http://slought.org/content/11028.

37 Vincent Hausman, "Envisioning the (W)hole World 'behind Things': Denying Otherness in *American Beauty*", *Camera Obscura* 55, vol. 19, no. 1, 2004, p. 114.

38 See Gay Hawkins, "Plastic Bag: Living with Garbage", *Intl. Journal of Cultural Studies*, 4, 1, 2001, p. 7.

39 Sam Mendes, "Commentary", *American Beauty*, DVD, dir. Sam Mendes (2000: Los Angeles, CA: Universal Studios 2003).

40 Italo Calvino, "La poubelle agrée", *The Road to San Giovanni*, trans. Tim Parks, New York, Pantheon Books, 1993; *La Strada di San Giovanni*, Milano, Arnoldo Mondadori , 1993.

41 See Ruth Cruikshank, "It could be argued that *Les Glaneuses* and *Deux Ans* are undercut by an anesthetizing focus on gleaning as art, or that they provide film maker and viewer alike a refuge from the suffering of the excluded", "The Work of Art in the Age of Global Consumption: Agnès Varda's *Les Glaneuses et la Glaneuse*", *L'Esprit Createur*, 47, 3 (2007), p. 36. I disagree with this interpretation.

Envoi: What Should We Do with Our Stuff?

Stuff Theory is a genealogy of possessed materiality. Its project has been to delineate the contact zones between marginal subjects and their stuff in late modernity as sites rife with the potential for generating productive hybrids and what Latour calls "quasi-subjects quasi-objects." It makes the case for recognizing the artefactuality of both subject and object. Its starting point is the volatile and changing status of materiality in late modernity, and the continued possibility of critique. Today, capitalism's system of organizing the contact points of subject and the material world has never been more pervasive, whether as Debord's mirage-like "Spectacle," Taussig's more Deleuzian, interflowing, and multiply networked "Nervous System," or Koolhaas's delirious, manufactured consumer-scape of "Junkspace." On the one hand capital works to contain and reassign materiality to the secondary space it has occupied in the western metaphysics, and on the other it mimics the hybrid, and reproduces the very mobility and unlimited dynamism and productivity of stuff. This book has focused on the moments when stuff, as the overflow and outré of this apparently well ordered commodity-object cornucopia, spills over and becomes visible in a series of flashes. I consider the particular conditions that make these moments of visibility possible or impossible, and examine what the new versions of contact between subject and materiality reveal to us.

If the radical potential of the previous stages of materialist analysis is indeed exhausted, as some new materialists would have it, what should we do with our stuff? And what should a stuff theory do? Certainly it must do more than contemplate materiality itself in all its splendor, or trace the networks, circulation, and exchanges in the circuits of power in order to theorize their ontology. For a start, it should commit itself to naming, differentiating, and understanding the political and individual effects—and the costs—of this ontology. It should understand reality in order to imagine how to change it. It's the plasticity of matter, which is also our own plasticity, that can actually change the world, and can make us radical (again), unsatisfied with ontologies. It's a matter of learning how to use the deflagratory power of plasticity, to take responsibility, in order to be true materialists. To begin to track this power, we need to trace the histories of materiality—not just the history of theories of materialism, but of the down-and-dirty contacts between subjects and objects in the everyday.

Here, the modernist interwar era is key, and not only as the time of a new thinking on objects and commodities. The modernist moment matters because its historical-economic-cultural conjuncture, as Perry Anderson points out,[1] allows a view of reality as incomplete—it is the period when systematic rationality was caught off guard. The modernist aesthetic of the object deeply contributes to this view. Modernism envisions and represents reality as fragmentary and incomplete, in the image of what Michael Taussig, in *The Nervous System*, calls "the world as Swiss cheese."[2] The "holes" in the system show its weakness and lack of stability, and at the same time point to the possibility of resistance. Early twentieth-century modernity, as also shaped by modernist aesthetics, is the final moment in the course of the century when the system of objects which more and more pervasively closes ranks upon the mass of modern consumer-subjects by the 1950s, is shown as open and vulnerable. This is the moment when stuff announces most audibly the possibility of experience, social change, and futurity. Baudrillard's apocalyptic view of contemporary culture, by the 1960s, points to the increase throughout the century of capitalism's alienating power, which affects the everyday experience of millions of people. However, as this book shows, the saturation of experience by the commodity is always in tension with a different force, the force of hybrid materiality and its adversarial potential, visible at specific historical conjunctures when the unevenness of the system momentarily breaks down and shows its irrationality and lack of closure. At such moments the hybrid can emerge. Aesthetics illuminates these crises by producing alternative visions of things aimed at queering realist mimesis and the coherence of the sign.

What is to be done, then, when the vision of "the world as Swiss cheese" is more and more difficult to recognize, when geocapital reaches into every aspect of life, so that people's bodies and even affects are continually transformed into value, while their defunct stuff falls out of it? Think of the international commerce of organs, or the highly transnational contemporary circulation of the body of the prostitute as object. Consider how the superseded subject, now resurrected into the identity of the credit-card holder, is continually invited to see the world through the fetishistic objectivity of the commodity, presented as the last outpost of human freedom. What is to be done when commodification is everywhere, and the commodity, now viral, is apparently nowhere, its solidity and materiality increasingly dispersed in forms of consumption that have become supremely spiritual? This is the conclusion reached by Sze Tsung Leong's claim, in *The Harvard Guide to Shopping*, when he proposes "In the end there will be little else for us to do but shopping."[3] If the object is left, as Donna Haraway insists, with style, the subject now only has the wan satisfaction of "lifestyle," consuming her own lack of satisfaction *as* pleasure. We see through the artifice of the commodity and our own subjection to the seductive imperatives of contemporary culture: comfort, happiness, sedation, the anaesthetic identification with the object, in a reality where shopping, far from being the height of materialism, has become a "spiritual" activity. "As for consumption ... as Marx feared, [it] has become altogether spiritual. Materiality is here a mere pretext for our exercise of the mental pleasures," as Jameson puts it.

This "spirituality" again signifies a disembodied refusal of materiality that is consumerism's logic. The work of the new materialism definitely refuses this. It wants to return us to a new awareness of the sensuousness of matter, and as such it has great and even utopian potential to change how we relate to materiality once and for all. Yet this new apprehension of matter as dynamic and alive needs to be more than a vitalist ontology. Instead, the reality of how human subjects are alienated from matter and its terrific, implacable weight must be a part of the equation. The point of hybrid materiality, and of the stuff theory which we use to study it here, is to replace the anaesthetic identification with the object, or the theorization of some sublime matter capable of living a life of its own, with a nuanced account of an unstable, impure traffic between subject and object, or even between different materialities. This traffic affirms their hybridity and multiplies their contact zones and entanglements in a way, as Malabou suggests, that might help us "not to replicate the caricature of the world," but rather to expose it and contest it.

The spirituality of shopping, through which we consume our own unhappiness, makes the question of exploring all new ideas on materiality, and especially the question of new kinds of contact, as yet unimagined, between subject and object, even more urgent. Against this "spirituality" we need to reclaim materiality as a form of hybridity and quasi-subject quasi-object contact which might challenge us to live without the philosophic safety net of human exceptionalism *and* make a new politics possible. This option has been taken up for a long time by all the hybrids that the western order of things doesn't allow into its approved systems of representation, and which have only recently begun to be recognized. *Stuff Theory* wants to contribute to this recognition, and at the same time affirm that there's much more left to us than shopping.

Notes

1 Perrry Anderson, "Modernism and the Revolution," in *Marxism and the Interpretation of Culture*, Cary Nelson and Lawrence Grossberg eds., Chicago: University of Chicago Press, 1990.
2 Michael Taussig, *The Nervous System*, New York, Routledge, 1992, p. 154.
3 Quoted in Fredric Jameson, "Future City", *New Left Review* 21, May–June 2003, p. 77.

Index